Roller Hockey

Skills and Strategies for Winning on Wheels

by
Greg Siller

A Division of Howard W. Sams & Company

Published by Masters Press
A Division of Howard W. Sams & Company
2647 Waterfront Pkwy E. Dr, Suite 100, Indianapolis, IN 46214

Printed in the United States of America.

97 98 99 00 01 02 10 9 8 7 6 5 4 3 2 1

Library of Congress Cataloging in Publication Information

Siller, Greg, 1960- .
Roller hockey: skills and strategies for winning on wheels / by Greg Siller.

p. cm.
Originally published: Ridgecrest, CA : Pro Learning Systems, c 1995.
Includes bibliographical references (p. 272)
ISBN 1-57028-118-1
1. Roller hockey. I. Title.
[GV859.7.S55 1997]
796.21--dc21 97-7369
CIP

Dedication

To Mary; thanks for ALL of your time, understanding, expertise, and encouragement during the nearly 15 months that it took to put this book together. Now let's go paint the town!

To Erin Marie; this book became our project, with me writing mine and you "writing" yours. Soon you'll be able to read this one. Now we've got time to shoot the puck around.

To Luke MacGregor; this book is almost as old as you are. P.S. It's amazing that I even finished it with you banging on the keyboard, trying to imitate Daddy. Keep working on your slap shot.

To Richard James, our newest addition; soon you'll be able to get up on your wheels.

To my parents; thanks for all of your love and devotion. Getting up at 5:00 in the morning to drive me to hockey practice was a sacrifice that I greatly appreciate.

I love you all! Greg

Greg Siller has done a great job providing a book that is very thorough and yet user friendly to coaches of all levels. This book provides excellent diagrams and key insights to help teach the necessary skills to develop players of all ages.

Dan Brennan — USA Hockey Inline Programs Coordinator

Coaches, players and parents alike will find that Greg has covered all of the key points in this tell-all roller hockey book. There are ideas in this book that even the pros will find beneficial. To sum it all up, it's a must to read and must to have!

Dan Delaney — General Manager/Director of Player Personnel, Empire State Cobras, RHI
Professional Roller and Ice Hockey Scout

This is far and away the most comprehensive and advanced rolley hockey manual in publication. A must for players and coaches who aspire to reach the next competitive level.

John E. Black — Head Coach/Director of Hockey Operations, Sacramento River Rats, RHI

Credits

Cover Photo ©John Lyman
Cover Design by Christy Pierce
Text Layout by Kim Heusel
Edited by Kim Heusel

Table of Contents

Acknowledgments

Mary
top notch editor-in-chief

Jim
long-distance editor and hockey mentor (four goals in one game is still tough to beat)

Ann
innovative ideas and marketing strategies (get this on the best seller list quickly Mom!)

Ken
my teammate, reviewer and marketer (thanks for your action photos)

Keith
for your encouragement and action photos

Peggy
for watching the kids and labeling photos (a negative job well done)

Bill
for networking and contacts (am happy!)

Dick and Maureen
support and encouragement and the minigetaways

Don at The Sports Asylum
for the ideas and encouragement

The Ridgecrest Roadies Roller Hockey Team
for being my sports models — what a crew — roll on

Chet
for the entertaining comics

To Masters Press
for giving me this opportunity

To all of my coaches
thanks for your time, thanks for the learning

Preface

I grew up in Michigan and played ice hockey in Michigan, Ohio, Maryland, Washington, D.C., Virginia and Canada. When I eventually found myself living in a remote California desert town, it became quite obvious to me that my days playing this sport were limited. It was a two- or three-hour drive to the closest ice rink, so practicing and playing games was basically out of the question.

I satiated my hockey craving by watching the Los Angeles Kings and other teams on various sports channels and my brother Keith sent homemade videos of the Detroit Red Wings and the Bruise Brothers. Although this temporarily satisfied my hockey fix, it just wasn't the same as playing. Fortunately, the inline skating craze began, and with a bonus check I received from work, I purchased my first pair of inline skates, a pair of Rollerblade Lightenings. Although it took a little getting used to, it was great to move around on skates again. Now all I needed was a group of interested players to get a game going. To my surprise, I was put in contact with Mike McDonald, another ice player who had been organizing some weekly inline games. Once I saw how much fun this mix of ex-ice and youth roller players were having, I knew I also wanted to be involved!

After playing for a while, I started coaching and officiating. As expected, there was not much information on the market about the sport. Many consumers were purchasing ice hockey books and videos to help them learn about the game of roller hockey. I saw the huge void in the area of roller hockey information as a challenge, and on June 14, 1994, I began a 15-month journey which has introduced me to you.

I decided to write this book to educate people on this exciting sport of roller hockey — both nationally and internationally; to fill a much needed niche; to gain academic knowledge on coaching, officiating, roller hockey and ice hockey to complement my years of playing experience; and to learn how to publish a book.

My qualifications to write, review and edit this book include more than 25 years of experience playing ice hockey in the U.S. and Canada, roller hockey, coaching and officiating. I know what it takes for a coach or player to become proficient. The information in this book contains what I have learned supplemented by various recognized ice hockey publications.

In addition, I hold BSEE and MBA degrees. These two triumphs have taught me what it takes to analyze and understand both technical- and people-oriented processes. A requirement for my MBA degree was to publish a project. This experience provided me with the opportunity to plan, research, develop, review, edit and publish my first "book". Also, for the past five years I have developed several training programs for the company that I work for. This has taught me what it takes to analyze a need and fill that need; in this case, this book on roller hockey.

Who would have guessed on those chilly weekend mornings driving with my family to a hockey tournament in Michigan's Upper Peninsula that I'd produce this labor of love? Those early childhood lessons from playing hockey, values of teamwork, competition, discipline and practice, are reflected in my daily life. Here's to the healthy, physical and mental enjoyment of this exciting sport called roller hockey!

1

The Exciting World of Roller Hockey

Highlights

This chapter introduces you to the exciting world of roller hockey. The topics in Chapter 1 are presented to orient each coach, player and enthusiast to the following:

So what is this game of roller hockey all about?

- *roller hockey's past, present and future*

What is required to get started?

- *playing surfaces*
- *player equipment*
- *should you use a puck or ball?*
- *nets*
- *the role of officials*
- *playing time*
- *roller hockey sanctioning*

Where do we go from here?

— Let the good times roll —

Congratulations on your purchase of the most comprehensive and informative book written on the sport of roller hockey. *Roller Hockey: Skills and Strategies for Winning on Wheels* was written to:

- Provide coaches with the necessary tools to introduce the fundamental and advanced concepts and strategies of the game of roller hockey, plan for the season, evaluate and select the right players, and ensure individual player and team improvement through the use of proper practice and feedback techniques.
- Teach beginning players the proper fundamentals that will provide immediate skill development as well as the best foundation for future skill development.
- Improve the playing ability of any roller hockey player so that he or she can get the most out of practice time and quickly move to the next skill level.
- Provide the enthusiast with the necessary information to understand and enjoy the exciting and rapidly expanding sport of roller hockey.
- Most importantly, provide a framework to ensure that learning about competition, sportsmanship, teamwork, and individual and team potential is done in the best manner possible. The most valuable lessons in life come through the experiences that each of us goes through. Participation by parents, coaches, officials, league directors, fans and sponsors is essential to creating this safe and fun framework that will help provide the opportunities to experience these valuable lessons.

So What Is This Game Of Roller Hockey All About?

Roller Hockey's Past. The sport of playing hockey on wheels has been around for quite a few years. Back in the 1930s and '40s, organized hockey playing on wheels was a great way to emulate a favorite player from the National Hockey League (NHL). Using a roll of electrical tape as a puck, a stick and a pair of strap-on roller skates, kids were afforded the opportunity to skate, shoot and score on wheels, like their NHL heroes on ice. During the late 1970s and '80s, in-line skates began being developed as a training tool for ice hockey players during their off-season as well as an alternative activity for the health conscious mind-set of Americans. Manufacturers such as *Rollerblade* began developing in-line skates designed to appeal to leisure skaters, trick skaters, speed skaters, and current and potential hockey players. As people found out how easy and fun skating on in-lines was, popularity soared. Pickup hockey games were being played again as they were in the '30s and '40s, only this time incorporating current equipment technologies. The World Roller Hockey League (WRHL) was formed to capitalize on the popularity of playing hockey on in-line skates and continued through 1993. During 1992, the Roller Hockey International (RHI) was established and eventually absorbed the WRHL to form a unified and cohesive roller hockey organization.

Roller Hockey's Present. The sport is rapidly approaching its 10-year mark and showing no sign of aging. As a result of its popularity, permanent rinks are now being built specifically to house league and tournament play. With millions of people playing and more joining every day, teams are competing all over the country, as well as the world. Countries that have begun organized roller hockey play include Canada, Japan, Germany, Great Britain, Australia, Sweden, Switzerland and Spain. Because of its accessibility, roller hockey is the fastest-growing sport in the United States and Canada. It can now be found in almost any parking lot in North America. Since roller hockey minimizes physical contact (focusing more on the non-checking fundamentals) as compared to its ice hockey counterpart, the sport is being enjoyed by a larger segment of both sexes. Girls' and women's teams are playing, as well as coed teams. In this book, I use the terms he or him to refer to one player's actions. These terms can be easily substituted to she or her when providing instruction to a particular player. I am very fortunate to have a young daughter who is just about the age to start playing, and if she is interested in playing roller hockey, I will fully support that endeavor! Roller hockey is played based on the fundamentals of skating, stickhandling and puck control, passing and receiving, shooting, and positional play; skills at which just about anyone who practices can become proficient.

The game of roller hockey, in its current form, is played using rules derived from ice hockey, with modifications made to allow for more offensive play, fewer line calls (offside and icing), and one less player on each team. The player positions consist of a goaltender, two players on defense and two forwards (as compared to three for ice hockey). With fewer players, roller hockey is designed to utilize the more open playing surface to showcase skating, passing and puck control skills.

Roller hockey, like ice hockey, is a team sport. The true notion of a team implies that each and every athlete has a vital role to play in determining the nature and character of the team while working to achieve the team's objectives. The game of roller hockey is also a game of one-on-one. Many one-on-one situations occur when two players are involved in puck possession. The puck carrier must continually find solutions to defensive actions by employing stickhandling, skating, passing and/or body deception techniques. At the same time, non-puck carriers must attempt to get into an open position to receive a pass while being covered by an opponent. Learning to play roller hockey is really about learning and improving your own abilities as well as integrating your abilities with other members of the team. It is a game within a game, and teamwork as well as individual play decide both games.

Roller Hockey's Future. As more facilities become available for the sport, organized roller hockey will continue to grow at quantum paces, both inside and outside of the United States. Roller hockey will become more integrated into college and high school athletic programs as well as city-sponsored programs. In addition, competition among world roller hockey teams should allow for this sport to be added to the Olympics. The ability of roller hockey players to effectively play ice hockey, and vice versa, will also improve the caliber of play in both sports. The great element about roller hockey is that whether you have a full facility or just a parking lot, the game is always ready to be played.

What Is Required To Get Started? Before organizing a league or playing a sanctioned roller hockey game, knowledge and possession of the following items is crucial to your success: playing surfaces, player equipment, puck/ball, nets, officials (for sanctioned games), playing time options and information on sanctioning organizations.

Playing surfaces. The playing surface can be located outdoors and unprotected from the natural elements (a parking lot), outdoors and partially enclosed (a permanent outdoor rink with boards), or a fully enclosed indoor facility (the way of the future). Five playing surfaces described in this section are blacktop, smooth cement, plastic tile, wood and coated surface.

- The most skated-on surface is asphalt, commonly called blacktop. Blacktop covers streets, parking lots and school yards across North America. Its major advantages are that it is relatively inexpensive, holds up well even in harsh climates and works well with the wheels that come with most in-line skates. The major disadvantages are that the surface is fairly rough and it softens when it gets hot, requiring the players to work harder.
- Another frequently skated-on surface is smooth cement. This is mainly found in ice rinks when the ice is melted away. It is not the same texture that sidewalks are made of; it is smoother. Because it is smooth, most pucks work very well on this surface. The main disadvantage is cracking that can occur over time.
- Over the past couple years, plastic tile floors have been developed and used over a cement or asphalt base. With interlocking tiles, large areas of playing surface can be laid down and taken up fairly easily. The tiles come in various colors so that lines, goal creases and face-off dots can be created without paint or tape. The most popular of these systems goes by the trade name of *Sport Court*. The puck slides extremely well on this type of surface, as it is slicker than blacktop or cement. Also, these plastic tiles can absorb some of the force of a fall and allow a player to slide a little when he or she has fallen. Special wheels have been created (and are recommended) that grip this type of playing surface better than stock wheels.
- A wooden floor is another type of playing surface, and is available at roller skating rinks. This surface is very durable if taken care of properly, lasting 50 or 60 years. The cost of this type of playing surface is the major consideration.
- Another surface that has gained popularity is a coated surface, one of which goes by the trade name *Roll On*. The underlying playing surface (generally smooth cement or wood) is coated with the product using one of the available levels of friction, ranging from gritty to smooth. A minor disadvantage with this type of playing

surface is that the puck does not slide as well as it does compared to a tiled surface.

The size of playing surfaces varies, but most rinks are close to a 2-to-1 ratio of length-to-width. Maximum rink dimensions are 200 feet by 100 feet, while a small rink would be130 by 65. Most sanctioned rinks fall somewhere in between. The playing surface is divided into two sides or zones as shown in Figure 1-1. The side occupied by a team's goaltender is known as the *defensive zone*. The side occupied by the opposing team's goaltender is known as the *offensive zone*. After each period or half, the goaltenders change ends of the rink which also changes the side of the playing surface the defensive and offensive zones are located for each team.

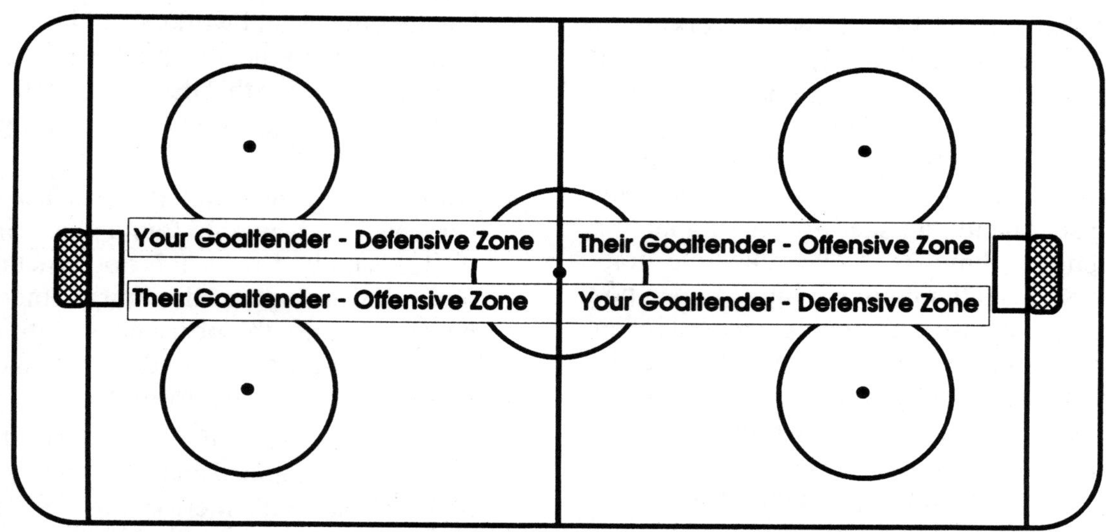

Figure 1-1; Playing Surface Layout

Player Equipment Requirements*	Cost
Skates	$40 - $400
Stick	$10 - $80+
Head protection (hockey helmet)	$20 - $75
Face protection (full face cage or shield)**	$20 - $70
Mouth guard	$3 - $10
Elbow pads	$15 - $70
Hand protection (hockey gloves)	$20 - $150
Knee/shin protection	$20 - $100
Cup and supporter (male) / Pelvic protection (female)	$10 - $30
Jersey	$15 - $100+
Shoulder pads***	$25 - $100+
Hockey pants and socks***	$55 - $100+
Roller hockey pants and hip protection***	$55 - $100+
Equipment bag	$20 - $75

* For specific requirements of your league or sanctioned event, consult appropriate rule book. ** For players over the age of 18, face protection is not required but is recommended. *** May represent additional equipment.

Goaltender Equipment Requirements*	Cost
Skates	$40 - $400
Stick	$10 - $80+
Hockey helmet and full face cage	$50 - $300+
Mouth guard	$3 - $10
Glove	$50 - $250+
Blocker	$40 - $200+
Leg pads	$45 - $400+
Cup and supporter (male) / Pelvic protection (female)	$10 - $30
Jersey	$15 - $100+
Arm and Chest Pads (Uppers)	$100 - $300+
Hockey pants and socks	$55 - $100+
Sweats (optional)	$5 - $25
Equipment Bag	$20 - $100

Player equipment varies depending upon whether or not you are playing in a game that is sanctioned by one of the recognized roller hockey organizations. As a minimum, a player will require skates and a stick to play in a pickup game. However, after a few falls on the playing surface (road rash), most players and/or parents realize that additional equipment is well worth the investment. For a sanctioned game, the sanctioning body sets minimum equipment requirements. Local leagues can require equipment in addition to the minimum equipment required by the sanctioning organization. For most sanctioned games and tournaments, the above-listed player equipment is required. In addition to the listed equipment, estimates of individually purchased retail equipment costs are provided. If a complete equipment package is purchased, the buyer should be able to receive a 10 percent (or more) discount.

Goaltender's equipment varies less between pickup games and sanctioned events. Goaltender's equipment requirements consist of:

Skates are the most important piece of equipment a player requires. They take the most pounding and should be the most durable and comfortable piece of equipment you own. Without a pair of in-line skates, there can be no roller hockey. I recommend that you talk to a few players or coaches to see which skates they prefer and why. Some stores also rent in-line skates. Rent a couple of different pairs for a weekend to evaluate. After becoming knowledgeable on a few particular models, find a knowledgeable salesperson, and try on several brands and sizes of skates. Choose a skate that is comfortable and the right size. A skate that is too loose will not provide you with much support, while a skate that is too tight *will* leave you in pain and not allow for some growth, if you are still growing. Skate sizes rarely equate directly to (American) shoe sizes, in fact, an equivalent skate size is usually one size smaller than your shoe size (if you wear a size 7 shoe, you will probably take a size 6 skate). Choose a skate that matches your needs for price, weight, durability, how often you play and on what type of playing surface you use. Skates are made up of four major components: the boot, chassis, wheels and bearing system.

- The **boot** is made of molded polyurethane (or other plastic), leather, nylon or a combination of the three. Polyurethane boots (which come with a liner) are generally better for younger players because of the support they give to the ankles. Molded boots also hold up better under adverse playing conditions and are better suited for outdoor play. Nylon and leather boots provide the flexibility needed for more experienced skaters, and are similar or identical to ice hockey boots. Skates are tightened using either laces or buckles. Laces are generally provided with nylon or leather boots, while buckles are provided with molded boots.
- The **chassis**, or frame as it is sometimes called, is attached to the boot and holds the wheels.

The chassis is either made of glass-reinforced nylon, polyurethane, aluminum or an alloy. Most new skates come with the nylon frame, however many manufacturers are now offering the aluminum/alloy frame as part of their newer lines. Other manufacturers provide these frames as after-market equipment. When considering the purchase of skates with an aluminum/alloy frame versus the nylon frame, the trade-off is simple — you pay more for lightness and strength with the aluminum/alloy frame. When purchasing skates with either type of chassis, consider the option to use 72mm (millimeter) wheels or 76 mm wheels (see next section on wheels) and the option to rocker your wheels (most in-lines skates are made with a slight rocker, as shown in the left side of Figure 1-2). Rockering the wheels can provide the skater with the ability to turn and start better by allowing him to move the center of gravity of the skates backward and forward. In addition, the fewer the number of wheels that contact the ground at any one time, the smaller the friction zone. Rockering an inline skate usually means moving the middle two wheels down to a lower level on the chassis than the two end wheels. This result is a curved appearance to the wheels when viewed from the side (right side of Figure 1-2). Another approach is to use one 72mm wheel as the front wheel of the skate and use three 76mm wheels for the remaining wheels. If you don't have the option to rocker your skates, you may feel like you are skating a little flat-footed.

- **Wheels** are defined by two attributes — diameter and durometer. **Diameter** represents the height of the wheel in millimeters. Most wheels come in diameters of 72mm and 76mm (one inch equals 25.4 millimeters). The smaller wheels are quicker in starting and maneuverability while a little slower in overall glide speed. Your skating style will determine which size is best for you. If you generally take short quick strides, a smaller wheel might work better, whereas long strides will work better with a larger wheel. **Durometer** represents the hardness of the wheel. For roller hockey, the best durometer will range from 76A, a softer wheel, to 86A, a harder wheel. Generally, the harder wheels are faster and the softer wheels grip the surface better. Another thing to remember is that while soft wheels will give you a smoother ride, they will also wear out faster. 81A is a good middle point for either indoor or outdoor skating and are the durometer wheels that come with most new skates.

  Don't buy a pair of skates only for the wheels that come with them. Roller hockey is hard on wheels and tends to wear them out quickly, so expect the replacement cost to be a part of the sport. Since the wheels wear out, you will have the opportunity to try several types, and I recommend you do so. If you are not confident with your ground-to-wheels connection, you can't expect too much from your game.

- The **bearing system** consists of bearings, axle and mounting hardware. Inferior **bearings** (on cheaper skates) spin less, wear out faster and force you to work harder. The high-performance or precision bearings found on better models spin more freely and permit you to skate more effi-

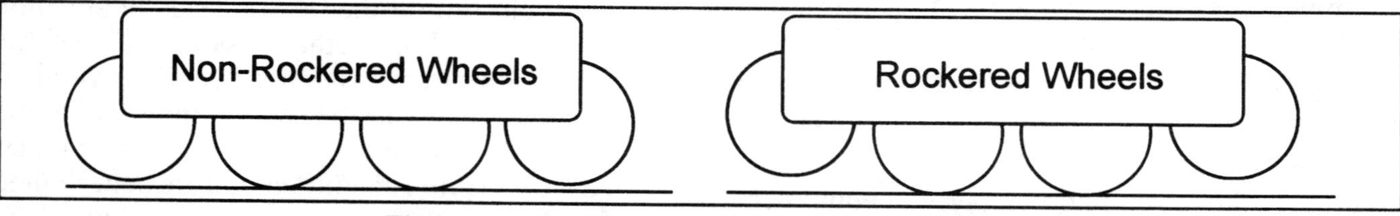

Figure 1-2; Non-Rockered and Rockered Wheels

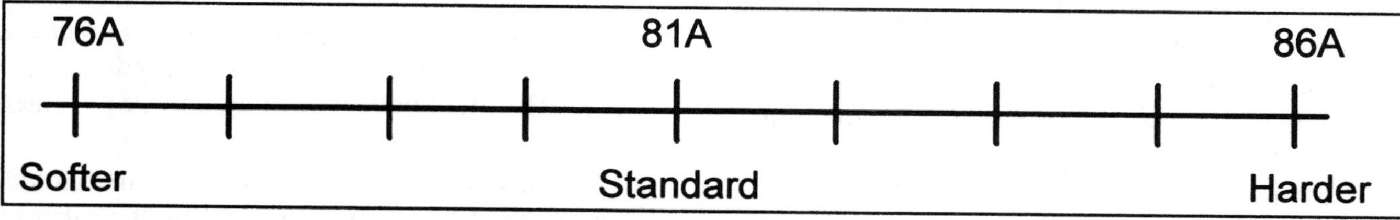

Figure 1-3; Wheel Durometer

ciently. Bearings are rated by their precision, or Annular Bearing Engineering Council (ABEC) rating. Bearings for roller hockey generally come in ABEC ratings of 1, 3 and 5 with 5 being high-performance. The difference between an ABEC 1 and an ABEC 5 bearing may not be greatly noticeable, but will depend upon the distances you travel without stopping. Your bearings should last for at least one season or more. **Axles** are required to support a player's weight and to keep the bearings separated, and are made of plastic, aluminum or stainless steel. By upgrading your axles to aluminum or stainless steel, a reduction in friction will be noticed. The difference can be demonstrated by conducting a simple spin test. Cradling one of your skates upside down, spin a wheel with your thumb and count the time until it stops. Do the same thing after replacing the stock plastic axles; there should almost be a doubling in spin time. Because of the metal to metal contact, friction is reduced, resulting in increased speed and more return for the same effort. Two types of **mounting hardware** consist of flush mount, and the bolt and nut system. Indoor rinks usually require flush hardware so their floors don't get damaged when a player falls.

Skate maintenance is required to keep your investment in top condition. Before you go skating, there are a few things that should be done to ensure that your skates give you everything that you purchased them for. If your:

- Hardware is not tight, tighten with an Allen wrench or manufacturer-recommended tool.
- Wheels move from side-to-side, replace the bearing system.
- Wheels do not move freely, clean your bearing system.
- Wheels are worn, rotate or replace.
- Laces or buckles are not in proper condition, repair or replace.

■ The **stick** is the second most important piece of equipment in the roller hockey player arsenal. It is used to help the player stick handle, pass, shoot and knock the puck off an opponent's stick. The stick comes as a single unit or can be purchased as a separate shaft, blade and end plug (this second type is not currently commercially available for a goaltender's stick). The shaft is the portion of the stick that the player holds onto. The blade is the portion of the stick that comes in contact with the puck when stickhandling, passing or shooting. The heel is the portion of the blade closest to the player and the toe is the portion of the blade farthest from the player. The end plug is actually a plug of wood four to six inches in length that can be put into the upper portion of a separately purchased shaft and allows an increase in overall stick length. Three types of sticks/shafts are discussed in this section — wood/fiberglass, aluminum and composites.

Wood or wood/fiberglass sticks have been around since the early days of ice hockey. The stick is made from woods such as ash, hickory or aspen, and combined with fiberglass in unique manufacturing processes to create a stick with the lowest unit cost.

Today, many players use a stick with an aluminum shaft. Introduced in the late 1980s, it has added a whole new dimension to stick selection. Not only can it reduce overall cost because of fewer broken sticks, but it is light weight for quick shooting. Aluminum manufacturing also allows producers to make the shafts more uniform than a wood/fiberglass stick. A wood/fiberglass blade (other types are also available) is added to the shaft to complete the stick. These sticks (shaft and blade) are priced higher than most wood/fiberglass models.

Composite shafts are a more recent entry into the stick market and are formed from combining materials such as graphite, fiberglass and Kevlar. The graphite and fiberglass provide strength while the Kevlar is used for dampening. Composite sticks strive for consistency, durability, a more responsive feel than aluminum sticks. A wood/fiberglass blade is added to the shaft to complete the stick. Most composite sticks (shaft and blade) are priced higher than the wood/fiberglass and many aluminum sticks.

Choosing a stick should be based not only on how it is manufactured but on how it feels in your hands (gloves). It is very important that you choose a stick that feels right and is correct for your skating and stickhandling style. Factors to consider include weight, shaft thickness, shaft flexure, length, blade curvature and lie. A good rule of thumb for proper **stick length** is to place the stick upright in front of your body with the toe resting on the floor. With skates on, the proper length occurs when the end of the shaft reaches just below your chin (or your nose while not on skates). The **lie** of a stick corresponds to the angle between the shaft and the blade/playing surface. Stick lies are commercially available in lies between 5 and 7. The smaller the lie, the smaller the angle. For example, a lie 5 stick requires a player to lean his upper body more when shooting than with a lie 7 stick. A test for the proper stick lie is to have the player stand on skates in a normal stance with the stick blade on the playing surface in front of him. If the heel of the blade is off the playing surface, a higher lie should be used. If the toe of the blade is off the playing surface, a lower lie should be used. Goaltender sticks are rated with lies around 30, which means that the shaft is more upright than the sticks described above.

Should you use a puck or ball? The decision to use a puck or ball should be based on the playing surface that you are using. A hockey ball is most effective when the surface is rough, such as with asphalt or rough concrete, as found in many parking lots. This is because the ball can roll over the surface imperfections whereas a puck would slide over some imperfections and roll over others. When moving to a surface that is smooth or semismooth, such as with some cement parking lots and all indoor arenas, a puck is most effective. A puck allows a player to shoot and pass more accurately than with a ball due to its rotational stability and shape. The puck is also designed to slide on the playing surface, whereas a ball is designed to roll on it. For this reason, the puck is easier to keep in contact with the stick which allows for easier puck control.

Nets. Roller hockey requires two goals or nets which can be made from metal or PVC piping. Shooting the puck past the goal line and into your opponents net provides your team with one point. As long as your team has more points at the end of the game, you win. The size of each net for adult play is generally 72 inches between goal posts and 48 inches from the playing surface to the top of net. Smaller nets are generally used for younger players.

The role of officials, both on and off the playing surface, is to make sure that the game is played in a safe manner according to league rules. Game officials generally consist of two referees (on the playing surface) and a scorekeeper (off the playing surface). The referees are required to operate without bias to make sure that the game is played in an orderly manner. When deliberate actions or words which are deemed unsafe or in violation of the rules are seen or heard from players, coaches or fans, a warning or penalty is assessed. Penalties require a team to place the violator in the penalty box for a specified period of time (usually two or three minutes but this can be extended based on the severity of the infraction). The role of the official off the playing surface is to record goals, assists and penalties, and to ensure that the game is played in the allotted time.

Playing time varies according to the specific rules of each league. Sanctioned games generally call for a minimum rink time of 45 minutes to a maximum of one hour. Rink time begins from the moment a team enters the playing surface to the moment it exits the playing surface after the handshake at the conclusion of each game. Playing time includes a three- to five-minute warm-up period prior to the beginning of each game, followed by either two 17 to 22-minute halves, three 15-minute periods or four 12-minute quarters. Most leagues play running time (the clock is started and continues until the period ends), however leagues have the option of incorporating stop time (the clock is stopped at each stoppage of play and started again at the drop of the puck) during the last few minutes of a game when the score differential is two goals or less.

Roller hockey sanctioning is performed by organizations recognized to do so. In the United States, major sanctioning organizations and their phone numbers (at this printing) are listed below. These organizations can help you get a league started, provide insurance coverage and keep you informed on events in the world of roller hockey. Fees range from $20 to $35 per year.

- USA Hockey Inline (an organization under USA Hockey, the national governing body for ice hockey in the U.S.); 719-599-5500.
- United States Amateur Confederation of Roller Skating (USAC/RS); (the national governing body for roller hockey in the U.S.); 402-483-7551.
- International Inline Skating Association (IISA); 404-728-9707.
- Other organizations that can provide assistance in setting up leagues include the YMCA,

YWCA, city parks and recreation departments, and local roller and ice rinks.

Where do we go from here? Now that you have been introduced to the evolutionary sport of roller hockey, you are ready to see what's in store for the rest of the book. The remainder of the book is organized into four phases. The first phase is covered in Chapter 2, *Coaching: Developing Your Team's Winning Program*. The remaining three phases of the book are segmented according to the three phases of roller hockey player development — individual skills, integrated individual and positional skills, and team skills. Chapters 3 through 6 contain specific information on teaching players the individual skills of roller hockey: *Skating and Rink Conditioning*, *Stickhandling and Puck Control*, *Passing and Receiving*, and *Shooting and Scoring*. Chapters 7 through 9 cover the integrated individual and positional skills: *The Dominant Defense*, *The Forward Faction* and *Goaltending at Ground Zero*. The last three chapters, 10 through 12, cover team skills in *Defensive Zone Team Play*, *Offensive Zone Team Play* and *Getting the Most Out of Your Special Teams*. Following Chapter 12 is the *Coaches' Toolbox*. The Toolbox contains many vital tools that allow the coach to perform player evaluations and to obtain team and individual statistics, both critical to providing effective feedback and plan improvements for the team as well as individual players.

Beginning with Chapter 3, each chapter has been developed using a consistent and straight-forward approach that provides the most effective path for learning and teaching.

- The first section, entitled *Discussion*, introduces the reader to the chapter concepts.
- The second section, entitled *Fundamentals*, covers fundamental concepts that each player must become proficient at if a solid roller hockey foundation is going to be built. Pictures, tables and diagrams are provided so the reader can *see* as well as read the correct techniques.
- The third section, entitled *Advanced Techniques*, allows the coach and players to learn the techniques required to move individual players to the next level of roller hockey. As in the *Fundamentals* section, pictures, tables and diagrams are used to enhance the learning and understanding process.
- The fourth section of each chapter contains the *Siller Player and Team Evaluation Profile©*. This profile provides the coach and/or player with the tools to monitor specific progress throughout the season via the collection of both quantitative and subjective data that will aid the coach in gauging individual and team improvement, or areas requiring further improvement.
- Following the profile section are two sections containing drills. These two sections are where the *rubber meets the road* in terms of putting roller hockey techniques into practice. The drills are divided into *Fundamental Drills* and *Advanced Drills*, which correspond to the information described in the *Fundamentals* and *Advanced Techniques* sections, respectively.
- The final section in each chapter provides the reader the opportunity to test his or her knowledge of roller hockey and of coaching. The *Recap* is a short, but effective tool designed to stimulate the reader's learning by focusing on specific topics in each chapter.

I hope that you have enjoyed (and learned) a little bit about roller hockey from what you have read so far. I guarantee that you will learn and be able to use something from each of the next 11 chapters to improve your current coaching or playing skills. Remember, the goal of the this book is to provide you with vital information in each chapter so that you can use it to develop the best *Skills and Strategies for Winning on Wheels!*

2

Coaching: Developing Your Team's Winning Program

Highlights

This chapter addresses the coach's many roles and responsibilities in the development of individual players and the roller hockey team. Chapter 2 presents the following information:

What Does it Take to Be a Good Coach?

The Three Player Development Phases of Roller Hockey

- *individual skills*
- *integrated individual and positional skills*
- *team skills*

General Rules Of The Game

Planning For A Successful Season

Siller Player and Team Evaluation Profile

Evaluating and Selecting Your Winning Team

Time To Practice — Time To Improve

- *practice organization*
- *learning styles and variety*
- *when should you scrimmage?*
- *varying the skill emphasis during the season*

Scouting Your Opponents

Game Time

Game Evaluation Tools

- *statistics*
- *videotape*

Recap

You cannot teach a man anything; you can only help him find it within himself.
— Galileo —

There are three types of people: those who make things happen — these are the leaders; those who watch what happens; and those who wonder, "What happened?"
— Roger Kirkham —

What does it take to be a good coach?

Take a few moments and seriously think about this question. Look back at some of the coaches that you may have had or known and look around to see what kind of people are coaching today. With all of these coaches, there are certain attributes that make some better than others. Walter Gillet, in this excerpt, summarized the job of a coach in *What is a Coach?*:

> A Coach is a politician, judge, public speaker, teacher, trainer, financier, laborer, psychologist, psychiatrist and chaplain. He must be an optimist, and yet at times appear a pessimist, seem humble and yet be very proud, strong but at times weak, confident yet not overconfident, enthusiastic but not too enthusiastic.
>
> He must have the hide of an elephant, fierceness of a lion, pep of a pup, guts of an ox, stamina of an antelope, wisdom of an owl, cunning of a fox and heart of a kitten.
>
> He must be willing to give freely of his time, money, energy and family life. In return he must expect little, if any, financial reward, and little praise but plenty of criticism.
>
> However, a good coach is respected and is a leader in his community, is loved by his team, and makes lasting friends wherever he goes.
>
> He has the satisfaction of seeing young people develop and improve in ability. He learns the thrill of victory and how to accept defeat with grace. His association with athletes helps keep him young in mind and spirit, and he too must grow and improve in ability with his team.
>
> In his heart he knows that, in spite of the inconvenience, the criticism and the demands of his time, he loves his work, for he is The Coach.

Coaching is both a demanding and rewarding position. It is demanding due to the time and effort required. Coaching requires many technical and personal skills in addition to a sound coaching philosophy. It involves planning to win and learning from defeat. As a coach, you have the responsibility of teaching the skills of the game and, more importantly, making these learning experiences challenging and enjoyable for the players and yourself. These responsibilities require that you assume various roles to effectively get the job done, both on and off the playing surface. This is what makes coaching such a dynamic and challenging occupation. Rewards include the development of athletes' physical, mental, emotional and social skills, and the opportunity of participating, having fun and learning to work together for a common goal. Successful coaches do not seem to have any specific type of personality; they are as individual as the general population. However, all **good coaches have certain qualities** that allow them to perform effectively. These qualities include dedication, enthusiasm and humor; the ability to teach and lead; the ability to communicate effectively; good planning and organizational skills; and a knowledge of the sport. It is unrealistic to expect all coaches to be experts in all of these areas; nevertheless, every coach should be familiar with these qualities and constantly try to improve in each. It is expected that each coach will make mistakes. But with each of these mistakes comes an opportunity to understand what happened and to learn from them.

- **Dedication, enthusiasm and humor.** Good coaches are dedicated to coaching. The time involved in coaching can range from a minimum of five hours to more than 10 hours for each one-hour game played, and this does not include driving to the game and practices or any additional time spent coordinating with players, parents or the league. A lack of dedication can seriously affect the team as well as the athletes' view of the coach. By realizing up front that coaching can take up a lot of time, the coach has already overcome a big hurdle. Since the coach is going to be spending so much time involved in roller hockey, he might as well enjoy that time. The coach is a role model and being such should realize the importance of this position and be aware of the effect that he has on the players, parents, officials, fans and the general roller hockey community. That effect can be positive if the coach adds enthusiasm and humor to the dedication. Make sure you are enjoying the game yourself. Athletes will feel more relaxed if the coach is able to see humor in some situations. A coach who is serious on all occasions may put added pressure on the players and may not be able to relate as effectively to them. It is also important that the coach not take himself too seriously and start to believe that he is the only reason for the success of an athlete or a team. Pause and enjoy, laugh a little, and everyone around you will be more likely to have fun, too.

- **The ability to teach and lead.** A coach is a teacher and must have an understanding of basic learning principles and teaching techniques. If a coach perceives himself as an educator first and foremost, many positive things will occur for the players both on and off the playing surface. Coaches should attempt to study and adapt the good coaching techniques of successful coaches rather than just attempting to emulate their personalities. Each coach has his or her own personality, so always be yourself. In addition to being teachers, coaches must be leaders. Coaches have a tremendous influence on young athletes. Players form attitudes and values based on the behavior of the coach. A coach's behavior will set an example for what is acceptable and unacceptable. Take those opportunities to teach and lead your players and foster a sense of respect, honesty and competition. Many teams have a basic code of conduct in which guidelines and rules for behavior are set. Team guidelines are best set up when the players have input and agree with the coach on guidelines such as punctuality for practices and games or general conduct on and off the playing surface. It is usually up to the coach to enforce these guidelines, and in general, rules should not be too numerous or so inflexible that they can't allow for extenuating circumstances.

- **The ability to communicate effectively.** For the coach to be an effective communicator, he must understand his players and be able to relate to them. Not understanding the player's motives and *real* concerns is one of the major reasons for breakdown in the coach-player relationship. Effective communication between the coach and players is essential for a good relationship, and a player should feel that the coach is approachable. It is also important that the coach give fair treatment to the players on a team as they can quickly turn on him if they feel he has been unfair. One guideline that every coach should incorporate is to talk to every player at least once per week. This may only take 30 seconds or may take as long as 30 minutes. In both cases, the players will realize that the coach is watching and concerned about what they do as individuals and as a team.

- **Good planning and organizational skills.** Just as each coach asks his players to be prepared, the coach should also be prepared through the execution of proper planning and organizational skills. If the coach is not very effective at either of these skills, make sure that an assistant coach is. The old saying that *failing to plan is planning to fail* can be very true for a coach. As the team progresses through the season, many events need to occur. Coordination of tryouts, practices, games, tournaments and playoffs requires that the coach (or assistant) decide what needs to be done and why, how it should be done, who should do it, and when and where it will occur. A well-organized coach gives the players confidence and pride in the team.

- **Knowledge of the sport.** Being in a leadership position, the effective coach needs to understand what is involved in the sport of roller hockey. This includes knowledge of the rules, roller hockey strategies and the development of the players being coached. Knowing the rules is important because it allows the coach to understand what is required to win the game, and along with knowledge of roller hockey strategies, will allow the coach to determine *how* to win as well. A thorough coach will continually read, observe and use any methods at his disposal to further his knowledge of the sport. Reading this book is an excellent way to further your knowledge. Other good ideas include attending coaching clinics, watching coaching videos, taking coaching certifications and observing other team sports such as ice hockey, basketball, soccer or lacrosse to learn and utilize applicable techniques and strategies. This knowledge should be passed on to the players at the appropriate times and in the appropriate amounts to be most beneficial. If the coach is instructing young children or teenagers, he also needs to be aware of how these players are developing, both physically and emotionally. By understanding these phases, the coach will be able to deal with them knowledgeably.

The Three Player Development Phases of Roller Hockey

Developing good roller hockey players is similar to constructing a new home: It takes time but the finished product can be a work of art. Roller hockey players progress through three phases of player development. The first phase is to develop a solid foundation. This is important because everything is built on that foundation. If the foundation is weak in any area, the player will eventually have problems. This first phase consists of learning and applying the **individual skills** of roller hockey which consist of skating and rink conditioning, stickhandling and puck control, passing and receiving, and shooting and scoring. This phase concentrates on the physical development of the roller hockey player, while limiting the mental development to the basics of reacting to various stimulus presented by the coach and other players. Roller hockey is a game that requires sound individual skills that become the foundation for both the individual players and the team. These individual skills must be taught at an appropriate complexity level according to the **ability, age, physical and mental development (AAPMD) level** of each player. The AAPMD level determines the level of roller hockey maturity for a specific player.

The second phase of development consists of learning and applying integrated individual and positional skills. **Integrated individual and positional skills** apply the individual skills (skating and rink conditioning, stickhandling and puck control, passing and receiving, and shooting and scoring) to positional skills (forward, defense or goaltender). Players in this second phase of development use the appropriate skills to gain advantage over opponents, either offensively or defensively. On offense, this may mean creating a two-on-one attack; on defense, it may mean stopping a two-on-one attack; and for a goaltender operating defensively, it may mean making the big save on a breakaway. This phase balances mental development, in terms of reading a developing play, and physical development, in terms of reacting to what is read. **Reading and reacting** refers to the ability of the individual or positional unit to perceive the play (of both teammates and opponents) around them and to respond appropriately. This process essentially deals with a player's ability to perceive, decide and react to ever-changing situations during the course of a game. Total situational awareness and accurate perception form the basis upon which effective reading and reacting occur. An example of defensive reading and reacting occurs when the defensive unit (generally the left and right defensemen) reads that the opponents have gained control of the puck in their own end and are beginning to break out. The defensive unit could react by retreating out of that zone. An example of offensive reading and reacting occurs when the offensive unit (generally the left and right forwards) reads that the defensemen have gained control of the puck in the defensive zone. The offensive unit reacts by getting into position to receive a pass to start a breakout play. An example of goaltender reading and reacting occurs when the goaltender sees an opponent carry the puck behind the net. The goaltender would prepare to cover the far post and protect that portion of the net as the opponent comes around from behind the net on the far side. In all three cases, the players gather information from the action around them and respond to this information based upon their ability, experience and knowledge to coordinate their actions for a successful end result. Effective reading and reacting doesn't come from careful planning, but from plenty of practice. Given the speed at which the game is played, the number of players on the playing surface and the necessity of almost instantly integrating all the situational elements for that moment, this can become a very complex task.

While keeping in mind the AAPMD levels of the players, the coach should move the players from individual (phase 1) skills to integrated individual and positional (phase 2) skills. As stated in Chapter 1, learning to play roller hockey is really about learning and improving your own abilities (individual skills) as well as integrating your abilities with other members of the team (integrated individual and positional skills). It is a game within a game, and teamwork as well as individual play decide both games. Winning the individual and small group battles makes the difference!

The third phase of roller hockey player development consists of learning and applying team skills such as breakouts, forechecking and face-offs, as well as everything discussed in phases one and two. **Team skills** are the consolidation of individual and integrated actions used by all players on a team, with the objective of winning the game. In addition to reading and reacting, the third phase adds an-

Player Development Phases Checklist							
	Junior			Intermediate		Senior	
	7 and Under	8 to 9	10 to 11	12 to 13	14 to 15	16 to 17	18 and Over
Phase I — Ind. Skills							
Skating and Rink Conditioning							
Forward skating	1	2	2	3	3	4	4
Forward stopping	1	1	2	2	3	4	4
Backward skating	1	1	2	2	3	4	4
Backward stopping	1	1	1	2	3	4	4
Turns and crossovers	0	1	1	2	3	4	4
Transitioning	0	1	1	2	3	4	4
Stickhandling and Puck Control							
Open area	1	1	2	3	3	4	4
Around pylons	1	1	2	2	3	4	4
Head up	0	1	1	2	2	3	4
Passing and Receiving							
Forehand	1	1	2	3	3	4	4
Backhand	0	1	2	2	3	4	4
Receiving passes	1	1	2	2	3	4	4
Head up	0	1	1	2	2	3	4
Shooting and Scoring							
Wrist shot	1	1	2	3	3	4	4
Snap shot	0	1	1	2	3	4	4
Backhand shot	0	1	1	2	3	4	4
Slap shot	0	0	1	2	3	4	4
Rebounds	0	0	1	2	3	4	4
Phase II — I.I. and P.Skills							
Defense							
Stick checking/body blocking	0	0	1	2	3	4	4
1-on-1, 2-on-1, 2-on-2	0	1	2	2	3	4	4
Rushing	0	1	2	2	3	4	4
Third man in	0	0	1	2	3	4	4
Forwards							
1-on-1, 2-on-1, 2-on-2	0	1	2	2	3	4	4
Moving puck into offensive zone	1	1	2	3	3	4	4
Backchecking	0	1	2	2	3	4	4
Goaltenders							
Playing the angles	0	1	1	2	3	3	4
Glove/blocker/stick/pad saves	1	1	2	2	3	4	4
Controlling puck after a shot	0	1	1	2	3	4	4
Phase III — Team Skills							
Forechecking	0	1	2	3	3	4	4
Breakout	0	1	2	3	3	4	4
Face-offs	1	1	2	2	3	3	4
Scale: 0 = Not or Minimally Performed, 1 = Low Proficiency, 2 = Medium Proficiency, 3 = High Proficiency, 4 = Excellent Proficiency							

Figure 2-1; Player Development Phases Checklist

other dimension — anticipation or hockey sense. **Anticipation** is a combination of skill, intellect, judgment, intuition and experience, and is the one element that sets upper echelon roller hockey players apart from average roller hockey players. Anticipation is the ability to read a play, predict a teammate's or opponent's probable course of action, and execute the best option available.

As the season advances, and again depending on the AAPMD levels of the players, the coach should progress through phases one and two of the player development trilogy toward team skills. What becomes most important is the rate at which the coach introduces the new skills throughout the season. The objective is to gradually build into practice more elements that teach and challenge the players, forcing them to execute under conditions similar to an actual game. For instance, if you are working on a team skill such as a breakout play, you would begin by concentrating on the individual skills of passing and skating; then progress to the integrated individual and positional skills of passing, skating, and defense, and forward positioning in the defensive zone with no opposition. To conclude, you would practice the actual breakout play with an opposing line or incorporate it into a scrimmage, which would simulate gamelike conditions. Players will require a number of practices, focusing on aspects of each player development phase, before they become proficient at any team skill.

Figure 2-1, **Player Development Phases Checklist**, was developed to help coaches determine when specific skills should be taught to the players and at what complexity level. This information covers three of the four AAPMD level factors; age, physical and mental development. The fourth factor, ability, is taken into account in the section on Evaluating and Selecting Your Winning Team. To make the best determination of when a player should be taught a particular skill, first assess the player's ability using the Team Selection Checklist (Figure 2-2) and then use that information along with the age, physical and mental development information to determine which AAPMD level the player is in. For example, if a 13-year-old is just starting to play roller hockey, you may want to develop his skills in accordance with the junior level, as shown in Figure 2-1. After a couple of seasons, that player could catch up to his peers (who may have been playing since age seven) and can be taught skills at his nominal level.

Three levels are identified in Figure 2-1 with each level subdivided by age. The junior level is 11 years old and under (7 and under, 8 to 9, and 10 to 11), the intermediate level is 12 to 15 years of age (12 to 13 and 14 to 15), and the senior level is 16 years old and over (16 to 17, and 18 and over). The junior level is prepuberty, the intermediate level is going through puberty, and the senior level is approaching or at physical maturity. Some roller hockey players are more or less physically developed for their age compared to other players. This just proves that every roller hockey player is an individual and should be coached accordingly.

The numbers used in Figure 2-1 indicate the ratings of proficiency that the coach should expect as the players progress through the different player development phases and AAPMD levels. A 0 indicates that the skill is minimally performed by a roller hockey player at this level. A 1 indicates that this skill should be formally introduced to the players. Expect only low proficiency from this group. A 2 indicates that the coach can begin building upon some previous skill development and can expect medium proficiency from the players. A 3 indicates significant improvement in this skill. A player at this level should be expected to execute the skill with high proficiency. A 4 indicates that the skill should be executed at a high or near high tempo both consistently and accurately, and with excellent proficiency. It is important for the coach to understand the three AAPMD levels as well as the three player development phases and their roles in overall player development.

General Rules of the Game

Rules are defined by the sanctioning organization and league under which each team plays. If you have no rules, then there are no boundaries for the game, and it basically results in a free-for-all. **Rules are not made to impede the game, but to define it**. The coach should obtain a copy of the rules prior to each season, study them and make sure that each player has an understanding of what the rules mean. Turn this task into a competitive game and challenge each player with questions that require the player to interpret the rules under the specific situation described by the coach. The rules of the game are actually very simple: The team with the most goals at the end of the game wins! How your team obtains more goals than your opponent is the question that keeps all coaches searching for the perfect system.

Penalties are violations of the rules which are caused by actions of players, coaches or even fans. Penalties are generally allocated into six categories — minor penalties, major penalties, misconduct penalties, match penalties, penalty shots and goaltender penalties.

- *Minor penalties* are served by the player called for the penalty or by a player designated by the coach or captain when a team penalty is called. A minor penalty requires the designated player to go to the penalty box for two or three minutes (depending on the specific rules of the league). During this time, the penalized team will play one player short (three skaters plus a goaltender), while the penalized player remains in the penalty box until either the penalty time elapses or a goal is scored on the penalized team. Minor penalties are generally called for the following actions: unsportsmanlike conduct (verbal abuse, shooting the puck after the whistle), acting in an extreme manner (deliberate body checking, cross checking), attempting to injure (slashing, spearing), obstructing a player (holding, tripping), technical violations (use of an illegal stick, leaving the penalty box before the penalty expires) and delay-of-game (deliberately shooting the puck out of play, placing more than five players on the playing surface at one time).
- *Major penalties* are served for more severe infractions. A major penalty requires the designated player to go to the penalty box for five minutes (this time may vary slightly depending on the specific rules of the league). During this time, the penalized team will play one player short (three skaters plus a goaltender), while the penalized player remains in the penalty box until the penalty time elapses. Since this penalty is deemed more severe than the minor penalty, the offended team is allowed to score as many goals as it can during the penalty. Major penalties are generally called for actions that appear to intentionally injure another player such as fighting, repeated slashing or kneeing.
- *Misconduct penalties* call for the removal of a player, other than the goaltender, for 10 minutes. During this time, another member of the team is permitted to replace the penalized player. This type of penalty is designed to allow a player to *cool off*, to focus back on playing the game. A *Game Misconduct penalty* involves the suspension of a player or a team official for the remainder of the game in addition to the next game. The penalized team may replace the suspended player with a substitute. Again, this type of penalty is designed to remove any belligerent players so that the game can proceed and also serves as a warning to other players that if the same type of actions continue, future playing time will be jeopardized. A game misconduct penalty may be assessed for deliberate intent to injure an opponent. A *Gross Misconduct penalty*, a very serious penalty, calls for the suspension of a player or team official for the remainder of the game. The penalized team may replace the suspended player with a substitute. The player or team official, however, will not be allowed to attend further games until the particular incident has been reviewed by the league manager or the sanctioning disciplinary committee.
- *Match penalties* are similar to major penalties (the penalized team is short-handed for five minutes) except that the penalized player is immediately removed from the game and cannot return to the bench for the duration of the game. Again, these types of penalties are given to players who attempt to injure an opponent.
- A *penalty shot* is one of the most exciting calls in roller hockey. A penalty shot is called when the defensive team deliberately prevents an offensive player, while in a clear scoring opportunity, from getting a shot on net (such as when a defensive player throws a stick in an attempt to dislodge the puck from the offensive player's stick). During the penalty shot, all other players must return to their respective benches while the offended player skates in on the goaltender alone. The excitement level for both teams during this play is unbelievable.
- Goaltenders have unique circumstances when penalties are called. *Goaltender penalties* are generally served by a player other than the goaltender. When a goaltender receives a minor or major penalty, a designated team member, other than the goaltender, serves the penalty. This allows the goaltender to remain in the game while the team is penalized. If, however, the goaltender receives a game or match miscon-

duct penalty, the goaltender will be removed from the game and a substitute goaltender is required. Some teams only carry one goaltender, so trying to equip another player with the various equipment can be time consuming. The officials, in this case, will allow five or 10 minutes for a coach to identify and prepare a substitute goaltender.

Planning for a Successful Season

Team success, which usually reflects coaching success, is dependent on effective planning. A good plan eliminates and controls problems that inevitably arise by serving as a reference point during the season. If the plan is implemented with proper thought and detail, reference to the plan prevents uncontrolled changes made just for the sake of change. A written plan is the basis for everything the coach and team should do during the season. Developing your plan can be done in a day; improving upon it can take a whole season. Initially make your plan generalized, with few details. As the season progresses, revisit the plan and incorporate details that are desired. To develop your written plan, spend some time thinking about the following questions and then compile your responses. Although this list is not exhaustive, it should provide the coach with the guidance necessary to get started. Questions to consider are:

- Why is this team being put together?
- How will the team be chosen? Tryouts? Draft? Lottery?
- When should preseason start?
- How many preseason practices are required?
- What facilities are available for practice and games?
- How can parents/supporters be most effective?
- Is sponsorship available?
- Who can support the team in an assistant coaching role?
- If the team played last season, which players are available again this season?
- What type of players will be most effective for the team?
- What type of competition will you face?
- How will evaluations be used to improve specific players as well as the team?
- How many practices and games are going to be scheduled during the season?
- How will rink time be paid for? Are fund-raisers necessary?
- Are tournaments going to be entered?
- How will problem players be handled?
- How often will feedback be provided to each player/the team?

Siller Player and Team Evaluation Profile

The Siller Player and Team Evaluation Profile is a series of coaching tools consisting of several checklists and worksheets. These tools are designed to provide essential quantitative and subjective data that will aid the coach in **team planning, player assessment and improvement, and evaluation of the competition**. An example of one of these checklists is the Team Selection Checklist shown in Figure 2-2. This checklist is designed to evaluate potential players during tryout sessions in terms of specific individual skills, integrated individual and positional skills, and team roller hockey skills. Other checklists and worksheets are provided in this and subsequent chapters, and each focuses on specific criteria required to scout, develop, evaluate and improve player ability. Completed checklists and worksheets are shown throughout the book. The *Coaches' Toolbox* contains a blank copy of each checklist and worksheet and should be used by the coach to help plan and monitor a very effective season. Make copies and use them!

Evaluating and Selecting Your Winning Team

Evaluating talent and selecting a winning team is one of the more difficult tasks in coaching. The allocation of time spent during this phase is usually rewarded with the selection of a team that has plenty of potential. Remember that once the team is selected, the coach will be utilizing those players throughout the remainder of the season. Good coaches have a plan to evaluate athletes. This **evaluation criteria** can consist of previous observations, discussions with other coaches or players, specific skill tests, perceived potential, physical attributes and personality traits. If a player is haphazardly chosen, the coach will not know how this player fits into the team. Before the players suit up and skate, spend a minute or two talking with each of them. Use this time to note some of their personal characteristics. Characteristics to look for include general attitude and character, and self-confidence. A brief description of these attributes follows:

- General attitude and character describe the disposition and tendencies that set each player apart. This is important because it can give the coach a clue as to how a player may work with other players and how he might react under pressure; and could show if a player is enthusiastic, moody, or negative. Although attitude and character are not always as recognizable of traits as skating or passing, they are important because they do affect each player in different ways during different situations.
- Self-confidence is another attribute that affects each player. A player who is not confident in his abilities will perform less effectively than a confident player. By questioning each player about his abilities, the coach can gain insight into this important quality.

Once the players have completed their introductions, the coach should have them warm up and be evaluated. The evaluation process consists of running each player through a series of tests designed to determine his ability or skill level. These tests include individual, integrated and team tests, as well as scrimmages. During this evaluation period (generally referred to as a training camp or tryout), it is important that the coach use an evaluation form to capture information about each player. The **Team Selection Checklist** (Figure 2-2) was designed to provide the coach with a vital tool to evaluate potential players. Specific drills have been chosen from Chapters 3 through 12 and cover the three player development phases. The better and poorer players are usually quite evident during the skill tests, but selecting from the middle group of talent is where the Team Selection Checklist becomes extremely important. If the coach is using additional evaluators, he should meet with them prior to the tryout to discuss what he is looking for in the players and to make sure that each evaluator understands his or her role. After the tryout, the evaluators should meet to discuss and compare their observations. The Team Selection Checklist should be used as the basis of team selection and can be combined with any notes or videos to paint a fairly complete picture of each player. This evaluation method will allow the coach to make an informed decision to determine whether or not the player fits into the team plan.

In addition to the skills listed in the Team Selection Checklist, other areas to consider while the players are executing their skill tests are motivation, intensity, leadership, coachability and determination. A brief description of these attributes follows:

- Motivation — A highly motivated player will want to make the team, improve and succeed.
- Intensity — A player with intensity plays hard during practices and games.
- Leadership — Not every player can be a leader, but leadership skills are evident in successful players in varying degrees. Some players are quiet and lead by example, while other players are more vocal. Good teams have more than one leader and the leaders cooperate with each other and the coach.
- Coachability — Does the player accept the coach's direction and respect his authority? Most top players are very coachable as they wish to improve their skills and need the feedback and direction of the coach.
- Determination — Does the player show second effort when required or does he quit? Does he work hard both offensively and defensively?

A good coach will use all the information at his or her fingertips to select the winning team.

Time to Practice — Time to Improve

Once the individual players have been chosen, it is time to begin practicing as a team. What goes into a practice, how it is conducted and what is accomplished are critical to the learning and improvement process of the individual players and the team as a whole, and is essential to the development and character of the team. The more effective the practices, the more potent the team is likely to be, and this potency can be directly related to team success whether it is measured in improvement, winning or fun. **Four factors that the coach should consider** when planning a practice include: practice organization, learning styles and variety, when to scrimmage and varying skill emphasis during the season.

- **Practice organization.** Practices are a vehicle for learning new skills, improving existing ones and integrating both into a new and improved package. Practices should be conceived with the idea that players must be exposed to different situations and make choices on the best solution in the particular context of play. Players

Siller Player And Team Evaluation Profile©
Team Selection Checklist

Notes:	BENNY			WILL		ANDY			MARK		
Skating and Rink Conditioning											
Skating—forward/backward	9			8		8			9		
Stopping	8			8		8			9		
Turns and crossovers	9			8		7			9		
Transitioning	8			7		0			7		
Stickhandling and Puck Control											
Open area	8			9		0			9		
Around pylons	7			8		0			8		
Passing and Receiving											
Passing—forehand/backhand	9			8		6			8		
Give-and-go	8			7		0			8		
Receiving—forehand/backhand	7			7		0			8		
Shooting and Scoring											
Wrist shot—forehand/backhand	8			8		0			8		
Snap shot	8			7		0			8		
Slap shot	8			6		0			8		
Rebounds	7			7		0			7		
Defense											
Stick checking/body blocking	9			0		0			0		
1-on-1, 2-on-1, 2-on-2	8			0		0			0		
Rushing	9			0		0			0		
Third man in	8			0		0			0		
Forwards											
1-on-1, 2-on-1, 2-on-2	0			8		0			8		
Moving puck into offensive zone	0			8		0					
Backchecking	0			7		0			10		
Goaltenders											
Playing the angles	0			0		7			0		
Glove/blocker/stick/pad saves	0			0		8			0		
1-on-1, 2-on-1, 2-on-2	0			0		8			0		
Controlling the puck after a shot	0			0		8			0		
Team											
Forechecking	0			8		0			9		
Breakout	9			7		0			7		
Face-offs	7			7		8			7		

Scale: 0 = Not Performed, 1-3 = Low Proficiency, 4-6 = Medium Proficiency, 7-9 = High Proficiency, 10 = Excellent Proficiency

Figure 2-2; Team Selection Checklist

must be taught the importance of using their physical as well as mental skills during practices and games. The coach should let the players try (and fail or succeed) during a practice. Practice will reinforce what the coach has already told them. By trying and failing, the players have learned what doesn't work. By trying and succeeding, the players have learned what does work. In both cases, learning has taken place. To make the most of limited practice time, the coach must have a plan of what needs to be accomplished. This plan should be based upon the current AAPMD level of the players, where the team is in the season, the level of competition in the league, and recent practice or game feedback. The coach should organize each practice on paper before it begins. Assistant coaches are essential during both practices and games. Both coaches should go over the practice plan prior to the actual practice so that each understands his or her role. The assistant coach should be active in providing feedback to the players and should have specific duties to support the coach. The assistant coach can direct the warm-up and conditioning part of the practices, and in some situations run certain drills. Here is a good way to organize your practices:

1. Define the objectives of each practice. Players are apt to remember more, learn easier and work harder when they have definite objectives.
2. Choose specific drills to best implement the objectives. When executing these drills, plan to use the entire playing surface. If the drills are localized in one area (such as the offensive zone), then split the team and have the assistant coach take half of the players and the head coach the other half. Design in time to provide feedback to individual players as well as the team. This time will also provide the players with a minute or two to rest between drills, drink some water and process what they just learned. Build some competition into the drills. Competitive drills will challenge the players and provide fun and added intensity.
3. Specify how much time to spend on each part of practice; warm-up, individual skills, integrated individual and positional skills, team skills, scrimmaging and cool-down.
4. Perform the various drills. When presenting a new drill, the coach should cover five steps:
   a. Describe the drill. This can be done verbally, using excerpts from this book, and with diagrams that will clarify the verbal or written information.
   b. Demonstrate the drill.
   c. Perform the drill.
   d. Evaluate the drill.
   e. Provide feedback. The coach should provide immediate feedback to individuals or groups of players so that they fully understand whether they met the objectives or how they need to improve.
5. Close out the practice by providing some generalized feedback and information for the next practice or game. Keep a record of all practices in terms of objectives, accomplishments and areas for improvement. This will provide a team development history which the coach can review periodically to compare against the season plan.

- **Learning styles and variety.** Different people learn in different ways; there are those who learn best from seeing (visual); those who learn best from hearing (auditory); and those who learn best from actions and movements (motor). Every person is some combination of these; in fact, approximately 60 percent learn best visually, 25 percent learn best by hearing and 15 percent learn best through motion. This information should be vital to the coach's planning methodology. Using a combination of visual and auditory presentation, the coach will effectively reach 85 percent of the players. This is why video has been so effective in the coaching of athletes and learning in general. The smart coach will determine which learning method(s) his individual players require and organize the learning accordingly. In addition to learning styles, the coach should be aware that athletes' learning capacity is most effective during the first 20 to 25 minutes of a practice. This is because athletic learning requires a large portion of mental and physical energy. An experienced coach will notice that as the players' energy level and enthusiasm decrease, so does their attention to detail. Accordingly, new material (requiring the most mental and physical development) should be taught during the early part of the practice.

  Keep players' interest and enthusiasm high by adding variety and competition to practices.

Player Development Phases	Preseason	First Game to Midseason	Midseason thru playoffs
Individual Skills	**60%**	**25%**	**20%**
Warm-up Period	as required	as required	as required
Skating and Rink Conditioning - Ch. 3	25%	10%	5%
Stickhandling and Puck Control - Ch. 4	15%	5%	5%
Passing and Receiving - Ch. 5	10%	5%	5%
Shooting and Scoring - Ch. 6	10%	5%	5%
Integrated Individual and Positional Skills	**30%**	**45%**	**45%**
Defense - Ch. 7	10%	15%	15%
Forwards - Ch. 8	10%	15%	15%
Goaltending - Ch. 9	10%	15%	15%
Team Skills	**10%**	**30%**	**35%**
Defensive Zone Team Play - Ch. 10	5%	10%	10%
Offensive Zone Team Play - Ch. 11	5%	10%	10%
Special Team Play - Ch. 12	0%	5%	5%
Scrimmage Play	0%	5%	10%
Cool-down Period	as required	as required	as required

Table 2-1; Percentage Of Time Spent On Skill Emphasis During The Season

When interest is high, the players' learning rate and capacity are increased. Variety can include adding new or modified drills periodically. Competition can be added to any existing drill where two or more players execute the drill simultaneously. If the coach incorporates these factors into each practice, he will be amazed at the work effort from his players.

- **When should you scrimmage?** A **scrimmage** is a controlled intrateam game designed to execute various team skills in a gamelike manner at a pace consistent with the competition. To be effective, a scrimmage should always be organized with a purpose. Before the scrimmage, each player should be told what the focus is and then given feedback at appropriate times. Scrimmaging without a definite plan will not result in the most effective player and team development and is not the most effective use of time. The decision to scrimmage should be based on the level of player development and the coach's decision that the specific skills necessary to execute the scrimmage have been practiced enough. Through specific individual, integrated individual and positional drills, team development can take place. Through the execution of a scrimmage, all of these skills can be integrated into gamelike scenarios. The coach must moderate the amount of scrimmage time with the amount of specific skill development time to ensure that proper player and team progression takes place.

- **Varying the skill emphasis during the season.** A typical roller hockey season is divided into three time frames: preseason, first game to midseason and midseason through playoffs. During these time frames, different percentages of time should be allocated to the three player development phases since this allows the **most effective learning** to take place.

During the preseason, approximately 60 percent of the time should be spent on individual skill development, 30 percent should be spent on integrated individual and positional skill development, with the remaining 10 percent spent on team skill development, as shown in Table 2-1. The emphasis on individual skill development should be continued throughout the season but especially stressed at the start of the season and at any time the players seem to be on a plateau of development.

During the first game to midseason time frame, the coach must establish practice priorities depending on what has happened in the games. He should study the needs very carefully and organize his practice time accordingly. For example, if the team is doing well on offense but showing defensive weaknesses, he should emphasize defensive work. A typical practice might be 25 percent individual skill development, 45 percent integrated individual and positional skill development, and the remaining 30 percent spent on team skill development.

During the midseason through playoff time frame, it is more important than ever to have an evaluation of the team needs, as demonstrated by the season's play, and then work to strengthen these needs on a priority basis. During the late season, when the players have been working hard for some time, keep them interested through lots of variety, competition and innovation when practicing the more repetitive phases of the game. A typical practice might be 20 percent individual skill development, 45 percent integrated individual and positional skill development, and the remaining 35 percent spent on team skill development.

Scouting Your Opponents

Careful planning for upcoming games gives the coaches and players a sense that they are ready. A well-prepared team knows what it is capable of doing and what to expect from the opposition. Scouting is the **process of gathering information about an opponent** by observing a practice or game against another team. Scouting the opposition should be done as close to your game date as possible. Trends and changes in tactics are reasons the latest game of the opposition should be viewed. Figure 2-3, **Scouting Information Worksheet**, has been designed so that the scout can capture data and provide an analysis of the opposition. Data gathered covers all major components of a team: offense, defense, goaltending, strategies, strengths, weaknesses and overall observations. Discuss this data with your team and use it to fortify your strengths and shore up your weaknesses.

Game Time

Now it is time to put all of the practice to the test: it's game time! **The coach's role** during this time frame is to ensure that the game plan is relayed to the team and the team is mentally ready to play. During the pregame meeting, the coach should cover the game strategy and the opponent's strengths and weaknesses according to the latest scouting report. Additionally, the coach should make sure that all players are mentally ready to play at 100 percent for the entire game. There is no way that a team is going to improve physically just prior to a game, but the mental component can be guided so that the players are all focused. Having done all this, the coach must be ready to make quick decisions on playing personnel throughout the game and must have a *feel* for which players are playing well during that particular game. It is important for a coach to decide before the game which players he is going to use in certain situations, such as power play or penalty killing roles. The coach also needs to consider the starting lineup, changing lines, the tight game, when to use a timeout and taking care of injuries.

- **The starting lineup.** Deciding which players start the game is primarily based on the coach's strategy. If the strategy is conservative, the coach should start a more defensive line. If the strategy is aggressive, the coach should start a more offensive line. A good start, even more important than the first goal, can do a lot to set the tone for the rest of the game. This will instill high initial team morale and get everyone into a smooth, working groove. Generally, it is recommended to keep the first shift for each line short so that all of the players get into the game (and into their groove) early.
- **Changing lines.** The question of when to substitute forward units, defensive units or whole lines is the most difficult game-time job of the coach. The coach can often gain an advantage or even defeat a team with superior overall skill through intelligent player substitution. On the other hand, a small lead can quickly vanish when poor line changes occur. It is important for the coach to change players at appropriate times. It is best to change lines or units during a stoppage of play or when your team has control of the puck and is moving into the offensive zone. It is not advisable to change a line or unit when

Siller Player And Team Evaluation Profile© Scouting Information Worksheet		
Scouted By: *The Big Cheese* **Date**: *5/5/95*	**Team #1**: *Eighteen Wheelers* **Location**: *The Palace*	**Team #2**: *Rolling Thunder* **Score**: *6 - 3*
Team Attribute	**Team #1**	**Team #2**
Style at start of game	Slow, team #1 hesitant	Moderate pace, not aggressive
Face-off strategies and effectiveness	Basic lineups, no real strategy. #14 and #27 are the teams best. Win about 40% of face-offs.	#18 wins most face-offs. He moves puck back to defense and breaks.
Goaltending style and effective-ness	Standup style. Excellent glove, weak on low stick side. Covers most rebounds.	Goes down a lot. Excellent on low shots. Weak on high shots. Gives up many rebounds.
Defensemen	#2 plays-the-puck. #8 and #3 are solid and move the puck well. The rest are average.	The team is weak on defense except for #44. He is very good all around — offense and defense.
Forwards	#14 and #55 are best combina-tion. Others average.	#18 and #17 are best combina-tion. Others average.
Defensive Zone Play — cover-age, breakout, backchecking	Play mostly zone defense. #8 and #3 set up effective breakout. Some backchecking.	Man-to-man defense. #44 sets up effective breakout. Others average. Some backchecking.
Offensive Zone Play — forechecking, offensive defensemen	#55 very good forechecker. #3 moves in as third forward on many plays.	#17 is a good forechecker. #44 always ready to move in as third forward.
Description of goals	2 low stick side. 2 low glove side. 1 wrap around power play goal. 1 five-hole deke.	All three goals scored up high on blocker side.
Power play strategies and effectiveness	#14/55/27/8/3 rotate on power play. They take their time. Scored 1 goal in 4 chances.	#18/17/44/23 comprise power play. Had many shots. 0 goals in 2 chances.
Penalty killing strategies and effectiveness	#55/8/3 comprise penalty killing unit. Out of position too much. No goals while penalized.	#18/17/44 comprise penalty killing unit. Aggressive. 1 goal was scored while penalized.
Players to watch	#14/55/27/8/3	#18/17/44/23
Team strengths	Penalty killing. Speed. Third man in.	Forechecking.
Team weaknesses	Breakout and backchecking.	Power play. Defense.
General comments	Should be able to beat team #1 by slowing pace of game and controlling #14 and #55.	Should be able to beat team #2 by covering #18 on offense and avoiding #44 on defense.

Figure 2-3; Scouting Information Worksheet

the play is deep in your defensive zone because then your opponent will have a player advantage. Changing *on the fly* (changing a line during active play as opposed to during a stoppage of play) allows the coach to make specific changes anytime during a game and should be practiced.

It is important that the players know which unit is going on the playing surface next. There are several different systems for calling players for the next shift but in most cases player names are adequate. Once the coach has called the next line or unit, it is the players' responsibility to know who they replace and to get onto the playing surface at the right time. It may be wise to have the head coach call the line changes and personnel adjustments and the assistant coach provide feedback to the players. It is important that the head and assistant coaches are coordinated so that each understands his role behind the bench. Other coaching considerations are:

- If you are playing against a team that you have never played before, try various line combinations initially until the proper line combinations are evident.
- The length of a particular shift depends on many factors, however the most efficient shifts are between 45 and 75 seconds of playing time (not including play stoppages). Any time longer than that usually results in significantly reduced performance.
- If a line or unit is playing well, the coach may consider keeping it out a little longer than normal (maximum of 90 seconds playing time). If a line is not performing as expected, get it off of the playing surface, give feedback, motivate the players and then send them out again in their normal rotation with renewed focus and intensity.

■ **When to use a timeout.** The coach should always be aware of the momentum of the game. If your team is not playing well, has more than one poorly timed penalty called against it or has a couple of quick goals scored on it, the coach needs to employ a strategy that will change the negative momentum. Changing the momentum of the game by varying your line combinations may be a good strategy; however, if this strategy is not successful, then a timeout may be necessary. A timeout forces both teams to cease playing for a period of time (generally one minute) and allows your team to relax, receive feedback and focus on a new strategy (or be reminded of the original strategy). The timeout is advantageous because it can have a positive effect on your momentum, or at least neutralize most of your opponent's momentum. At best, it will recharge your players and allow them to get back into the game. At worst, it will stop the decline in momentum and give your team a fighting chance to get back into the game. Use your timeout wisely as each team only has one per game.

■ **Injuries** are an unfortunate side effect of being active. Injuries in roller hockey can be a result of not wearing proper protective gear or not warming up properly; but most injuries are due to some type of impact with the boards, another player, the net or the playing surface. Two types of injuries covered in this section are strains and sprains. Strains are a stretch, tear or rip in the muscle or muscle tendons (which hold the muscle to the bone). Strains are usually due to overuse or over extension. A sprain occurs when ligaments, which connect one bone to another bone, become stretched or torn. A *pop* or *snapping* sensation is a probable symptom of a severe sprain or strain. In either case, pain, swelling, temporary loss of mobility and/or weakness may result.

The treatment for both strains and sprains is the same; use the **RICE** method. RICE stands for Rest, Ice, Compression and Elevation. *Rest* enables the body to go through the physiological changes needed for healthy healing without putting further stress on the affected area. *Ice* (or an ice pack) causes a reduction in circulation to the region where it is being applied. This reduces the amount of fluid/blood that accumulates, which ultimately reduces the swelling. Do not apply ice directly to the affected area; always use a plastic bag or towel. Never use heat on an acute injury as it increases circulation, which aids in swelling. *Compression* also prevents further swelling by squeezing out accumulated fluid. This is usually done with an elastic bandage. *Elevation* of a swollen area uses gravity to move fluid away from the injured area. Also, when elevated, localized blood pressure is reduced, which helps minimize swelling and pain. After the swelling has disappeared, moist heat can be applied; whirlpools, hot tubs, hot showers, moistened hot towels or chemical hot packs work best. In both cases, follow up with a physician because there is no way to differentiate a strain or sprain from another injury without an X-ray. The prepared coach should keep various **supplies in his coaching bag**; these include extra wheels, bearings, tape, pucks, tool kit, helmet and skate hardware, notebook, ice packs, ibuprofen, ace bandage and towels.

Game Evaluation Tools

Evaluating each game is important to the coach as it provides objective and subjective information on the performance of the team as well as each player to support improvement. In addition to the coach's observations, **two game evaluation tools** should be employed —statistics and video.

- **Statistics** are an important tool to help coaches assess what is happening during a game and to help understand what happened after the game. If compiled accurately, they can be an important aspect in the success of a team. During a game, strategy can be devised or altered depending on the coach's interpretation of specific statistics. If statistics indicate a situation where individual players can improve specific play (such as shooting more), the coach should provide immediate feedback to those players. After a thorough review of the game, the coach can also use statistics to help plan upcoming practices by emphasizing weak areas. Over a longer period of time, statistics can show trends which will help the coach determine the strengths and weaknesses of individual players, the team as a whole and opponents.

  It is very important that statistics be used wisely by the coach and not become negative to the players by continually emphasizing what they are doing wrong. They should be used positively to point out individual and team improvement areas as well as to plan and change strategies during and after a game. With younger players, game statistics should be secondary to learning the basic fundamentals and having fun. A sequence of pertinent statistics, rather than just goals and assists, will point out the importance of all aspects of the game and the value of different types of players on the team. The Siller Game Statistic Worksheet (Figure 2-4) has been designed to provide the coach with 13 essential raw and computed statistics to aid in team improvement and planning. The six raw statistics include:

1. **Shots on net** records the number of shots that reach the goaltender or go into the net. For your team, the location of the shot and the player executing the shot can be recorded. This data is used to determine if your team is getting shots from high- or low-percentage scoring locations. It is also used to determine the number of shots your opponents are taking, which can show how effective your team's defensive play is.
2. **Goals** are recorded to determine both your team's and your opponents' top goal scorers. This will help the coach make sure that high scorers are on the playing surface at times when goals are needed. It will also alert the coach when the opponent has its high scorers out or when your team has a defensive breakdown.
3. **Assists** are recorded to determine each team's playmakers. It will also provide the coach with some information about which line combinations are better than others.
4. **Plus/Minus** is recorded to determine the players who are on the playing surface when a goal is scored. If your team scores, each player on the playing surface gets a +; if the opposing team scores each player gets a -. This statistic is recorded while playing at full strength, on the power play (PP) or while penalty killing (PK). A trend will develop if certain lines are on for an unusual number of goals for or against. Use this data to determine the strong and weak defensive or offensive pairs.
5. **Face-offs won/lost** are recorded to determine the number of face-offs won or lost during the game. This statistic will alert the coach to which units need to work on face-off skills more during practice. It can also document who your best face-off players are so that you can use them in critical situations.
6. **Penalty minutes** are recorded to determine which players are most often penalized and for how many minutes. Playing short-handed, when only four attackers are available to begin with, is a definite handicap. Although some

penalties are worth taking (interfering with a player who has an excellent scoring opportunity), most penalties are a sign of tired and/or frustrated players. In either case, improvements should be made to reduce your team's penalty numbers.

The seven computed statistics include:

7. **Points** (goals plus assists) are computed to determine which players should be used more when your team is behind and needs to put points on the board. It will also alert the coach when the opponent has its pointgetters out.
8. **Shooting percentage** is a statistic and is computed to determine the team's scoring effectiveness. To calculate this percentage, divide the number of goals scored (No. 2) by the number of shots on net (No. 1). A shooting percentage higher than 20 percent is very good.
9. **Save percentage** is computed to determine the effectiveness of your goaltender (and defense). This statistic alone will not provide enough information to determine whether a goaltender played well or poorly, but combined with the coaches' observation, will make a good assessment. To calculate this percentage, subtract the opposing team's shooting percentage (goals/shots) from 100 percent. A save percentage higher than 90 percent is very good.
10. **Face-off win percentage** is computed by dividing the number of face-offs won by the total number of face-offs attempted. If this statistic shows a win percentage of less than 35 percent, a definite increase in face-off skills should be incorporated into your practices.
11. **Penalty killing percentage** is computed to determine the effectiveness of your team's penalty killing unit (or the opponent's power play effectiveness). To determine this percentage, subtract the number of times your team was scored upon while in a penalty killing role from the total number of penalty killing opportunities, and then divide this number by the total number of penalty killing opportunities. Seventy-five percent or better is considered very good.
12. **Power play percentage** is computed to determine the effectiveness of your team's power play unit (or the opponent's penalty killing effectiveness). To determine this percentage, divide the number of goals scored while on the power play by the number of power play opportunities. Thirty percent or better is considered very good.
13. **Shot distribution** is computed to determine the percentage of players on the team who had shots on net during the game. A low percentage indicates that only a few players had shots on net and the coach should reinforce the importance of shooting during the next practice and game. To determine this distribution, divide the number of players who had shots on net by the total number of players on the team (exclude the goaltender). Fifty percent or better is considered very good.

- **Video** technology provides another game evaluation tool that can be used by coaches for training camp evaluations during the preseason and for postgame analysis during the season and playoffs. During training camp, it is useful to videotape scrimmage games, especially if the coach is undecided on the selection of particular players. The videotape can be used to isolate specific player skills which can help the coach make a more informed player assessment. Following a game, the coach can review the videotape and reassess scoring chances, offensive or defensive breakdowns, and other specific team and individual play. Highlights from the videotape can be shown to the team before the next practice. These highlights should point out areas where the team has played competently or exceptionally as well as areas requiring improvement. It is both an eye-opening and learning experience for a player to see how he looks from an outside perspective. Only the player can truly explain why he reacted in a particular manner; only he can provide the reason for his decision, based upon what he read at that time. This video experience, if properly utilized, can be an invaluable learning tool for both coaches and players, so use it wisely.

Siller Game Statistics Worksheet©

Roadies **vs.** *The World* **Score:** *12-2 Win* **Location:** *Ridgecrest* **Date:** *6/16/95*

No.	Player	Shots	Goals	Assists	Points	+/- PP PK	Face-offs Won\Lost	Penalty (mins)
4	MacGregor	7	2	1	3	+6/-1PK	9/6	
17	Millar	5	1	2	3	+6/-1PK	1/0	
77	Siller	5	2	1	3	+6/-1PK		1 (3)
15	Palmer	4	1	1	2	+6		1 (3)
18	Gallagher	1		2	2	+1/+1PP	5/2	
9	Lewis	3	2		2	+1/+1PP	8/8	
19	Mazur	1	1	1	2	+1/+1PP		2 (6)
49	Donohue	1		1	1	+1/+1PP		
22	Decker	4	1	1	2	+3	0/1	
55	Buckey	4	1	1	2	+3	8/8	
33	Johnson	3	1		1	+3		
69	Quinn	1		1	1	+3		
1	Collman							1 (3)
TOTALS		39	12	12	24	+41	31/25	5 (15)

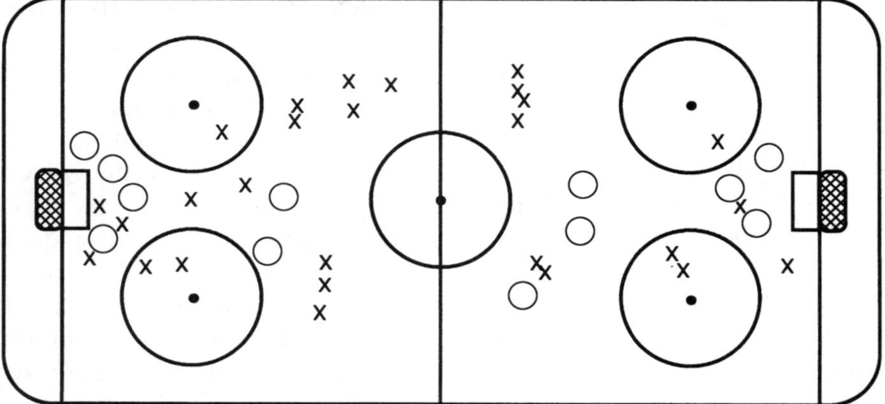

O represents goals; X represents shots

Opponent's Stats
2 Goals Scored #7 Power Play #16 Full Strength
Shots — 28
Penalties — 5 for 15 min.

Shooting Percentage .... 12/39 = 30.8%	**Penalty Killing Percentage** .... 4/5 = 80%
Save Percentage .... 100% - 2/28 = 92.9%	**Power Play Percentage** .... 1/5 = 20%
Face-off Win Percentage ...... 31/56 = 55.4%	**Shot Distribution** .... 12/12 = 100%

Notes: All players played very well. On offense, the shot selections and locations were excellent. The defense moved up into the play and because of that, 5 of the 12 goals were scored by defensemen. On defense, the forwards were backchecking and the defense executed three or four poke checks on potential scoring opportunities. Both opponents goals were scored by an open man left in front of the net, one at full strength (#16) and one while playing one man short (#7). Our goaltending was very effective, stopping 92.9% of the shots. Next practice need to work on a more effective breakout play and defensive play in front of the net.

Figure 2-4; Siller Game Statistics Worksheet

Recap

After reading and studying the material in this chapter, you should be able to answer the following questions:

1. List and describe some of the qualities of a good coach. Why are they important?
2. Describe the three player development phases of roller hockey. How does each phase differ?
3. What does a player's AAPMD level determine?
4. Define reading and reacting and provide three examples of how it is used.
5. What information does the Player Development Phases Checklist (Figure 2-1) provide the coach? How can it best be used?
6. Why are roller hockey rules important? What can happen without them?
7. Why is team success dependent upon effective planning? What happens if your team does not have a plan?
8. What types of tools are provided in the Siller Player and Team Evaluation Profile? How will they help prepare you and your team for a successful season?
9. What are some criteria that can be used to evaluate and select a team? How can the Team Selection Checklist (Figure 2-2) be used as part of the selection process?
10. Describe four factors that the coach should consider when planning a practice. Why is it important to vary the skill emphasis of player development during the season?
11. What is a scrimmage? How can it be used most effectively?
12. What are the benefits of scouting your opponent? How will the Scouting Information Worksheet (Figure 2-3) be used to prepare your team during the season?
13. What is the coach's role prior to a game? What are some of the factors that a coach needs to consider during a game?
14. List the supplies that a prepared coach carries in the equipment bag.
15. Describe two game evaluation tools. How can each of these tools assist the coaching staff with planning and player improvement?

3

Skating and Rink Conditioning

Highlights

This chapter addresses the importance of skating and conditioning while on the playing surface. Chapter 3 presents the following information:

Discussion

Fundamentals

- *forward skating*
  - *starting*
  - *moving forward*
  - *stopping*
  - *turning and crossovers*
  - *transitions*
- *backward skating*
  - *starting*
  - *moving backward*
  - *stopping*
  - *turning and crossovers*
  - *transitions*

Advanced Techniques

- *power slide*
- *jumping*

Siller Player And Team Evaluation Profile — Skating And Rink Conditioning

Drills

Advanced Drills

Recap

A journey of a thousand miles must begin with a single step.

— Chinese Proverb —

He who stops being better stops being good.

— Oliver Cromwell —

Discussion

Skating is the most important fundamental since skating is what players do most! During an average roller hockey game, a player can skate up to two miles, but poor line changes can increase that distance. This is why developing and perfecting skating technique is important. Skating is the foundation on which everything else is built. Proficient skating will make any player more capable of performing the other skills presented in this book. A roller hockey player whose skating is technically sound will skate fast, be hard to move off the puck, tire less rapidly and be able to learn many skating moves without great difficulty. The player whose skating has even one technical imperfection can be seriously handicapped. One reason that many *good* roller hockey players may never make it to the professional level is that, although they skate a lot, much of it is done haphazardly. Little attention is given to developing correct technique. **Effective skating** can only be achieved by working hard at drills specifically designed to develop and improve posture, balance, efficient movement, speed, endurance and, ultimately, confidence.

Posture is important in any form of athletics and in roller hockey refers to the general body position of the skater. The stomach should be comfortably drawn in and the chest held high. This position gives muscles around the lower abdomen and hips room to move freely and efficiently. A high chest avoids cramping of the lungs and heart space and enables these important organs to perform efficiently. This may seem a little awkward at first, but continued practice will soon make it second nature.

When the skater moves forward, his knees should be slightly bent and his upper body a little ahead of his hips. This gives him maximum forward drive. This forward body lean should not be overemphasized because balance and maneuverability will be compromised. Players who skate with their body upright not only lose forward drive but also appear to *run* on their skates due to high skate lift. Experiment until you coordinate the factors that give maximum speed together with a feeling of balance and comfort. Anywhere from 10 to 25 degrees of upper body forward lean is sufficient.

Most of us have a natural sense of balance that allows us to stand on both feet without falling over. In most cases we can also stand on one foot at a time. Walking involves being in and out of balance, shifting weight from one foot as you support it with the other. The same principle holds true on skates. Just as you learned how to find your balance and walk, you can do the same on in-line skates.

Any player can develop top level skating efficiency if he works hard and applies correct methods. Efficient skating can be developed by incorporating good (correct and efficient) habits and eliminating bad (incorrect and inefficient) habits. The intelligent player and coach will continually try to improve skating, and will regularly check style and technique to enhance good habits and eliminate bad ones.

Body type contributes to differing levels of speed, endurance and overall conditioning. Some players have the type of muscles that generate speed. Others have muscles that cannot move quite as fast, but move at a good rate of speed for longer periods of time. The slower, endurance players will have to work harder at quickness than the speedier players. However, quicker players tend to tire more easily or work effectively only in spurts. This is why a team which was outskated in the first period can turn around and outskate the opposition during the last period. By paying close attention to your skating technique, you can work on specific techniques to improve your speed, endurance and overall conditioning. Since speed is about 25 percent mental, the player who consciously drives himself past the natural tendency to take things easy will skate faster than a player who makes no such attempt. This extra drive or desire comes from the fact that you have developed confidence in your ability to *push the skating envelope* and take your skating ability further than you have before.

At first, having skates on your feet may seem a little awkward. You will be about three or four inches taller and will not have the stability you are accustomed to when standing on your feet. Your muscles may be straining to keep your legs from sliding out from under you and your brain may be telling you, "this is not natural." Don't let your mind confuse you. The more you put on your skates, stand and move, the more natural it will feel and the more confident you will feel. Remember, confidence is a state of mind. Don't get frustrated if you don't get it at first, just keep practicing!

Fundamentals

This section covers the fundamental forward and backward skating techniques of starting, moving, stopping, turning and crossovers, and transitioning from forward to backward skating and backward to forward skating.

V-start

Crossover Start

Stride-Then-Glide

Forward Skating

Starting

The **front start or V-start** is effectively employed immediately following a face-off. The position from which you can get going in the least amount of time is with your skates shoulder width apart and turned slightly outward (V position), weight distributed evenly on both legs, knees slightly bent, stomach in, chest high, upper body leaning comfortably forward and head up. The whole body should be loose and relaxed since relaxed muscles move more quickly and efficiently than tensed muscles.

When starting, pick your left skate (for this example) up a couple of inches off of the playing surface and move your hips slightly forward. At the same time, push off hard with the inside edge of your right skate and extend your right leg fully to obtain maximum thrust, then put your left leg back on the playing surface and glide. The right leg is then brought around to the front along with the right hip. The left skate is now turned slightly outward and fully extended using the inside edge of your left skate to obtain the necessary thrust. Your right leg is placed back on the playing surface to glide. Each cycle in this process takes a fraction of a second to complete. The first four to six strides should be as short and quick as you can make them, then you can gradually lengthen your stride to normal length. The short strides are required to get you up to speed as quickly as possible.

The **side start** is used in situations when your side or back is facing the direction in which you want to go. This could occur in the offensive zone when the opponents have started to break out and you need to get back into the play. The ability to start quickly in this situation is extremely important.

To initiate the side start, turn your hip and shoulder in the direction that you want to move (to the right side in this example). With your knees slightly bent, lean so that most of your weight is on your left leg and pick up your right skate a couple of inches off of the playing surface. Push off with the inside edge of your left skate as you place your right skate on the playing surface in the direction of travel. After you push off, bring your left hip and leg around in the direction of travel. Your right leg should now be ready to thrust you forward as the cycle continues.

The **crossover start** is used in similar situations as the side start. To initiate this start, turn your hip and shoulder in the direction that you want to move (to the right side in this example). With your knees slightly bent, lean so that most of your weight is on your right leg. Swing your left leg around and over your right skate. Push off with the outside edge of your right skate as you place your left skate on the playing surface in the direction of travel. After you push off, bring your right leg around in the direction of travel. Your left leg is now ready to thrust you forward as you place your right skate on the playing surface, and the cycle continues. As with all starts, the first four to six strides should be as short and quick as you can make them, then you can gradually lengthen them. You should practice starting from either side until you are confident in your abilities in both directions.

Moving forward. Once you have started moving forward, it is important to be able to continue moving forward using what I call the **stride-then-glide** technique. The body is leaned forward to place the weight over the glide (front) leg. The upper body and the upper portion of the glide leg should form an approximate 90-degree angle. The skate of the stride leg (the leg that is pushing) is turned outward and extended. Try to develop a smooth stride with maximum thrust from the stride leg. As the stride leg is returned from extension, it is brought to the front and assumes the role of the glide leg. The stride leg should be kept close to the playing surface as it is returned from extension. The glide leg now assumes the role of the stride leg and extends outward to continue the forward movement. This stride-then-glide pattern is continued until you have reached your forward destination. As you move, allow for a natural arm swing, but do not overswing the arms which could interfere with efficient forward motion. Excess motion is a waste of energy and may cause a reduction in the forward speed.

Here are some additional steps to keep in mind while moving forward:

- Bring your skates close together after each stride. If your skates are wide apart, you are only pushing off with a limited amount of distance with every stride; and distance equates to power. Bring your skates close together and start your stride from a center position to increase the length of your pushoff.
- Keep your knees flexible and relaxed. The only time the knee should be straightened is during the stride. Flexible knee action enables the skater to sustain good balance, glide smoothly, and provides the ability to change direction or maneuver quickly.
- Develop weak muscles. Many players do not skate properly because there is a muscular weakness in some part of their body (i.e., around the ankles) that prevents efficient performance. When this is the case, the player often unconsciously makes some adjustment in style in an attempt to use a stronger muscle. The solution is to develop the muscles. Every roller hockey player, no matter how strong he or she seems to be, should do special exercises designed to strengthen, stretch and flex the muscles used in skating.
- Relax. When trying to move quickly, some skaters grit their teeth, thrust their head forward and tighten every muscle in their bodies, tiring themselves needlessly and spoiling the efficient skating action. Controlled relaxation is very important. Keep your determination firm but your muscles loose. When you tighten a muscle not being used in the skating action, it interferes with the action of the muscles that are supposed to work and throws a greater strain on your heart and lungs, which must force more blood to these muscles.
- Never lift your skates more than a couple of inches off the playing surface. Many beginning roller hockey players have a bad habit of lifting their skates high off the playing surface after completing the thrust. This wastes energy and takes away speed and balance. Make sure that when the thrust is completed, the skate comes forward again close to the playing surface.

Stopping

The **T-stop** is one of two fundamental stops described in this section. The T-stop is a slow stop that can be used when coming to the bench when a shift is over or by a defenseman when he slows down behind the net to set up a breakout play. Begin by using one of the starting techniques described above and then glide. Place your weight on your left skate (for this example), and slowly lift your right skate and turn it perpendicular to your direction of travel (sideways). With both knees bent, slowly drag the wheels of your right skate and increase the pressure until you stop. Keep your upper body square in the direction of travel. Practice this with both the right and left skates.

The **two-skate stop** technique is designed to stop the player quickly in order to avoid a defender, change position, or stop and come back down the playing surface while backchecking (skating back toward your defensive zone while covering an offensive player). This is important because the faster you can stop, the sooner you can get back in the play or the easier you can get away from an opponent.

Two-Skate Stop

This stop is made by swinging the upper body and hips quickly at a right angle to the direction of travel. As this occurs, the player should turn both skates quickly in the same direction, bend the knees, and press his weight down so that the wheels grip the playing surface. As you are stopping, shift your weight from the outside edge of the inside skate to the inside edge of the outside skate. Stay low upon completion of the stop to keep your balance. Learn how to stop facing both directions.

Turning and Crossovers

Turning and crossovers are used to change direction efficiently without stopping. The **two-skate turn** is the most basic turn and requires very little technique. Once you know which direction you want to turn, look to see if you have a clear path, bend and point your knees into the turn, and allow the outside edge of your inside skate and your inside shoulder to guide you through the turn. Keep your shoulders level and place most of your weight on your inside leg. For wide turns, your weight should be distributed on your middle two wheels. When making a tighter turn, your weight should be distributed on your back two wheels. Practice this turning technique to both the right and left.

The **power turn** (scooting) is a turning technique that can be used to maintain or gain speed. It is generally a move that can be used to great advantage when carrying the puck around a defender in the offensive zone.

Place most of your weight on one leg (the left leg for example) slightly bending the left knee, and then give a series of quick, hard thrusts using the inside edge of the right skate. This action moves the skater quickly forward and, in this case, also to the left.

The **crossover** enables the skater to change direction quickly. It is the best movement to use to get back into the play in the least amount of time without stopping. Crossovers can also be used by a defenseman when going behind the net to start a breakout play.

To perform this move, take a few strides, bend your inside knee (the left if crossing over to the left), put most of your weight on your left leg, swing your body forward and to the inside of the turn, and bring your right leg (and skate) around and over the left leg (and skate) in the direction that you want to go. Push toward the outside of the turn with the outside edge of your left skate to continue momentum while turning. As your right skate makes contact with the playing surface, lift your left skate around and behind your right skate, then use your right leg to provide thrust. If you have developed the correct technique, your actions will look like a scissoring action with one leg pushing and the other leg pulling. The faster you go when making the crossover, the more you must bend your inside knee and place your weight on this leg. If you perform the move properly you can do it at a very high speed.

Left Crossover

In general, the more you bend at the waist and lean into the turn (while keeping your shoulders level), the more extreme the turn will be. The taller you stand, the straighter you will go. As you get better, your turns will become sharper and your circles smaller. Eventually you will be able to make hairpin turns with ease. Don't forget to practice turning in both directions.

Transitions

Transitions are a means of reversing your orientation while continuing in the same direction without actually stopping. It is an advantage for the offensive player and is a necessity for defensive players. The secret of being able to transition is in developing the ability to shift your weight quickly and maintain proper balance. Players with a better natural sense of balance and coordination will be able to perfect the technique more quickly than the average player; however, anyone can develop this skill through practice.

Forward-to-backward. Initiate this technique while skating with your knees bent and your weight on the balls of your feet. Once you decide to transition, in a clockwise direction in this example, pick up your right skate, lean slightly forward over your left skate and turn your body quickly clockwise 180 degrees. As you turn your body, your right leg is swung around behind you from your right side to your left side. As your body and leg swing around, pivot in the same direction on the back two wheels of your left skate. When turning your body, make sure you snap your hips and shoulders around, as this action is the key to a quick transition. The backward skating action starts the moment your right skate completes its swing into position and is placed onto the playing surface in the direction you want to go. Practice transitioning in both clockwise and counter-clockwise directions.

Backward Skating

Starting

The **figure-eight** start is a basic start used by beginning in-line skaters. This technique requires a similar starting position to the front or V-start except that the toes of the skates are pointed inward (inverted V) and the upper body is leaning slightly back. The movement of the skates is from a toes inward to toes outward position. This is accomplished by simultaneously moving both skates in a continuous figure-eight pattern. This technique is not the most effective backward starting technique but it will get you started in the direction that you want to go.

The C-start technique is an excellent way to start moving backward with power. Begin with your skates shoulder-width apart, knees bent, weight slightly back on your rear wheels and the upper body leaning slightly back. Make a large semicircular motion or C using the inside edge of your left skate by pushing outward with your left leg. After completing the C with your left leg, bring your skates back together. Make a C using the inside

Backward C-start

edge of your right skate and bring your skates back together. Continue making the C patterns and you will be moving and gaining speed. Remember to keep your glide skate straight. To achieve maximum power and speed, try to develop maximum stride leg extension with each stride. Speed will improve with strong leg action. Don't forget to look behind you.

Moving Backward. Skating backward utilizes the same movements that were described in the C-start section above. Once you have initiated your C-start, you can continue to use it while moving backward. The skill level reached by many backward skaters is far from the level that could be achieved if more time were spent on it. This is why so many coaches find it difficult to find good backward skating defensemen. Skating backward should be practiced by all players on a team and especially defensemen. A backward skater who has good agility and mobility will be able to defend very efficiently against most puck carriers.

Stopping

The **backward curl stop** is used mostly by defensemen when the play begins to transition out of the defensive zone and into the offensive zone while the defenseman is still skating backward. To perform this stop while moving backward, cut a wide arc using the inside edges of both skates by turning the heels of your skates outward. Slowly turn the heels of your skates in and move the insides of the knees out away from each other. As the heels of your skates approach each other, lean forward so that your center of gravity is ahead of your skates. Force the inside edges of your wheels hard onto the playing surface and slowly move your body back toward the upright position. At this point, your skates should be in the V position. Once stopped, you are now ready to use the V-start technique described earlier to begin moving forward and back into the play.

Turning and Crossovers

The **two-skate turn** is similar to the forward two-skate turn with the only differences being that you are skating backward and you will bend and point your knees to the outside as you turn. As with its forward counterpart, practice this turning technique both to the right and left.

The **crossover** is the most efficient way to turn while skating backward. If you want to go to the left while moving, lean into the turn while keeping your shoulders level, place most of your weight on your left leg, and bring your right skate across and in front of the left skate. As the right skate comes over, drive the outside edge of the left skate underneath and across your body. It is important to push the left skate under to full extension using the outside edge of your wheels. At the completion of the left skate extension, your weight should be transferred to your right leg. Push out with the right skate using the inside edge and bring the left skate back to its original position. Both legs need to work together in a scissoring motion with one leg pushing and one leg pulling. The power and acceleration is developed by the pushing action from the inside edge of the outside leg and the outside edge of the inside leg. When performed correctly, the backward crossover ends in a powerful stride. Be aware that you can easily pick up speed.

Backward-to-forward transitions. This transition is similar to the forward-to-backward transition described earlier. Once you decide to transition, in a clockwise direction for example, pick up your left skate, lean slightly forward over your right skate and turn your body quickly clockwise 180 degrees. As you turn your body, your left leg is swung around in front of you from your left side to your right side. As your body and leg swing around, you pivot in the same direction on the back two wheels of your right skate. The forward skating action starts the moment your left skate completes its swing into position and is placed onto the playing surface in the direction you want to go. Practice transitioning in both clockwise and counter-clockwise directions.

Advanced Techniques

Two advanced skating techniques covered in this section include the power slide and jumps.

The **power slide** is an advanced stopping technique that allows a player to retrieve a puck from the corner while keeping his eyes on the action around him and can be used while skating either forward or backward. This stop should only be attempted after you have mastered all of the fundamental stops described earlier.

While skating forward, pivot on your right skate (for this example) so that the heel of that skate is pointing in the direction of travel. Keep most of your weight on your right leg. Bend your right knee so that your upper and lower leg form a 90-degree angle. At the same time, swing your left leg around, extend it in the direction of travel, and begin to lay the side of your left skate and the wheels down on the playing surface. The side of your skate and wheels will slide along the playing surface until you stop. If you only place the wheels on the playing surface, you might twist your ankle. To avoid this problem, lay *both* the inside edge of your skate and the wheels down. Practice stopping with either the right or left leg extended.

Power Slide

While skating backward, bend your right knee at a 90-degree angle. Extend your left leg in the direction of travel, and lay the side of your left skate and the wheels down so that they slide along the playing surface until you stop. Practice stopping with either the right or left leg extended.

Scissor and two-legged jumps. Being able to step or jump over fallen players is a skill that can be used to continue a play, and if used effectively in the offensive zone, can set up a scoring opportunity. There are two types of jumps used to clear a fallen player, the scissor jump and the two-legged jump. As the player comes within one or two feet of a fallen opponent, he can employ the scissor jump by moving most of his weight to one leg (left in this example), lifting the right knee and leg, and pushing off with his left leg so that the right skate is propelled over the opponent and lands on the playing surface on the other side of the opponent. The arms should be lifted as the knee of the forward leg comes up. As you land, bring the left skate over the opponent and continue skating. Problems with jumps occur when the rear leg is dragged after it pushes off to start the jump and collides with the fallen player. The two-legged jump is executed by merely jumping, with both skates, over the fallen player. As with the scissor jump, the landing should be cushioned with your knees.

Drills

Prior and subsequent to any of the drills described in this book, players should **warm up and cool down** by performing stretching techniques designed to lengthen and loosen the muscles associated with the feet, legs, back, arms and shoulders. These techniques will help prevent injuries during practices and games and will prevent some of the muscular tightness that follows the day after a practice or game.

For each drill, the coach should monitor proper technique and provide feedback. The **six factors** that should be monitored by the coach when evaluating each player's skating ability are posture, balance, efficient movement, speed, endurance and

Siller Player And Team Evaluation Profile©
Skating and Rink Conditioning Checklist

Evaluator: The Coach **Date**: 7/15/94 **Location**: The Pond

		Player Name							
Notes:	**MATT**		**SNOOP**		**BILL**				
Fundamental Skating and Rink Conditioning Techniques									
Forward Skating									
Front (V) Start	9		8		8				
Side Start	8		8		8				
Crossover Start	7		8		8				
Moving Forward	7		7		8				
T-Stop	9		9		9				
Two-Skate Stop	7		7		7				
Two-Skate Turn	**10**		9		9				
Power Turn (Scooting)	7		9		8				
Crossover	9		**10**		7				
Forward-to-Backward Transition	7		6		6				
Backward Skating									
Figure-Eight Start	7		7		8				
C-Start	6		6		7				
Moving Backward	8		7		7				
Backward Curl Stop	5		7		6				
Two-Skate Turn	8		8		7				
Crossover	8		8		7				
Backward-to-Forward Transition	8		8		7				
Advanced Skating and Rink Conditioning Techniques									
Power Slide (Forward)	**3**		**3**		7				
Power Slide (Backward)	**3**		**3**		7				
Scissor Jump	6		7		6				
Two-Legged Jump	6		6		6				
TOTAL SCORE	**148**		**151**		**153**				
AVERAGE SCORE	**7.0**		**7.2**		**7.3**				

Comments: Matt, Snoop, and Bill have demonstrated high overall skating proficiency with total scores of 148, 151, and 153 respectively and average scores of 7.0, 7.2, and 7.3 respectively. Matt's two-skate turn and Snoop's forward crossover are rated as excellent. Both Matt and Snoop need to improve their power slides.

Scale: 0 = Not Performed, 1 - 3 = Low Proficiency, 4 - 6 = Medium Proficiency, 7 - 9 = High Proficiency, 10 = Excellent Proficiency

Table 3-1; Skating and Rink Conditioning Checklist

confidence. Use the Skating and Rink Conditioning Checklist to monitor performance and plan improvements for each player.

When presenting a new drill for your team, the coach should cover the following five steps:

1. Describe the drill. This can be done verbally, using excerpts from this book and with diagrams that will clarify the verbal or written instruction.
2. Demonstrate the drill. This can be performed by one of the coaches or by a player who is already knowledgeable on the drill.
3. Perform the drill. The players should execute the drill when requested by the coach.
4. Evaluate the drill. The coach should evaluate each player's execution of the drill.
5. Provide feedback. The coach should provide immediate feedback to the individual or group of players so that the players fully understand whether they met the objectives or how they need to improve to meet the objectives the next time the drill is performed.

Drill 3-1; Finding Your Center. This drill is important because it helps each player find his or her correct stance and body lean. Lay your stick on the playing surface so that the front wheels from both skates touch the stick (to keep you from rolling forward). Stand straight up with your skates shoulder width apart, arms at your side and looking ahead. Slowly lean forward, without bending at your waist or knees, until your heels start to rise and you are about to lose your balance. Do not go so far as to fall over. Note how far forward you leaned. Now do the same movement leaning back (stabilize yourself by putting your arms out in front of you, if necessary). You probably leaned about 12 inches (about 30 degrees) in each direction.

What you have done is to define your natural center of balance on in-line skates. To increase this range of balance and permit better stability, repeat the first part of the drill; this time bend your knees and waist so that your nose, knees and toes are in a straight line. Keep your head up while doing this. You should have been able to lean more in both directions with a greater freedom of movement and a better sense of your own balance when bending your knees and waist. You are now in the proper upright skating position. The bent knees act as shock absorbers, while the forward curve of your upper body keeps your weight centered forward. The correct body position while skating will vary from player to player depending on your height, weight and upper-to-lower body ratio. Incorrect positioning can only result in improper balance.

Drill 3-2; Starting. This drill provides practice for the three forward starting techniques; the front start (or V-start), side start and crossover start. Position the team into three lines starting on the goal line. At the whistle, have the first player in each line take four strides and then glide using the front start (V-start) technique. Watch for proper technique and provide feedback. Have each player run through this drill at least three times. Next, have each player practice using the side start. Again, have the players take four strides and then glide. Watch for proper technique and provide feedback. The final time, have the players perform this drill using the crossover start. Again, have the players take four strides and then glide. The coach should check technique carefully during this drill and give each player guidance as to what the player needs to work on. However, do not spend *too* much time talking. It's best to keep the drill running quickly and smoothly.

Drill 3-3; Starting Efficiency. This drill gauges each player's starting efficiency. It is similar to drill 3-2 except that instead of taking four strides, each player takes two strides. Following the second stride, the player glides until he or she stops moving. Measure the distance that each player covers. Starting efficiency is directly related to the distance that each player moves. Each player also has the opportunity to see how efficient his teammates are, thereby creating a competitive environment. This drill can be used starting in the forward or backward directions. Keeping careful records on everyone's progress and posting results of the distances achieved using the Skating and Rink Conditioning Checklist will reap benefits and add interest to this and other drills.

Drill 3-4; Developing Powerful Starts. This drill is designed to improve each player's starting power. The goal in this drill is to go from a dead stop to full speed in the first six strides. If you're able to react quickly, it takes less than three seconds to reach maximum speed. Position the team into three lines starting on the goal line. Player number two in each line will hold onto the jersey of player number one. This increased load (on player number one) while starting requires the legs to work harder than normal, and will develop a more powerful starting technique. At the whistle, have the first player in each line take six strides while pulling the second player, and then glide. Have each player run through this drill at least three times. If this drill is used enough, it will become second nature for the players to execute the explosive starts which will allow them to get that extra step on their opponents during a game.

Drill 3-5; Backward Starting. This drill provides practice for the two backward starting techniques: the figure-eight start and the C-start. Position the team into three lines starting on the goal line. At the whistle, have the first player in each line take four strides using the figure-eight technique and then glide. The coach should monitor the players for proper technique and provide feedback. Have each player run through this drill at least three times. Next, have each player practice using the C-start. Again, have the players take four strides and then glide, after which the coach provides feedback.

Drill 3-6; Stopping. This drill provides practice for the two forward stopping techniques, the T-stop and the two-skate stop, as well as the backward curl stop. Position the team into three lines starting on the goal line. At the whistle, have the first player in each line start skating toward the other end of the rink. At the next whistle, the players should stop, using the T-stop, facing the right boards. When the whistle is blown again, the players start again. At the next whistle, the players again stop, facing the right boards. These steps are repeated so that the players practice between four to six stops by the time they reach the other end of the rink. Once the first line of players gets to the center line, the second line of players can begin the drill. When all players have completed this drill, start them back to the other end of the rink. This time have them stop facing the left boards. This will ensure that stops are practiced in both directions. Repeat the drill using the two-skate stop and while skating backward and stopping using the backward curl stop.

Drill 3-7; End-to-End. This drill combines starting, skating and stopping, as well as anaerobic (without oxygen) conditioning. It is an excellent drill to use during every practice as well as during player evaluations. Timing data can be recorded for each player using the Skating and Rink Conditioning Checklist and a periodic team assessment can be performed. This drill is performed by placing the team into two lines starting at the goal line. At the whistle, the first player in each line skates at about 85 percent intensity to the far goal line, stops and returns to the original goal line. The coach can either whistle the next players in line to go or allow the player just completing the skating to tap the next player in line to go.

Since the level of intensity is high, the players will need to rest for a sufficient time period so that their heart rates return to normal and the bodies are allowed to oxygenate properly. The **interval between skating and resting** should be 1:4 for high intensity drills such as this one. This means that the time it takes to complete one skating interval (skating to far goal line and back), should be multiplied by four to determine the amount of time required for resting. For example, if it takes 40 seconds to complete one skating interval, the player should be allowed to rest for 160 seconds before executing the drill again. Normally, the amount of time a player waits in line to start the drill again is sufficient to meet this criteria. The coach should run this drill so that a minimum of three skating intervals are performed by each player. Provide feedback to the players with respect to starting, leg extension during skating, stride efficiency and stopping technique.

Variations:

- Have the players perform this drill skating laterally across the width of the rink. In this case, the skating interval is shorter, so the resting interval will also be shorter. In this variation, the team could be divided into five lines and the drill could be run a minimum of six times.
- Using a competitive edge, this drill could be performed at the end of practice with the winner allowed to rest. The remainder of the team would continue the drill until one player is left.
- Skate forward to the far goal line, stop, and return to the original goal line skating backward.
- Have the players skate from the goal line to the center red line, stop, return to the original goal line, stop, skate to the far goal line, stop and then skate back to the original goal line and stop. This drill should be performed a maximum of three times.
- Have two lines skate up the middle of the rink, swing deep into the corners, stop, and return back along the boards.

Drill 3-8; Practice Warm-Up. This is a good half-speed warm-up drill for any practice. Skate forward once around the rink in a counter-clockwise direction and stretch the legs and body in preparation for the remainder of the practice. Skate a second lap around the rink backward in the same direction. Stop and skate forward in a clockwise direction for the third lap. Complete the drill by skating a fourth lap backward in the same clockwise direction.

Variations:

- Increase to three-quarter speed.
- Combine or incorporate this drill with ones from upcoming chapters (e.g., passing, shooting) to develop a balanced and complete pregame warm-up drill.

Drill 3-9; Two-Skate Turning. Position the team into three lines starting on the goal line. Place three pylons 25 feet before the center red line, place three additional pylons on the center red line and three more pylons 25 feet after the center red line as shown is the corresponding diagram. At the whistle, have the first player in each line skate counter-clockwise around each pylon using the two-skate turn as he moves toward the far goal line. This drill should be run at half speed initially until the players are confident in their turning abilities. Have each player run through this drill at least three times.

Variations:

- Have each player skate clockwise around the pylons.
- Increase the pace to three-quarter speed.
- Have the players skate backward and around the pylons, both clockwise and counter-clockwise.

Drill 3-10; Power Turns. Position the team into three lines starting on the goal line. Place three pylons 25 feet before the center red line and place three additional pylons 25 feet after the center red line, as shown is the corresponding diagram. At the whistle, have the first player in each line skate toward each pylon, staying about five feet to the right of the pylon. When the player is about five feet from the pylon, he should start the power turn (to the left), placing most of his weight on the left leg, and then give three or four quick, hard thrusts using the inside edge of the right skate. As the player passes around and beyond the first pylon, he should prepare for the second pylon. At this point, he should skate to the left of the pylon and when he is about five feet before the second pylon, he should begin the second power turn (to the right). This time he will place most of his weight on the right leg, and then give three or four quick, hard thrusts using the inside edge of the left skate. A demonstration of this drill is essential until the players are familiar enough with what is expected of them.

Variation:

- Have players reverse the turning order by starting with a right turn followed by a left turn.

Drill 3-11; Crossovers In A Figure Eight. Line the players up on the goal line and have them skate

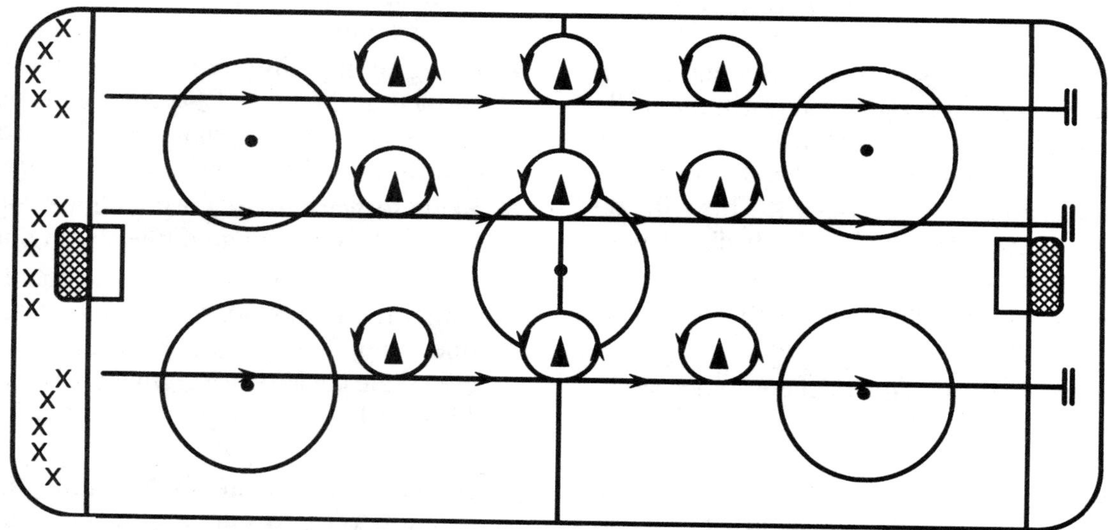

Drill 3-9; Two-Skate Turning

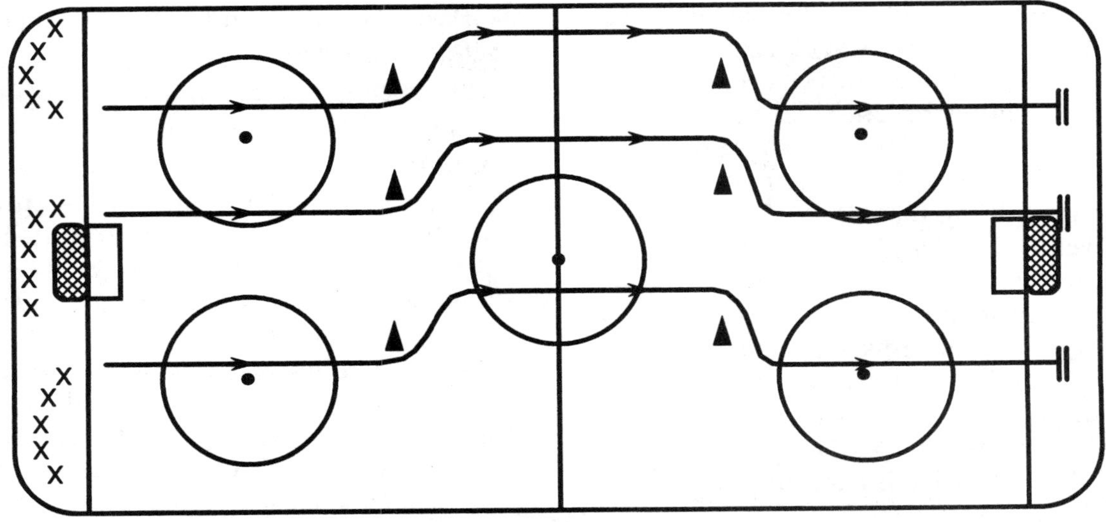

Drill 3-10; Power Turns

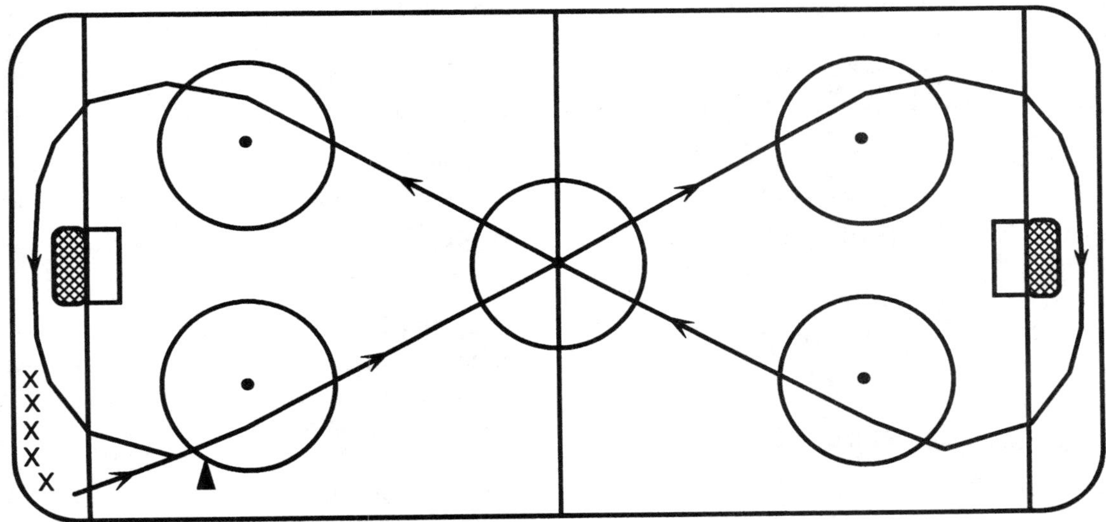

Drill 3-11; Crossovers In A Figure-Eight

forward one-by-one in a figure-eight pattern around the rink at about half speed, as shown in the corresponding diagram. Once the first player has skated about 25 feet (marked with a pylon), the next player should start. As the players skate around each net, they should employ the crossover turning technique. This drill forces each player to cross over to the left and to the right when going behind the nets and forces them to keep their heads up when they are crossing over the center red line (through the oncoming players).

Variations:

- Split the team into two groups, with one group on the near goal line and the other group on the far goal line. At the whistle, one player from each group performs this drill. Once the player has completed his figure eight, he taps the next player in line, and the next player performs this drill. This provides a competitive setting for the team.
- Perform the drill at three-quarter speed.
- Perform the drill skating backward at half or three-quarter speed. This drill is essential for all defensemen.

Drill 3-12; Zigzag. The zigzag, or double crossover, is an offensive move and is a variation of the crossover. It is a move used to get by a defender. It demands agility and balance and can be learned through regular practice. Divide the team into three lines on the goal line. At the whistle, have the players skate in a straight line. At the second whistle, have the players bring the left skate over in front of the right skate as if they were going to start a crossover to the right side. Just as the left skate hits the playing surface, bring the right skate around behind and over the left skate. The player should now be moving forward and slightly to the left. Have the players perform the zigzag at least twice each time they skate down the rink. Once the first player reaches the far goal line, the second player in each line can start the zigzag. As with power turns, a demonstration of this drill is essential until the players are familiar with what is expected of them.

Drill 3-13; Snake. Position the team into two lines starting on the goal line. Place a series of pylons on the playing surface in a pattern similar to the diagram below. At the whistle, the first player in each line skates at half speed down the playing surface, threading his way in and out of pylons. As they go down the playing surface toward the far goal line, the players should be cutting around each pylon. The drill is designed so that minimal straight-away skating is executed. Competition in this drill will key up interest and proficiency. The coach may want to time the players over the course and record the data using the Skating and Rink Conditioning Checklist.

Variations:

- Perform while skating at three-quarter speed.
- Perform while skating backward.
- Place the pylons in a pattern so that turns are tighter or sharper.

Drill 3-14; Sprint Skating. One of the best ways to train for roller hockey is to discipline yourself to do sprint intervals, working at 100 percent capacity by pushing your limits to develop speed, acceleration and stamina. This type of drill allows all-out effort for only a few seconds. It's physically strenuous, but simulates the energy demands when playing roller hockey. Set up pylons 15 feet before the center red line and 15 feet after the center red line next to the boards on both sides of the rink. Have the players skate around the rink in a clockwise direction. As each player reaches the first pylon, he should skate at 100 percent intensity until he reaches the second pylon. After he passes the second pylon, he can slow down, skate behind the net and prepare for the next set of pylons on the other side of the rink. This drill can be performed for about two minutes depending upon the level of team fitness.

Variations:

- Skate in a counter-clockwise direction.
- Skate backward in a clockwise or counter-clockwise direction.

Drill 3-15; Transitions. This drill provides half-speed practice for the forward-to-backward and backward-to-forward transitions. Position the team into three lines starting on the goal line. At the first whistle, have the first player in each line skate forward toward the other end of the rink. At the next

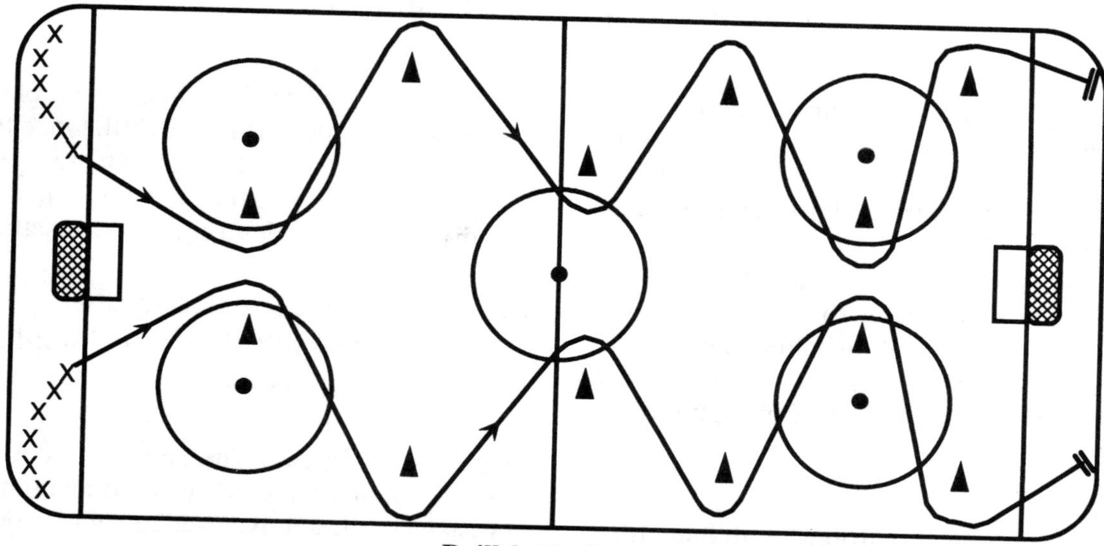

Drill 3-13; Snake

whistle, the players should transition in a clockwise direction to skating backward. The coach should repeat this action so that a minimum of four transitions are performed by each player (seven or eight is ideal). Repeat this drill so that each player has skated the length of the rink a minimum of four times.

Variations:

- Increase to three-quarter speed.
- Transition in a counter-clockwise direction.
- Transition using both clockwise and counter-clockwise movement.
- Start the players skating backward.

Advanced Drills

Drill 3-16; Power Slide. This drill provides half-speed practice for the power slide stop. Position the team into three lines starting on the goal line. At the whistle, have the first player in each line start skating forward toward the other end of the rink. At the next whistle the players should pivot on their right skate, place the left skate and wheels on the playing surface, and stop. At the next whistle the players should skate forward again toward the far end of the rink. At the next whistle the players should perform the power slide again. The players should complete at least three power slides as they skate from one goal line to the other. The coach should provide feedback to the players after each stop if necessary.

Variations:

- Increase to three-quarter speed.
- Pivot on the left skate and slide with the right.
- Alternate the pivot skate (right then left then right).
- Skate backward and execute the power slide.

Drill 3-17; Jumps. This drill provides half-speed practice for the two types of jumps: scissor and two-legged. Position the team into three lines starting on the goal line. Place sticks about 30 feet apart, parallel to the goal lines, all the way down the playing surface. At the whistle, have the first player in each line start skating forward toward the other end of the rink. As the players approach the sticks, they should jump over them using the scissor jump (right leg then the left). The players should repeat this process until they have reached the far goal line. When all of the players have completed one length of the playing surface, have them skate back to the original goal line using the two-legged jump.

Variations:

- Increase to three-quarter speed.
- Initiate the scissor jump with the left leg first.
- Place hockey bags on the playing surface so that the jump height increases.

Recap

After reading and studying the material in this chapter, you should be able to answer the following questions:

1. Why is developing and perfecting the skating technique so important?
2. What are the six factors that contribute to effective skating technique?
3. Which forward starting technique should you use immediately following a face-off? Why?
4. Define the *stride-then-glide* technique.
5. What technique will stop you quicker — the T-stop or the two-skate stop?
6. What are turns and crossovers designed to do?
7. Define transitions.
8. How will you use the Skating and Rink Conditioning Checklist to evaluate and improve individual players as well as the entire team?
9. What is the benefit of the warm-up and cool down prior to using any of the drills described in this book?
10. How can you measure a player's starting efficiency?
11. What is one method used to improve starting power?
12. What is the proper interval between skating and resting when performing high intensity skating drills?

Strategy Will Only Take You So Far!

4

Stickhandling and Puck Control

Highlights

This chapter addresses the importance of proper stickhandling and puck control. Chapter 4 presents the following information:

Discussion

Fundamentals

- *push*
- *side-to-side*
- *diagonal*
- *back-to-front*

Advanced Techniques

Puck Control

- *one-handed puck control*
- *puck control using the skates*
- *incidental body contact and puck control*
- *stickhandling while skating backward*

Siller Player and Team Evaluation Profile — Stickhandling and Puck Control

Drills

Advanced Drills

Recap

Ability is of little account without opportunity.
— Napoleon Bonaparte —

A wise man will make more opportunities than he finds.
— Francis Bacon —

Discussion

Stickhandling and puck control are skills required to maintain possession of the puck, advance the puck into the offensive zone, skate in close proximity to opponents without losing control of the puck, create open space in which the puck carrier (and team) can work and maneuver close-in on a goaltender to set up a scoring opportunity. **Stickhandling** is the process of moving the puck with the eventual goal of setting up a scoring opportunity. **Puck control** is the process of maintaining possession of the puck against one or more opponents and can be performed individually or as a team.

Although many roller hockey players possess good skating skills, when the puck is introduced, their level of skating ability drops off due to the added task of keeping the puck on their stick and moving it up the playing surface. A developing roller hockey player is not expected to learn the combined skills of skating, stickhandling and puck control overnight. Eventually, through much practice, each player must demonstrate that he can skate and perform equally well with or without the puck if he hopes to advance further. The skating ability of proficient roller hockey players does not drop off when they are in possession of the puck; they are proficient (either naturally or taught) skaters *and* puck carriers. One of the most important yardsticks for gauging the potential of players, particularly at a young age, is controlling the puck while skating.

To be able to learn and improve stickhandling and puck control skills, it is important to understand **proper body positioning**. The player stands with his skates shoulder width apart, knees bent and head up. The hands and wrists should be loose. The elbows should be kept well out from the sides of the body, the arms and shoulders should be as relaxed as possible, and the hands should be moved so that they are above the puck and in line with the puck and the body. If the elbows are too close to your body, and the arms and shoulders are stiff, you will not be able to efficiently move your hands and stick from side to side with the puck.

Proper placement of the hands on the stick is also very important. Placing the hands too close together on the stick creates a weak grip and decreases a player's stickhandling control, making the puck easier to knock away. The top hand (right hand for left-handed shooters) should be at the top of the stick just below the knob. The grip by the top hand should be firm, yet relaxed. The bottom hand (left hand for left-handed shooters) should be approximately **12 to 24 inches** below the top hand. The grip by the bottom hand should be somewhat loose, allowing the player to cushion the puck as he stickhandles. **An easy way to learn proper hand placement** is to place the top hand around the top of the stick. Next, place the elbow of the lower hand against the top hand and grasp the shaft of the stick with the bottom hand. This gives you a close approximation for proper hand position, allowing for strength, control and soft hands. ***Soft hands*** is a term for a player who has the ability to control and manipulate the puck quickly, accurately and consistently by *feel*. All great puck handlers have soft hands. When you see a player with soft hands stickhandling, it seems as if the puck is magically attached to his stick.

Positioning the puck correctly on the stick is performed by cradling the puck in a spot halfway between the heel and toe on the blade of the stick. When moving the puck, it should be feathered back and forth along the playing surface with a light, smooth touch in a series of short or long sweeps by rolling the wrists. There should be little or no noise created by the stick hitting the playing surface. Cushion the puck while you stickhandle. Be sure your weight is over the top of the puck. That is, if the puck is off to your right, then your body weight should be mostly on the right leg.

One problem players may have with any of the stickhandling and puck control techniques is **allowing the puck to roll off the blade of the stick**. This is caused by incorrectly positioning the blade of the stick (by the hands and wrists). When the bottom edge of the blade is allowed to slant toward the puck, there is a tendency for the puck to roll or jump off of the blade. When the top edge of the blade moves too far over the puck, there is a tendency for the puck to flip over the blade. When the toe of the blade points outward to the side instead of straight ahead or slightly inward, the puck can easily roll off of the blade. The toe of the blade should be turned in toward the puck so that it will not roll off the end of the blade.

Along with correct body positioning and hand placement, proper positioning of the head and eyes represents the third building block for effective control and handling of the puck. **Proper head positioning** allows the player to more accurately *read* (or perceive) the playing environment by providing the player with the necessary information to *react*. The common expression *keep your head up* is often used by coaches to refer to the importance of players *reading* what is ahead of them. More recently, the expression *look over your shoulders* is being used to stress the importance of players being aware of what is in front, to the side and behind them simply by moving their heads. The intent is to develop players' peripheral vision rather than just line-of-sight vision, thus increasing the quality of the *read* and the likelihood of a good *reaction*. Total situational awareness and accurate perception form the basis upon which effective stickhandling and puck control occur.

Ideally, the puck carrier should attempt to have his body and head in such a position so as to maximize his vision, both peripheral and line-of-sight, recognizing that this is not always possible in tight playing situations. Skilled puck carriers have an ability to find open spaces because they constantly try to "face the play" or place themselves in the best possible position in relation to their teammates and opponents. Once a player has learned the skill of controlling the puck on his stick, without looking at the puck too often, he will then be able to look ahead and increase his scope of vision, awareness and options.

Fundamentals

There are four basic stickhandling and puck control techniques covered in this section. These include the push, side-to-side, diagonal and the back-to-front.

The **push** is the most basic of all stickhandling and puck control techniques. It consists of pushing the puck ahead of the player by about four feet or so, and then skating after it. This process is repeated as the player skates to a desired location. The push is an efficient way to move the puck when you have a lot of open space to work in and allows the player to concentrate on skating and gaining speed. It is not recommended for use when opponents are within 10 feet due to the increased probability that possession of the puck will be jeopardized. Beginners should keep both hands on the stick when executing this technique.

Side-to-Side Stickhandling

The **side-to-side** is the most commonly used stickhandling technique. The player starts off by moving the puck from side to side using a sweeping motion in a path that varies from one foot to as wide as you can reach with your stick and arms. The puck is moved to one side, then the stick is lifted over and ahead of the puck to cup it, and then the puck is moved back again. When lifting the stick at the end of the sweep, let the puck move a little ahead of the stick blade so that it is not flipped by the stick as the stick is lifted. The player who moves the puck only as far as is needed to avoid an opponent's stick or some other obstacle has an advantage because any unnecessary movement can slow forward speed and makes it more likely to lose control of the puck.

The **diagonal** applies many of the same principles as the side-to-side technique. The player starts off by moving the puck on a diagonal line from approximately the front-and-center position to the left (or right) side approximately even with the left (or right) skate. As the puck is brought back along the diagonal, the stick is then lifted over and ahead of the puck to cup it, and then the puck is moved back to the front-and-center position again. The shoulders and waist turn so that they are as square as possible to the path of the puck while it is moved along the diagonal. The top arm is carried well away from the body with the elbow pointing along the direction in which the puck is being moved. The lower arm is also kept away from the body and the elbow points along the direction of the puck travel, but in the opposite direction to the upper arm.

The **back-to-front** technique is performed by bringing the puck to the left (for this example) side of the body and about a foot behind the left skate; turning the shoulders and waist well to the left, and then moving the puck from that point to a point about a foot or two in front of that skate. The lower hand and arm should be close to the side, with the elbow well bent and pointing behind. The top hand and arm should be placed well away from the body with the elbow up and pointing perpendicular to the direction of puck travel. This is the most difficult of the four stickhandling and puck control techniques, but regular practice will enable you to improve the amount and accuracy of control. This technique does not allow the player to move the puck on a very wide path back to front because of the cramped arm position.

Diagonal Stickhandling

Back-to-Front Stickhandling

Advanced Techniques

There are four advanced stickhandling and puck control techniques that are covered in this section. These include one-handed puck control, puck control using the skates, incidental body contact and puck control, and stickhandling while skating backward.

Puck Protection. In many playing situations, it is necessary for the puck carrier to focus on protecting the puck in order to maintain puck control. Puck protection also allows you to *buy time* until a teammate is available to provide support or you successfully get by the defender. **Puck protection** is a process in which the puck carrier keeps his body between the defender and the puck to maintain control of the puck. It is most commonly used in tight coverage situations such as near the corners, along the boards and around the net.

In certain situations where you do not have the puck but will soon gain possession, the idea of puck protection should start before you even get the puck. This is accomplished by placing your body in between the puck and the eventual defender. Other times, as you get closer to the puck, you may decide to lift the opponent's stick, use your arm to keep the defender away or use your skates to control the puck. All of these techniques are useful forms of puck protection.

One-handed puck control is a technique that has two uses: to obtain the widest possible puck travel while stickhandling and to advance past a defender while keeping a defender away with your free hand. To get the widest possible side-to-side puck travel, the player can release the lower hand and use only the top hand on the stick. This technique is relatively easy to learn going one way — to the right if you are a left-handed shooter — but few players can do it equally well to both sides. Moving the puck to one side, releasing the lower hand, bringing the stick back and then doing the same to the other side will give the player the widest possible path for controlled puck travel.

To advance past a defender, a player should move to the outside of the defender, lean slightly into the defender, and with his inside arm, keep the defender from trying to obtain possession of the puck without holding the defender. The inside arm should be firmly held out to keep the defender from getting too close to the puck while the outside arm and hand control the stick and puck. Both of the one-handed puck control techniques are excellent methods to keep control of the puck during a one-on-one encounter.

Puck control using the skates. Controlling the puck with your skates may seem awkward, but may be the only choice available when you are in the corner with an opponent, have lost the puck off your stick, or have broken your stick and must discard it. This skill makes excellent use of your skates and is a technique that is carried over from soccer. Three different skate puck control methods are discussed below:

1. **Between the skates.** When moving the puck between the skates, it is important to move the puck in the direction that you want to travel. This is accomplished by turning the toe of your skate outward approximately 45 degrees, bringing your leg forward so that the middle wheels of your skate make contact with the puck. Move the puck forward with one skate and then with the other. This is very similar to the push technique described earlier in the chapter and should be practiced with both skates.
2. **Skate-to-stick.** This method allows you to move the puck ahead to your stick with the same motion described in No. 1. If you happen to overskate the puck, bring one skate directly behind you so that the wheels are perpendicular to the direction you are traveling. Move your leg forward and make contact with the puck to move it up to your stick. It is important to practice with both skates so that you will not miss an opportunity.
3. **Stick-to-skate-to-stick.** This method allows the puck carrier to shield the puck with his skates for an instant while he defeats the opponent. The puck carrier passes the puck directly back to his skates and then returns it to the stick from his skates, not allowing the opponent to gain control of the puck.

Incidental body contact and puck control. Although most amateur roller hockey leagues do not permit body checking, incidental and accidental body contact are part of the game. Incidental and accidental body contact occur when two (or more) players are trying to obtain control of the puck and their bodies make contact. This could happen during both offensive and defensive play in the corners or when one player is trying to force another player off of the puck. To compensate for incidental body contact, focus on keeping your balance. To do this, lean your body in the direction of the other player. This will compensate for the added force from that opponent and allow you to remain standing or skating. After the body contact occurs, continue controlling the puck while reading for an opportunity.

Stickhandling while skating backward. This form of stickhandling involves skating backward or transitioning to skating forward while controlling the puck. It can be performed using the push, diagonal or back-to-front moves described in the fundamental section. The puck must always be drawn toward the body during the execution of this technique or the player could lose control of it. This is an essential skill for any above-average defensemen and can be used by a clever forward as well.

Siller Player And Team Evaluation Profile©
Stickhandling and Puck Control Checklist

Evaluator: The Coach | **Date**: 7/15/94 | **Location**: The Forum

	Player Name										
Notes:	**KEN**		**GREG**		**KEITH**		**JIM**				
Fundamental Stickhandling and Puck Control Techniques											
Push	**10**		**10**		**10**		**10**				
Side-To-Side	9		8		**10**		9				
Diagonal (Left Side)	8		8		8		8				
Diagonal (Right Side)	5		5		5		5				
Back-To-Front (Left Side)	4		5		6		6				
Back-To-Front (Right Side)	**3**		**3**		**3**		**3**				
Advanced Stickhandling and Puck Control Techniques											
One-Handed Puck Control	7		6		7		9				
Puck Control Using The Skates											
• between the skates	5		5		6		5				
• skate-to-stick	7		5		6		7				
• stick-to-skate-to-stick	5		4		4		4				
Incidental Body Contact and Puck Control	7		7		5		7				
Stickhandling While Skating Backward	**2**		**3**		**2**		**3**				
TOTAL SCORE	**72**		**69**		**72**		**76**				
AVERAGE SCORE	**6.0**		**5.8**		**6.0**		**6.3**				

Comments: Ken, Greg, Keith, and Jim have all demonstrated medium overall stickhandling and puck control proficiency with total scores of 72, 69, 72, and 76 respectively and average scores of 6.0, 5.8, 6.0, and 6.3 respectively. All players scored excellent on the push. Keith scored excellent on the side-to-side. All players need to improve on the back-to-front (right side) and stickhandling while skating backwards areas.

Scale: 0 = Not Performed, 1 - 3 = Low Proficiency, 4 - 6 = Medium Proficiency, 7 - 9 = High Proficiency, 10 = Excellent Proficiency

Table 4-1; Stickhandling and Puck Control Checklist

Drills

To develop skill at moving the puck in the various patterns, you must execute them over and over again, both stationary and while moving, until control is perfected. The secret of good stickhandling and puck control is practice. If you devote a few minutes to each drill every day, the results will soon show in your game; it will be time well spent. A basic repertoire of stickhandling skills will give you the dexterity to control the puck in any pattern required to carry it up the playing surface or past an opponent. Once you can move the puck through all the various drills in this chapter, at full speed and with full control, you will find your skill and confidence at manipulating the puck during games will have improved tremendously.

Several stickhandling and puck control drills have been provided in the following two sections that can be used by any coach or player to enhance current skill levels. The drills cover the material discussed in this chapter as well as some effective variations. When first trying these drills, begin slowly and don't worry about keeping your head up. Watch the puck to make sure you're in control and executing the drills correctly. As you practice and see improvement, pick up the pace and begin keeping your head up more of the time. Your peripheral vision will allow you to keep the puck in view while you keep your head up. It also allows you to see a large percentage of the playing surface in the direction your head is turned. If you lose the puck during these drills, stop, pick it up and continue on.

Drill 4-1; Stationary Puck Control — Part 1. For this drill, the coach or designated player should demonstrate the three fundamental stationary stickhandling techniques discussed earlier (side-to-side, diagonal and back-to-front). Divide the players into two lines approximately 10 feet apart, stretching from goal line to goal line. When the coach points his hand to the side, the players should stickhandle side to side. If the left hand is pointed down, the players should stickhandle on a diagonal and to the left. If the right hand is pointed straight ahead, the players should stickhandle using the back-to-front technique on the right side. The coach should also verbally call out the specific puck control techniques along with using the various arm movements. The emphasis of this drill in the early part of the season should be on the side-to-side technique. During the season, all three techniques should be practiced and mastered.

Drill 4-2; Stationary Puck Control — Part 2. Divide the players as described in Drill 4-1. At the whistle, the players begin using the side-to-side technique, making four short, four medium and four wide movements. Next, the players execute the diagonal puck control technique with four moves on the left side and then four moves on the right. This is followed with the back-to-front technique, executing four moves on the left side and four moves on the right. Perform the diagonal technique again, making four moves to the right side and four moves to the left. The drill is finished with four medium movements using the side-to-side technique. This drill is a real challenge to the player who enjoys precision puck control and it offers a fun and interesting variety as well as invaluable training.

Drill 4-3; Developing Soft Hands. There are two great ways to develop soft hands. First, practice stationary stickhandling with your eyes closed. You can repeat Drills 4-1 and 4-2 to do this. Remember to keep a firm grip on the stick with your top hand and a relaxed grip on the stick with your bottom hand. If you don't have soft hands with your eyes closed, you will notice that the puck will quickly slide off the blade of your stick. After some practice, you should feel as if the puck is a part of your stick, and you won't have to look down as often. Your head and eyes will be up looking for an open receiver or a shot on net.

Another way to develop soft hands is to improve your hand-eye coordination. In this portion of the drill, a ball or puck can be used. Flip the ball or puck up with the blade of your stick and try to bounce it repeatedly off the blade without allowing the ball or puck to fall. Concentrate on keeping the distance the puck or ball bounces in the air as short as possible. If you can bounce the puck or ball five consecutive times, you are doing well; 10 consecutive times and you are doing excellent.

Moving Drills

These drills teach players to coordinate both stickhandling and skating maneuvers. For each drill, the coach should watch the players for proper technique and provide feedback. The **six factors that**

should be monitored by the coach when evaluating each player's stickhandling and puck control ability are body balance, body positioning, hand positioning on the stick, head and eye positioning, keeping the puck on the stick, and skating technique. Use the Stickhandling and Puck Control Checklist to monitor performance and plan improvements for each player. Don't forget to use proper warm-up and cool-down techniques prior and subsequent to performing any of the drills.

Drill 4-4; Stickhandling Around The Rink. This drill provides players an opportunity to coordinate their skating and stickhandling skills before they begin some of the other drills. It also provides the coach an opportunity to preview the players and is an excellent beginning stickhandling drill to evaluate current or potential talent. Players skate clockwise around the rink, at half speed, while carrying the puck. The coach should provide feedback to the players on the six stickhandling and puck control factors described above.

Variations:

- Skate in a counterclockwise direction.
- Skate at three-quarter speed.

Drill 4-5; Stickhandling End-To-End. Divide the players into three lines approximately 10 feet apart, starting on the goal line, as shown in the corresponding diagram. Have the players stickhandle down the playing surface to the far goal line at half speed, using the push fundamental stickhandling and puck control technique. The skating speed of the players should be controlled so that they can focus on moving the puck forward. Once all of the players have skated to the far goal line, have them return to the original goal line. Continue this drill until all players have completed skating at least four lengths of the rink.

Variations:

- Use the side-to-side, diagonal or back-to-front techniques.
- Skate at three-quarter speed.

Drill 4-6; Stickhandle and Breakaway. This drill is the maneuver a player should use when he gets a breakaway. Divide the players into three lines as described in the previous drill. At the coach's whistle, have the players stickhandle at half speed to the center red line using the side-to-side technique, then move the puck to the far goal line using the push technique.

Variations:

- Use the diagonal or back-to-front techniques while skating to the center red line.
- Skate at three-quarter speed.

Drill 4-7; Puck Control and Turns. This drill provides practice making turns while controlling the puck. Set up the pylons in a pattern shown in the corresponding diagram. Divide the players into two lines starting on the goal line. At the whistle, the first two players in each line skate in and out of the pylons to the far goal line, at half speed, using any of the four fundamental stickhandling and puck control techniques (push, side-to-side, diagonal and back-to-front).

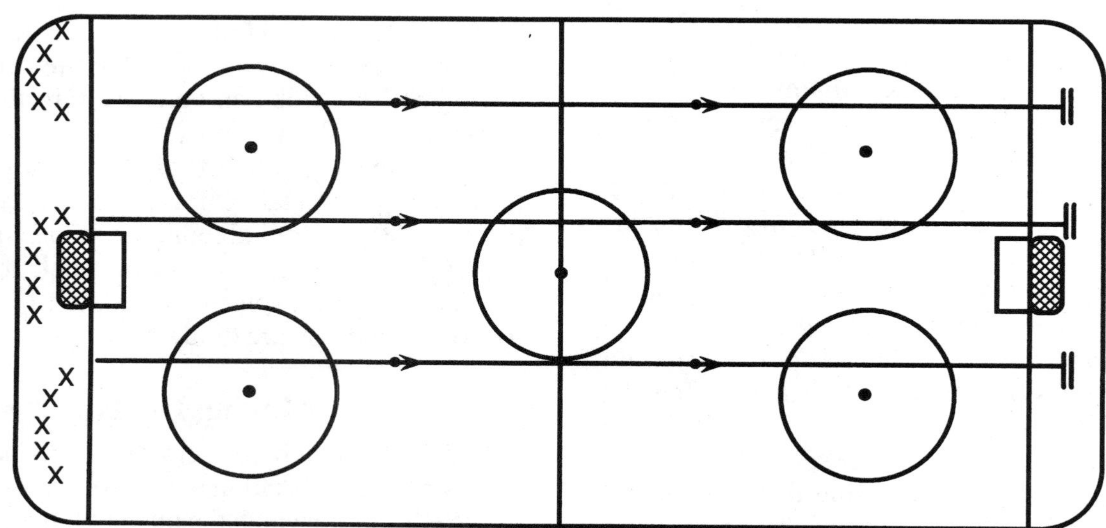

Drill 4-5; Stickhandling End-To-End

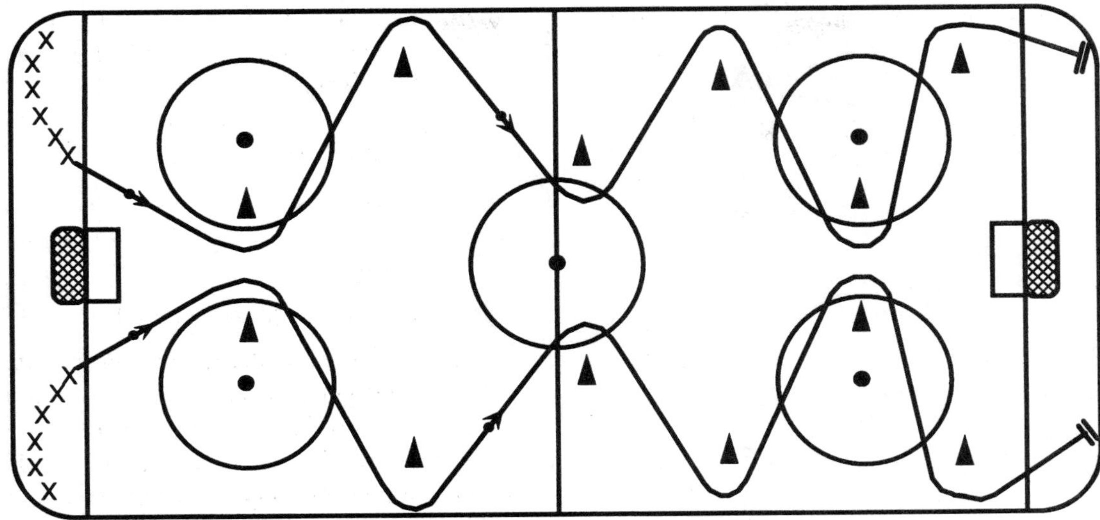
Drill 4-7; Puck Control and Turns

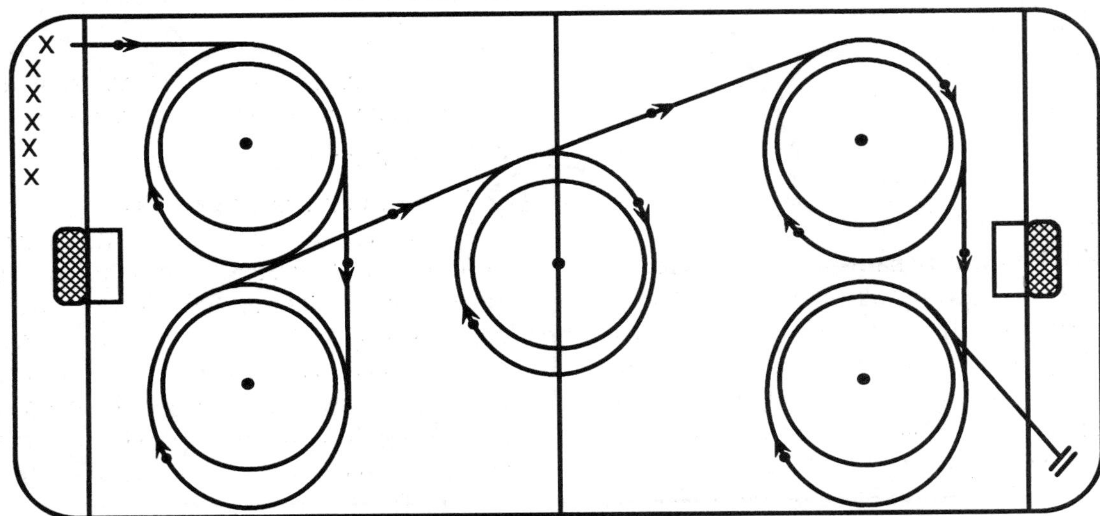
Drill 4-8; Puck Control and Circles

Variations:

- Skate at three-quarter speed.
- Vary the pylon pattern.

Drill 4-8; Puck Control and Circles. This drill provides practice circling while controlling the puck. Form one line at the goal line. Players skate, at half speed, clockwise around each of the five face-off circles or (pylons) while stickhandling. The coach should provide feedback to the players on the six stickhandling and puck control evaluation factors described earlier.

Variations:

- Perform in a counterclockwise direction.
- Vary the turning pattern so that both clockwise and counterclockwise circles are completed.
- Skate at three-quarter speed.

Drill 4-9; Puck Control and Stops. This drill provides practice for stopping while controlling the puck. This may be necessary to change direction quickly while avoiding a defender. Set up pylons in the pattern shown in the corresponding diagram. Divide the team into two lines starting at the goal line. At the whistle, players skate, at half speed, to each pylon and stop, facing the right boards. At the next whistle, the second players in each line start the drill, while the first players continue on to the second pylon. All players should continue stopping facing the right boards.

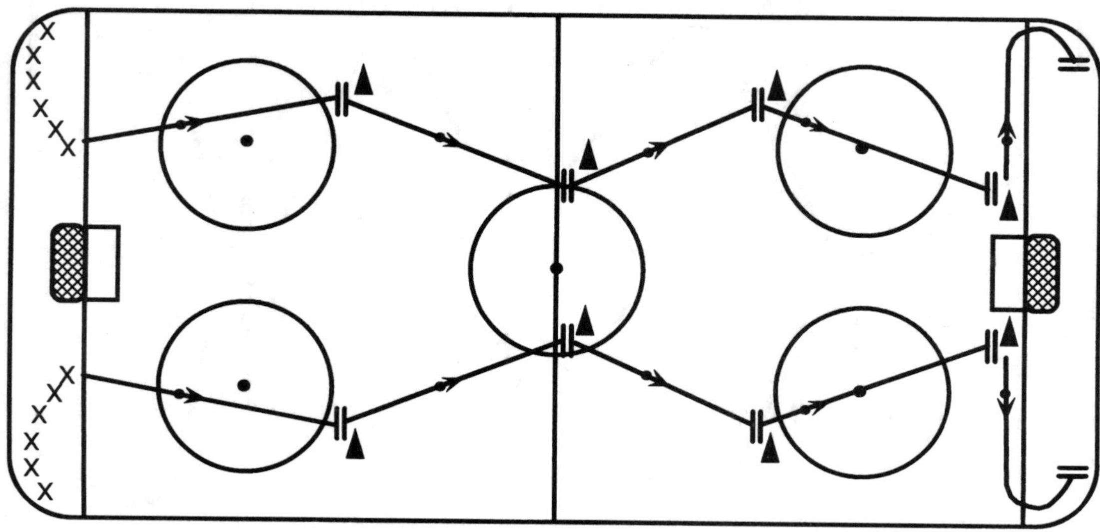

Drill 4-9; Puck Control and Stops

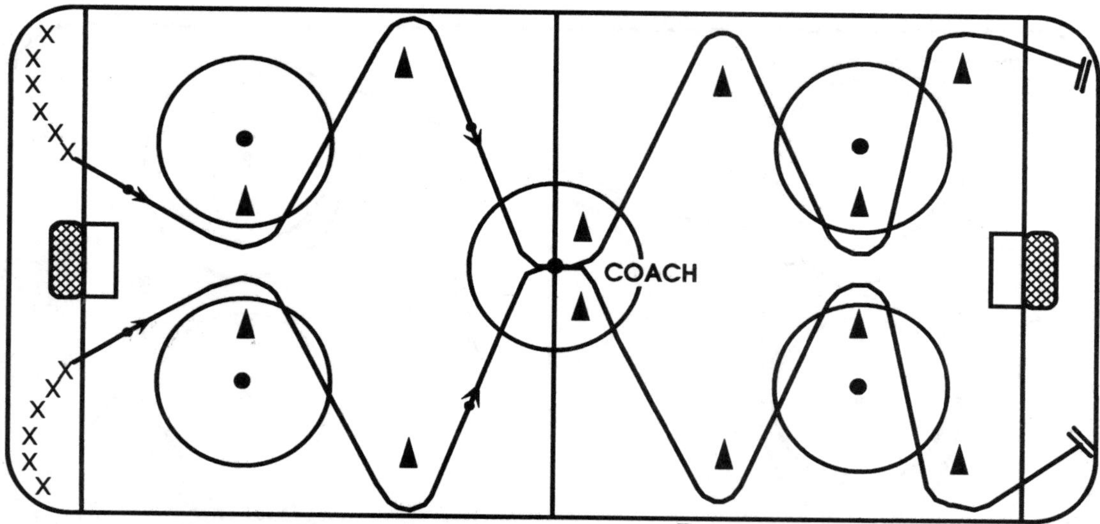

Drill 4-10; Puck Control and the Coach

Variations:

- Vary the pylon pattern.
- Skate at three-quarter speed.
- Stop facing the left boards.
- Vary the stopping position from right to left.

Drill 4-10; Puck Control and the Coach. This drill is an excellent variation of the previous drill but warrants its own description. It provides practice making turns while controlling the puck as well as some reading and reacting by the players based on the coach's signal. Set up the pylons in a pattern shown in the diagram below. Divide the players into two lines starting on the goal line. At the whistle, the first player from the bottom line skates and stickhandles (using the push or side-to-side technique), at half speed, in and out of the pylons toward the far goal line. As he reaches the center red line, the coach provides a signal (either with the hand or the stick) as to which way the player should proceed. If the coach points to the left, the player will proceed down the left side of the rink; if he points to the right side, the player will proceed down the right side of the rink. At the second whistle, the first player in the top line begins skating, following the same approach. Players should alternate from the bottom line to the top until all players have completed the drill.

The benefit of this drill is that it provides some realistic exposure to game situations. As the puck handler moves the puck toward the goal, the coach acts as a defender by providing information to the puck handler as to which way he should turn to get past the defender. The puck handler is forced to keep his head up at this crucial time (relying on his soft hands and peripheral vision), *read* the defender (coach) and *react* to the cues he receives to move past the defender (coach). In a real game, the puck handler will have to choose which direction to move to get past a defender based on his stickhandling, puck control ability and the cues the defender provides to the player. This drill will begin to instill learning and confidence in the players with respect to their ability to defeat a defender in a one-on-one situation.

Variations:

- Skate at three-quarter speed.
- Vary the pylon pattern.
- Add one or two additional "coaches" to force the player to *read and react* additional times.

Drill 4-11; Zigzag. This drill combines the actions of a couple of previous drills. Set up the pylons in a pattern shown in the diagram below. Divide the players into two lines starting on the goal line. At the whistle, the first two players in each line skate, at half speed, to each pylon and circle it in a clockwise pattern on their way to the far goal line.

Variations:

- Skate at three-quarter speed.
- Vary the pylon pattern.
- Circle the pylons in a counterclockwise pattern.

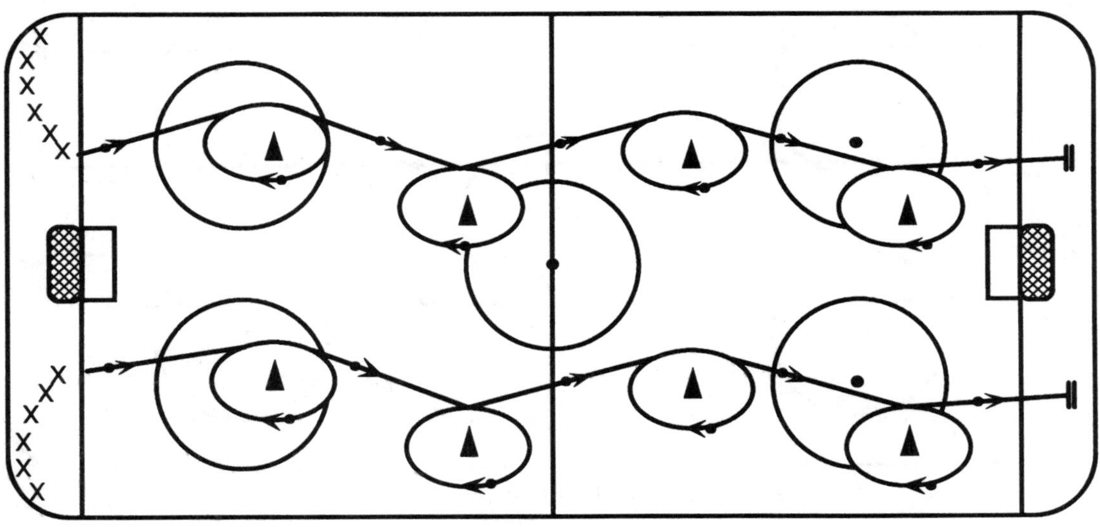

Drill 4-11; Zigzag

Advanced Drills

Drill 4-12; One-Handed Puck Control. For this drill, the coach or designated player should demonstrate one-handed puck control using the side-to-side technique. While practicing the side-to-side technique, release the lower hand and use only the top hand on the stick to obtain the maximum puck extension from the body. Move the puck to one side, release the lower hand, bring the stick back and then do the same to the other side. Practice this drill while stationary and moving.

Drill 4-13; One-Handed Puck Control Past a Defender. This drill is designed to provide the puck handler with experience advancing past a defender. Divide the team into two groups, placing one group in the lower left corner of the rink and the other group in the upper right corner, as shown in the corresponding diagram. Select four defenders (X), whose job it is to place their sticks in the puck handlers path as the puck handler skates by, and position them according to the corresponding diagram.

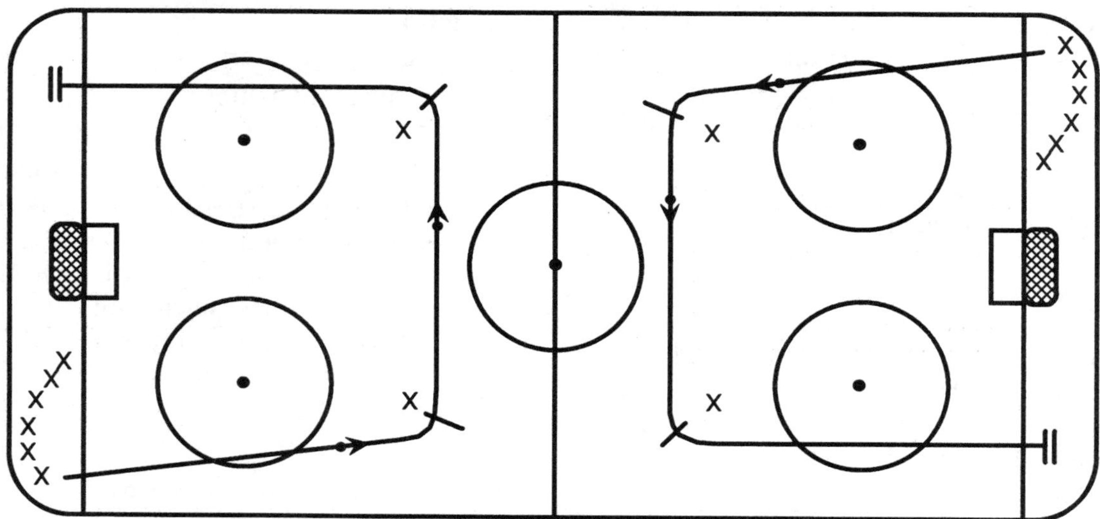

Drill 4-13; One-Handed Puck Control Past a Defender

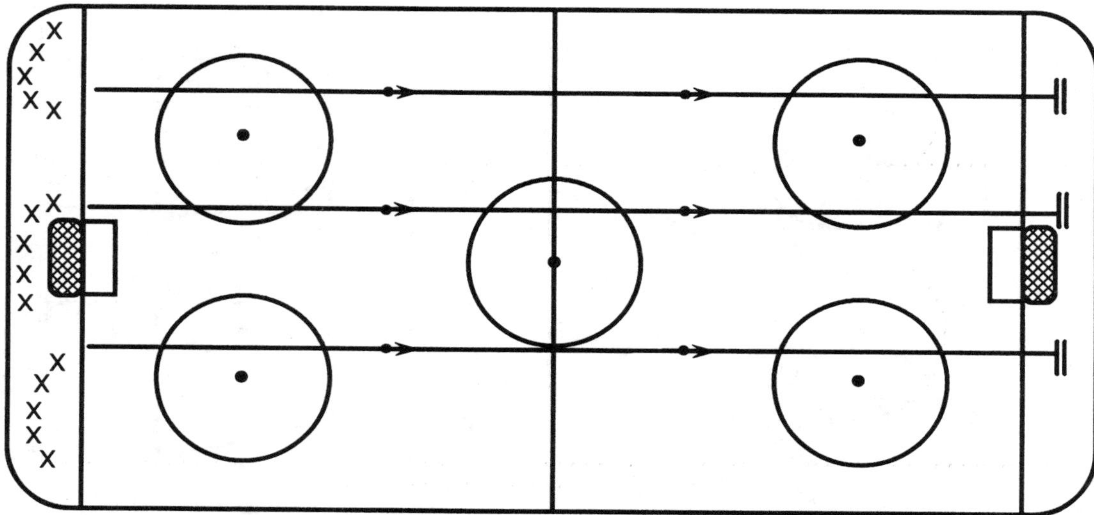

Drill 4-14; Puck Control Using the Skates

At the whistle, the first player in each line moves the puck toward the defender at half speed. As the puck handler gets within six feet of the defender, the defender will move his stick toward the puck handler in an attempt to knock the puck off of the puck handler's stick. As the puck handler approaches the stick, he should lean slightly into the defender, and with his inside arm, move the defender's stick out of striking range without actually holding the defender's stick. The puck should be controlled with the outside arm using a sweeping motion.

Variations:

- Execute in a clockwise direction.
- Execute at three-quarter speed.
- Rotate defenders.

Drill 4-14; Puck Control Using the Skates. This drill teaches players to control the puck with their skates. Divide the players into three lines starting on the goal line, as shown in the corresponding diagram. At the whistle, the first player in each line moves the puck toward the far goal line, at half speed, using the between-the-skates puck control technique. The puck is moved forward with one skate, and the action is repeated with the other skate. During this drill, provide feedback on the players' balance, direction of puck movement and consistency of body movement.

Variations:

- Execute at three-quarter speed.
- Repeat the drill using the skate-to-stick and stick-to-skate-to-stick puck techniques.

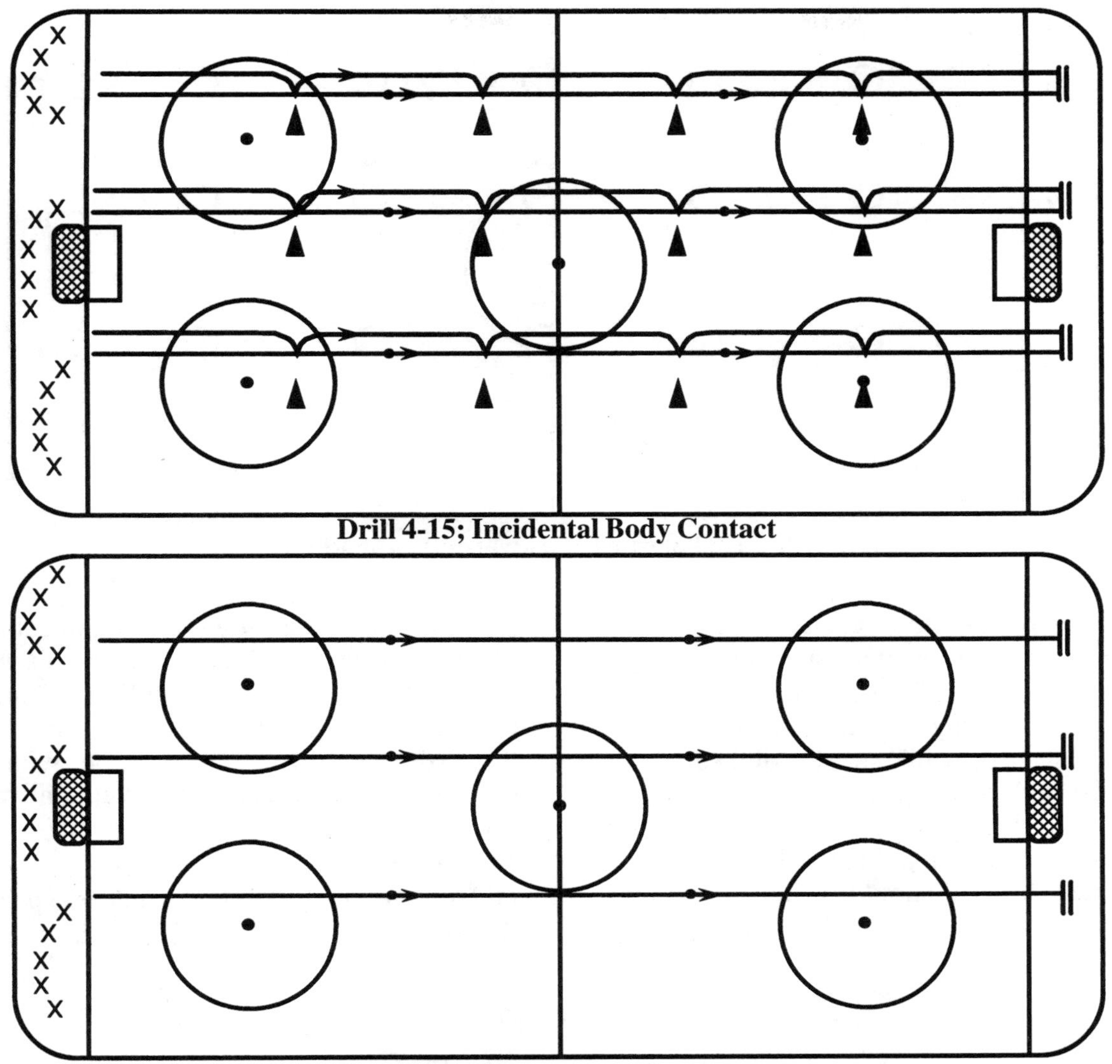

Drill 4-15; Incidental Body Contact

Drill 4-16; Backward Stickhandling

Drill 4-15; Incidental Body Contact. Divide the players into three lines approximately 10 feet apart, starting on the goal line, as shown in the corresponding diagram. Pair up the first and second players in each line next to each other. The first player will be the puck handler and the second player will be the defender. At the whistle, each of the three pairs should begin skating, at half speed, toward the far goal line. At each pylon the defender should move toward the puck handler and moderately bump him and then return to his normal skating route as shown in the corresponding diagram. Continue this drill until all players have completed both the defender and the puck handler roles at least once. Make sure that the bumping is not exaggerated. The goal of this drill is to develop confidence in the players' balance and ability to maintain control of the puck during incidental body contact.

Variation:

- Execute the drill at three-quarter speed.

Drill 4-16; Backward Stickhandling. Divide the players into three lines approximately 10 feet apart, starting on the goal line as shown in the corresponding diagram. Have the players stickhandle down the rink to the far goal line, at half speed, while skating backward. The skating speed of the players should be controlled so that they can focus on keeping possession of the puck. Once all of the players have skated to the far goal line, have them return to the original goal line. Continue this drill until all players have completed skating at least four lengths of the rink.

Variation:

- Skate at three-quarter speed.

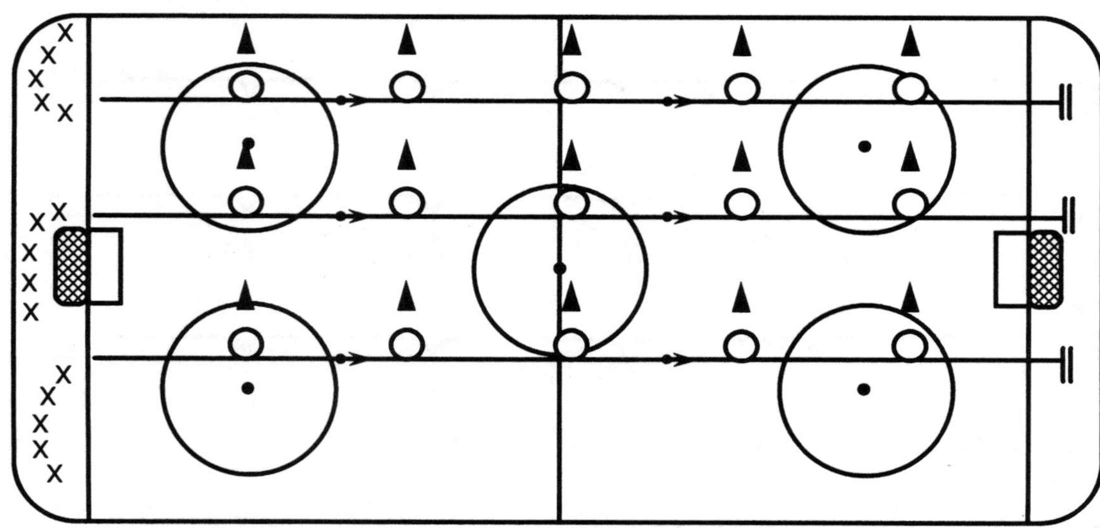

Drill 4-17; Forward-Backward Stickhandling

Drill 4-17; Forward-Backward Stickhandling. Divide the team into three lines starting at the goal line, as shown in the corresponding diagram. At the whistle, the first players in each line should skate forward, at half speed, while stickhandling until they reach the first pylon. At the first pylon, they should transition to skating backward. This transition process is continued at each pylon until they reach the far goal line. The drill should be performed once without the puck to familiarize the players with the pattern. The coach should provide feedback to the players on keeping the puck close to their bodies during the transition and angling the stick blade toward the center of the transition circle. Expect this drill to be difficult at first, but with practice, the level of player confidence and ability will improve.

Variations:

- Execute the drill at three-quarter speed.
- Start the drill skating backward.

Recap

After reading and studying the material in this chapter, you should be able to answer the following questions:

1. Why are stickhandling and puck control skills required?
2. Define stickhandling.
3. Define puck control.
4. Describe the proper body positioning used during stickhandling and puck control maneuvers.
5. What is the proper distance between the hands when holding a stick? What technique can be used to quickly position your hands on your stick?
6. Define *soft hands*. How can *soft hands* be developed (review Drill 4-3)?
7. What causes the puck to roll or jump off the stick of a player carrying the puck?
8. Why is it important to emphasize keeping a player's head up when carrying the puck? Answer this question in conjunction with the terms *read* and *react*.
9. Define the four fundamental stickhandling and puck control techniques.
10. Define puck protection. How is it used?
11. When would you be required to control the puck with your skates?
12. How will you use the Stickhandling and Puck Control Checklist to evaluate and improve individual players as well as the entire team?
13. During the execution of all stickhandling and puck control drills, what six factors should be monitored by the coach so that proper feedback can be provided to the players?

5

Passing and Receiving

Highlights

This chapter addresses the importance of effective passing and receiving. Chapter 5 presents the following information:

Discussion

Fundamentals

- *forehand sweep*
- *backhand sweep*
- *snap pass*
- *flip pass*
- *around-the-boards pass*
- *give-and-go*
- *receiving passes*

Advanced Techniques

- *bank pass*
- *open area pass*
- *drop pass*
- *touch pass*
- *reverse*
- *weave*
- *skate pass*
- *receiving passes*

Siller Player and Team Evaluation Profile — Passing And Receiving

Drills

Advanced Drills

Recap

A man can fail many times, but he isn't a failure until he begins to blame somebody else.
— John Burroughs —

Defeat is not the worst of failures. Not to have tried is the true failure.
— George E. Woodberry —

Discussion

Passing

Passing is the **quickest and most effective** way to move the puck up the playing surface because puck movement is faster than player movement. There are **many reasons for passing** the puck during a roller hockey game: to quickly bring the puck out of the defensive zone, to defeat a defender, to create a numerical advantage (i.e., 2-on-1 or 3-on-2) or to set up a great scoring opportunity. Each type of pass serves a unique purpose in terms of catching the opposition off guard and gaining positional advantage. The speed and change in flow provided when making a pass allow the offense to open up many exciting opportunities to get the puck into a scoring situation.

After deciding on a particular receiver, **three factors** to consider when executing an effective pass are accuracy, timing and deception. A fourth factor is what you do after the pass is made.

Accuracy. This is probably the most important aspect to passing. Accuracy is determined by the ability of the passer to read the speed and intended direction of the receiver in relation to his own speed (if the passer is moving). Once the passer gauges any difference in relative speed, he can lead the receiver with a pass that should arrive at the same location and time as the receiver's stick. Being able to accurately and consistently put the puck on a receiver's stick will allow you and your team to effectively employ many individual and team strategies.

Timing. Deciding when to pass should be based on improving your team's offensive situation. If a teammate is in a better position than you are, you should always pass the puck. This rule is most frequently broken when the puck carrier chooses to carry the puck past a defender when there is a teammate up ahead or he decides to hold onto the puck too long, allowing a defender to get too close. The consequences to these decisions are that the open player has to continue to try and stay open or, in the case of the close-in defender, the puck could be intercepted, deflected by a stick or skate, or blocked. It is better to make the pass too soon and ahead, than too late and behind. The only time a pass is not the best play is when the defender gives away his intention of trying to intercept the pass or if the receiver is too close to a defender to receive the pass. If it will improve your team's situation, pass the puck!

Deception. Many players spoil their passing attempt because they *telegraph* their intention. **Telegraphing a pass** occurs when the passer is looking at the potential receiver and lining up the passing play without any deception. This not only allows the receiver to know where the pass will be made, but the defenders as well. A good idea before attempting a pass is to *read* the coverage, then *react* with a deceptive move to fake or confuse the defenders. This could be a quick fake, as if you were going to carry the puck yourself, and then pass the puck to the receiver. A factor in using deception is peripheral vision. Good playmakers have excellent peripheral vision, to the side (and down) when looking ahead. This enables them to line up a receiver without giving away their intention by looking directly at the receiver. By employing deceptive techniques, you will provide a receiver with additional time and space to set up many scoring situations.

When you pass, break! One of the most common individual faults after making a pass is failing to stay in the play. Players often make a pass and then watch to see what happens without taking any further action. The moment the player makes the pass, he should get into position for a return pass, break for the net or decoy a defender away from the play. By breaking fast after the pass has been made, you create many options for your team. If you remove yourself from the play, you reduce the options for your team.

Receiving

The **role of the receiver** in the passing-receiving combination consists of three basic tasks: to locate an open area on the playing surface to receive the pass, to communicate to the passer that you are or will soon be available, and to capture the pass effectively.

To locate open space and become available for a pass, a potential receiver should move to an open area on the playing surface that is, in general, in the direction of the play. Many times a receiver needs to deceive the defender so that he can get open.

This is accomplished by using body fakes, changing direction or varying speed. Just as a passer needs to avoid telegraphing his pass, a receiver must also attempt to camouflage his moves to get open.

Receivers also have the responsibility of indicating to the puck carrier whether they are open or not open for a pass. This information can be either verbal or nonverbal. Calling the player by a first name or nickname can be effective, but opponents may know this name. Nonverbal cues can be audible, such as tapping your stick on the playing surface or the boards, or silent, such as raising your stick or pointing to the open space that you intend to move to. A potential receiver must never give up trying to get into the open, even though the passer may have missed him the first time around. Receivers must appreciate the task faced by the puck carrier in attempting to make a pass, given the forechecking pressure (when the attacking team applies pressure to the defending team in the defending team's zone) and the speed of the game. This is why receivers need to be patient and keep trying to find open space. Timing your arrival to an open space by controlling your speed and direction is the key to successfully supporting the puck carrier and getting open.

Capturing the pass is the third role for the receiver. Receiving a pass requires practice and *soft hands*. ***Soft hands*** was described in Chapter 4 with respect to stickhandling and puck control. It is also a passing and receiving term used to define how a player receives a pass. If the pass bounces off the stick of the receiver, the player is said to have *hard hands*. If the player is able to cushion the puck using his arms and a relaxed grip of the lower hand, that player has *soft hands*. Sometimes, soft hands may not be enough to receive a pass since passes are not always perfectly on-target. Receivers should also expect to make some type of adjustment, such as reaching for the puck, angling toward or away from the puck, slowing down or speeding up, or using the skates to redirect the pass onto the stick when attempting to receive a pass. In many situations, this also means that the receiver must protect the puck from a defender once it is received. Controlling and protecting the puck from your opponents will allow you more time to execute your next move, whether it is passing, stickhandling or shooting. Even before the pass is completed, the receiver should have some idea of his next move, such as driving for the net, passing, shooting or carrying the puck. Anticipating the next action is a skill that all great roller hockey players have.

Fundamentals

All roller hockey players should become familiar with the various types of passes and the time and place to use each. Nine basic passing and receiving techniques are covered in this section — the forehand sweep, backhand sweep, snap pass, flip pass, around-the-boards pass, give-and-go and three methods for receiving passes.

Forehand sweep. The forehand sweep pass is the most commonly used pass and is designed to be used when deceiving a defender is not important. The sweep pass is also the most accurate pass due to its relative simplicity of movement. To execute the forehand sweep pass, the puck should be cradled with the blade of the stick angled slightly over it. The puck should be at the center of the blade, with the blade positioned approximately even with the back skate (left skate for a left-handed player). As the player begins to pass, weight transfers from the back skate to the front skate. As the back leg extends, the lower hand pushes the stick toward the receiver and the upper hand pulls the top of the stick back toward the body. The puck should be released with the blade at a 90-degree angle to the direction the puck is to travel and the follow-

Forehand Sweep

Backhand Sweep

Snap Pass

through should be low. Speed comes from the quickness of the arms and wrists during the pushing and pulling process, the weight transfer from the back skate to the front skate, twisting of the upper body toward the receiver and the distance the puck travels while on the blade. **Accuracy** is strictly a function of the follow-through. The straighter the follow-through, the more accurate the pass. **Puck height** is controlled by the height of the follow-through. If the follow-through of the stick blade is low, the puck will remain low.

Backhand sweep. The same fundamentals are used with the backhand sweep pass as with the forehand sweep, only the puck is started off the backhand side of the stick. The puck begins well on the backhand side, with the blade positioned approximately even with the back skate (right skate for a left-handed player). As the back leg is extended, weight shifts from the back skate to the front skate and the lower hand pulls the stick toward the receiver while the upper hand pushes the top of the stick away from the body. As with the forehand sweep, the follow-through controls the accuracy and height of the puck. The backhand sweep may appear more difficult to perfect, in part due to the use of curved sticks, but with practice, it is an effective and deceptive passing technique.

Snap pass. If there is little time in which to make a pass or if the puck carrier wants to make a quick, unexpected pass in the midst of a stickhandling pattern, he should use the snap pass. The snap pass is executed using a quick snap of the wrists with no sweeping motion. To make this type of pass, the lower hand and wrist snaps the stick toward the receiver while the upper hand and wrist snaps the top of the stick toward the body. The blade of the stick should have a short follow-through in the direction of the receiver. The stick is brought back slightly from contact with the puck and then snapped. This technique results in a quick, hard pass. It is very easy to loft this type of pass if the puck carrier does not remember to keep the blade of his stick along the playing surface during the follow-through or if the upper hand is snapped downward instead of straight back toward the body. The player who can use the snap pass effectively will find it a big advantage because he will be able to make the pass without giving away his intention. The gain in quickness and deception by using the snap pass is at the cost of some accuracy, as the snap pass is generally not as accurate as the sweep pass.

Flip pass. The flip pass or saucer pass is used when the puck carrier cannot make a direct pass to a receiver due to a barrier between the passer and the receiver, such as an **opponent's stick**, a fallen defenseman or goaltender. The key to executing the flip pass is the rotation of the puck, which is created by rolling the puck from the heel of the stick blade to the toe as the pass is made. This will ensure that the puck lands flat and does not bounce or roll. Some players try to flip the puck up into the air using the lower edge of the stick blade against the back of the puck. If this occurs, the puck will move end over end, and when it lands, it bounces or rolls, and is difficult to receive.

The pass begins with the puck on the heel of the stick blade, with the blade positioned approximately even with the back skate (left skate for a left-handed player). Using the same technique described in the sweep pass, move your arms and hands across your body, rolling the puck from the heel to the toe of the blade. As the puck comes within an inch or two of the toe of the blade, roll your wrists toward the receiver and release the pass. The height of the pass is controlled by the angle of the stick blade at the release point. The normal height of a flip pass is from 6 inches to 2 feet. For shorter passes, a softer touch is more important than speed. For longer passes, puck speed comes from the quickness of the arms and wrists during the pushing and pulling process and the distance the puck travels while on the blade. The follow-through is shorter for the flip pass than with the sweep pass; therefore, it is critical that the puck is released at precisely the right time.

Around-the-boards pass. This type of pass allows a passer to indirectly reach a receiver who is not available for a direct pass because he is blocked by a defender (X) as shown in Figure 5-1. It is particularly effective when used by a defenseman (D) to quickly move the puck from behind his net to an open forward (F) who is positioned along the boards or when the offensive team's defenseman (D) decides to dump the puck into the offensive zone to a forward (F) breaking into the offensive zone on the far side of the play. The around-the-boards pass is most effective when using either the forehand or backhand sweep or the snap passing techniques. The pass should be low and not too hard so that the receiver can handle it. Figure 5-1 depicts both the defensive (left side of figure) and the offensive (right side of figure) versions of this pass.

Give-and-Go. The give-and-go is not really a single pass but a play consisting of two passes. The first pass is from a moving player to a stationary player and the second pass is from the stationary player back to the moving player, as shown in Figure 5-2. This technique is a very effective means for a puck carrier to beat an opponent by passing the puck at the appropriate moment and then receiving the puck back after he gets around him. The give-and-go is most effective when working on a two-on-one situation (two offensive players versus one defender). Use this technique during a breakout play, where the defenseman (D) moves the puck from behind the net (left side of figure). If the defenseman is being challenged by a defender (X), the defenseman can pass the puck to a nearby forward (F), skate past the defender and receive a return pass from the forward when he is in the clear. A variation of the give-and-go is where no return pass is received (center of figure). This play requires both offensive players to play the situation as a typical give-and-go. Instead of obtaining the return pass, the moving player (D) acts as a decoy, taking the defender (X) with him and creating space for the puck carrier (F).

The secret of successfully receiving a pass involves two factors: the angle of the stick blade and *soft hands*. To receive a pass either on your **forehand** or **backhand** side of the stick blade, the top edge of the stick blade should be angled slightly over the puck and perpendicular to its direction of travel as puck contact is made. The blade of the stick can be angled over the puck by turning the wrists toward the direction of travel, forming a

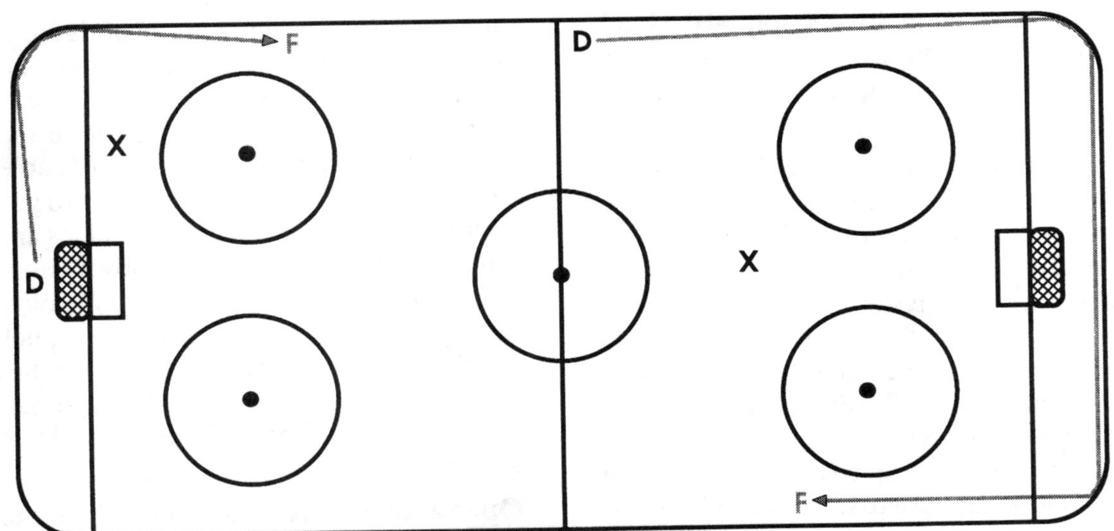

Figure 5-1; Around-The-Boards Pass

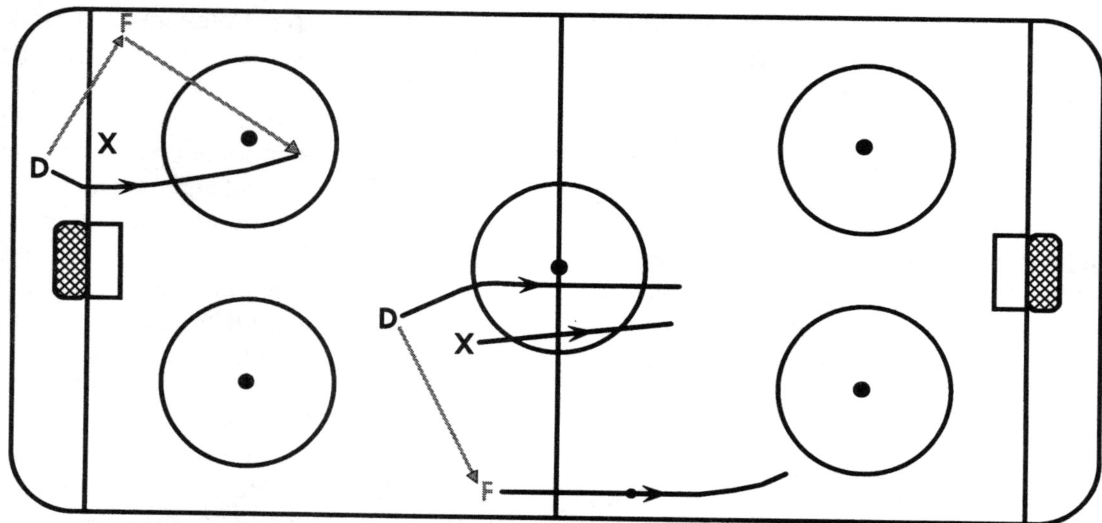

Figure 5-2; Give-And-Go

pocket that will hold the puck and help prevent it from sliding off the blade. During the initial contact with the stick blade, it is important to cushion the puck using your arms and the relaxed grip of the lower hand as shock absorbers. *Soft hands* are required when receiving a pass as they provide the cushioning effect that allows the puck to be cradled onto the stick. Even if the proper angle is used, without *soft hands*, the puck will bounce off of the stick blade and a turnover could result.

Receiving a pass too far ahead requires a player to lean forward and place most of his weight on the left leg (when reaching with his right arm). Extend the right arm toward the puck, slightly twist the upper body to the left to get those few extra inches of reach and attempt to cradle the puck onto your stick. This technique adds an additional three to six feet to your reach. When receiving a pass while skating down the boards, another method to obtain a puck that is too far ahead is to let the puck bounce off of the boards and then skate after it.

Advanced Techniques

There are nine advanced passing and receiving techniques that are covered in this section — the bank pass, open area pass, drop pass, touch pass, reverse, weave, skate pass and two methods for receiving passes.

Bank pass. The bank pass is an indirect passing technique that uses the same principles as a bank shot in pool and allows the offensive team (team with the puck) to defeat a defender using the boards or to reach a player who is not available for a direct pass. The bank pass can be used by a defenseman to pass the puck behind the net and off the boards to another defenseman (left side of Figure 5-3); to defeat a defender by employing a version of the give-and-go passing technique in which the player banks the puck off the boards, moves around the defender, and retrieves the puck himself (lower portion of figure); or to pass the puck from a defenseman to a forward who is not available for a direct pass (upper right portion of figure). The puck is generally kept on the playing surface and is passed at varying angles without being passed too hard. Although the bank pass depends on the passer's judgment, timing and accuracy, it is an extremely safe and effective means of passing to yourself or a teammate when normal passing lanes are blocked. Around the goal line, it also allows you to pass the puck from one side of the rink to the other without hitting the net or having to pass the puck through the slot (defined as the shaded area in the diagram) area when in your own end. This pass can be made using either the forehand sweep, backhand sweep, snap pass or flip pass.

Open area pass. A puck carrier will encounter situations where no receivers are available to accept a pass. In this case, one option is passing to an unoc-

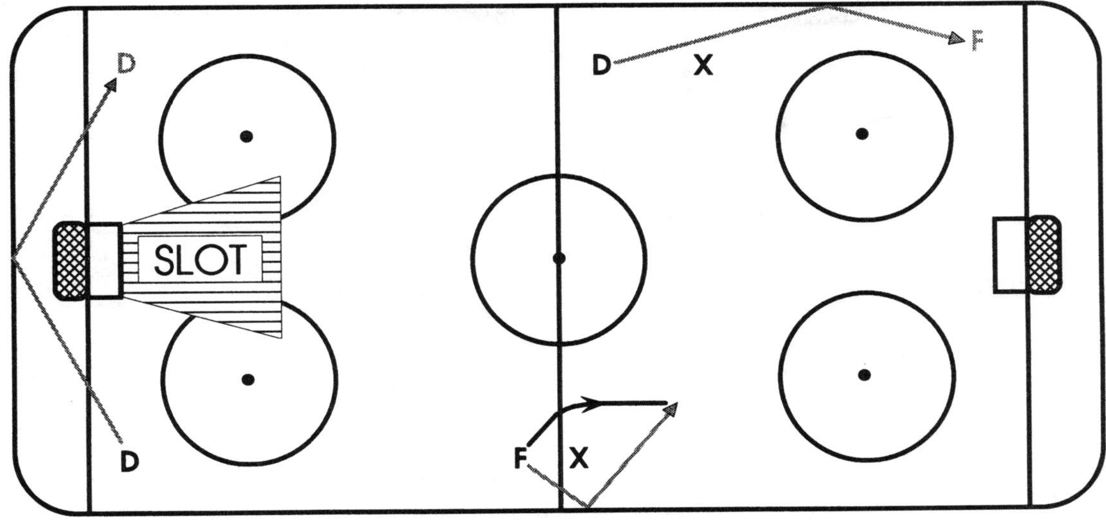

Figure 5-3; Bank Pass

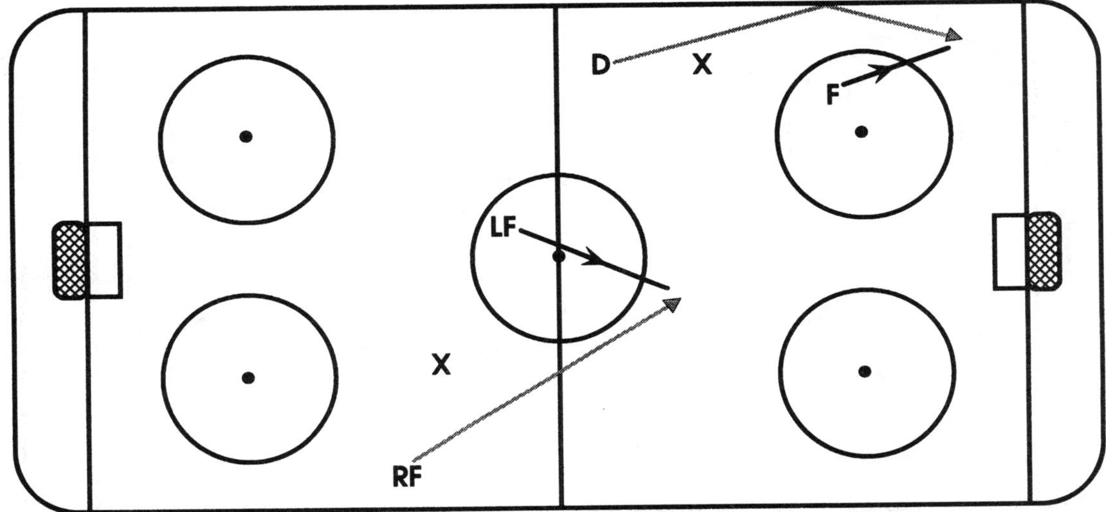

Figure 5-4; Open Area Pass

cupied space on the playing surface. Passing to an open area (also known as a spot pass) requires anticipation or what roller hockey players called hockey sense. The passer reads that an area is an open space in which a potential receiver would be the first to access, and the receiver reacts by anticipating that the pass will be directed into the open area and heads there. Both players are using anticipation to coordinate their actions for a successful pass. An open area pass can either be off the boards or just into open space. In Figure 5-4, the right forward (RF) cannot directly pass the puck to the left forward (LF) due to the defender (X). The RF makes an open area pass to the right of the center face-off circle. The LF reads the play and reacts by breaking to the open area to receive the pass.

In the second example, the defenseman (D) uses a combination bank pass and open area pass to reach the forward (F) who is breaking toward the goal line.

Drop pass. The drop pass is an effective technique used to deceive an opponent (left side of Figure 5-5) or to set up a screen shot on the goaltender (right side of figure). The drop pass requires a puck carrier to leave the puck or very softly pass it behind him a short distance to one of his teammates. The player executing the drop pass can either move into an open area for a return pass, keep an opponent from moving toward the receiver (similar to a pick in basketball) or screen the goaltender so that the receiver can take a shot on net without the goaltender fully seeing it. In the left side of the figure,

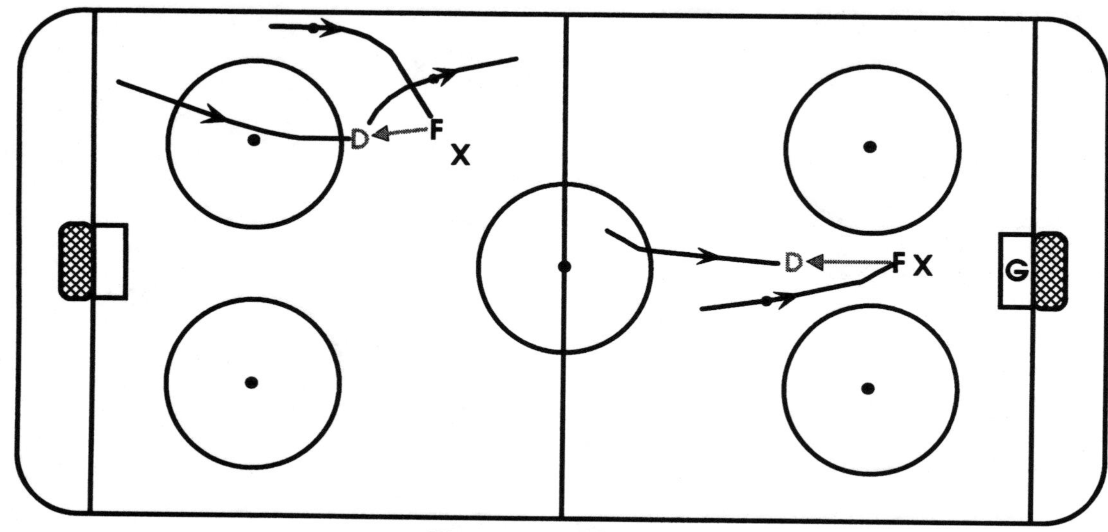

Figure 5-5; Drop Pass

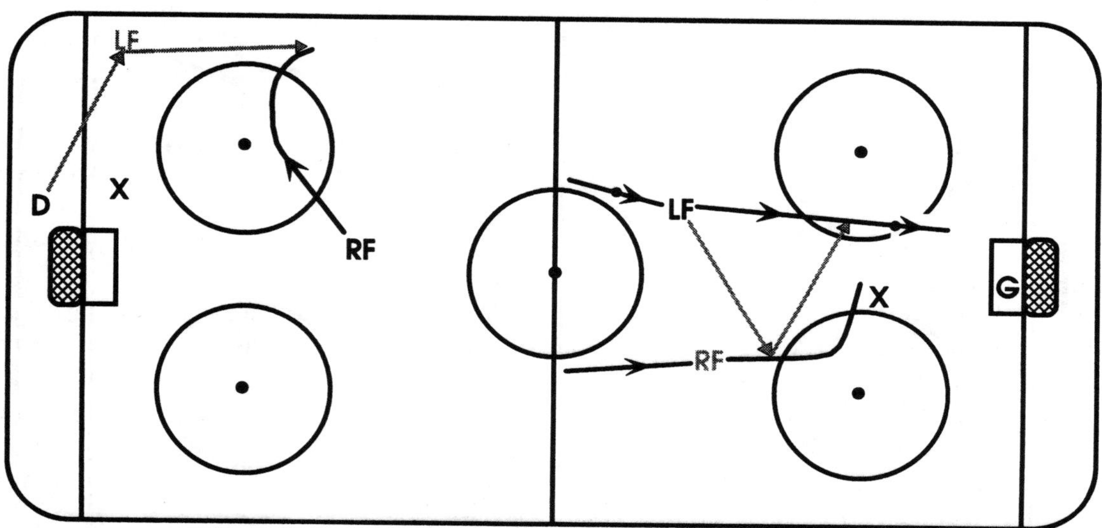

Figure 5-6; Touch Pass

the forward (F) is breaking out toward the center of the playing surface and encounters a defender (X). The defenseman (D) reads to the situation and reacts by moving up into the play. F makes a drop pass to D, and F then acts as a decoy to draw X away from the play. D completes this play by cutting left and advancing up the playing surface.

In the other example, F cuts straight toward X and makes a drop pass to D. In this case D can use both X and F as a screen by shooting low to one corner of the net or he can cut left or right and take a quick shot on the goaltender in an attempt to surprise him.

Touch pass. The touch pass or one-time pass is really just a redirection of the puck. This pass is mainly used when the puck carrier wishes to make a quick pass to a teammate or to quickly return a pass to the original passer. Because the touch pass redirects the puck to another player in a short time, opponents are often unable to adjust quickly enough to defend against this play, creating many quick break and scoring opportunities. No other form of passing is as rapid and deceptive. Given the speed of today's game, roller hockey players are using this pass more frequently as another means of gaining advantage over the opposition. In Figure 5-6, the defenseman (D) passes the puck to the left forward (LF), who executes a touch pass to the right forward (RF), who is cutting to the boards and up the playing surface in order to initiate a breakout play.

In the second example, LF carries the puck into the offensive zone and passes the puck to RF who executes a touch pass back to LF. In this example, quickness of the play fooled the defender (X) into covering the RF, leaving the LF to carry the puck toward the goaltender for a scoring opportunity.

Reverse. The reverse pass is really an offensive play that involves two players, the puck carrier and a potential receiver, coming from opposite directions and moving on a parallel course toward each other. As the players move toward each other, the puck carrier can choose to execute a drop pass to the receiver or continue to skate with it, electing not to pass the puck. If no pass is made, the non-puck carrier would act as a decoy and attempt to draw the defender away from the puck carrier. In both cases, the defenders will have a short amount of time to decide what to do. The reverse play can be very effective when the puck carrier is under pressure from a defender and is designed to confuse the defense.

In the left side of Figure 5-7, the left forward (LF) is carrying the puck toward the center of the playing surface, trying to move past the defender (X) who is skating just a few feet away. The right forward (RF) *reads* the situation and *reacts* by skating on a parallel course to the LF in order to receive a drop pass. As LF and RF pass each other, LF executes a drop pass to RF. LF continues skating, acting as a decoy by taking the defender with him. RF is now ready to continue the offensive attack and head into the offensive zone.

In the right side of the figure, the forward (F) is carrying the puck in an attempt to avoid the defender (X) covering him a few feet away. In this situation, the defenseman (D) moves up into the play by skating in a path parallel and opposite to F. As the players pass each other, F makes a drop pass to D. Again, F acts as a decoy and takes X with him, leaving D to move the puck into a scoring opportunity.

Weave. The weave, or crisscross, consists of two players angling toward each other and eventually crossing paths with the objective of creating open space for the puck carrier. The weave is a play designed with three passing options. The first option consists of actually passing the puck prior to weaving, shown in Figure 5-8. A pass is made, followed by a change in position between the passer and receiver, with the passer cutting across and behind the receiver. In Figure 5-8, the right forward (RF) carries the puck toward the center of the playing surface as a backchecking defender (X) attempts to cover him. The left forward (LF) *reads* the coverage and *reacts* by weaving or crossing in front of RF. Once LF is in position, RF passes the puck to him, they cross paths, and RF takes the defender with him, acting as a decoy.

The second option consists of holding the puck with no pass being made as the players cross paths. The third option consists of weaving and then passing the puck, and is just the opposite of the first option. All three options are designed to have the same effect — confuse the opposition and defeat any defenders.

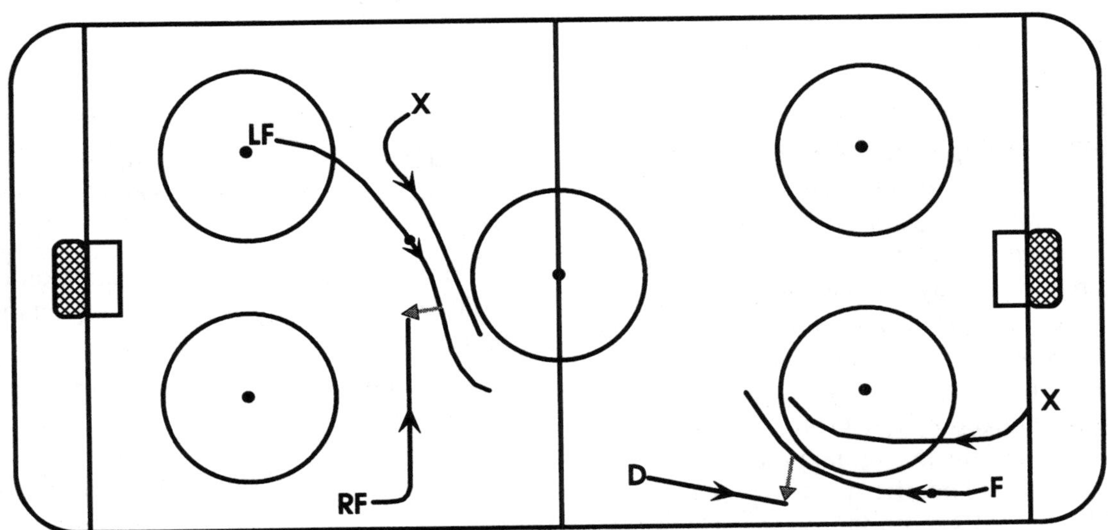

Figure 5-7; Reverse

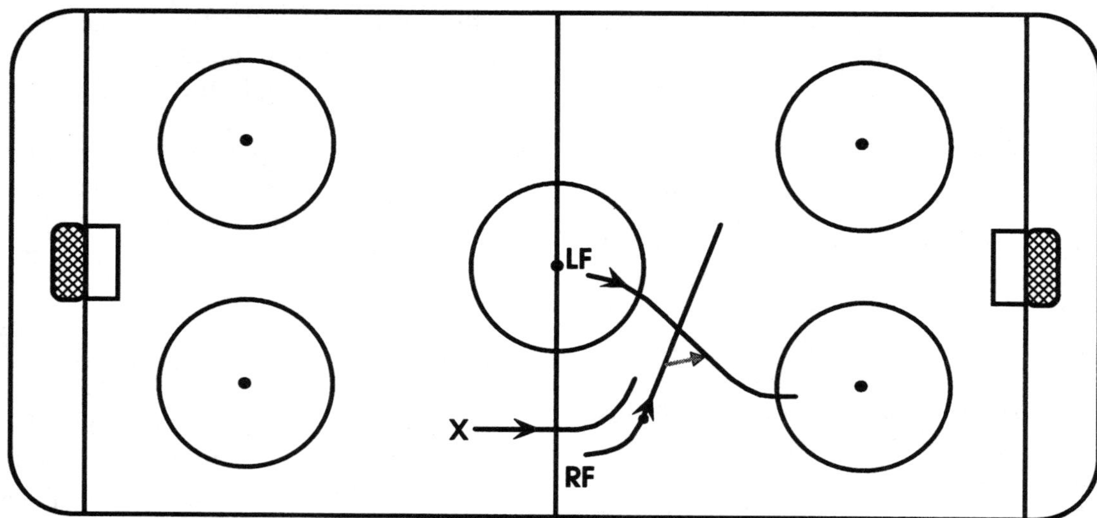

Figure 5-8; Weave

Skate pass. There are situations in roller hockey where the skate pass can be quite effective in addition to the only option available. For example, when your stick is tied up and players are competing for the puck with their skates. The only alternative is to use your skate to move and/or pass the puck into an open area or directly to a teammate. Many close battles for the puck can be won with the proper use of a player's skates.

Receiving a pass with the skates. To receive a pass with your skates, put most of your weight on the non-receiving skate and lean slightly to that side. This will free up the use of the other skate for receiving the puck. If you are skating forward and want to receive a pass with your skates from a passer who is even with or behind you; slightly lift and turn the receiving skate so that the toe is pointing inward and deflect the puck up to the blade of the stick. If you are not moving, turn your skate so that it is at approximately a 90-degree angle to the direction of the puck. As the puck hits your wheels, it will bounce off and you can retrieve it with the blade of your stick. Practice is definitely required to master this technique.

Receiving a pass in the air. Not all passes are textbook perfect and stick-to-stick. Occasionally, a pass must be received a few inches or a few feet off of the playing surface. In this case, the receiver should attempt to knock down a low, in-the-air pass with the blade of the stick using a downward slapping motion. When the pass is being received around or above the knees, attempt to knock it down with the glove or body and then move it ahead with the blade of your stick.

Drills

Passing and receiving drills should be selected to enable the players to adjust to as many passing and receiving situations as possible, using different types of passes, executed at various speeds between the passer and receiver. Players that have developed a high level of passing-receiving ability are well on their way to becoming proficient roller hockey players. Virtually any of these drills in the next two sections can be organized by any group of players, either on their own or during actual practices. As the coach discovers the specific needs of his players, he can select the drills required for specific player improvement. The coach should employ the Passing and Receiving Checklist to monitor performance and plan improvements for each player throughout the year.

For all stationary drills, the coach should monitor and provide feedback to the players on the following **four factors**:

1. Keeping the head up to locate the target.
2. Passing accuracy.
3. Controlling the height of the puck during the pass.
4. Cushioning the puck after receiving the pass.

Siller Player And Team Evaluation Profile©
Passing And Receiving Checklist

Evaluator: The Coach **Date**: 8/15/94 **Location**: The Arena

	Player Name											
Notes:	**TERRY**		**TAD**		**DON**		**BIRK**					
Fundamental Passing and Receiving Techniques												
Passing												
• Forehand Sweep	9		8		9		9					
• Backhand Sweep	8		8		8		8					
• Snap Pass	6		5		5		5					
• Flip Pass	6		5		5		5					
• Around-The-Boards Pass	**10**		**10**		**10**		**10**					
• Give-And-Go	8		8		8		8					
Receiving												
• Forehand	8		7		9		7					
• Backhand	6		6		8		6					
• Too Far Ahead	7		8		6		6					
Advanced Passing and Receiving Techniques												
Passing												
• Bank Pass	7		6		7		6					
• Open Area Pass	5		5		6		4					
• Drop Pass	7		5		6		8					
• Touch Pass	**3**		**3**		4		4					
• Reverse	6		6		5		6					
• Weave	7		7		5		6					
• Skate Pass	5		5		**3**		**3**					
Receiving												
• Off The Skates	4		4		4		4					
• In The Air	7		7		6		6					
TOTAL SCORE	**119**		**113**		**114**		**111**					
AVERAGE SCORE	**6.6**		**6.3**		**6.3**		**6.2**					

Comments: Terry, Tad, Don and Birk have all demonstrated medium overall passing and receiving proficiency with total scores of 119, 113, 114 and 111, respectively, and average scores of 6.6, 6.3, 6.3 and 6.2, respectively. All players scored excellent on the around-the-boards pass. Terry and Tad need to improve on the touch pass. Don and Birk need to improve on the skate pass.

Scale: 0 = Not Performed, 1 - 3 = Low Proficiency, 4 - 6 = Medium Proficiency, 7 - 9 = High Proficiency, 10 = Excellent Proficiency

Table 5-1; Passing and Receiving Checklist

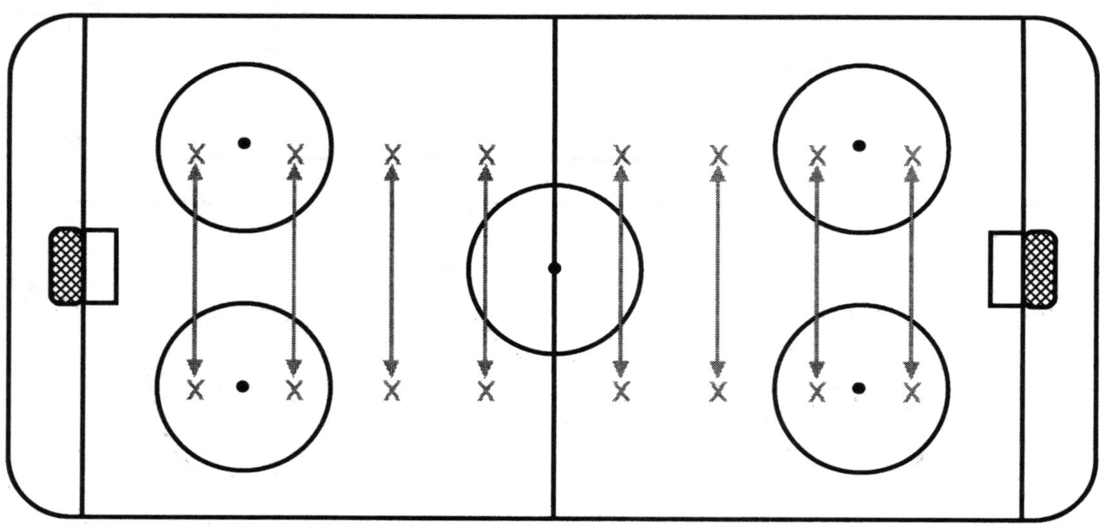

Drill 5-1; Stationary Passing And Receiving

During the moving drills, the coach should monitor and provide feedback to the players on the following **eight factors:**

1. Skating ability with the puck.
2. Keeping the head up to locate the target (reading the play).
3. Knowing when to pass.
4. Passing accuracy.
5. Controlling the height of the puck during the pass.
6. Getting into proper position to receive a pass (reacting by varying speed and direction).
7. Cushioning the puck after receiving the pass.
8. Controlling the puck after receiving the pass.

Drill 5-1; Stationary Passing and Receiving. This drill is designed to provide practice with four of the fundamental passes described earlier; the forehand sweep, backhand sweep, snap pass and flip pass. The players should spread out lengthwise along the playing surface, with half the team on one side of the rink and half on the other, as shown in the corresponding diagram. The distance between players should initially be about 20 feet. Have the players start off passing using the forehand sweep, making slow and easy passes. During this drill, the coach should monitor and provide feedback to the players on the four passing and receiving factors denoted earlier.

Variations:

- Use the backhand sweep, snap and flip pass.
- Increase the distance between players.
- Increase the speed of the pass.
- Have all players receive passes on their backhand.

Drill 5-2; Passing the Circle. Players, in groups of four or five, form three circles or enough circles to include all the players. The diameter of the circles should be approximately 20 feet as shown in the corresponding diagram. The puck is given to one of the players in each circle. At the whistle, the players pass the puck in a clockwise pattern, using the forehand sweep technique.

Variations:

- Use the flip, snap and backhand sweep passes.
- Increase the distance between players.
- Increase the speed of the pass.
- Have all players receive passes on their backhand.
- A competitive theme can be introduced to see how many players in each circle can pass the puck in 30 seconds. If the puck gets loose, it should be regained as quickly as possible and the pass sent on to the player who was to have received the next pass.

Drill 5-3; Passing and Receiving While Moving. This drill is designed to provide practice on four of

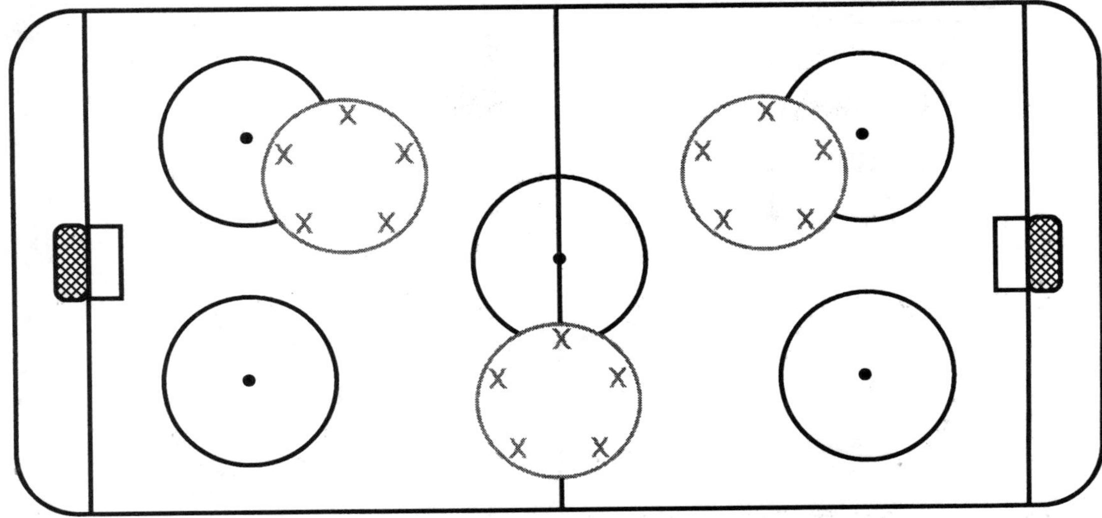

Drill 5-2; Passing The Circle

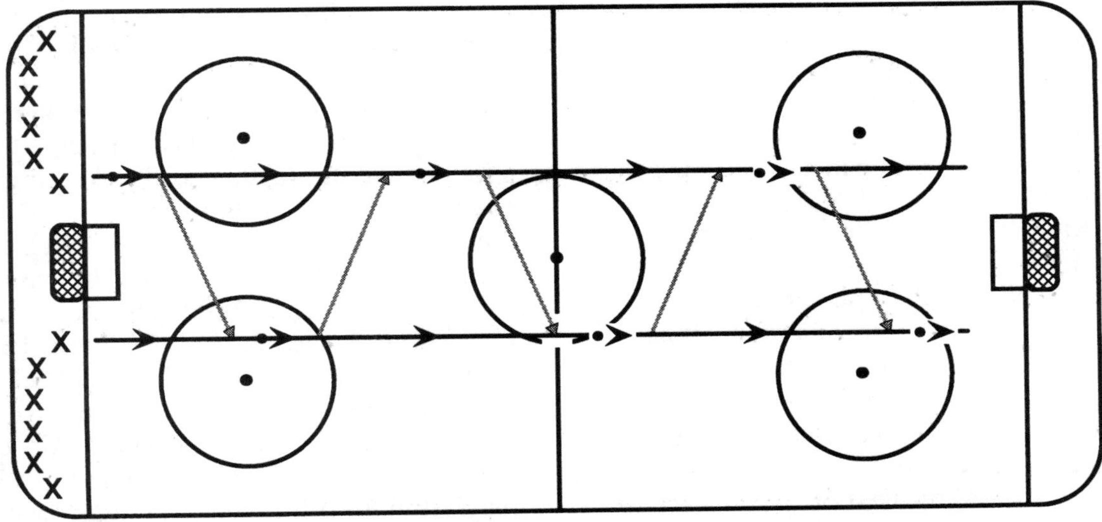

Drill 5-3; Passing And Receiving While Moving

the fundamental passes while skating: the forehand sweep, snap, flip and backhand sweep. Divide the players into two lines about 20 feet apart, starting on the goal line as shown in the corresponding diagram. While skating the length of the playing surface at half speed, have the players make slow and easy passes using the forehand sweep technique. Five passes should be attempted. Once the entire team has completed the drill going in one direction, have the players start off in the other direction. The coach should make sure that the first pass by each player is accurate. If it isn't, have the players start over again. It is important that the players get used to starting off each passing and receiving drill accurately. It will force them to set a standard for the remainder of the drill and for all passing plays described in subsequent chapters. During this drill, the coach should monitor and provide feedback to the players on the eight passing and receiving factors stated earlier.

Variations:

- Use the backhand sweep, snap and flip pass.
- Increase the distance between players.
- Increase the speed of the pass.
- Increase the players' speed to three-quarter speed.
- Have all players receive passes on their backhand.

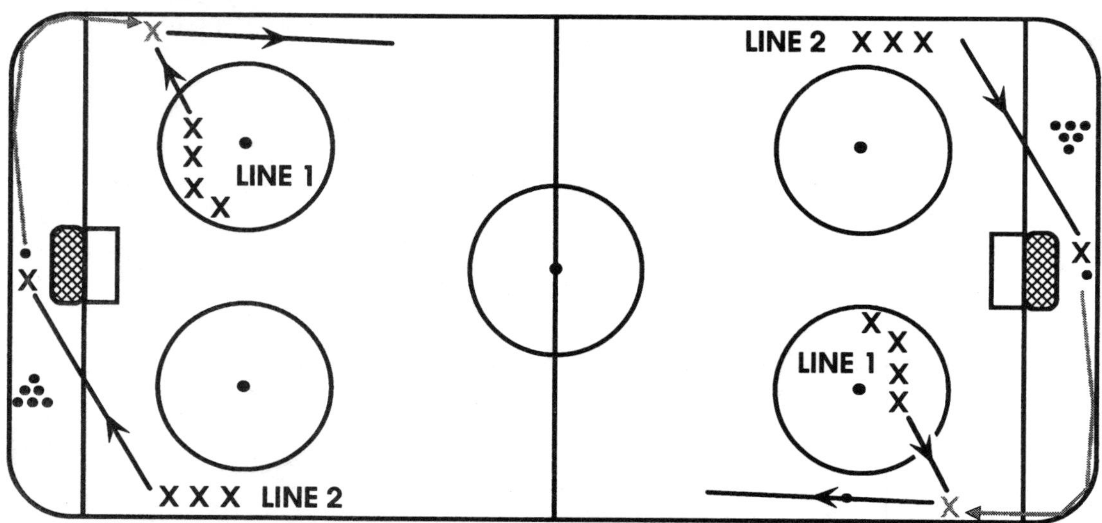

Drill 5-4; Around-The-Boards Pass

Drill 5-4; Around-The-Boards Pass. This drill teaches both the technique of passing along the boards and of receiving a board pass. Divide the players into two groups and place half at each end of the rink. Divide each group in half and place half in line 1 and the other half in line 2 (as shown in the diagram). At the whistle, the first player from line 1 skates to the boards and positions himself so that he is facing the net. The first player in line 2 skates behind the net, picks up a puck and executes a half-speed around-the-boards forehand sweep pass to the player along the boards. The player along the boards receives the pass and begins skating toward the center red line with the puck. Once he starts skating with the puck, the next players in each line should begin the drill. It is important to keep the passes on the playing surface until each player develops the proper technique for making and receiving this type of pass. Make sure that each player has the opportunity to participate in both line 1 and line 2.

Variations:

- Increase the pass speed to three-quarter.
- Use the backhand sweep and snap pass.
- Pass the puck so that it is off the playing surface when it reaches the player from line 1. When the pass is off the playing surface, the player should attempt to knock it down with the blade of his stick, skate or glove depending on the puck height and then move toward the center of the playing surface.

Drill 5-5; Peripheral Vision Drill. Although this type of vision is, to a large degree, inherited, peripheral vision can be improved through practice. Once a player realizes that he can actually see quite a lot without turning his head or looking down, he can begin using this ability. This drill will help the players make accurate passes without giving away their intention by telegraphing the pass, a useful skill in deceiving an opponent. First, line up the players across the rink, as shown in Drill 5-1. While stationary, have them pass the puck back and forth to each other while keeping their eyes straight ahead. The coach should provide feedback to each player on keeping his head up and passing accuracy. After the drill, spend a minute to get feedback from the players as to the field of vision and any problems they encountered. Work on instilling confidence in each player's ability to pass and receive the puck without directly looking at it.

Drill 5-6; Give-And-Go. The give-and-go drill is designed to develop the player's accuracy in passing and receiving when on the move. This drill also aids the stationary player in taking and receiving passes from a moving teammate. It is an excellent drill to be used as part of a breakout play. Four players are stationed lengthwise along the boards, about 20 feet from the center red line, and should all face toward the spot where the puck carrier starts. Divide the remaining players into two groups and place them behind each net (as shown below). At the whistle, the puck carrier in each line takes three half-speed strides and then makes a forehand

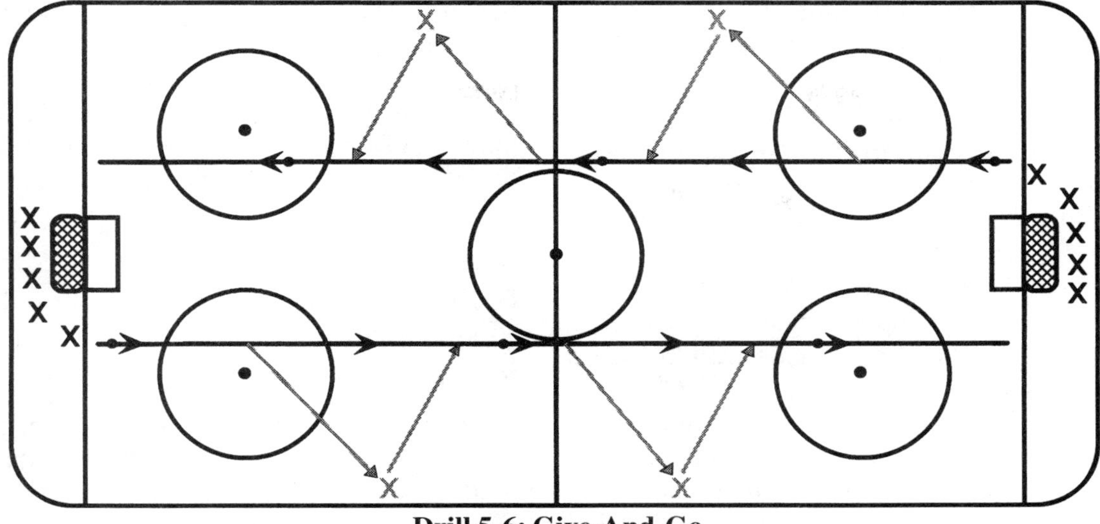

Drill 5-6; Give-And-Go

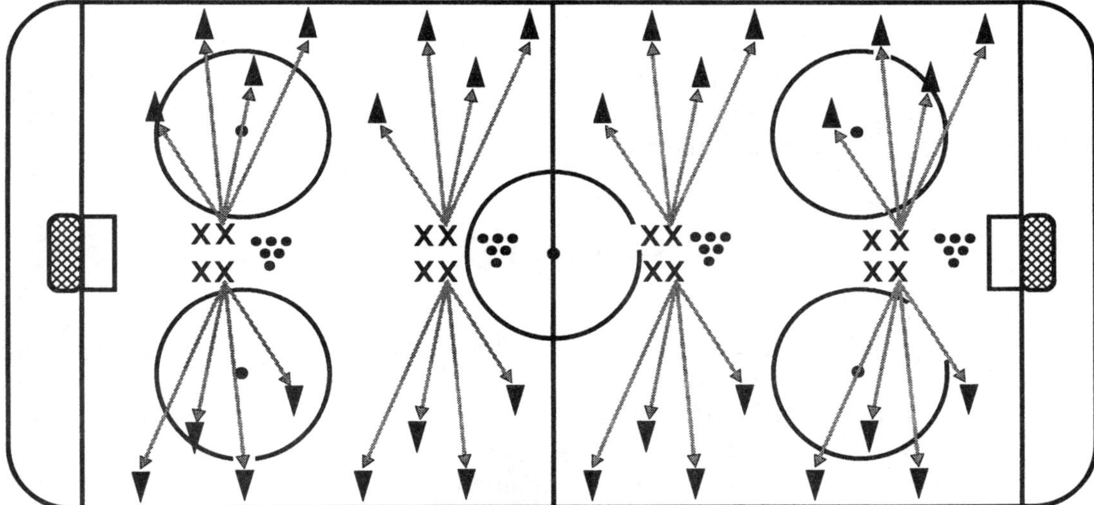

Drill 5-8; Target Practice

sweep pass to the first stationary player along the boards. The stationary player returns the puck to the original puck carrier with a sweep pass. The puck carrier continues by taking three strides and repeats the play with the next stationary player. After all players have gone through the drill, exchange the stationary players for players who have completed the moving portion of the drill and start again. During this drill, the coach should monitor and provide feedback to the players on the eight passing and receiving factors stated earlier.

Variations:

- Increase the speed of the pass.
- Increase the players' speed to three-quarter.
- Utilize the flip, snap and backhand sweep passes.
- Have all stationary players receive passes on their backhand.

Drill 5-7; Keep Away. Group the team into four player units. Select one of the four players to be the defender in the middle, while the other three players form an offensive triangle. Play a game of keep away. When the defender gains possession of the puck, the member of the triangle who lost the puck becomes the defender. If the offensive triangle keeps possession of the puck for more than one minute, the players can switch roles to keep the tempo going and to allow each player to perform the defender role. Passes should be made using the flip pass when attempting an over-the-stick pass and with the forehand sweep pass for under-the-stick and between-the-legs passes. Players should also practice this drill using the backhand sweep pass as their passing and receiving confidence increases.

Drill 5-8; Target Practice. To test the passing accuracy of the players and to bring in variety and competition, target receivers, such as pylons, can be set up and used to test the passing accuracy of the players. These target receivers can be placed along the playing surface with the objective of each player to try and hit as many targets as possible using the forehand sweep pass made from a specific location. Use the Passing and Receiving Checklist to test the players first, then give them a few weeks of practice and test them again. It will quantitatively demonstrate the positive effect that specific and focused practice has on each individual player as well as the team.

Divide the team into pairs and position them as shown below. Set up four pylons for each pair, varying the distance and passing angle of each. At the whistle, have one player in each pair pass a puck at each pylon. Have each pair keep track of the number of pylons hit. Next, have the other player in each pair do the same. At this point the coach should provide some feedback to each player in terms of passing accuracy and follow-through. Have the players perform the drill at least one more time with the coach recording the scores and comments for each player.

Variations:

- Execute passes using the snap, flip or backhand sweep techniques.
- Vary the positioning of the pylons.
- Incorporate competition. Execute the drill. Eliminate all players who hit less than two of the four (or three of the four depending on the level of talent) pylons. Have the remaining players repeat the drill. Eliminate the players who hit less than two of the four (or three of the four) pylons. Continue until there is a winner.
- Set up the drill like Drill 5-5; Give-and-Go. Have the players skate and pass the puck at the targets instead of at stationary players.

Advanced Drills

Drill 5-9; Stationary Bank Pass. The bank pass drill is designed to teach the players to use the boards as an option while passing. Position the players around the rink as shown below. The players, working in pairs, direct the passes to each other by banking the puck off the boards. Passes should initially be made using the forehand sweep technique while keeping the puck on the playing surface. For the drill, the coach should monitor and provide feedback to the players on passing accuracy and cushioning the puck after receiving the pass.

Variations:

- Execute passes using the snap or backhand sweep techniques.
- Receive passes on the backhand.
- Execute passes so that they are received off the playing surface, using the stick, glove or skate.
- Increase the distance between the pairs, both away from the boards and away from each other.
- Have the receiver use his skate to receive the pass and then move it up to his stick blade.

Drill 5-10; Skate Pass. Practice passing the puck between two players using only the skates. Set up this drill similar to Drill 5-3, Passing and Receiving While Moving, and keep the players about 10 feet apart as they skate.

Drill 5-11; Bank Passes While Skating. Divide the players into two groups and position them as shown in the corresponding figure. At the whistle, the first player in each line skates, at half speed, toward the far goal line executing four bank passes to the boards and receiving his own pass back. Passes should initially be made using the forehand sweep technique while keeping the puck on the playing surface. During this drill, the coach should monitor and provide feedback to the players on the eight passing and receiving factors stated earlier.

Drill 5-12; Touch Pass. Divide the players into groups of three (X1, X2 and X3) and position them as shown in the corresponding diagram. At the whistle, X1 passes the puck using the forehand sweep to X2 who redirects the puck (without stopping the momentum of the puck) to X3. This com-

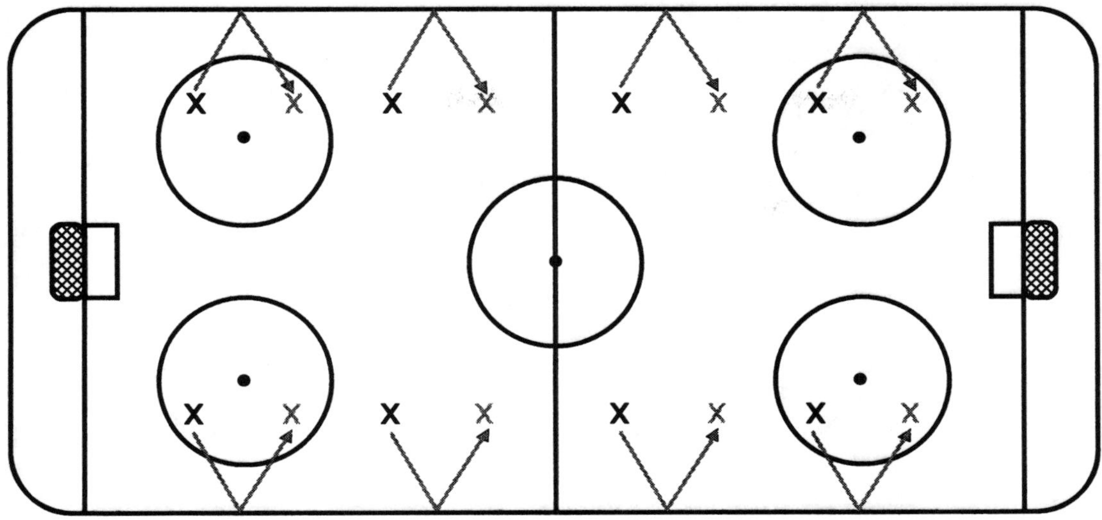

Drill 5-9; Stationary Bank Pass

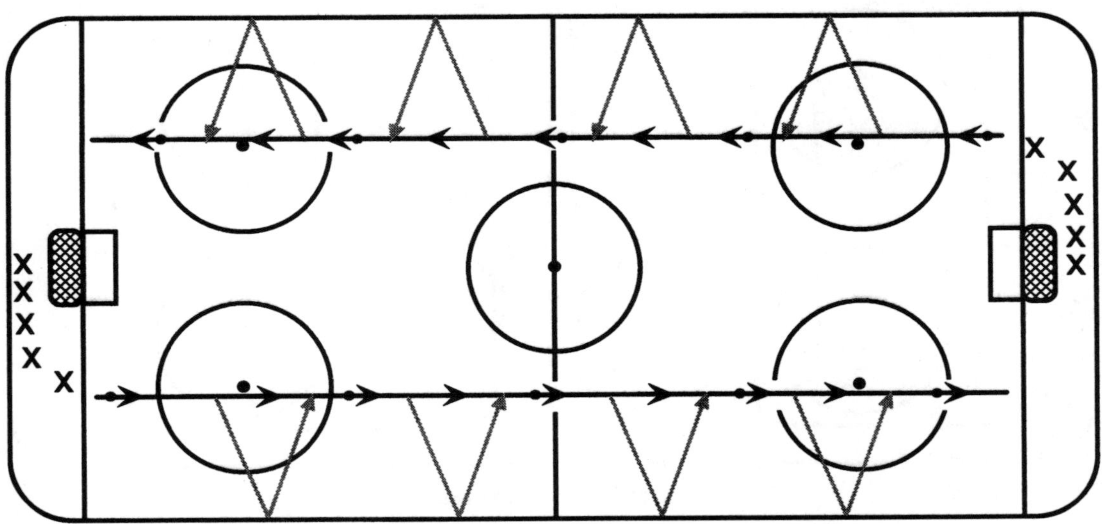

Drill 5-11; Bank Passes While Skating

pletes the first cycle. X3 now passes the puck to X1, who redirects the puck to X2. The drill continues for 10 cycles or until the coach stops the drill.

Drill 5-13; Reverse. Divide the team into two groups and position them at the goal line as shown in the corresponding diagram. The group on the top of the diagram starts off with the puck and will always turn closest to the pylon, with the other group making a wider radius turn around the pylons. At the whistle, the first players in each line begin skating at half speed. As the players move around the pylons and approach each other, the puck carrier executes a pass to the receiver. The players should be skating in paths about five feet apart at that point. The players skate around the next pylon and as they approach each other, the new puck carrier executes a pass to the original puck carrier. This reverse pattern continues one more time so that a total of three passes are made. Once all players have completed the drill going in one direction, they should complete it going in the other direction.

Variations:

- Increase skating to three-quarter speed.
- Have the receiver use his skate to receive the pass and then move it up to his stick blade.

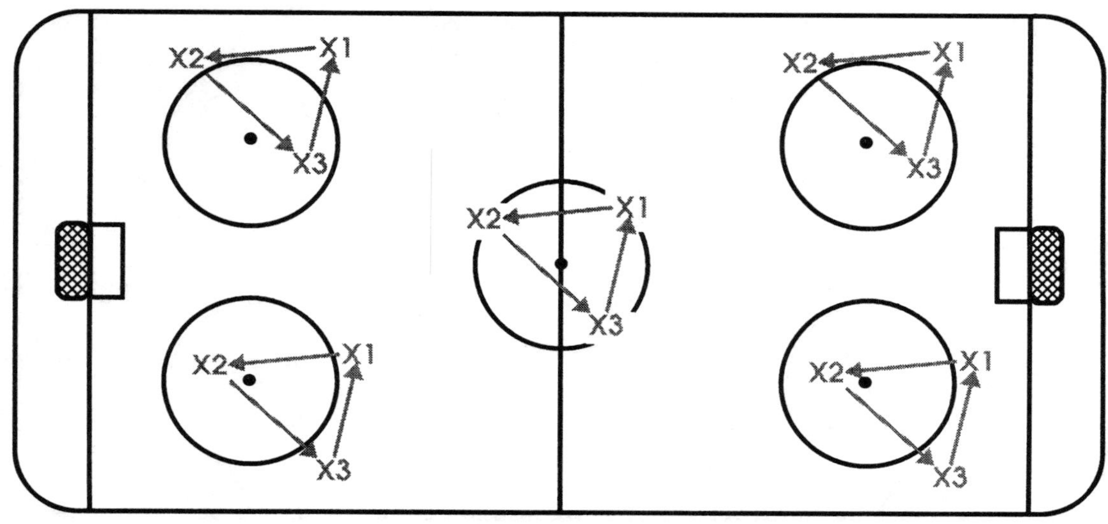

Drill 5-12; Touch Pass

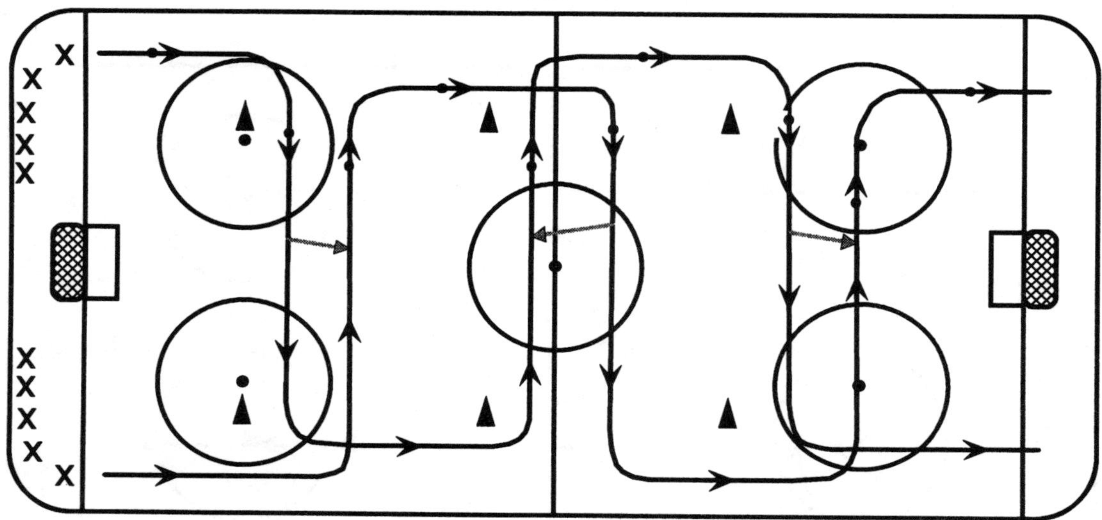

Drill 5-13; Reverse

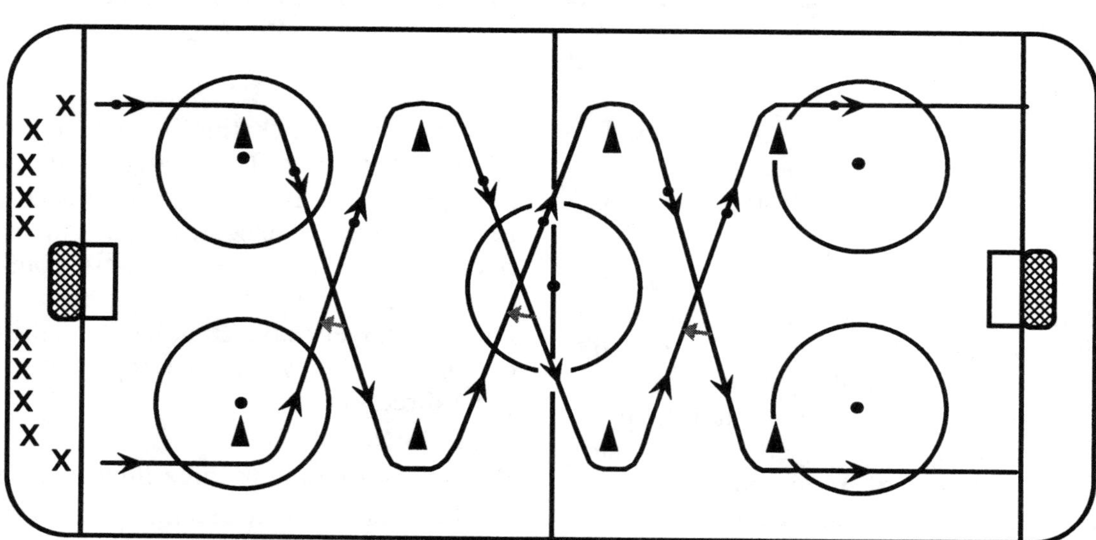

Drill 5-14; Weave

Drill 5-14; Weave. Divide the team into two groups and position them at the goal line as shown in the corresponding diagram. The group on the top of the diagram starts off with the puck. At the whistle, the first players in each line begin skating at half speed. As the players move around the pylons, the puck carrier will cut in front of the non-puck carrier and execute a drop pass to that receiver. The players skate around the next pylon and as they approach each other, the new puck carrier executes a drop pass to the original puck carrier. The players continue the weave pattern one more time so that a total of three drop passes are made. Once all players have completed the drill going in one direction, they should complete it going in the other direction.

Variations:

- Execute at three-quarter speed.
- Use an open area pass.
- Have the receiver use his skate to receive the pass and then move it up to his stick blade.
- Have the non-puck carrier cross in front of the puck carrier and take a pass.

Recap

After reading and studying the material in this chapter, you should be able to answer the following questions:

1. Why is passing the quickest and most effective way to move the puck up the playing surface?
2. Cite four reasons for passing the puck.
3. What are the three factors associated with effective passing?
4. What is meant by telegraphing a pass?
5. What should a player do after he passes the puck?
6. What are the three basic roles of a receiver in the passing-receiving combination?
7. Define *soft hands* in terms of pass receiving.
8. List and describe the six fundamental passing techniques.
9. List and describe the two fundamental pass receiving techniques.
10. What controls the accuracy and height of a pass?
11. What pass should be used to get the puck over an opponent's stick?
12. List and describe the seven advanced passing techniques.
13. List and describe the two advanced pass receiving techniques.
14. How will you use the Passing and Receiving Checklist to evaluate and improve individual players as well as the entire team?
15. During the execution of all stationary passing and receiving drills, what four factors should be monitored by the coach so that proper feedback can be provided to the players? For moving drills, what eight factors should be monitored?

JOIN THE FUN.
JOIN THE EXCITEMENT.
-JOIN A NO CHECK ROLLER HOCKEY LEAGUE NEAR YOU!!
HEY COACH, CAN OUR LINE START?

6

Shooting and Scoring

Highlights

This chapter addresses the exciting topic of shooting and scoring. Chapter 6 presents the following information:

Discussion

Fundamentals

- *wrist shot*
- *snap shot*
- *flip shot*
- *backhand wrist shot*
- *backhand flip shot*

Advanced Techniques

- *slap shot*
- *rebounds*
- *shooting off the back leg*
- *deking the goaltender*
- *breakaways — shoot or deke?*
- *screen shot*
- *one-time shot*
- *deflections*
- *scoring slump*

Siller Player and Team Evaluation Profile — Shooting and Scoring Checklist

Drills

Advanced Drills

Recap

Obstacles are those frightful things you see when you take your eyes off your goal.
— Henry Ford —

Big shots are only little shots who keep shooting.
— Christopher Morley —

Discussion

Scoring a goal is the ultimate offensive play and the objective of almost every player. No game can be won unless your team puts the puck into the net more times than your opponent. Skill at *anything* is only a group of correct habits formed through practice. Any roller hockey player can **develop effective goal scoring skills** by practicing drills designed to develop these specific shooting and scoring principles. To recognize an opportunity is one thing, but to consistently capitalize on those opportunities takes effective practice, and plenty of it!

Shooting and Scoring Technique

An effective shooting and scoring technique is the main ingredient for scoring goals. **Effective shooting and scoring** consists of shooting accurately from a high-percentage location, releasing the puck quickly with speed and power, and using the correct shot.

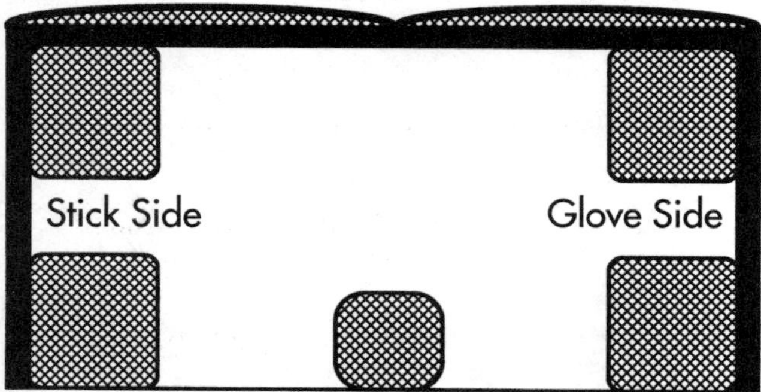

Figure 6-1; Portable Goaltender

Shooting Accuracy. Just as accuracy is a vital fundamental of baseball, basketball, football and soccer, so it is with roller hockey. A shot executed with a quick release and good speed is worthless unless it is directed at the net. The puck must be on target to have any chance of scoring. But great scorers do more than just shoot the puck in the direction of the goal. Great shooters pick their spots. They aim at the holes the goaltender leaves open while positioned in the crease. Normally, these **five locations** are the top right and left corners, bottom right and left corners, and occasionally between the legs (also known as the *five hole*), as shown in Figure 6-1. By practicing and using the right techniques at the rink, on a tennis court, basketball court or driveway, you are guaranteed to improve your consistency and overall shot placement.

To **control the accuracy of the puck**, the player must depend on his eyes and follow through with the stick. It is through these two factors that accuracy is controlled. When the player is approaching the net for a shot on goal, he should keep his eyes on the net to find an opening, then direct his muscles so that the puck moves accurately toward the opening using an effective follow-through. In some cases, a quick glance downward at the puck may be required to ensure that the puck is in the proper position with respect to the stick blade, but this extra step can be reduced and eliminated with practice. It doesn't matter from what distance or angle a puck is shot, accuracy improves when watching the target area rather than looking at the puck and stick at the moment of the shot.

Three methods can be practiced to **develop shooting accuracy**. (1) Shots can be made from different distances and angles in order to place the puck in different areas of the net past the goaltender. (2) A portable goaltender (see Figure 6-1) or target system can be used without an actual goaltender in the net. A portable goaltender is a device that partially covers the opening of the net. It has openings in the four corners and the five hole. This practice device can be built or purchased. The portable goaltender is used to train a shooter to shoot the puck consistently into areas of the net that have the most probability of scoring. (3) A combination of the first and second approaches can be used. Use the portable goaltender initially during the practice with a short period of shooting on the actual goaltender to finish off the workout. Applying the accuracy gained during the target practice to an actual goaltender provides a competitive angle along with gamelike experience.

Figure 6-2 shows the **location and percentages of goals** scored on a typical goaltender, based upon general observation of hundreds of ice and roller hockey games. Although goals are scored in the white area as well, this information provides the coach and players with some concrete payback when planning and executing shooting practices. As shown in the figure, the greatest percentage of goals were scored below knee level (70 percent), with more goals going in on the goaltender's stick side (60 percent) than on his glove side (30 percent). The top corners should not be neglected, since many times the goaltender is sprawled across the playing surface, leaving the upper corners open.

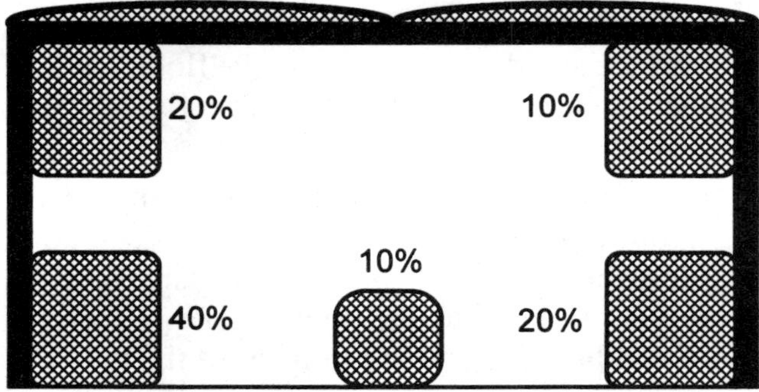

Figure 6-2; Scoring Location and Percentages

Positioning. Positioning is the second main factor in scoring. Positioning refers to a player's location with respect to the goaltender and net when a shot is released. **Most goals** are scored from five to 25 feet out, and directly in front of the net; with the majority of those goals coming from between 10 to 15 feet out. That ideal distance changes according to the goaltender's positioning in front of the net, the goaltender's skill level and the shooter's skill level. The ideal time to shoot is when you are far enough away from the goaltender to prevent him from cutting off any open net, but not close enough to give him the minimum reaction time to make his move once you shoot.

Many young roller hockey players have a habit of moving in too close before they shoot because they believe that they need to be as close to the net as possible to score. This habit is probably the **number one reason** why scoring opportunities are missed, since it allows the goaltender added time to react. Correcting that problem, by staying far enough out from the goaltender, can raise your goal scoring average.

To improve your goal scoring stature and that of your team, get into a high-percentage scoring position before shooting. If you are not able to get into a good position, look for a teammate who may be open in such a position. If you cannot see anyone and cannot maneuver into position, shoot low at the goaltender's feet and go in for the rebound. Figure 6-3 shows **position and percentage information of typical goal scoring locations**. The numbers represent the percentage of goals scored by location on the playing surface. Approximately 60 percent of goals are scored from the middle slot, 30 percent (15 percent on each side) of goals are scored from the area of the face-off circles and 10 percent (five percent on each side) of goals are scored from the extreme angles between the lower portion of the face-off circle and the goal line. As with Figure 6-2, this information is based upon general observation of hundreds of ice and roller hockey games. Although goals are scored from other locations as well, this information should be used by a coach to focus player positioning for scoring. The moment a player gets the puck and has a chance to score, his first thought should be to get into position. Once in a good position, the odds start to swing in his favor and against the goaltender.

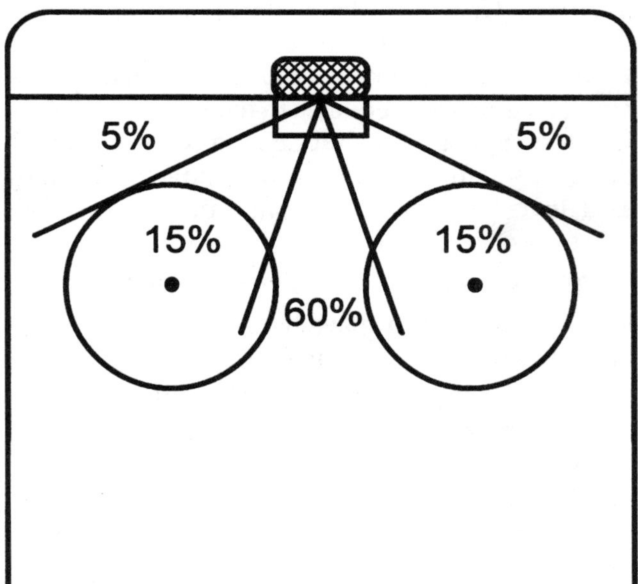

Figure 6-3; Scoring Location and Percentages

Quick Release. Players who possess a quick release can regularly **catch the goaltender off-guard**. There are **two methods** to release the puck quickly. The first method is the one-time shot (similar to the one-time pass described in Chapter 5), where the goaltender rarely has a chance to face the shooter and prepare himself for the shot. This is frequently the case when the puck comes from behind the net or across the slot and the goaltender has to face the shooter already in action. The second method is when the goaltender is clearly focusing on the puck carrier but is tricked by an unexpected shot. The shooter didn't *telegraph* (give away the intention to shoot) the shot. The shot was hidden or camouflaged among his skating and stickhandling action. One of the most effective ways of concealing the release of your shot is to shoot in stride. Basically, this means that you release the puck without changing the rhythm of your skating and stickhandling.

Speed of the puck. The speed with which a player moves the puck toward the net is an important factor in scoring goals. Goaltenders are often beaten by the velocity of the puck simply because of the human limits to reaction time. A well-placed shot, released from a high-percentage scoring area with adequate speed is almost impossible to stop. Emphasis should be placed on the development of as much speed as possible during practices, because the faster the puck goes, the less time the goaltender has to react. As the roller hockey player progresses through the various levels of play, from beginner to advanced, it is quickness rather than strictly pinpoint accuracy that equates to the most success for shooters. **Speed of a shot** depends on the strength and the execution of the shooting movement. Many excellent shooters with fast shots do not have massive upper bodies but their shooting movement, like the swing of a golfer, is coordinated and smooth.

Players can **develop speed** both off and on the playing surface. Off the playing surface, speed can be developed using exercises that strengthen the forearms and wrists. On the playing surface, power can be developed in three ways. The first method requires that the shooter make a conscious effort to consistently shoot as hard as possible. This will train the body to react to a shooting opportunity in a consistent way: powerfully. The second method requires the use of a power stick. Power sticks can only be used for practice, not during a game. A power stick is a normal stick that has been modified by adding extra weight to it. Modifications could include adding small weights to a normal shaft, or making a metal shaft and attaching a normal wooden stick blade to it. The benefit of the power stick is that it increases the muscular load involved in shooting, therefore developing more muscular power, like weight training. A power stick improves hand, wrist and forearm strength, and combined with the first method (consciously shooting hard all the time), will allow any player to increase the speed at which the puck approaches the net. The third method is to use a puck that is heavier than a normal roller hockey puck. This would generally be an ice hockey puck that has been modified by adding plastic pegs, used by most roller hockey pucks, so that the puck slides easily along the playing surface and does not damage the floor. Using a heavier puck provides the same benefits as using the power stick.

Type of shot. The type of shot to use during a scoring opportunity has a great deal to do with creating the element of surprise, noting the position of the goaltender at the time the puck carrier is about to shoot and how far you are in front of the net. The wrist and flip shots are the two shots to use when a player does not want to *telegraph* the shot, since they do not require a back swing. The wrist shot is the **most accurate** shot, whether the player is moving or stationary. **In the slot area**, the wrist, flip and snap shots are preferable to the slap shot. This is not only because there is little time to release a shot due to the number of players in the slot, but also because the shooter is normally going for accuracy as well.

Farther **away from the slot**, the slap shot can be more effective. If a player has time to wind up with a big backswing, the slap shot sends the puck traveling faster than any other shot. If the player does not have time to wind up, his preferable option is the snap or wrist shot, which reduces the time of execution.

The backhand shot should also be considered as an effective shot to use. Players who shy away from using their backhand shot are committing a serious error. **Backhand shots** surprise goaltenders because they can be very deceiving and most goaltenders are unaccustomed to them. Develop accuracy and confidence in your backhand shot and the results will speak for themselves. The backhand flip is an essential shot to master if you are thinking of deking a goaltender.

Fundamentals

There are five fundamental shots that every roller hockey player should become proficient at — the wrist shot, snap shot, flip shot, backhand wrist shot and the backhand flip shot.

The **wrist shot** or sweep shot is the most common and most accurate shot in roller hockey. It is named because of the action of the wrists as it is performed, and is similar in execution to the sweep pass described in Chapter 5. To utilize the wrist shot, start with your feet a little wider than shoulder width apart, weight predominantly on your back leg (left leg for a left-handed shooter), knees slightly bent and your body leaning over a point in front of the puck. The puck should be placed in the middle of the stick blade, even with your back skate. Any deviation from this position will result in a loss of power. Your eyes should initially focus on the puck and then, as you move through your swing, on your target. Eventually, with practice, you should not have to look down at all when executing this shot.

The lower hand should be between 12 and 24 inches below the upper hand; experiment with the spread of your hands until you find the best distance for you. With a forward motion, transfer your weight from your back leg to your front leg and quickly move the puck toward the target. The lower arm pushes the stick toward the target while the upper arm pulls the top of the stick toward your chest. At the start of the shot, keep your wrists cocked back. Then, just before the puck begins to move out in front of you, snap the wrists, putting every ounce of forearm and wrist strength you have into it. As the puck moves forward, make sure you do not pull away from the shot by letting your head and shoulders come up and away from the puck. Instead, keep your momentum moving toward the target until the puck has left your stick blade. Keeping the wrists stiff all through the shooting action is a common fault that makes it impossible for the player to obtain maximum speed and accuracy.

After the puck leaves your stick blade, make sure you allow your stick to **follow through** smoothly until it is pointing at the target. Do not stop it with a jerking motion. To keep this shot low, keep the shaft of the stick ahead of the blade and follow through after the shot with your blade on the playing surface or just a little above it. To lift the puck, let the blade of the stick come through until it is ahead of the shaft and let your blade follow through to the height required.

The **snap shot** is an abbreviated version of the slap shot and is used when a player wants to get a quick, hard shot on net. When stickhandling, this shot can also be used effectively to catch a goaltender by

Wrist Shot

Flip Shot

surprise, since it can be executed in stride. The **snap shot is a valuable** weapon because it is quick and accurate from up to 30 feet away from the net. The snap shot follows the same basic principles as the wrist shot with the following exceptions. Bring the puck to a point even with the heel of your front skate. Quickly draw the stick back about 12 to 30 inches (no higher than the thigh) and with a forward motion, transfer your weight to your front leg, snap the wrists and quickly move the puck toward the target using a short follow-through. Although this shot may not be as accurate as the wrist shot, a player with strong, flexible wrists and forearms can get remarkable speed into a snap shot and thus reduce some of the disadvantage of it not being as accurate.

The **flip shot** is used when the player is very close to the goal and is most effective **when the goaltender is flat on the playing surface** in front of the net. The flip shot is one of the hardest shots to effectively master. This fact is demonstrated over and over during the season when you see players fail to flip the puck over a goaltender who is flat on the playing surface, with an otherwise open net. The shot is performed by using a very short shooting action. The blade of the stick is placed just behind the puck with the top edge of the blade over the puck. The upper arm pulls the stick down and back toward the body, while the lower wrist is flipped toward the target and the upper wrist is flipped away from the target. This brings the bottom edge of the blade forward, contacting the puck,

Backhand Flip Shot

and brings the puck up off of the playing surface. The blade follows through to the height slightly below the knees. It is the action of the wrists and upper arm that flips the lower edge of the blade under the puck, providing the quick lift needed to send the puck over the goaltender and into the net.

Backhand wrist shot. This shot is very valuable when a player is angling toward the net on either his forehand or backhand side. The average player tends to neglect backhand shooting, preferring to shoot from his forehand when possible; even during practices or scrimmages. This is a mistake because goal scoring opportunities will be added if the backhand is utilized.

The shooting principles for the backhand wrist shot are similar to the forehand wrist shot. The only difference is that when shooting, the lower arm provides the pulling action while the upper arm provides the pushing action (just the opposite of the forehand wrist shot).

Backhand flip shot. This shot is similar to its forehand counterpart described earlier, except that the upper arm pushes the stick down and away from the body, while the lower wrist is flipped toward the target and the upper wrist is flipped away from the target. The backhand flip shot is an excellent shot to use when the goaltender is down on the playing surface and the shooter has the puck on his backhand side.

Advanced Techniques

Eight advanced shooting and scoring techniques covered in this section include slap shots, rebounds, shooting off the back leg, deking the goaltender, breakaways, screen shots, one-time shots and deflections.

Slap shot. The slap shot is one of the most emulated shots in all of roller hockey and scoring a goal with one is comparable to baseball's home run. The slap shot is valuable because the puck can be shot at greater speeds, from greater distances, than any other shot, and is an effective tool when used properly by a defenseman. A good low slap shot from a defenseman will give forwards good scoring opportunities by allowing them to redirect the puck and capitalize on rebounds. However, the gains in speed and distance are sacrificed for some accuracy and release quickness.

The body position for the slap shot is similar to that of the snap shot, only more exaggerated. Start with your feet a little wider than shoulder distance

Slap Shot

apart, weight evenly distributed between both legs, knees slightly bent and your body over the puck. The puck should be placed in the middle of the stick blade with the puck at a point just inside the heel of your front skate (right skate for a left-handed shooter). Once you have identified your target, your eyes should focus back on the puck and then as you move through with your swing, focus back on the target. Your lower hand should be about 20 to 30 inches apart from your upper hand. Experiment with the spread of your hands, however, until you find the best one for you.

To execute the slap shot, the stick is drawn back to at least shoulder height, the lower wrist is cocked back, the upper wrist is turned inside toward your body and your weight is shifted slightly to the back leg. On the downswing, the weight shifts to the front leg, the wrists move forward and the lower arm pushes the stick forward to the target while the upper arm pulls the top of the stick back toward the body. As the stick is brought in contact with the playing surface, tighten the lower hand around the shaft so that there is no give in your grip when the blade hits the playing surface. The stick contacts the playing surface in a downward motion just before it hits the puck, usually one to two inches from the puck, which causes the shaft to bend in the middle. The force unleashed by the straightening out of the shaft, the motion of the arms and wrists, along with the rotation of the upper body, helps to propel the puck at speeds that approach 100 mph! Keeping the wrists stiff through the shooting action is a **common fault** that makes it impossible for the player to get maximum speed and accuracy. **Strength** in the arms, shoulders and wrists is essential in shooting the slap shot. This precludes many **younger players** from executing effective slap shots. The slap shot should only be developed after all of the fundamental shots described above have been mastered. After the puck has gone, make sure you allow your stick to follow through to the target. Let the blade of the stick follow through until it is pointing at the target. As with other shots, the puck height is controlled by the height of the follow-through.

Rebounds. Another way to pick up more goals is to get into the habit of **following in on your shot** as quickly as possible to take advantage of any rebounds that may occur. The average goaltender allows many rebounds, especially from low shots. If you follow in quickly, these rebounds can be turned into additional scoring opportunities. Study the goaltender to see how the rebounds come out from his pads, stick, blocker or skates. This information is important because it gives you clues regarding just where to follow up. If you are not in position for a shot and have no one to pass to, keep your shot low so that you or your teammates around the net can get any rebounds. Avoid the bad habit of shooting and then watching to see what happens.

A good play, when you are at a bad angle, is to flip the puck so that it will land at the goaltender's feet, and then follow in quickly. A quick follow-up may result in picking up a rebound or may unsettle the goaltender. Flipping the puck instead of shooting hard will give you time to follow it in. Also, using your skates to get control of a rebound allows a player to get control of the puck when his stick is initially tied up by a defender.

Timing, quickness and strength to move into position in front of the net are essential factors in obtaining rebounds. With limited space and defensive coverage by the opponents in the slot, you must be strong on your skates, work your way to the puck, anticipate the shot from your teammate (if your teammate is the shooter), obtain the rebound and shoot the puck. Sometimes the forward can anticipate where a rebound might go, but the two keys to obtaining rebounds are to position aggressively in the scoring area (based on the trajectory of the original shot) and to focus on puck movement while keeping your stick on the playing surface. The determination to drive the rebound home is the mark of a good scorer and should be a main feature in all rebound drills.

Shooting off the back leg. Normally, a right-handed shooter will release a wrist or snap shot off his left skate (front skate). Advanced players should be able to shoot the wrist shot and snap shot off either their left or right leg in order to get a shot off quickly and to confuse a goaltender. To shoot either shot off of the back leg, simply keep your weight on the back leg as you shoot the puck. The follow-through is shorter than either the normal wrist or snap shots as the player is not in a stable position and is vulnerable to imbalance. All good goal scorers are able to shoot the puck off either leg since in many cases there is no time to relocate your footing when receiving the puck in a shooting position.

Deking the goaltender. Deking (pronounced deek-ing) is the skill **used to defeat a goaltender** during a one-on-one confrontation. Using exaggerated and camouflaged player and puck movement, it is designed to pull the goaltender out of position to create a scoring opportunity. It is important to get as much practice as possible using deking drills on a goaltender. In games or scrimmages, the player gets only a few chances to go in alone on goal. He will not be able to develop a great deal of skill and confidence unless opportunities are provided during practice drills. An excellent plan is to give each player a certain number of breakaways, putting the drill on a competitive level by keeping a check on the number of goals scored and the type of deke used during each drill using the Shooting and Scoring Checklist. This will also give the coach information on the player's progress throughout the season. Try using a specific deke on your own goaltender and then check with him to see how your moves can be improved. The information could be obtained in the form of asking your goaltender the following questions:

- Is your fake convincing?
- Do you start your deke too soon or late?
- Do you have any habits that give away your intentions?

Another way is to get the goaltender on your team to try to stop you in different ways, sliding out one time and standing up the next. This will give you a chance to see what moves are most effective against different goaltending styles. Effective deking begins well before the puck carrier is near the goaltender and consists of **five attributes**: analyzing the goaltender, controlling puck carrier speed, keeping the puck moving, watching for an opening and executing a specific deke.

Analyzing the goaltender. Players should study opposing goaltenders at every opportunity in order to **determine weak and strong points**. The goaltender should be watched carefully during the pregame warm-up and as play progresses. When sitting on the bench, a player can learn a lot about the opposing goaltender (and his teammates) if he watches carefully. Most players just watch the game and fail to look for information they can use to their advantage the next time they are on the playing surface. The coach should also make a point of collecting this data through scouting reports and passing it on to his players prior to each game. When scouting a goaltender, answer the following questions and you will have at least one strategy to defeat that opponent. These questions should also be answered during each game.

- Does he go down to the playing surface often and what moves get him down there?
- Is he good with his hands?
- Which hand is best?
- Is he better to one side (stick side or glove side)?
- Does he give rebounds off his stick, skates or pads?
- Does he stay in his goal or come out to cut off the angle?
- Does he keep his legs together or apart?
- Does he cover the short side or leave it open on shots to the far side (see Figure 6-4)?
- Does the goaltender purposely leave openings or fake a movement in order to draw shots?

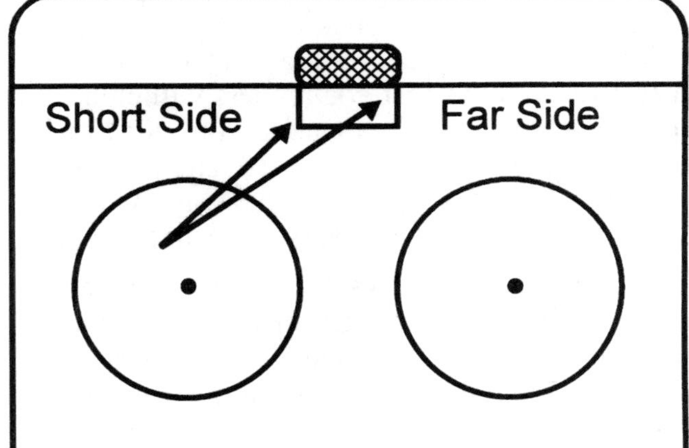

Figure 6-4; Short and Far Side Shooting

Controlling puck carrier speed. Slow down a little to effectively deke a goaltender and provide time for a fake. This makes the goaltender more nervous and can provide a mental edge. It also gives you a chance to maneuver in a way that would be impossible if you moved in at full speed. Failure to get set for a deke is one reason players miss when a scoring opportunity arises. They come in at top speed and, unless everything is executed perfectly, their chance to score may be gone before they know it. One way to avoid this is to take it slow.

Keeping the puck moving. The player who develops a high level of puck control and skating skills is prepared to do a good job deking the goaltender. Moving the puck is effective because, although it may not make the goaltender actually move his body, it will make him move his eyes. As a player approaches the goaltender with the puck, the goaltender's eyes focus on the puck and the stick blade, and move to what is called a *level*. When the eyes are on the level, they are most efficient and can follow the puck very well. If they have to move to a new level, due to rapid puck movement, there is a short period of adjustment. This is why a curveball or forkball is harder to hit than a fastball in baseball. So when a player keeps the puck moving and then executes a deke, a shot should be made as soon as possible after the deke so that the goaltender's eyes do not have time to move to the next level.

Watching for an opening. When deking the goaltender, the puck carrier should keep his eyes on the goaltender and manipulate the puck by feel as much as possible (that means keeping your head up). As soon as the goaltender is drawn out of position, the shooter's eyes should focus on an opening where the player can put the puck. An effective way to create an opening is to force the goaltender to move laterally. Even the best goaltenders will create an opening when they have to move from side to side. If you get the goaltender to move laterally and he opens the legs, shoot it there right away. When this is executed correctly, it is very difficult to stop.

Executing specific dekes. Nine types of dekes are presented in this section. Experiment with this list and then vary some of the tactics to create some of your own. This tailoring process allows each player to incorporate specific moves that he is proficient at. The dekes presented here include the forehand shift, backhand shift, forehand five-hole, backhand five-hole, backhand-to-forehand shift, forehand-to-backhand shift, short side shot, far side shot, and the fake shot and shift.

- **Forehand shift.** This deke is performed by skating directly toward the goaltender with the puck in front of you. About six feet from him, move quickly to your forehand and move the puck completely around the goaltender before he has a chance to get set, then shoot. It is not necessary to get your body past the goaltender, just the puck. Watch the goaltender's leg pad. Most roller hockey goaltenders cannot get their leg pad fully extended and over to the goal post before a quick move is made. But if the goaltender does, flip the puck over the pad.
- **Backhand shift.** This deke is performed like the forehand shift except you move to your backhand and then move the puck completely around the goaltender. This type of deke requires good backhand skills. Practice your backhand shot so that you will be comfortable with this maneuver.
- **Forehand five-hole.** This deke is similar to the forehand shift deke described above except instead of moving the puck completely around the goaltender, you slip the puck between the goaltender's legs. If the five-hole is not available, move the puck completely around the goaltender (the forehand shift).
- **Backhand five-hole.** This deke is performed like the one above except you move to your backhand side and slip the puck into the five-hole. As with the forehand version, if the five-hole is not available, move the puck completely around the goaltender (the backhand shift).
- **Backhand-to-forehand shift.** Now we are starting to get a little more technical. In performing this move, the puck carrier keeps the puck in front of him as he skates toward the net. About six feet away from the goaltender, shift the puck to your backhand as if you are going to shoot, and instead of letting the puck go, slip it quickly to your forehand side and shoot for that side of the net. This maneuver is effective when the goaltender moves with the first shift.
- **Forehand-to-backhand shift.** This is the opposite of the backhand-to-forehand shift described above. You move to the forehand, and then move to the backhand and shoot. Again, this maneuver is effective when the goaltender moves with the first shift.
- **Short-side shot.** Use this play when moving across the front of the net. As the player cuts in toward the net, he fakes a shot to the far side of the net. Just before he releases the puck, slide the puck to the short side and shoot.
- **Far-side shot.** This is the opposite of the short-side shot. As you cut across the front of the net, fake a shot to the short side, and then move and shoot to the far side.
- **Fake shot and shift.** Like the other dekes described above, this deke can be employed using your forehand or backhand. This deke consists of a faked shot aimed in one direction, from

about six feet out, quickly followed by the real shot aimed in another direction. For example, the player could fake a shot to the right side and end up shifting and shooting to the left. This deke is very effective because even if the fake shot is not pointed in any special direction, it frequently causes the goaltender to tighten up. It is not only a good way to fake the goaltender, but is also a good move to use to get by a defender.

Breakaways — shoot or deke? One of the most exciting moments in roller hockey occurs during a breakaway — one player versus the goaltender. This becomes even more dramatic during a penalty shot, overtime or a shootout. The puck carrier skating toward the goaltender is faced with a decision to shoot or deke. The puck carrier should not decide prior what he will do or carry the puck in such a way as to give away his intentions to the goaltender. Normally, when a player decides to deke, the puck is in front of him and when he intends to shoot, it is on his side. Ideally, the player should **keep the puck between these two positions** (front and side) until after the decision is made. This is very important — just ask an experienced goaltender. It is also important to keep the player's individual preferences in mind. Certain players possess deadly accurate shots, and their instincts and experience should naturally sway them to think of shooting as they approach the net. There is no problem with this kind of mind-set, but always leave your options open in case, for example, the goaltender comes way out of the crease, leaving you with minimal shooting area.

Having **confidence** is not only important during breakaways, it is also fundamental to playing the game. Coaches must constantly attempt to instill confidence in their players. If a player is going to score goals, he must have confidence in himself and believe that he can score goals. A player's negative thoughts and self-doubts are often a goaltender's best friend.

When a player breaks in alone on a goaltender, he must decide whether to deke the goaltender or shoot. In deciding this, there are **several factors to consider**:

- What is your strong point? A shot or a deke?
- Is there time to go in for a deke or is there an opponent coming toward you?
- How is it easiest to beat the goaltender?
- Does the goaltender stay back in the net or come out and challenge? Is your shooting *on* tonight or are you having an *off*-night?
- What did you do on any previous chances?
- Are you winning or losing?
- As Clint Eastwood would say, do you feel lucky, well do ya puck?

The answers to these questions should help decide your strategy. You must know yourself and know your opponent to make a reasonable decision. If you know the goaltender is easier to beat with a deke, go in and try to fake him. If your shooting has been off, deke. If you shot the last few times you were in on goal, try a deke to keep the goaltender from getting set.

If you can shoot better than deke, then shoot. If you are experiencing trouble stickhandling, lay off the deke and shoot. If you tried to deke him before, try a shot because he may be expecting you to come right in again. Once you have decided to shoot, you must then decide what kind of shot to use. Should it be high, low, stick side, glove side or in the five-hole? The first choice should be to shoot below the knee, preferably about ankle-high or even right along the playing surface. The shot can be in either corner or in the five-hole (see Figure 6-2 for percentages). The majority of the time, the low shot will be the best. Low shots are harder to stop, give better rebounds and are easier to place. Most goaltenders say that they are the hardest shots to handle.

The second choice is to use a shoulder-high shot in either corner. This type of shot is a good one to use against goaltenders who crouch very low when getting set for the shot, butterfly goaltenders, goaltenders who have a hard time handling high shots or who are slow with their hands (goaltending styles are presented in Chapter 9). It is also the best location to use if the goaltender is down on the playing surface. To stop a shoulder-high shot the goaltender must move his glove hand or blocker a long distance in order to stop the shot. Usually the goaltender keeps his glove hand at his side, which means he must raise it almost a foot to stop a shoulder-high shot. One of the things that makes a shoulder-high shot take second place to the low shot is that there is more margin for error. If the shot is just a little too high, it will go over the net;

if it is just a little too low, it will be in the waist to chest area, which is normally an easy save.

Remember also, that as you get closer to the goaltender, the open net area you have to shoot at gets smaller. And if you are coming in on an angle, you have significantly reduced your shooting area over a straight-on shooting situation. For those reasons, it is best to shoot from directly in front of the goal so that you can shoot to either side of the goaltender. When the shot comes from directly in front of him, the goaltender has to wait and see which side the puck is going before he can effectively move.

Screen shot. Players around the net should also think of screening the goaltender when a shot is taken. The player in front of the net can also divert defenders and create a certain amount of commotion to distract the goaltender, who is trying to keep his eyes on the puck. The screener should also be looking for any possible rebounds. Puck carriers skating into the offensive zone must also learn how to use the opposing defenseman as a screen. If this maneuver is properly executed, the defenseman can totally or at least partially obscure the vision of the goaltender. This can be a particularly effective play in a one-on-one situation.

One-time shot. The one-time shot is really a combination pass and shot and is similar to the touch pass described in Chapter 5. The type of shot that can be used with the pass can be any one of the shots described in this chapter but mainly consists of the snap and slap shots. Along with the normal slap shot, this shot creates much excitement due to its difficult execution and results when it is properly executed. The one-time shot relies on one major factor, **timing**, to be executed effectively. As a pass is made to the shooter, the shooter readies himself. Instead of receiving the pass, the shooter draws his stick back and times the travel of the pass so that the shooter's follow-through with the blade of the stick coincides exactly with the arrival of the puck. When the puck reaches the shooter, he one-times (redirects) the pass by shooting. This type of shot is very deceptive because as a goaltender attempts to follow the puck on the playing surface, it is moved from one location to the net usually before the goaltender has a chance to prepare himself for the shot. This is frequently the case when the puck comes from behind the net or across the slot and the goaltender moves to face the shooter already in action. Roller hockey players are using this shot more frequently as another means of gaining advantage over the opposition.

Deflections. Many goals are scored by a player changing the direction of the puck using the blade of the stick. To deflect or redirect a puck, it is important to get into a good position. There are three locations in which deflections work effectively: directly in front of the net, off to either side of the net and a couple feet away from the goal line. When in front of the net, the player should attempt to block the goaltender's view of the shot (screen shot) and be available to redirect a straight-on shot to the corner of the net. When off to the side of the net, the player should be watching the shooter with his body turned slightly toward the shooter for a forehand deflection and with his back turned slightly toward the shooter for a backhand deflection. In all cases, the blade of the stick should be angled down to deflect the puck downward and angled up to deflect the puck upward. Keep a tight grip on the stick for all deflections.

Scoring Slump. Just as a hitter in baseball will suddenly go into a hitting slump for *no apparent reason*, a roller hockey player can also find himself in a scoring slump. The puck hits the post, hits a skate and is deflected wide, or the goaltender seems to go on a hot streak and stops everything. A slump can discourage a player and spoil both determination and spirit. Analyze the play of someone in a scoring slump and you'll probably find that he has developed some bad habits in his shooting technique or strategy. He may be pressing too hard and is too tense to perform at peak efficiency or he may be getting lazy. When a player hits a slump he should keep a determined and optimistic attitude, see if his fundamentals are sound, and work with the coach to do all that is possible to make sure his technique is not at fault. The Shooting and Scoring Checklist and drills provided in this chapter are excellent tools to improve performance and to correct existing deficiencies. Don't put the slump down to bad breaks and leave it at that; continually work toward improvement!

Siller Player And Team Evaluation Profile©
Shooting And Scoring Checklist

Evaluator: The Coach | **Date**: 9/21/94 | **Location**: The Pond

	Player Name											
Notes:	**ANN**		**ERIN**		**LUKE**		**RJ**					
Fundamental Shooting and Scoring Techniques												
Wrist Shot - low	**10**		**10**		**10**		**10**					
Wrist Shot - high	7		8		8		8					
Snap Shot - low	8		8		8		8					
Snap Shot - high	6		5		5		5					
Flip Shot - high only	5		5		5		5					
Backhand Wrist Shot - low	6		6		6		5					
Backhand Wrist Shot - high	5		5		5		5					
Backhand Flip Shot - high only	4		**3**		4		**3**					
Shooting Power Test - This test lists the distances the 8-pound target block has been moved, from 5 feet, with a forehand wrist shot, snap shot, and a backhand wrist shot, in inches.	41” 44” 25”		36” 39” 22”		37” 39” 23”		34” 40” 22”					
Advanced Shooting and Scoring Techniques												
Slap Shot - low	7		7		6		6					
Slap Shot - high	7		6		6		6					
Rebounds	5		5		7		5					
Shooting Off The Back Leg	7		5		6		7					
Deking the Goaltender	5		4		4		4					
Breakaways	5		5		5		5					
Screen Shot	6		6		5		6					
One-Time Shot	7		7		5		6					
Deflections	5		5		5		5					
TOTAL SCORE	**105**		**100**		**100**		**99**					
AVERAGE SCORE	**6.2**		**5.9**		**5.9**		**5.8**					

Comments: Ann, Erin, Luke and RJ all have demonstrated medium overall shooting and scoring proficiency with total scores of 105, 100, 100 and 99, respectively, and average scores of 6.2, 5.9, 5.9 and 5.8, respectively. All players scored excellent on the low wrist shot. Erin and RJ need to improve on the backhand flip shot.

Scale: 0 = Not Performed, 1 - 3 = Low Proficiency, 4 - 6 = Medium Proficiency, 7 - 9 = High Proficiency, 10 = Excellent Proficiency

Table 6-1; Shooting and Scoring Checklist

Drills

Shooting and scoring drills should be selected to enable players to adjust to as many shooting situations as possible, using different types of shots, executed at various speeds and angles. To develop skill at shooting and scoring, you must execute over and over again, both stationary and while moving, until your shots become perfected. The secret to shooting and scoring is practice. If you devote a few minutes to each drill every day, the results will soon show in your game. As the coach discovers the particular needs of his players, he can select the drills required in order for the players to improve. The drills in this chapter include the components of skating, stickhandling and puck control, passing and receiving, and shooting and scoring.

For all stationary drills, the coach should monitor and provide feedback to the players on the following **seven factors**:

1. Position of the puck on the stick blade.
2. Location of the puck in relation to the skates and body.
3. Distance between the hands on the shaft of the stick.
4. Distance the stick is drawn back (snap shot only).
5. Movement of the legs, arms and wrists while shooting.
6. Position of the head and eyes.
7. Follow-through of the stick and arms toward the target.

During the moving drills, the coach should monitor and provide feedback to the players on the following **11 factors**:

1. Skating ability with the puck.
2. Getting into a high-percentage scoring position (depending on the drill).
3. Position of the puck on the stick blade.
4. Location of the puck in relation to the skates and body.
5. Distance between the hands on the shaft of the stick.
6. Choosing the correct shot for the correct distance and angle from the goaltender and net.
7. Distance the stick is drawn back (snap shot only).
8. Movement of the legs, arms and wrists while shooting.
9. Shooting off of the front or back leg.
10. Position of the head and eyes.
11. Follow-through of the stick and arms toward the target.

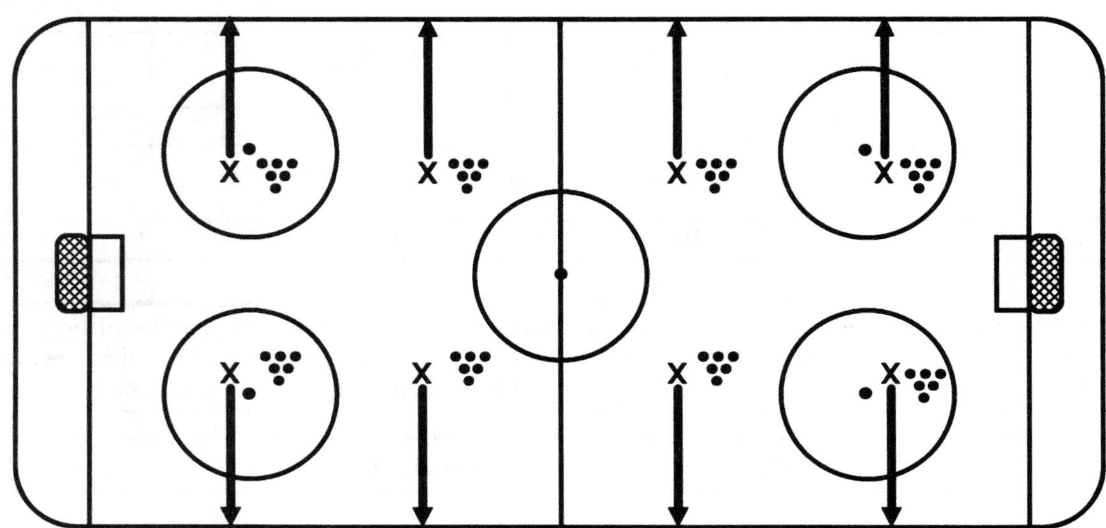

Drill 6-1; Stationary Shooting Against The Boards

Drill 6-1; Stationary Shooting Against The Boards. This drill provides practice shooting three of the five fundamental shots against the boards: the forehand wrist shot, snap shot and backhand wrist shot. Position the players along the length of the rink, about 15 feet from the boards, as shown in the diagram. Have them practice executing the forehand wrist shot first. During this drill, the coach should monitor and provide feedback to the players on the seven stationary drill factors listed earlier.

Variations:

- Use the snap shot and backhand wrist shot.
- Practice shooting 10 high shots, 10 low shots, then alternate high and low shots.
- Mark targets on the boards, low and high, and have the players shoot for the marks. Score the players and keep track of their progress using the Shooting and Scoring Checklist.
- Increase the distance of the players from the boards to 20 feet; to 25 feet.

Drill 6-2; Stationary Shooting On Net. This drill provides shooting practice for three of the five fundamental shots (the wrist shot, snap shot and backhand wrist shot) on net. Five players set up in a semicircle about 15 feet from the net and will shoot from that position. At the whistle, player X1 executes a forehand wrist shot. At the next whistle, player X2 performs the same shot. The players should wait to shoot until the coach blows the whistle so that the goaltender has a chance to get set for each shot. After each player shoots one puck, he retrieves it and begins the drill again.

Variations:

- Alternate the shooting pattern (i.e., X5-X4-X3-X2-X1, X1-X5-X2-X4-X3, or X5-X1-X4-X2-X3).
- Vary the distance that the shots are taken from. The minimum distance should be 10 feet and the maximum distance should be 30 feet, depending on the type of shot and the skill level of the players.
- Use a target goaltender.
- Have the players alternate the position that they shoot from so that they can get practice shooting from different angles.

Drill 6-3; Stationary Shooting On Net — Flip Shot. To develop proper execution for the forehand and backhand flip shots, position the players in the sequence described above and about 5 feet in front of the net. From this position, the objective is to put the puck into the flat part of the top netting. Use an equipment bag in front of the net to block any low shots. This drill does not require the goaltender, although one (or a target goaltender) can be used.

Drill 6-4; Turning And Shooting. This drill provides practice making turns while controlling the puck and shooting. Set up the pylons in a pattern shown in the corresponding diagram. Divide the players into two lines starting on the goal line. At the whistle, the first player in line 1 skates in and out of the pylons at half speed, and then shoots on the goaltender using the forehand wrist shot. After

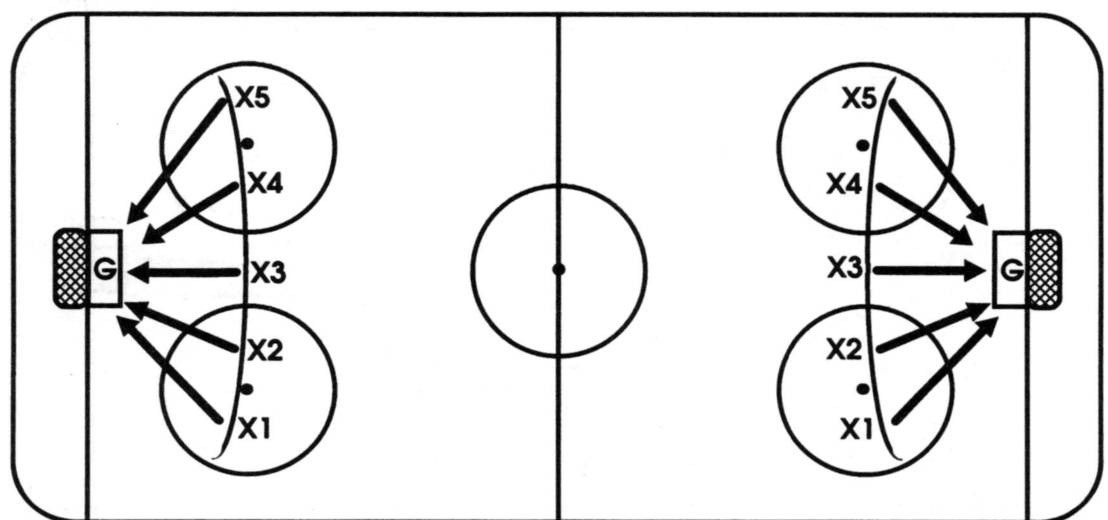

Drill 6-2; Stationary Shooting On Net

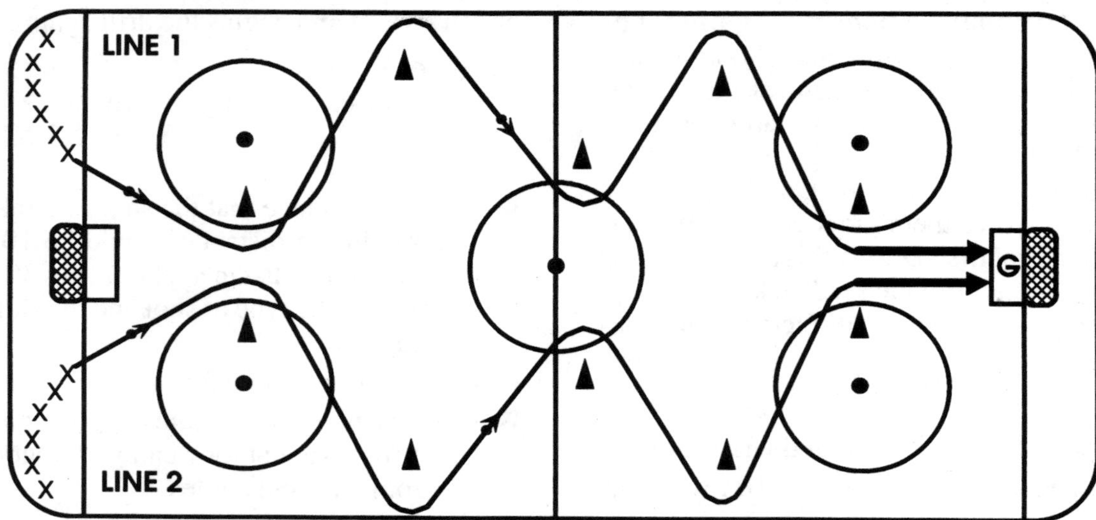

Drill 6-4; Turning And Shooting

the player in line 1 takes a shot, the first player in line 2 does the same. Continue until all of the players have completed the drill.

Variations:

- Use the snap shot, backhand wrist shot, forehand flip shot and backhand flip shot.
- Skate at three-quarter speed.
- Vary the pylon pattern.
- Use a target goaltender.

Drill 6-5; Zigzag. This drill combines the actions of a couple of previous drills. Set up the pylons in a pattern shown in the corresponding diagram. Divide the players into two lines starting on the goal line. At the whistle, the first player in line 1 skates at half speed to each pylon and circles it in a clockwise pattern. After the last pylon is circled, move into position in front of the net and shoot using a backhand wrist shot. After the player in line 1 takes a shot, the first player in line 2 does the same. Continue the drill until all of the players have completed the drill.

Variations:

- Use the snap shot, forehand wrist shot, forehand flip shot and backhand flip shot.
- Skate at three-quarter speed.
- Vary the pylon pattern.
- Circle the pylons in a counterclockwise pattern.
- Use a target goaltender.

Drill 6-6; Stopping And Shooting. This drill provides practice stopping while controlling the puck

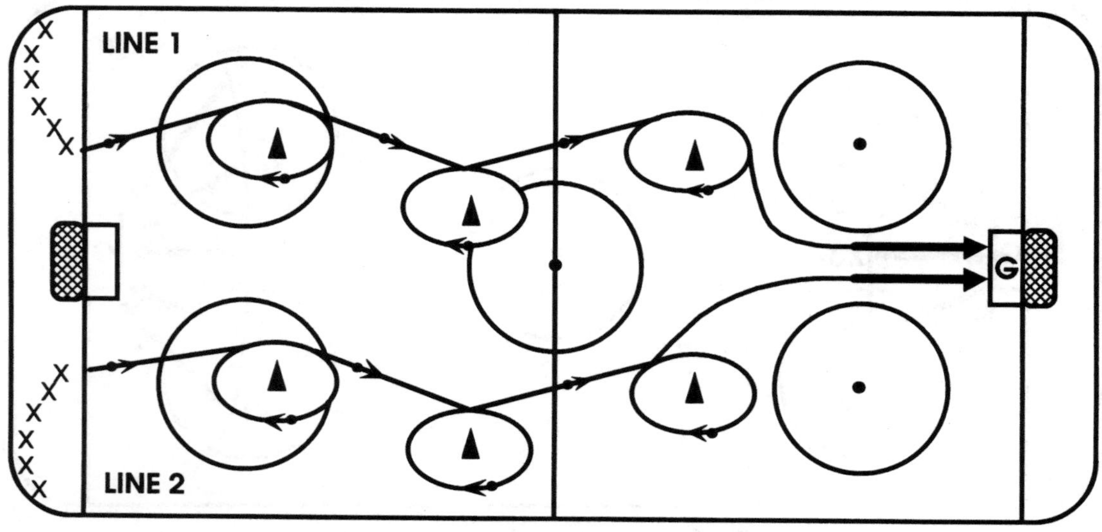

Drill 6-5; Zigzag

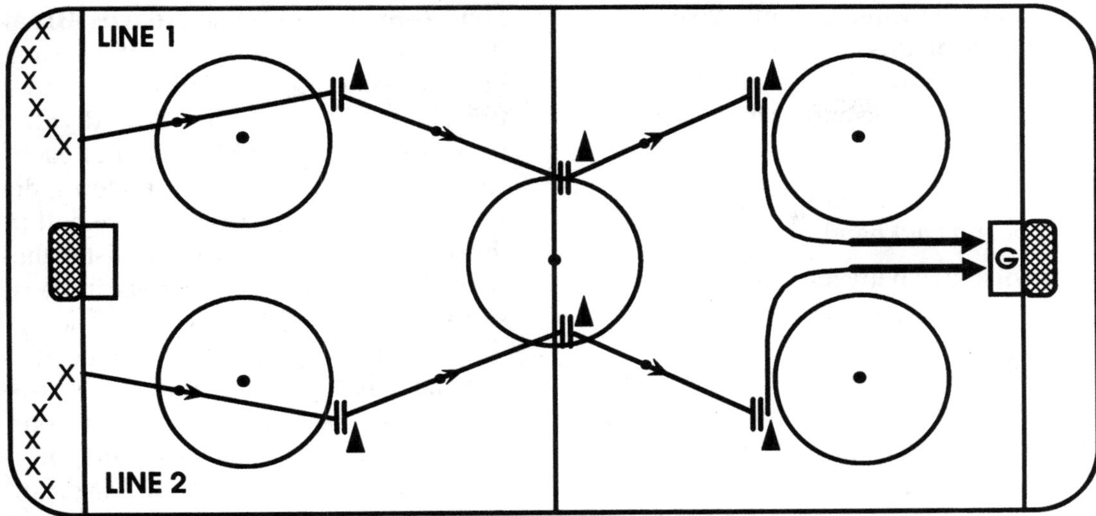

Drill 6-6; Stopping And Shooting

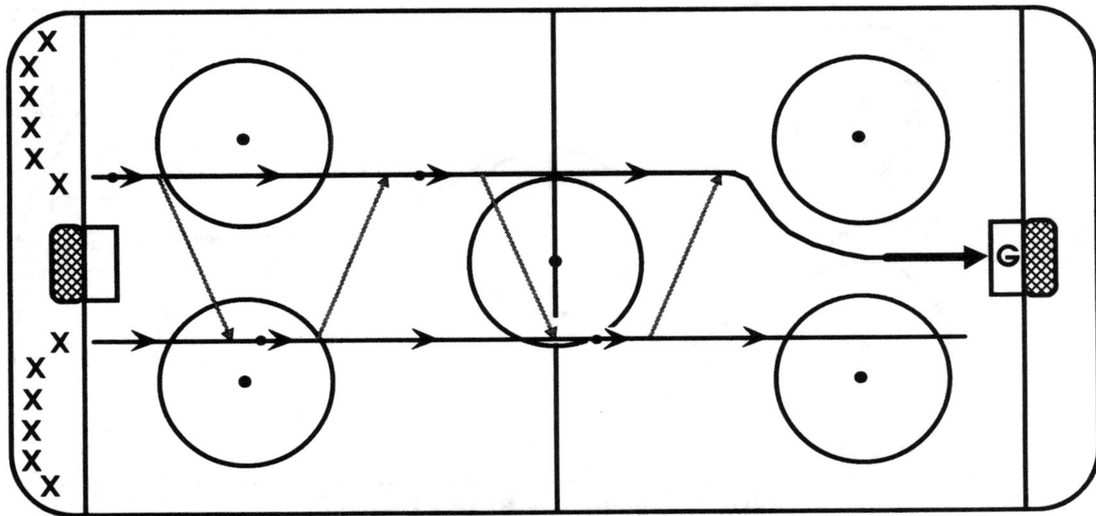

Drill 6-7; Skating, Passing And Shooting

and shooting. This may be necessary to change direction quickly to avoid a defender. Set up pylons in a pattern shown in the corresponding diagram. Divide the team into two lines starting at the goal line. At the whistle, the first player in line 1 skates at half speed to each pylon and stops, facing the right boards. After the last stop is made, move into position in front of the net and shoot using a snap shot. After the player in line 1 takes a shot, the first player in line 2 does the same. Continue the drill until all of the players have completed the drill.

Variations:

- Use the forehand wrist shot, backhand wrist shot, forehand flip shot and backhand flip shot.
- Vary the pylon pattern.
- Skate at three-quarter speed.
- Stop facing the left boards.
- Vary the stopping position from right to left.
- Use a target goaltender.

Drill 6-7; Skating, Passing And Shooting. This drill is designed to provide practice skating, passing and shooting. Divide the players into two lines about 15 feet apart on either side of the net, starting on the goal line as shown in the corresponding diagram. While skating the length of the playing surface at half speed, have the players make slow and easy passes. Four passes should be attempted. The coach should make sure that the first pass by each player is accurate. If it isn't, have the players start over. Once the players have completed the four passes, the player with the puck should take a forehand wrist shot. During this drill, the coach should monitor and provide feedback to the players on the 11 moving drill factors listed earlier in this chapter.

Variations:

- Use the backhand wrist shot, snap shot, forehand flip shot and backhand flip shot.
- Increase the distance between players.
- Increase the speed of the pass.
- Increase the players' skating speed to three-quarter for the next three drills.
- Have all players receive passes on their backhand.

Drill 6-8; Around-The-Boards Breakout. This drill teaches the technique of passing along the boards, receiving a board pass, skating with the puck and shooting. In this drill, divide the players into two groups and place half at each end of the rink as shown in the corresponding diagram. Divide each group in half and place half in line 1 and the other half in line 2. At the whistle, the first player from line 1 skates to the boards and positions himself so that he is facing the net. The first player in line 2 skates behind the net, picks up a puck and executes a half-speed around-the-boards pass to the player along the boards. The player along the boards receives the pass, skates toward the far net and executes a forehand flip shot. Make sure that each

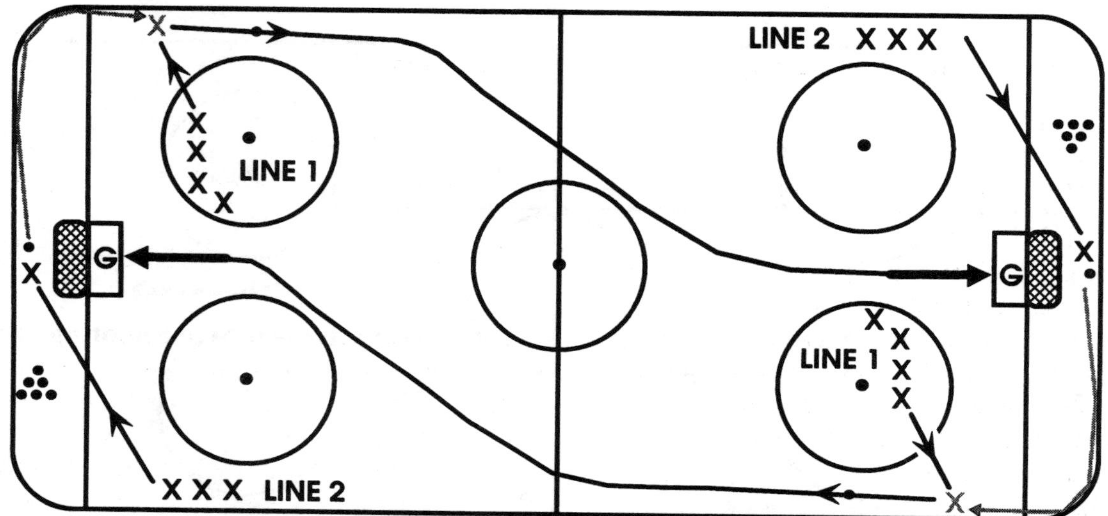

Drill 6-8; Around-The-Boards Breakout

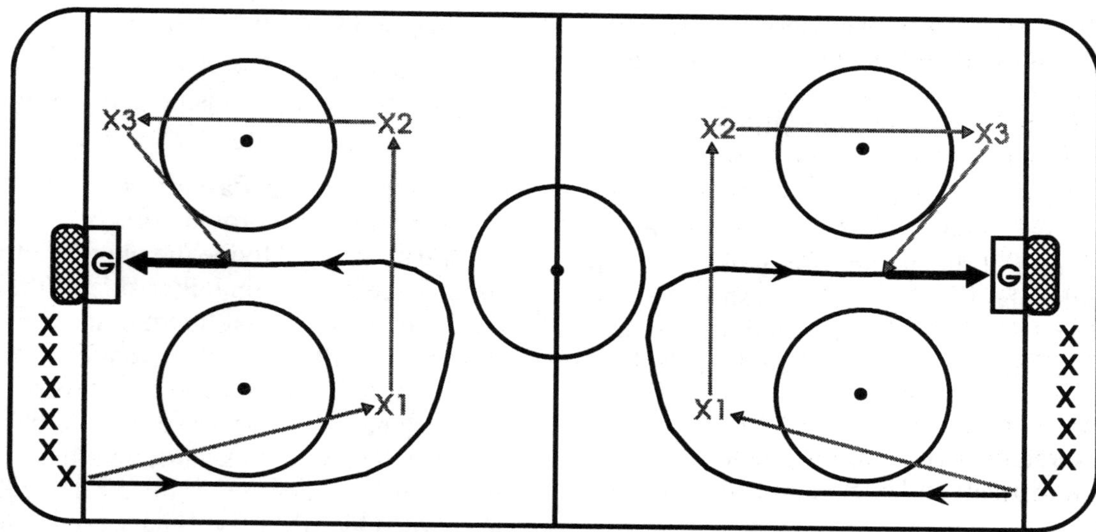

Drill 6-9; Box Passing and Shoot

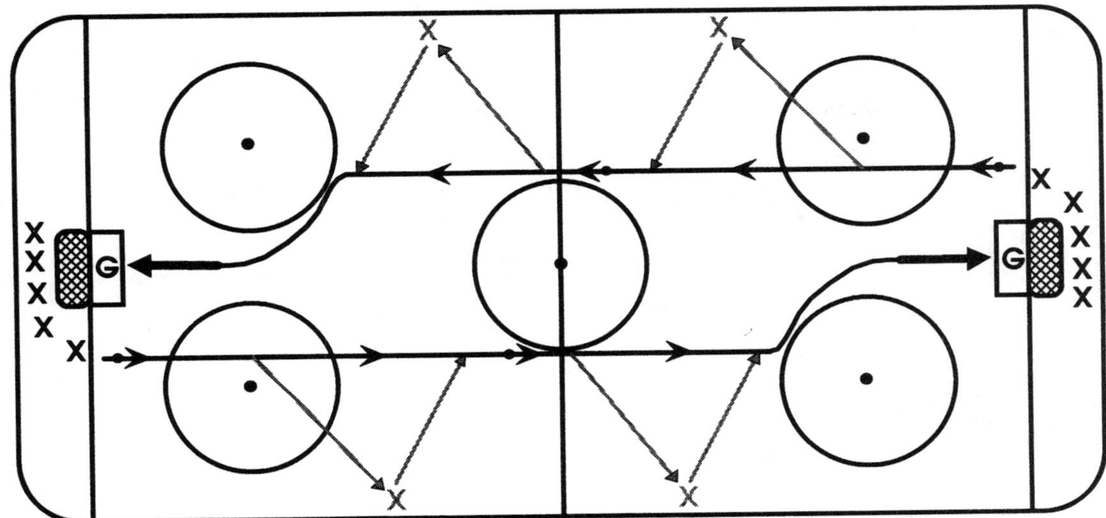

Drill 6-10; Give-And-Go Shooting

player has the opportunity to participate in both lines 1 and 2.

Variations:

- Use the forehand wrist shot, backhand wrist shot, snap shot and the backhand flip shot.
- Pass the puck so that it is off the playing surface when it reaches the player from line 1. When the pass is off the playing surface, the player should attempt to knock it down with the blade of his stick, skate or glove, depending on the puck height, and then move toward the center of the playing surface.

Drill 6-9; Box Passing and Shoot. This drill is an **excellent pregame drill** as it provides all players the opportunity to skate, pass and shoot. Divide the team into two lines starting at the goal line as shown in the corresponding diagram. Select three players from each line and position them at locations X1, X2 and X3 about 25 feet apart. At the whistle, the first player in each line passes the puck to X1 and begins to skate at half speed around the outside of player X1 and then toward the net. In the meantime, player X1 receives the puck and passes it to X2 who passes it to X3. When the skater is 25 feet from the net, X3 executes a pass to him. The skater receives the pass and executes a forehand wrist shot. After the shot, the skater moves to X3, X3 moves to X2, X2 moves to X1, and then the next player in line becomes the skater. Continue the drill until all of the players have completed one cycle.

Variations:

- Use the backhand wrist shot, snap shot, forehand flip shot and the backhand flip shot.
- Have all players (including X1, X2 and X3) receive passes on their backhand.
- Increase the distance between X1, X2 and X3 to 30, 35 and 40 feet.

Drill 6-10; Give-And-Go Shooting. This drill is designed to develop the player's ability to skate, pass, receive and shoot. Four players are stationed lengthwise along the boards about 20 feet from the center red line, and should all face toward the spot where the puck carrier starts. Divide the remaining players into two groups and place them behind each net as shown in the corresponding diagram. At the whistle, the first player in each line skates with the puck and takes three half-speed strides, and then passes the puck to the first stationary player along the boards. The stationary player returns the puck to the original puck carrier. The puck carrier continues by taking three strides and repeats the play with the next stationary player. Once the player receives the second pass, he should head toward the net and execute a snap shot. After all players have gone through the drill, exchange the stationary players for shooters and start again. During this drill, the coach should monitor and provide feedback to the players on the 11 moving drill factors listed earlier in this chapter. Ensure that all players have the opportunity to practice both the skating and stationary portions of this drill.

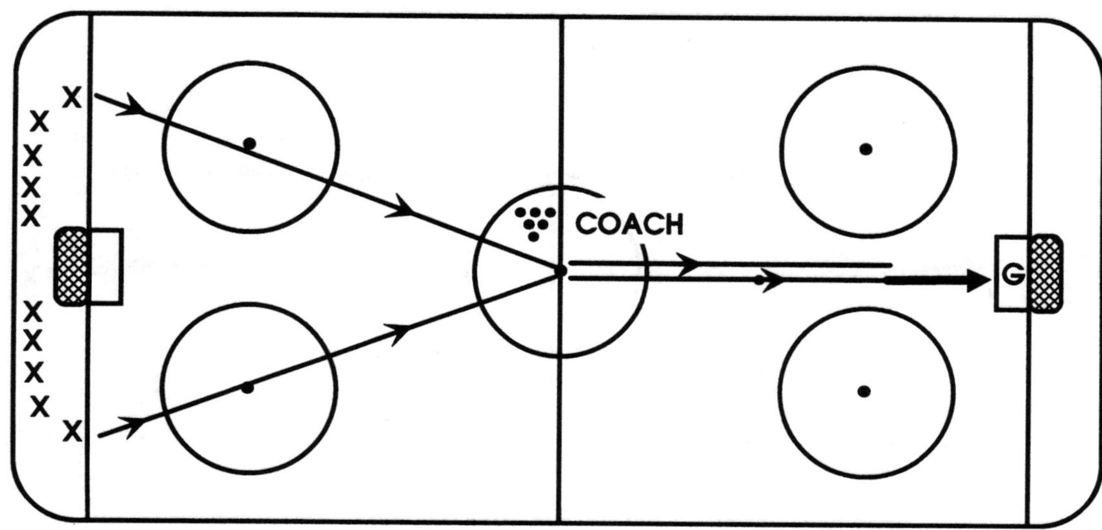

Drill 6-11; Race For The Puck

Variations:

- Have players maneuver around pylons as they progress toward the net.
- Use the forehand wrist shot, backhand wrist shot, forehand flip shot and the backhand flip shot.
- Increase skating speed to three-quarter.
- Use a target goaltender.
- Have all players (including stationary ones) receive passes on their backhand.

Drill 6-11; Race For The Puck. Divide the team into two groups and place them on the goal line about 25 feet apart. The coach positions himself at the center face-off circle and places one puck on the face-off dot as shown in the corresponding diagram. At the whistle, the first player in each line starts skating at full speed toward the puck. The first player to reach the center face-off circle picks up a puck and skates for the net as the second player tries to keep him from getting a good shot away. This drill provides realistic breakaway situations for the shooter, defender and goaltender.

Drill 6-12; Shooting Power Test. An excellent way to test a player's shooting power and at the same time get the players into the habit of putting full effort into their shooting action is to use this power test. The focal point of this drill is a target block that the players will shoot at. A block of wood or a strong wooden box can be used. The bottom surface of the target block should be flat and covered with felt of similar material so that it can move without damaging the playing surface. The dimensions of the target block can range from 12 to 18 inches on each side and should weigh no more than 10 pounds for senior players and no more than 5 pounds for junior players. The box can be weighted with just about any object, but cement-filled or steel weights are recommended. A bull's eye can be painted on one side of the block to add some personality to the box. Two or three blocks are recommended to keep the drill moving and player enthusiasm up.

Place the blocks at the center red line about 10 feet apart. The first players take their positions 5 feet from the target blocks. Have the players execute a forehand wrist shot with the intent to move the target blocks as far back from the center red line as possible. The farther it goes, the more power is indicated. This drill can be done with any shot listed in this chapter. The coach should use the Shooting and Scoring Checklist to record the name of the shooter, type of shot used, distance the shooter is from the target block, weight of the target block and distance the target block moved. Keep records for each player and monitor improvement throughout the season.

Variations:

- Shoot while skating toward the target.
- Increase the distance between the players and the target block.
- Increase the weight of the target block.
- Increase the competitive angle by forming the players into groups and measuring the total distance moved by each group.

Advanced Drills

Drill 6-13; Slap Shots. This drill provides shooting practice for the slap shot. Five players set up in a semicircle about 25 feet from the net and shoot from the positions shown in the corresponding diagram. At the whistle, player X1 executes a slap shot. At the next whistle, player X2 performs the same shot. Players should wait to shoot until the coach blows the whistle so that the goaltender has a chance to get set for each shot. After all five players have shot, they retrieve the puck and begin the drill again.

Variations:

- Alternate the shooting pattern (i.e., X5-X4-X3-X2-X1, X1-X5-X2-X4-X3, or X5-X1-X4-X2-X3).
- Vary the distance from which the shots are taken. The minimum distance should be about 20 feet and the maximum distance should be about 40 feet, depending on the skill level of the players.
- Use a target goaltender.
- Alternate the position from which the players shoot so that they can get practice shooting from different angles.

Drill 6-14; Rebounds. Divide the team into two groups and place them at the center red line near the boards. Select one player from each group (X1) and position them in the corners as shown in the corresponding diagram. Player X1 will be the shooter for this drill and the first player in the line will be the trailer, following X1 in for a rebound. At the whistle, player X1 skates toward the center red line and then around the pylons. As he passes the second pylon, the first player in line passes the puck to him. Both players skate at half speed in on net and X1 executes a snap shot at the pads of the goaltender from about 15 feet out. As X1 peels away from the net, the trailer retrieves the rebound and executes a forehand wrist shot on net. The trailer will become the shooter for the next cycle and the shooter goes to the end of the line at the center red line. This drill gets the players used to following in after a shot so that if a rebound becomes available, a second scoring chance is created. Study your own goaltender to see how he or she allows rebounds from the pads, stick, blocker or skates.

Variations:

- Have the shooter use the forehand wrist shot and backhand wrist shot.
- Have the trailer use the backhand wrist shot, forehand flip shot and the backhand flip shot.
- Increase skating speed to three-quarter.
- Have all players receive passes on their backhand.
- Add the give-and-go play.

Drill 6-15; Shooting Off The Back Leg. This drill can be performed using almost any of the skating and shooting drills described in this chapter. While

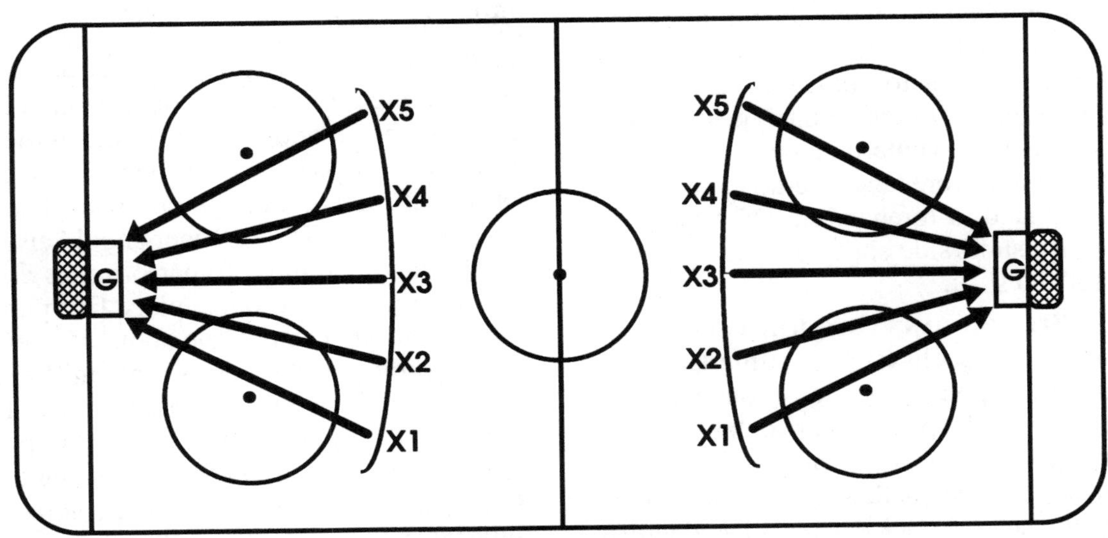

Drill 6-13; Slap Shots

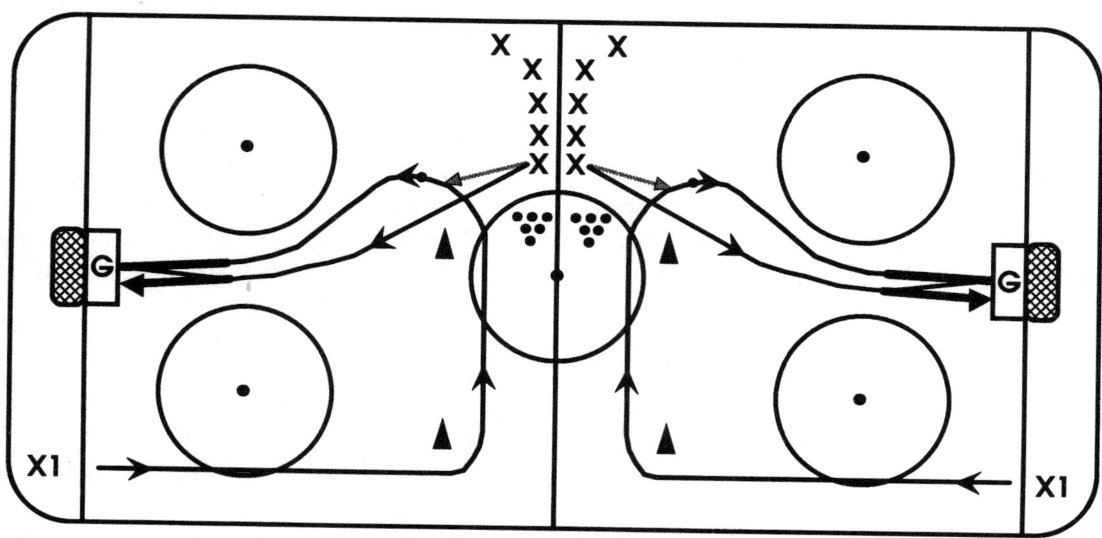

Drill 6-14; Rebounds

skating in on the goaltender, simply keep your weight on the back leg as you shoot the puck in stride. Keep the follow-through short so that you don't become unbalanced.

Drill 6-16; Deking The Goaltender. This drill can be performed using almost any of the skating and shooting drills described in this chapter. During the approach to the net, the player should control his speed so that there is ample time for a specific deke. Keep the puck moving so that the goaltender doesn't have a chance to get set; watch for a specific opening to use the deke. Practicing deking on a goaltender is the only way to develop confidence in a player's ability since there are few opportunities in most games to execute these moves. The coach can keep track of a player's progress by recording the number of goals scored and the type of deke used during each drill using the Shooting and Scoring Checklist. Make sure that the players talk to their own goaltender to get his advice on improving the deking technique. Nine types of dekes to have the players execute include the forehand shift, backhand shift, forehand five-hole, backhand five-hole, backhand-to-forehand shift, forehand-to-backhand shift, short side shot, far side shot, and the fake shot and shift.

Drill 6-17; Breakaways. This drill is excellent preparation for a gamelike or overtime shootout situation in which a player is one-on-one with the goaltender. As with the previous drill, this drill can be performed using almost any of the skating and shooting drills described in this chapter. During the approach to the net, the puck carrier is faced with a decision to shoot or deke. As with the deking drill, the player needs to control his speed, keep the puck moving, keep the puck between the front and side so as not to give away his shooting or deking intention, watch how the goaltender positions himself and watch for a specific opening to shoot or deke. Practicing breakaways on a goaltender is the only way to develop confidence in a player's ability. The coach can keep track of a player's progress by recording the number of goals scored and whether a shot or deke was used during each drill using the Shooting and Scoring Checklist. Refer to Figures 6-2 and 6-3 when explaining this drill as it will remind the players of the highest percentage scoring and shooting locations. Work this drill so that players have the opportunity to execute a breakaway from a straight-on position and from different angles.

Drill 6-18; Screen Shots. This drill is designed to provide practice shooting on a goaltender who is screened by an opponent. The role of the player in front of the net is to block the view of the goaltender or at least create a certain amount of commotion to distract him. The screener should also be looking for any rebounds. To perform this drill, divide the team into two groups; place five players from each group in a semicircle about 15 feet from the net as shown in the corresponding diagram. The remainder of each group should move to the corner, with one player from this group playing the first screener. The screener should stand on a path between the net and the shooter, with the legs a little wider than shoulder width apart. At the whistle, player X1 executes a low forehand wrist shot toward the net. The screener should attempt to screen the goaltender and not block the shot. The coach should stress to the shooters that the intent of the drill is not to shoot the puck as hard as they can or to shoot without aim. The shooters should originally keep the puck low, shoot with medium speed and aim for a location in either corner or between the legs of the screener. This will allow the screener to develop confidence in the shooter's ability to control the location and speed of the puck. At the next whistle, player X2 executes the same shot. After the first five shots have been taken, the screener moves to X1, the next player in the screener line moves to the screener position in front of the net, X5 takes a place at the end of the screener line and X1, X2, X3 and X4 shift one position.

Variations:

- Use a snap shot, backhand wrist shot and slap shot.
- Shoot both low and high shots.
- Execute the shot at full speed.
- Vary the distance that the shots are taken from. The minimum distance should be 15 feet and the maximum distance should be 40 feet, depending on the type of shot and the skill level of the players.

Drill 6-19; One-Time Shots. This drill is actually two drills in one, both variations of the one-time shot. Divide the team into two groups and place them at the center red line as shown in the corresponding diagram. The group on the right is di-

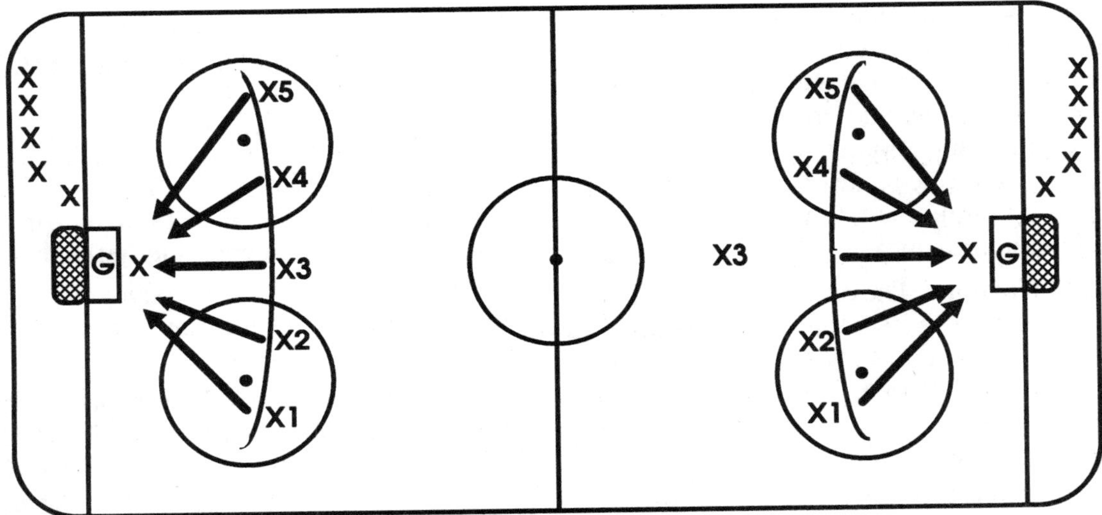

Drill 6-18; Screen Shots

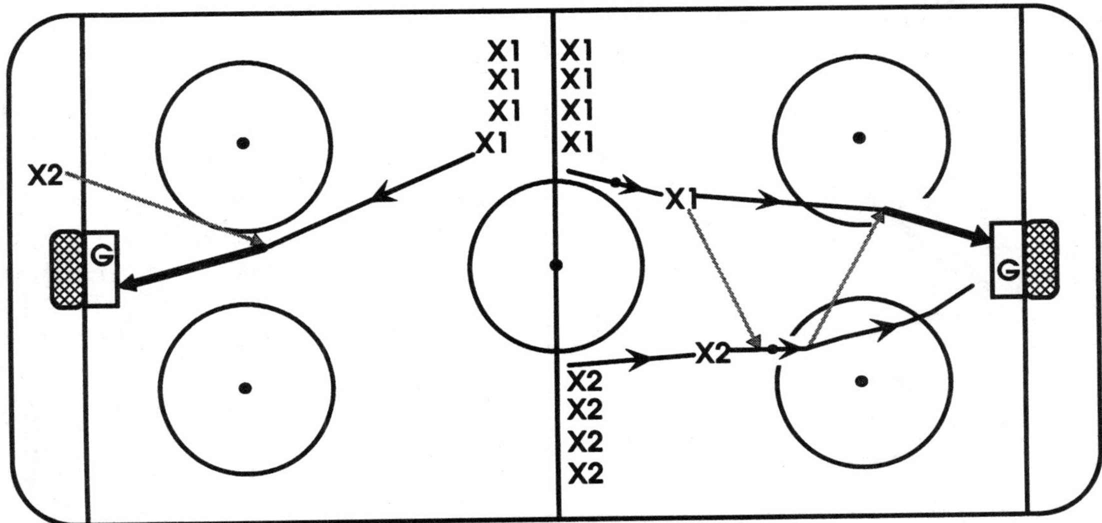

Drill 6-19; One-Time Shots

vided into two lines (X1 and X2) and placed near the boards at each end of the center red line. Start the drill by having the first player in X1 and X2 skate three or four strides and then have X1 pass the puck to X2 who will return the puck to X1. As the puck nears X1, he one-times (redirects) it toward an open area in the net. Players in X1 and X2 should alternate lines once each player has completed the cycle.

The group on the left will also line up along the center red line (X1). Choose one player (designated X2) and position him about 5 feet from the net and behind the goal line. Start this drill by having the first player from X1 skate toward the net, with X2 passing the puck to X1 when X1 enters the slot. As the puck nears X1, he one-times it toward an open area in the net. Players in X1 and X2 should also alternate once each player has completed his cycle. After both the left and right groups have completed their cycles, have them switch sides. This drill relies on timing to be executed properly. Perfecting this shot requires a lot of practice. If you practice this drill, you will see the results from the surprised goaltenders who rarely have time to move across the crease to stop the quick shot.

Drill 6-20; Deflections. The purpose of this drill is to practice deflecting shots from various locations and angles into the net. Divide the team into two groups and place five players from each group in a semicircle about 20 feet from the net. The remainder of each group should move to the corner, with one player from this group playing the first deflector. The role of the deflector is to redirect the puck from its original path into the net. The deflector should stand about 3 feet from the goal post and just outside the goal line. At the whistle, player X1 executes a low forehand wrist shot toward the net. The deflector attempts to redirect the puck from its original path, just inside the goal post, past the goaltender and into the net. The shooters should originally keep the puck low and shoot with medium speed. This will allow the deflector to develop confidence in the shooter's ability to control the location and speed of the puck. At the next whistle, player X2 executes the same shot. After the first five shots have been taken, the deflector moves to X1, the next player in the deflector line moves to the deflector position at the side of the net, X5 takes a place at the end of the deflector line, and X1, X2, X3 and X4 shift one position.

Variations:

- Use a snap shot, backhand wrist shot and slap shot.
- Shoot both low and high shots.
- Execute the shot at full speed.
- Move the deflector to the front of the net (he will act as a screener and deflector) and to the opposite side of the net.
- Introduce deflectors on either side of the net and then both sides.
- Vary the distance that the shots are taken from. The minimum distance should be 15 feet and the maximum distance should be 40 feet, depending on the type of shot and the skill level of the player.

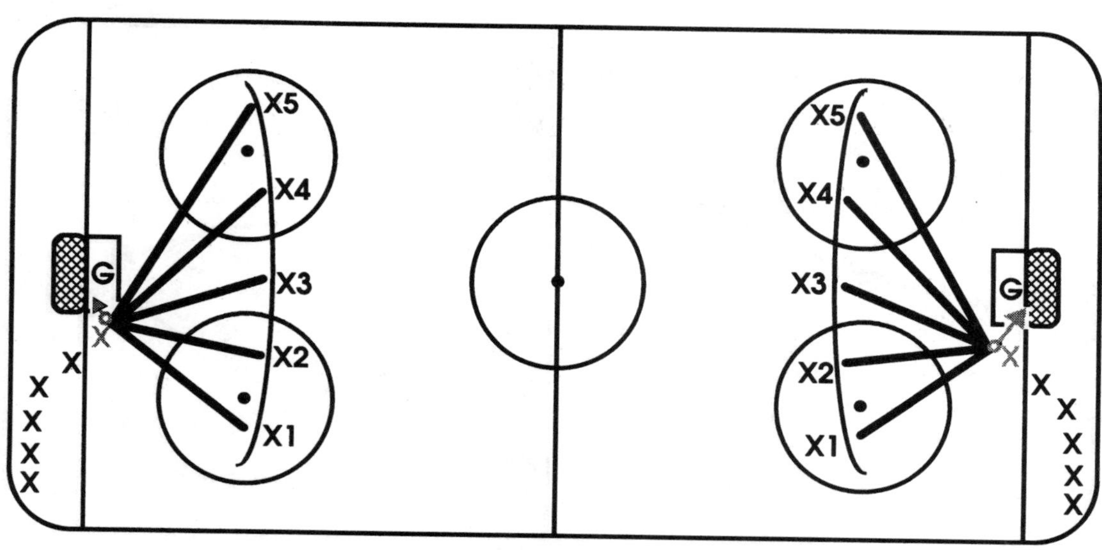

Drill 6-20; Deflections

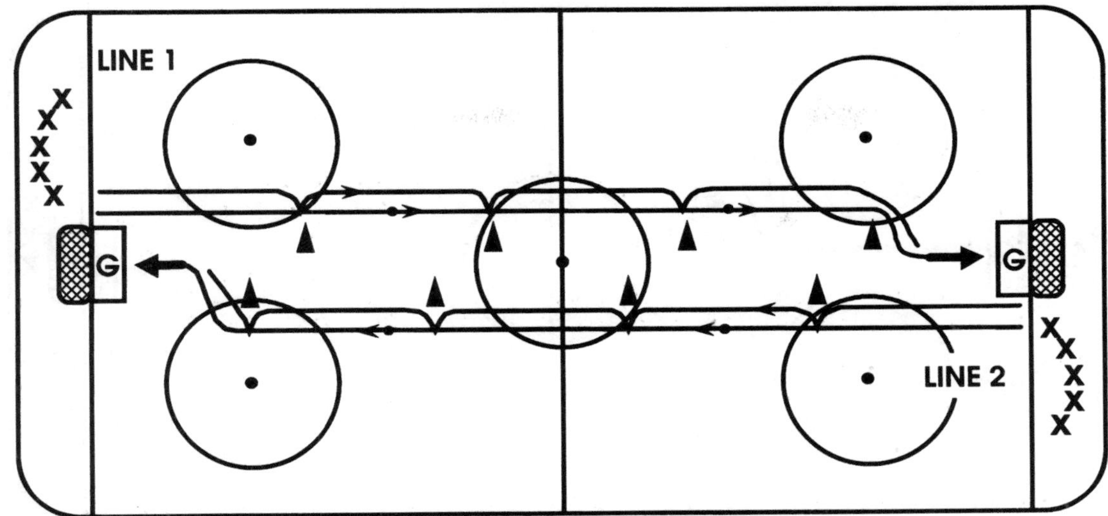

Drill 6-21; Incidental Body Contact While Shooting

- Have the deflector skate to the corner of the net before deflecting the shot.

Drill 6-21; Incidental Body Contact While Shooting. The goal of this drill is to develop confidence in the player's balance and shooting ability during incidental body contact. Set up the pylons as shown in the diagram below. Divide the players into two lines approximately 15 feet apart and on either side of the net, starting on opposite goal lines. Pair up the first and second players in each line. The first player will be the shooter and the second player will be the defender. At the whistle, each of the two pairs should begin skating at half speed toward the far goal line. At each pylon, the defender should move toward the shooter and moderately bump him and then return to his normal skating route. After the fourth pylon, the shooter should move into the slot for a forehand wrist shot while the defender attempts to dislodge the puck from the shooters stick. Continue this drill until all players have completed both the defender and the shooter roles at least once. Make sure that the bumping is not exaggerated.

Variations:

- Execute the drill at three-quarter speed.
- Use a target goaltender.
- Use a snap shot, backhand wrist shot and slap shot.

Drill 6-22; Bank Passing And Shooting. Divide the players into two groups and position them as shown in the corresponding diagram. At the whistle, the first player in each line skates at half speed toward the far goal line, executes three bank passes to the boards and receives his own passes. After receiving the third bank pass, the shooter moves into the slot area and executes a snap shot.

Variations:

- Use the forehand wrist shot, backhand wrist shot, forehand flip shot, backhand flip shot or slap shot.
- Increase skating speed to three-quarter.
- Retrieve any rebounds and shoot or execute a deke on the goaltender.

Drill 6-23; Reverse. Set up the pylons as shown in the corresponding diagram. Divide the team into two groups and position them at the goal line. The group on the top of the diagram starts off with the puck and will always turn closest to the pylon, while the other group makes a wider radius turn around the pylons. At the whistle, the first players in each line begin skating at half speed. As the players move around the pylons and approach each other, the puck carrier executes a pass to the receiver. The players should be skating in paths about 5 feet apart at that point. The players skate around the next pylon and as they approach each other, the new puck carrier executes a pass to the original puck carrier. As the players round the third pylon, they break for the net. The puck carrier passes the puck to the shooter who executes a snap shot on net. The other skater moves in to retrieve any rebounds released by the goaltender. Once all players have

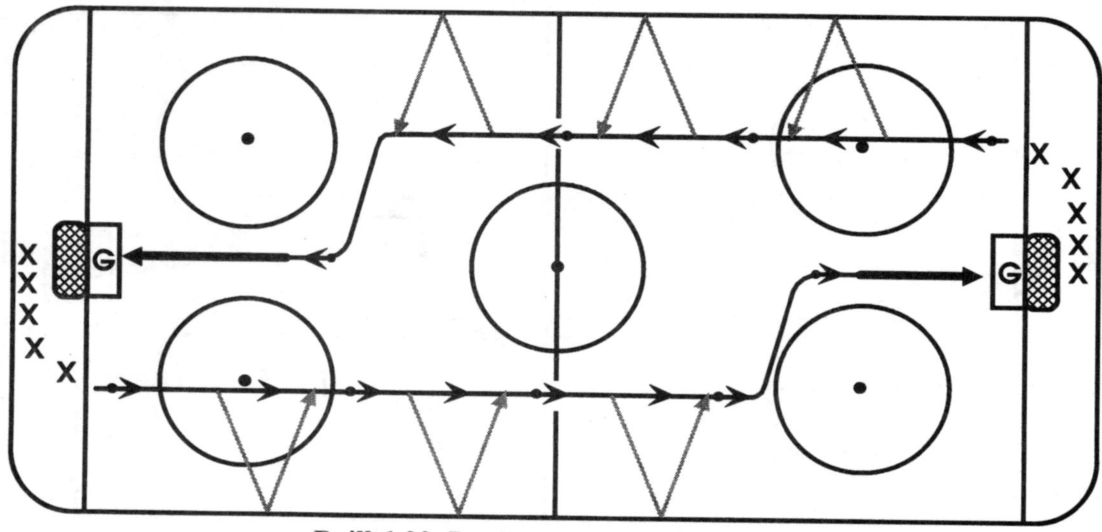

Drill 6-22; Bank Passing And Shooting

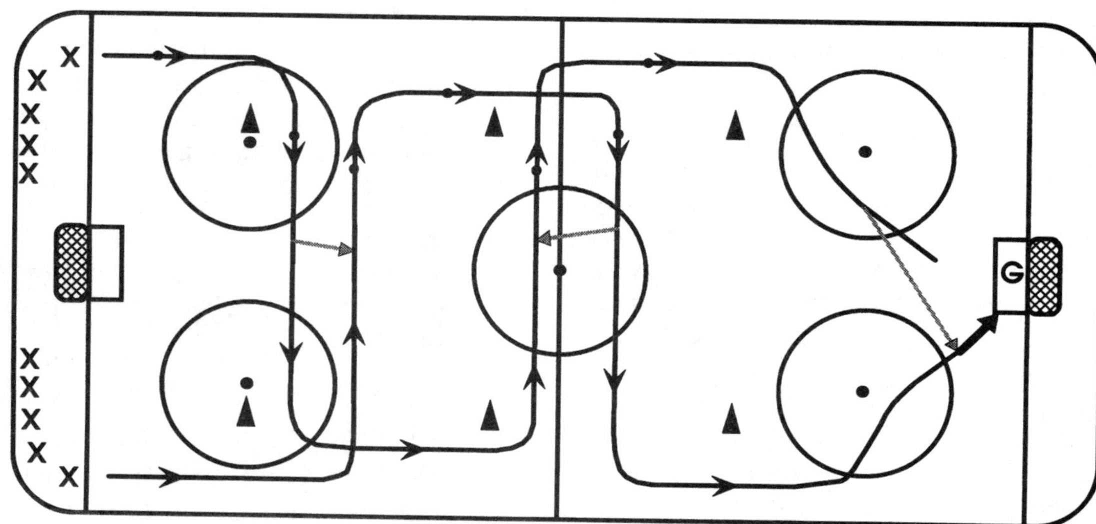

Drill 6-23; Reverse

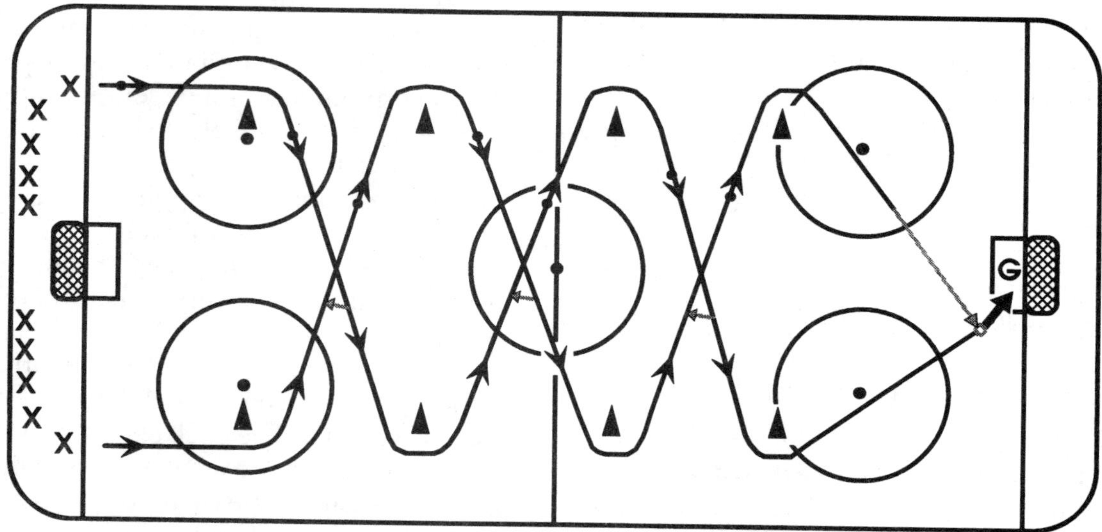

Drill 6-24; Weave

completed the drill going in one direction, they should complete it going in the other direction.

Variations:

- Increase skating to three-quarter speed.
- Use the forehand wrist shot or backhand wrist shot.
- Have the shooter execute a one-time shot as he receives the puck.
- Deke the goaltender.

Drill 6-24; Weave. Set up the pylons, divide the team into two groups and position the players at the goal line as shown in the corresponding diagram. The group on the top of the diagram starts off with the puck. At the whistle, the first players in each line begin skating at half speed. As the players move around the pylons, the puck carrier will cut in front of the non-puck carrier and execute a drop pass to that receiver. The players skate around the next pylon and as they approach each other, the new puck carrier executes a drop pass to the original puck carrier. This player continues the weave pattern one more time so that a total of three drop passes are made. As the players round the last pylon, the player without the puck breaks for the net. The puck carrier passes the puck to the shooter who deflects the puck on net. Once all players have completed the drill going in one direction, they should complete it going in the other direction.

Variations:

- Increase skating to three-quarter speed.
- Have the puck carrier execute a forehand wrist shot, snap shot or slap shot, and have the non-puck carrier retrieve any rebounds.
- Have the puck carrier pass the puck to the other player and deke the goaltender.

Recap

After reading and studying the material in this chapter, you should be able to answer the following questions:

1. How does a roller hockey player develop effective goal scoring skills?
2. What are five components of an effective shooting and scoring technique?
3. Where are the five most popular shooting locations on net?
4. What two factors control shooting accuracy?
5. What three methods can be used to develop shooting accuracy?
6. What is the average percentage of goals scored in each of the five locations?
7. From what distances are most goals scored?
8. What is the number one reason why many scoring opportunities are missed? Why?
9. Where is the number one position on the playing surface to shoot from? Number two positions? Number three positions?
10. Why is a quick release important? What are the two methods to release the puck quickly?
11. What two factors control puck speed? How can a player improve these two factors?
12. Which one of the six shots presented in this chapter is the most accurate? Why is the slap shot not recommended in the slot area? Why is the slap shot effective from longer distances than other shots? Why is a backhand shot effective?
13. What are the five fundamental shots described in this chapter?
14. Why is the follow-through important?
15. From what distance is the snap shot valuable?
16. When is the flip shot best utilized?
17. List and describe the eight advanced shooting and scoring techniques.
18. What is a common fault that makes it impossible for a player to get maximum speed and accuracy on a slap shot? What physical attribute is necessary to execute the most effective slap shot? Why is it difficult for many younger players to execute an effective slap shot?
19. What is one method to obtain additional scoring opportunities after an initial shot is made?
20. Define *deking*. What five attributes contribute to effective deking?

21. Why is analyzing a goaltender so important? How can goaltender data be obtained? By whom?
22. List and describe the nine types of dekes described in this chapter.
23. Where should a player carry the puck, in relation to his skating position, when he is on a breakaway? Why is confidence so important during a breakaway? What are some of the factors that a player should consider when on a breakaway?
24. What are three roles of a screener on a screen shot?
25. Why is the one-time shot so difficult to perfect?
26. Name three locations on the playing surface where a deflection works effectively.
27. What are three things a player should do to get out of a scoring slump?
28. How will you use the Shooting and Scoring Checklist and the drills provided in this chapter to help improve individual and team shooting and scoring performance and correct existing deficiencies?
29. For all stationary drills, on what seven factors should the coach monitor and provide feedback to the players? For all moving drills, on what 11 factors should the coach should monitor and provide feedback to the players?
30. What drill is an excellent pregame drill? Why?
31. What drill can be used to test a player's shooting power? What are the benefits of a shooting power test? How should the Shooting and Scoring Checklist be used with this drill?

7

The Dominant Defense

Highlights

This chapter addresses the role of the dominant defense and the integrated individual and positional skills required of this position. Chapter 7 presents the following information:

Discussion

Fundamentals

- *skating*
- *stickhandling and puck control*
- *passing and receiving*
- *shooting*
- *communicating with your partner(s)*
- *defensive reading and reacting*
- *using the stick and body to strip opponents of the puck*
- *covering opponents in the defensive zone*

Advanced Techniques

- *learning the opponents' patterns*
- *blocking shots with your body*
- *fake shot*
- *one-time shot*
- *rushing*

Siller Player and Team Evaluation Profile — Defensive Player Checklist

Drills

Advanced Drills

Recap

Our strength grows out of our weakness.
— Ralph Waldo Emerson —

The wisest mind has something yet to learn.
— George Santayana —

Discussion

The play of the defense is an important factor in the success of any roller hockey team. The **primary role of the defense** is to help prevent goals, give your goaltender a clear and equal chance at stopping shots, break up any attack that your opponents may have and to participate on offense. Defensive strategy is situational in nature and is based on playing the percentages. This means that it is better to force an opponent to take a shot from farther out, compared to close in, because a greater percentage of long shots are stopped than close ones. Playing the percentages also means forcing shots from an angle rather than directly in the slot. This is particularly evident when the opposition has an outnumbered attack, as in two-on-one or three-on-two situations. Providing the goaltender with a clear and equal chance at stopping shots means controlling the slot area. Controlling the slot is important because of the high percentage of scoring opportunities in that area. Defensemen accomplish this by using their bodies, arms and sticks (legally) to contain or move opponents who are in the slot area looking for a shot, pass, rebound or deflection. Breaking up an offensive attack is another important role. A defenseman accomplishes this by playing hard in the corners and behind the net against the opposing forwards, attempting to gain control of the puck or at least preventing the other team from gaining or maintaining control. Once the attack is broken up, the defenseman can gain control of the puck and begin to move the play toward the other end of the playing surface.

The goaltender must also become involved in defensive situations. This means that the defensemen and the goaltender must coordinate their efforts to strategically resist offensive attacks. Communication between the defense and the goaltender is essential. Too many times, through nonexistent or confusing communication, the goaltender is simply left to play the shot. If the goaltender and the defensemen play together, with each understanding the other's role, they will have an excellent chance of neutralizing any attack.

Offensive participation is another important responsibility of a defenseman in roller hockey. Because of its offensive design, roller hockey requires at least one of the defensemen to participate in the offense to provide additional scoring opportunities required to win the game. The defensemen participate by moving the puck up the playing surface and by becoming an extra attacker in the offensive zone. An important factor in knowing when to move up into the play or stay back is proper reading and reacting of each play. By being aware of the play around you and understanding what patterns exist, the defenseman has the information required to make a good judgment and can decide whether to move into the offensive play or whether it is time to maintain a defensive posture.

Fundamentals

The eight fundamental defensive techniques consist of the topics discussed in the last four chapters — skating, stickhandling and puck control, passing and receiving, and shooting, as well as:

- Communicating with your partner(s).
- Defensive reading and reacting.
- Using the stick and body to strip opponents of the puck.
- Covering opponents in the defensive zone.

Skating. Skating is an essential ingredient in the defenseman's formula for success. The skating techniques described in Chapter 3 should be practiced so that the defenseman develops confidence to expertly execute each technique. The ability to get off to a good start, both forward and backward, is crucial to any defenseman. Starts are used following a face-off, moving out of the offensive zone when the opposition is on the attack and going from the front of the defensive net into a corner to defend against an attacker. If the start is not effective, an opponent will be able to get one, two or even three steps on a defenseman. Review and practice drills 3-3 (Starting Efficiency) and 3-4 (Developing Powerful Starts) to improve the starting technique. Once the defenseman has started, forward

Defender

and backward movement should be continued using the stride-then-glide technique. A defenseman does not have to be the fastest skater on the team, but should be one of the most efficient. Mastering the stride-then-glide technique will make the defenseman a very efficient skater.

Transitions are the second most important skating technique for a defenseman to master. They are used by the defenseman when changing orientation while moving in the same direction. Transitions are used when covering an opponent coming into the defensive zone. As the attacker attempts to move past the defenseman, the defenseman changes his skating orientation from backward to forward in order to successfully defend against the attacker. Transitions can also be used starting out from the offensive end of the rink. As the defenseman reads that the opponents are moving on the attack, he can start skating forward toward the defensive zone and, once up to speed, transition to skating backward. One pitfall associated with this move is that you lose sight of the developing play as you skate toward your defensive zone and can only read what is happening when you transition or turn your head around. In any case, the transition must be smooth and performed confidently and quickly so as not to give the attacking team an extra edge.

Turning and stopping should be developed as an efficient means of changing direction. Stopping, if performed efficiently, is the most effective means of changing direction. Stopping can be used when the defenseman moves behind the net to set up a breakout play, when moving from a defensive corner to the front of the net to cover an attacker, or when coming off of the playing surface to the bench. The Power Slide and Backward Curl Stop should be practiced so that a defenseman can stop and retrieve the puck in the defensive zone while he reads the oncoming forechecking attack. Turning is used when moving the puck from behind the net, when avoiding a defender or when cruising in the offensive zone for a scoring opportunity. Making use of the crossover turn allows the defenseman to increase his speed and move laterally while skating either forward or backward. This helps the defenseman move around a defender (in an offensive role) or keep up with an attacker while skating backward (in a defensive role). Work on these skating fundamentals to develop confidence on the various playing surfaces that are used.

Stickhandling and Puck Control. Stickhandling and puck control are skills that help the defenseman (and his team) maintain possession of the puck. The stickhandling and puck control techniques described in Chapter 4 should be practiced so that the defenseman develops confidence in his ability to move and control the puck with precision. Stickhandling skills are used while moving the puck out of the defensive zone and into the offensive zone, with the eventual goal of setting up a scoring opportunity. Stickhandling skills should be practiced so that they can be accomplished while keeping the head and eyes up. Looking down at the puck is fine for momentary assurance that you still have control of the puck, but with practice, it should become the exception and not the rule. A defenseman should also develop soft hands so that he has the ability to control and manipulate the puck quickly, accurately and consistently by feel. Review Drill 4-3 (Developing Soft Hands) to perfect this ability.

Puck control consists of maintaining possession of the puck while skating in close proximity to opponents and can be performed either individually or as a team. Puck control also allows a defenseman additional time to execute. While moving around a forechecker, the defenseman can control the stick and puck with one arm while keeping a defender away with his other arm. When working against a defender for possession, control of the puck can be obtained using the skates. Once the puck is free, the defenseman can break away from the defender to advance the puck or allow a teammate to pick it up. Occasionally, incidental body contact will occur when carrying the puck. The defenseman should be strong enough on his skates to withstand the effect of the incidental body contact and still maintain control of the puck.

Another technique that the defenseman should practice is stickhandling while skating backward. As the defenseman skates forward into his defensive zone to retrieve the puck, he can transition to skating backward, retrieve the puck, read the opponent coverage, and determine whether he should carry the puck or pass it up the playing surface to a teammate (react). By skating backward and controlling the puck, the defenseman can gain information on how, where and when to best move the puck.

Passing and Receiving. Passing and receiving, used in conjunction with stickhandling and puck control, are essential to moving the puck out of the defensive end and into the offensive end. The passing and receiving techniques described in Chapter 5 should be practiced so that the defenseman develops confidence in his ability to expertly deliver or receive a pass. Passing is the quickest and most effective way for a defenseman to move the puck up the playing surface during a breakout play when being covered by a defender or while setting up a scoring play in the offensive zone. By using deceptive techniques such as body fakes and peripheral vision, the defenseman can avoid telegraphing his intentions to the defenders. After the defenseman makes the pass, he should get into position for a return pass or decoy a defender away from the play.

There are a variety of passes a defenseman can choose:

- The sweep pass is the most commonly used and most accurate pass.
- The snap pass is used in conjunction with stickhandling to quickly and deceptively move the puck to a teammate.
- The flip pass can be used to clear the puck out of the defensive zone when a breakout play is not working. It can also be used to pass the puck to a teammate over a stick or fallen defender.
- The around-the-boards pass allows the defenseman to quickly move the puck from behind his net to an open forward who is positioned along the boards.
- The give-and-go pass is used during a breakout play to move past a defender.
- The bank pass moves the puck behind the net and off the boards to another defenseman.
- The open area pass moves the puck to an unoccupied area of the playing surface to a teammate anticipating the pass.
- The skate pass can be used to move the puck to a teammate when the defenseman's stick is tied up.

When receiving a pass, the defenseman should read the defensive coverage and react by getting into an open area, communicating to the passer that he is available and receiving the pass effectively. A defenseman communicates with his teammates by pointing his sticks in the direction that he wants the pass to go, tapping it on the playing surface, raising it in the air, or calling a teammate's name or call sign. The defenseman should receive the pass using soft hands, described earlier in this book. In some cases, passes will not be on target and the defenseman will have to turn or reach to receive it. Other times, he will have to receive it with his skates or in the air.

Shooting. Shooting is where you get the most bang for your puck. A defenseman can develop effective shooting and scoring skills by utilizing the techniques described in Chapter 6. The ability of a defenseman to get off a good shot is crucial to the offensive game of roller hockey. When a defenseman is shooting, he should shoot accurately and, when possible, from a location that has a high-percentage opportunity of scoring (refer to Figures 6-2 and 6-3). Unless the defenseman is playing against a goaltender who remains low in the crease, such as a butterfly goaltender (more discussion on goaltenders in Chapter 9), has a clear opening up top or knows that the goaltender has a weak glove, he should keep his shots low. Low shots have a greater chance of being deflected, provide better rebounds and work more effectively when the goaltender is screened by a teammate or an opponent. Remember, puck height is controlled by the follow-through. If the defenseman has time to maneuver into a better position before shooting, he should move in toward the slot area. The moment the defenseman gets the puck and has a chance to score, his first thought should be to get into the best possible scoring position. If you are not able to get into a good position, look around for a teammate who may be open, and pass the puck to create a better scoring opportunity.

The type of shot used has a great deal to do with creating the element of surprise, noting the position of the goaltender at the time the puck carrier is about to shoot and how far you are in front of the net.

- The wrist shot is the most accurate shot in roller hockey and should be chosen when the defenseman is close to the goaltender (generally between 5 and 25 feet) or just needs to get a quick shot on net. Since this shot does not require a back swing, you can release the puck quickly.
- The snap shot allows the defenseman to get a quick, hard shot on net. When stickhandling in on a goaltender, this shot can also be used effectively to catch a goaltender by surprise, since it can be executed in-stride. The snap shot is a valuable weapon because it is quick and accurate from up to 30 feet away from the net.
- The flip shot is generally used when the defenseman is close to the goaltender (within 10 feet), such as when you have skated in to retrieve a rebound, and is most effective when the goaltender is flat on the playing surface in front of the net. Like the wrist shot, the flip shot can be executed quickly.
- The slap shot is valuable because a defenseman can shoot the puck at greater speeds and from greater distances than any other shot. As stated earlier, a good low slap shot will give forwards good scoring opportunities by allowing them to redirect the puck, screen the goaltender and capitalize on rebounds. This shot should only be used when the defenseman has enough time for the backswing. Also, since the slap shot requires a fair amount of upper body strength, it is not recommended for players under 10 years old.

Communicating With Your Partner(s). A **defensive unit** is defined as two players operating in a defensive role, and can include the goaltender or other players who are also functioning in the defensive role. The goaltender can be included due to his symbiotic role in supporting the defensive unit (such as informing a defenseman that an attacker is right behind him). Other players can be included depending upon the circumstances of the game (such as two defensemen and a forward who are operating in a penalty-killing role). For the purpose of this chapter, two defensemen are considered a defensive unit.

Working effectively as a defensive unit requires:

- Each defenseman to be knowledgeable of and able to execute the individual skills described above.
- The desire to perform as a team by complementing each other's skills.
- Experience—gained from playing with several defensive partners over time.
- Making mistakes — and learning from those mistakes.
- Most importantly, constructive communication between the members of the defensive unit as well as feedback from the coach, other teammates and practice/game videos.

Can you think of some other factors required of an effective defensive unit?

Knowledge, experience and mistakes are all interrelated capacities. Without knowledge, a defensive unit is bound to make mistakes but will gain experience. Without experience, a defensive unit may have knowledge but no one will know whether it is effective or not because the players have not played together. Without making mistakes, they wouldn't be human, and I'm not ready to discuss *alien roller hockey* (although it might make good tabloid reading). Mistakes are part of the game of roller hockey. Whoever makes the fewest mistakes is generally going to win the game. The point about mistakes is that if you do not learn from your mistakes you will continue making the same mistakes, and that demonstrates that the defensive unit is ineffective. Don't think about every move that is made because then you begin to second guess yourself (analysis paralysis). It is important, however, to be decisive and not worry about being wrong. When you do make a wrong decision, understand what improvements could have been made and use that new information the next time that situation occurs.

Communication is the exchange of information. The information exchanged is dependent upon the

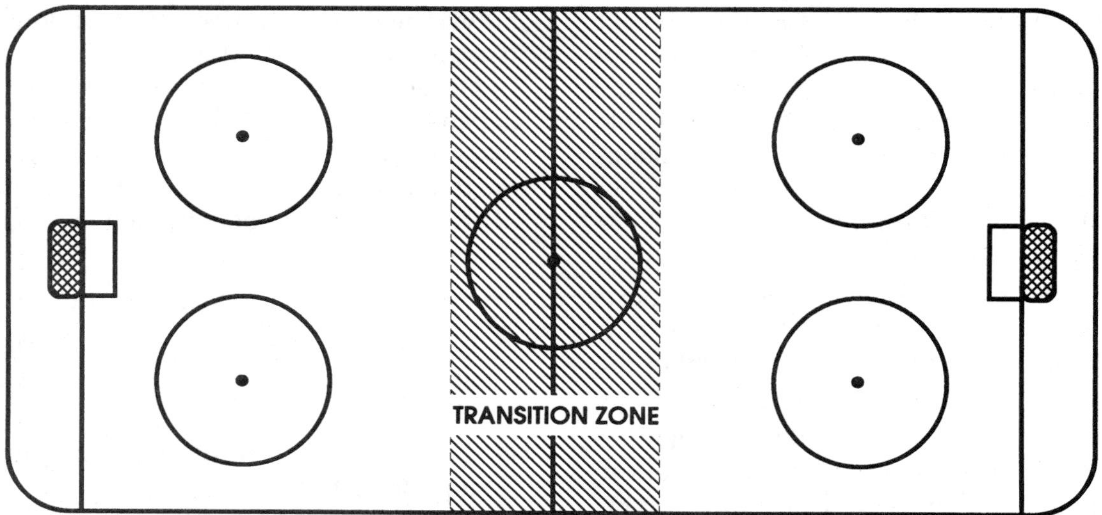

Figure 7-1; Transition Zone

personnel involved and the factors described above. Verbal communication is very important, but you shouldn't rely on it too much while on the playing surface. There are so many things happening so fast that it is impossible to tell your partner everything you are thinking. Spend time after each shift discussing the effectiveness of your defensive strategies and sharing information about opposing players. Knowledge of your partner's tendencies will often be the deciding factor as to who will initiate a defensive play or who will cover a particular attacker. Get to know your partner, but just as important, be realistic about your own abilities. Knowing your own strengths and weaknesses, and developing your game around them, is critical.

Defensive Reading and Reacting refers to the ability of the defensive unit to perceive the play of players around them and to respond appropriately. Total situational awareness and accurate perception form the basis upon which effective defensive reading and reacting occur. An example of defensive reading and reacting occurs when the defensive unit reads that the opponents have gained control of the puck in their own end and are beginning to break out. The defensive unit would react by retreating out of that zone. Another more aggressive example of defensive reading and reacting could occur when the same breakout play takes place, but one of the defensemen also anticipates that a pass is about to occur and reacts by attempting to intercept it. The other defenseman would move toward the transition zone (an area approximately 20 feet on either side of the center red line where team play is considered neither offensive nor defensive; see Figure 7-1) and set up in case his defensive partner does not intercept the pass. In both cases, the defensive unit gathers information from the players around them and responds to this information based upon their ability, experience and knowledge to coordinate their actions for a successful end result.

Zone of Play	Role	Objective (at full strength)
Defensive	Offensive	Breakout
Transition	Offensive	Move the puck into the Offensive Zone
Offensive	Offensive	Score
All	Defensive, Transitional	Gain Control of the Puck

Table 7-1; Reading and Reacting

Table 7-1 provides some simplified, yet effective, underlying information with respect to reading and reacting and should help the coach and players in determining the proper overall reaction for a particular read. In roller hockey, there are **four phases of the full-strength game**. The first phase occurs when you are in your defensive zone and are in an offensive role (i.e., you have control of the puck). Your objective should be to break out of your defensive zone. When you are in the transition zone and are in an offensive role, your objective should be to move the puck into the offensive zone. The third phase of the game occurs when you are in the offensive zone and in an offensive role. Your objective should be to score. The fourth phase occurs when you are operating in a defensive or transitional role. A transitional role is neither offensive nor defensive and occurs when neither team has definite control of the puck, such as when each team is trying to gain control of the puck immediately following a face-off. This could happen in any of the three zones and your only objective should be to gain control of the puck.

Using the Stick and Body to Strip Opponents of the Puck. As the last row of Table 7-1 shows, when the role of a team is defensive or transitional, its only objective should be to gain control of the puck. To help facilitate this objective, the stick and body can be used as effective tools to strip opponents of the puck and prevent them from scoring. Stick checking is a technique whereby a player (legally) uses his stick to prevent an opponent from maintaining or acquiring control of the puck. Discussion of five stick checking techniques follows:

1. The **poke check**, one of the most valuable defensive tools, is used in a one-on-one situation when the opponent is in close proximity (about six feet). Use the poke check when in front of, to the side of or behind an opponent. In executing the front poke check, the scenario has a defender skating forward toward a defenseman, who is skating backward, both heading into the defensive zone. The knees and elbows of the defenseman are bent and the elbows are close to the body. Both hands are held outward at a 45-degree angle so that the arms and body form a V-shape. This *defensive posture* allows the defenseman to use his stick and arms as defensive tools to disrupt the attacker. As the attacker begins to skate past the defenseman toward the net, the defenseman's stick is quickly poked toward the puck in an attempt to move it off the opponent's stick. The side poke check and poke check from behind are executed in a similar manner except the defenseman is at the side or behind the attacker. If the poke check is successful, then the defenseman or a teammate should try to gain control of the puck and begin an offensive attack. If the poke check is unsuccessful, the defenseman is still in position to contain the attacker. Perhaps the biggest mistake in performing the poke check is holding the stick too far out in front of the body just prior to execution. This does not allow the defenseman to get a good poke at the puck due to the limited range the stick can travel.
2. The **sweep check** is similar to the poke check. As the opponent closes in, the defenseman, in his defensive posture, moves the arm holding the stick in a sweeping motion across his body so that the blade of the stick moves in a half-circle toward the oncoming puck carrier. If executed properly, the defenseman's stick blade should come in contact with the puck or the opponent's stick, knocking the puck free. The main advantage of the sweep check is that it covers a lot of playing surface and, if the stick moves quickly, the puck carrier has difficulty avoiding it. The main disadvantage is that even when the puck is contacted it can be knocked some distance away from the play.
3. Use the **diving sweep/poke check** as a last resort when an opponent has gotten past the defenseman and is in a breakaway. Once the defenseman realizes that he has been beaten, he should **skate hard** to position himself just off to the side and in back of the opponent. Once you have the puck in sight, leave your feet in a diving motion, extend your arms and put the stick flat on the playing surface. Aim the stick and body at, or a little ahead of, the opponent's stick and attempt to knock the puck away. Do not knock the opponent's feet out from under him, since this could cause a tripping penalty or even a penalty shot. Too many times players who are beaten in a one-on-one situation stand around and spectate. Even though the defenseman who was just beaten may have the best seat in the house, this is no time to give up on the play. There are basically four outcomes in a situation like the breakaway described above: the opponent could lose the puck or overskate the net, the goaltender could make the big save while the defenseman is hustling back to pick up any rebound, the defenseman could hustle back to catch the opponent by making a diving sweep check or the opponent could score. I would definitely like to be hustling back and get involved in the second or third results as opposed to just spectating as the opponent moves in alone on my goaltender. **The Point: Never Stop Hustling! Stay Involved! It works!**

4. The **stick lift** is a good technique to use in front of the net when guarding an attacker or when the defenseman is skating alongside an opponent who has the puck or is about to receive the puck. Execute the stick lift by placing the blade of your stick under the lower shaft of the opponent's stick and quickly lift the opponent's stick about eight inches off the playing surface. Once the opponent's stick is lifted, retrieve the puck, turn and begin setting up an offensive attack. Even if the check doesn't work the first time, the defenseman is in a good position to execute it again. Every player should practice this technique because opportunities to use it always occur during games. Upper body and arm strength are important in this technique.
5. The **stick press** is similar to the stick lift except that the lower portion of the stick blade or shaft is pressed down onto the opponent's stick to keep the opponent from gaining possession or controlling the puck. Again, upper body and arm strength are important when using this technique.

Anyone who has ever played in a *no-check* roller hockey league knows enough to expect some physical contact, whether it is accidental, incidental or intentional. But how much you can give or have to take depends upon the players involved, the style of the game and the official's judgment. In no-check play, the defenseman must rely on proper body position, allowing the attackers to come to him and making contact only when the attacking player is very close. Two forms of intentional body contact are becoming more permissible in no-check roller hockey leagues:

- **Body blocking** is a form of body checking without the hard contact, and is used to slow the forward speed of an attacking puck carrier while eventually creating an opportunity to regain control of the puck. The approach to body blocking is to minimize the opponent's forward progress without interfering with it. A body block is similar to a basketball guard drawing a charge while standing his ground against an oncoming attacker, except in this case both players are moving. To execute an effective body block, the defenseman must *play the man* and not *play the puck.* **Playing the man** requires the defenseman to focus on the movement of the attacker (specifically his chest). By focusing on the player's chest, the defenseman can still see the puck, using his peripheral vision, and can use the stick checking techniques described above to gain control of the puck. **Playing the**

Stick Check in Front of the Net

puck requires the defenseman to focus on the movement of the puck. Since the puck moves faster than a player, focusing solely on the puck is nearly impossible (any defenseman who has been beaten by focusing on the puck can attest to this). As the defenseman plays the man, while moving backward and laterally, he positions himself so that the attacking puck carrier moves into him. The body block should only be continued for a second or two. If contact occurs any longer than that, or if the body block has been executed against a non-puck carrier, the defenseman is open for an interference penalty.

- **Riding the puck carrier out of the play** is a technique used along the boards to play an opponent off of the puck and eventually gain control of the puck. As the puck carrier moves into the defensive zone, the covering defenseman moves to force the puck carrier toward, and then along, the boards. At this point, the defenseman makes incidental body contact with the puck carrier using his hip and shoulder, retrieves the puck, and moves to make an offensive play. If you want to make the least amount of physical contact and still obtain the same results, make body contact with the attacking player's stick along the boards. This will have the effect of neutralizing the puck carrier's control of his stick while allowing you to gain control of the puck.

Covering an opponent in front of the defensive net is one of the most difficult tasks for a defenseman to perform in a no-check roller hockey league. You have to avoid interfering with the opponent when he doesn't have the puck and you can't be overly physical when he does have the puck. The objective when covering an opponent in front of the net is to stand your ground and prevent him from screening the goaltender, deflecting a puck into the net or receiving a pass or a rebound. This means that you may have to employ *some* intentional body contact on an opponent if he is trying to enter your space. **A player's space** is defined as an area surrounding your body with the horizontal component equal to the distance of your outstretched arms, generally two feet to the front, back and sides of your body. If you are standing your ground, you have the right to legally use your stick, arms and body to keep the opponent out of the space that you occupy. To effectively perform this task, you have to know where the play and the opponent are at all times. That means keeping your eyes on the play and rarely turning your back on the play to watch the opponent. This is important because you will not be able to read the play if your back is turned to it. If you read that a shot is going to be taken, you can react by clearing the opponent away from the net (out of your space). After the shot, you can use the stick checking techniques described above to ensure that the opponent does not get an opportunity to score. In covering an opponent in front of the net, the defenseman should stay close to him (within a stick's length) and position himself between the opponent and the puck or to the side of the opponent.

Covering Opponents in the Defensive Zone. Forcing the opposition into making bad plays is good defensive roller hockey and is critical in the defensive end. The assets of quickness and correctly reading a play will help prevent the attacking team from winning the battles in the defensive zone. As the oncoming attack moves into the defensive zone, the defensive unit has to consider just how to play the attack. The main question to answer is should you play a zone or man-to-man defense? This is addressed by first answering five additional questions:

1. Is your defensive partner with you and is he in the play?
2. How many open attackers are in the play?
3. Do you have any trailing support from your forwards?
4. Does the opposing team have any trailing support?
5. Which player has the best chance of scoring?

Answering these questions will help each defenseman decide how to position himself and to determine which player(s) to cover. Each defenseman needs to answer these questions as he moves around in the defensive zone by continually reading and reacting. Before we can answer the main question, zone and man-to-man defensive coverage needs to be defined. A **zone defense** is normally used when the attacking team has a numerical advantage in the defensive zone (i.e., three-on-two or two-on-one). Figure 7-2 depicts the left, right and central defensive zones that the defensemen need to patrol. In a zone defense with two defensemen, the left defenseman generally stays in his left zone and the right defenseman generally stays

Scenario	Trailing Support	Priority Play	Zone of Coverage
1-on-1	Opponent	Play the pass	Central Zone
1-on-1	Teammate or None	Play the man	Man-to-Man
1-on-2	Opponent, Teammate or None	Play the man	Play the man
2-on-1	Opponent or None	Play the pass	Central Zone
2-on-1	Teammate	Play the man	Man-to-Man
2-on-2	Opponent	Play the pass	Left and Right Zones
2-on-2	Teammate or None	Play the man	Man-to-Man
3-on-1	Opponent, Teammate or None	Play the pass	Central Zone
3-on-2	Opponent or None	Play the pass	Left and Right Zones
3-on-2	Teammate	Play the man	Man-to-Man

Table 7-2; Fundamental Defensive Zone Scenarios

in his right zone to cover attackers. In a zone defense with one defenseman, the single defenseman generally stays in the central zone to cover attackers. A **man-to-man defense** is normally used when the defending team has an equivalent number of players or a numerical advantage in the defensive zone (i.e., two-on-two or one-on-two). Figure 7-3 depicts a one-on-two scenario with the left defenseman utilizing man-to-man coverage (i.e., playing the man), by focusing on the movement of the attacker and not being concerned about which zone the attacker is in, while the right defenseman is ready to retrieve the puck and act as a backup for the left defenseman.

To answer the questions on trailing support, this term should be defined. **Trailing support from your teammates** refers to backcheckers, teammates who are skating back toward your defensive zone while covering or attempting to cover an offensive player. **Trailing support for the opposing team** refers to additional opponents who are entering the zone behind the initial play, to provide secondary attacking support. If neither team has trailing support, then there are no additional offensive or defensive players entering the defensive zone.

All of the information gained by reading the play is used in many scenarios. Ten scenarios are defined in Table 7-2 by whether the defensive unit is playing a one-on-one, one-on-two, two-on-one, two-on-two, three-on-one or a three-on two. The table defines the situational scenario; whether there is offensive, defensive or no trailing support; the priority play that the defensive player or unit should utilize (play the man or play the pass); and zones of coverage (Figure 7-2). **Playing the pass** requires the defenseman to maintain a position between two attackers with the intent of breaking up a pass, while covering the player with the best scoring opportunity.

A **one-on-one** scenario is defined as one attacker against one defender and usually consists of an opposing forward against a defenseman. As the defenseman moves with the attacker into the defensive zone, there are two scenarios that will be addressed — a one-on-one scenario with a trailing attacker and a one-on-one scenario with either a teammate trailing (backchecker) or no trailer (refer to Table 7-2). In the first scenario, the defenseman (XD) has read the oncoming play and determined that there is an immediate threat posed by the puck carrier (OF) and a potential threat posed by the trailing attacker (OF), as shown in Figure 7-4. This scenario requires the defenseman to:

- Play the pass as his first priority. Playing the pass requires the defenseman to maintain a position in the central defensive zone with access to both attackers. The intent is to break up a pass, while focusing on the player with the best scoring opportunity (this does not always mean the puck carrier).

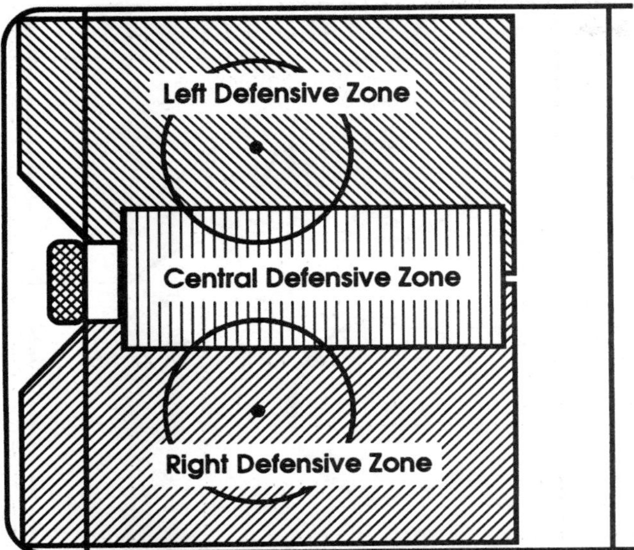

Figure 7-2; Zone Coverage

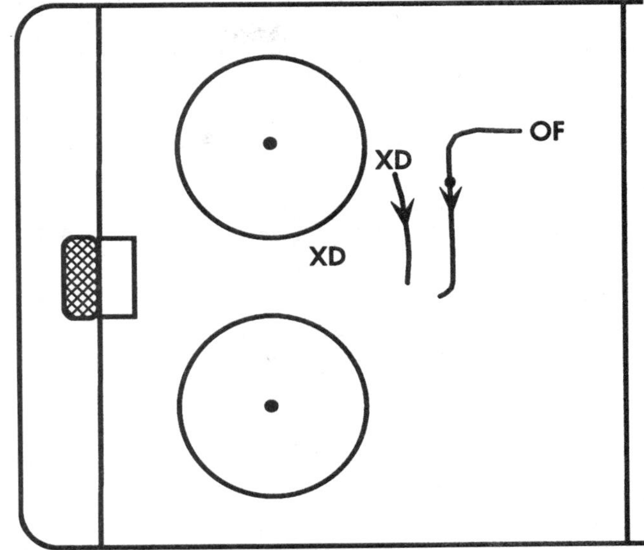

Figure 7-3; Man-to-Man Coverage

- Angle the puck carrier toward the boards as his second priority, forcing a low-percentage shot or a turnover, while constantly reading and reacting to the trailing attacker's positioning. If you are close enough to the puck carrier, try to use the stick checking techniques described earlier to knock the puck off his stick. Make sure that if he cuts toward the net, you stand your ground, allowing his body to move into yours (body blocking). If you are beaten, turn and skate toward the net, using the diving poke check if close enough to the attacker.
- Make sure that you aren't screening the goaltender if the puck carrier shoots, and that any rebounds are covered up or cleared. After a shot, the defenseman must not let the attacker slip past him for a second chance at scoring or regaining possession of the puck. If you gain control of the puck, begin a counterattack or clear it out of the defensive zone using a flip pass.

In the second scenario, the defenseman (XD) has read the oncoming play and determined that there is an immediate threat posed by the puck carrier (OF) and either help is on the way in the form of a trailing teammate or there are no additional threats, as shown in Figure 7-5. This scenario requires the defenseman to:

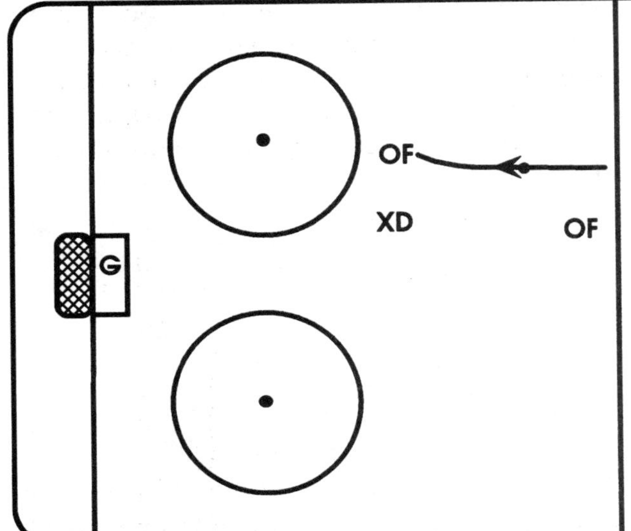

Figure 7-4; One-On-One With A Trailing Attacker

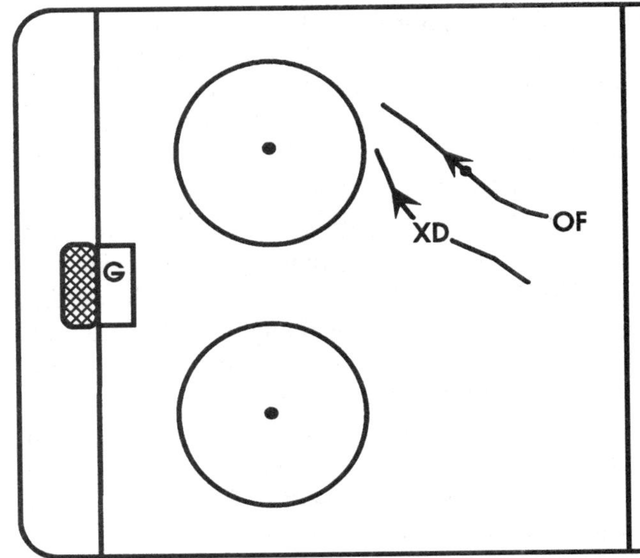

Figure 7-5; One-On-One With No Trailer

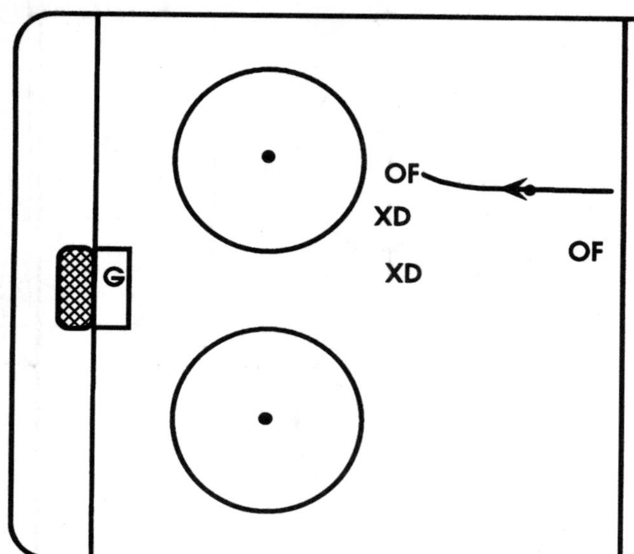

Figure 7-6; One-On-Two With A Trailing Attacker

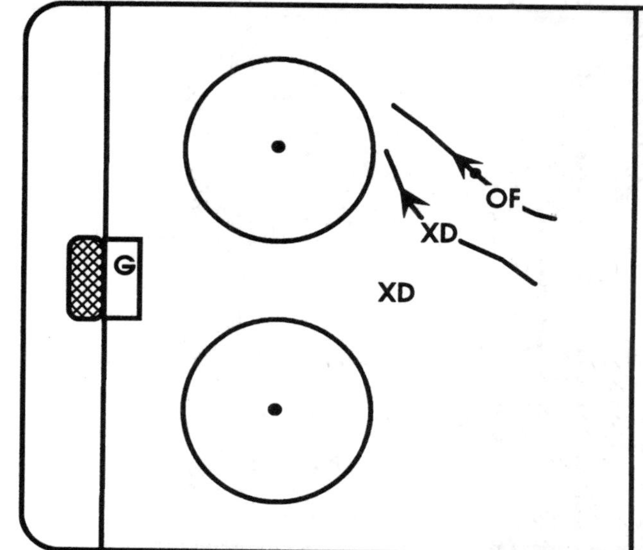

Figure 7-7; One-On-Two With No Trailer

- Play the man as the only priority, attempting to angle the puck carrier toward the boards again, forcing a low-percentage shot or turnover. By playing the man, the defenseman leaves the goaltender with a clear view of the puck. If the defenseman is playing the puck, he could potentially screen the puck from the goaltender. The defenseman should try to use the stick checking techniques to knock the puck off the puck carrier's stick. If the puck carrier cuts toward the net, use the body blocking technique to contain him.
- Make sure that you aren't screening the goaltender if the puck carrier shoots, and that any rebounds are covered up or can be cleared.

A **one-on-two** scenario is defined as one attacker against two defenders and usually consists of an opposing forward against two defensemen (the defensive unit). As the defensive unit moves with the attacker into the defensive zone, there are two scenarios that will be addressed — a one-on-two scenario with a trailing attacker and a one-on-two scenario with either a teammate trailing or no trailer (refer to Table 7-2). In the first scenario, the defensive unit (XD and XD) has read the oncoming play and determined that there is an immediate threat posed by the puck carrier (OF) and a potential threat posed by the trailing attacker (OF), as shown in Figure 7-6. This scenario requires the defensive unit to:

- Play the man. Although this scenario seems straight forward, if the defensemen are not communicating, problems can occur. This is exactly what happened to me and my partner on one occasion during the 1994 North American Roller Hockey Championships (NARCh) in St. Louis. Although we *usually* communicate very well, this particular time we both made the mistake of not communicating and anticipated that the other defenseman would cover the attacker. WRONG! The attacker went right between us. Not only were we beaten, but the attacker scored a goal as well. Anticipation is a good trait for a defenseman, but anticipation combined with communication is excellent. The defenseman closest to the puck carrier should call to his partner that he will play the man. The second defenseman will position himself so that he takes into account both the covered attacker and the trailing attacker, and acts as a safety net. The second defenseman needs to stay alert and ready to contain the puck carrier if he gets by the first defenseman.
- Make sure that you aren't screening the goaltender if the puck carrier shoots. After the shot, continue moving with the attacker, allowing your partner to pick up or clear any rebounds.
- Force the puck carrier to the outside and knock the puck off his stick with a stick check. If he cuts toward the net, execute a body block.
- Ensure that if a pass is made to the trailer, each defenseman covers one attacker. Communication is *essential* in this case.

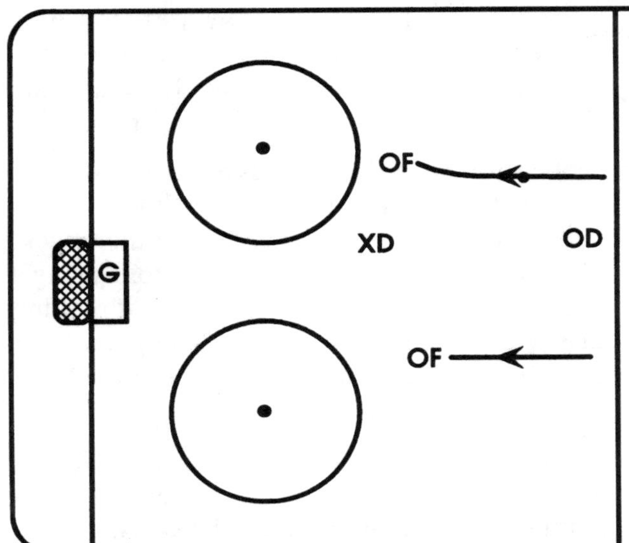

Figure 7-8; Two-On-One With A Trailing Attacker

In the second scenario, the defensive unit (XD and XD) has read the oncoming play and determined that there is an immediate threat posed by the puck carrier (OF) and help is on the way from the trailing teammate or there are no additional threats, as shown in Figure 7-7. This scenario also requires the defenseman to play the man, and is essentially the same as the scenario described above. The covering defenseman should aggressively stick check the attacker to knock the puck off his stick during this scenario while the other defenseman again acts as a safety net.

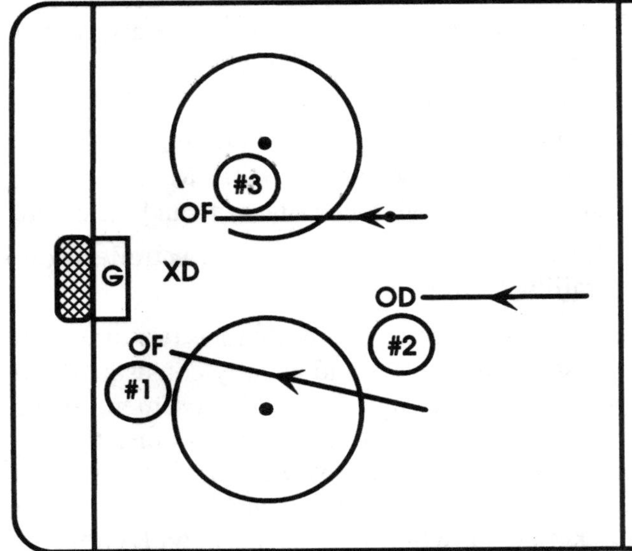

Figure 7-10; Covering The Most Dangerous Attackers

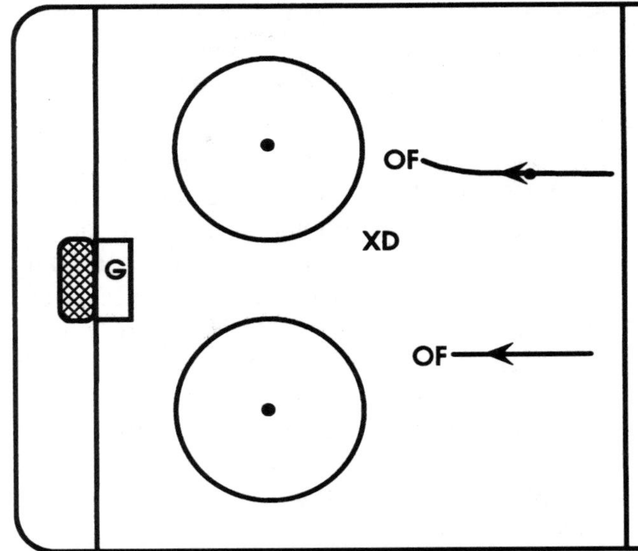

Figure 7-9; Two-On-One With No Trailer

A **two-on-one** scenario is defined as two attackers against one defender and usually consists of two opposing forwards against one defenseman. As the defenseman moves with the attackers into the defensive zone, there are two scenarios that will be addressed — a two-on-one scenario with a trailing attacker or no trailer, and a two-on-one scenario with a trailing teammate. In the first scenario, the defenseman (XD) has read the oncoming play and determined that both attackers (the puck carrier OF and the non-puck carrier OF) pose immediate threats, and either the trailing attacker (OD) poses

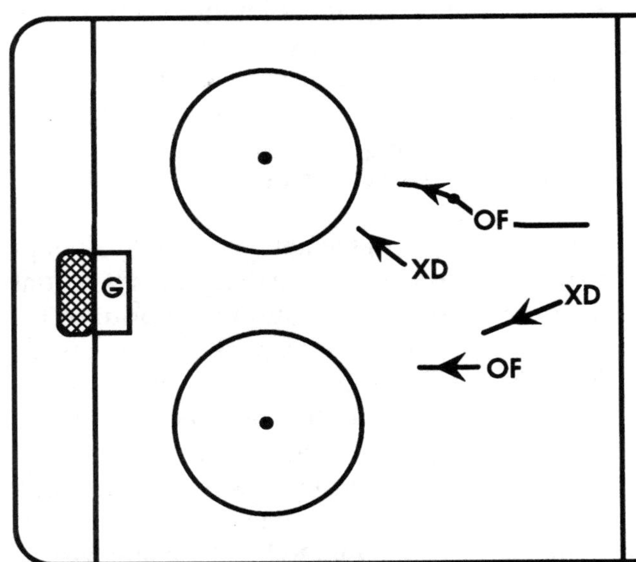

Figure 7-11; Two-On-One With A Trailing Teammate

a potential threat, as shown in Figure 7-8, or there are no additional threats, as shown in Figure 7-9. This scenario requires the defenseman to:

- Play the pass as the first priority either to the non-puck carrier or the trailing attacker. This is because a quick pass across the slot would not allow the goaltender enough time to slide across the crease to cover the open net, while an outside shot from the puck carrier can be effectively covered by the goaltender. During a two-on-one, the defenseman should not attempt to cover all of the attackers. If he tries to cover all of them (puck chasing), he ends up covering no one and the goaltender is left with confusion. A good rule of thumb when playing a two-on-one is to have the goaltender play the shooter and the defenseman play the pass. You can also think of this situation as the goaltender takes the outside shots and the defenseman takes the middle. Both approaches require the defenseman to contain the pass, remain in the central defensive zone and utilize the goaltender in a specific role. Quickness, fast thinking and execution are a defenseman's greatest assets when facing an outnumbered attack. The ability to relax under pressure is very important. If you get too uptight, you are more prone to make mistakes. If you can relax, think clearly and react quickly, you will be right more often than not.
- Angle the puck carrier toward the boards as the second priority, forcing a low-percentage shot or a turnover while constantly reading and reacting to the non-puck carrier's positioning. While attempting this, it is important not to turn your back on the play for very long, because you lose the ability to read and react to the positioning of the non-puck carriers. If the puck carrier cuts toward the net, you should attempt to play the pass to the most dangerous potential attacker. Figure 7-10 shows the prioritized locations to cover when the puck carrier cuts toward the net. The most dangerous potential attacker (No. 1) would be positioned on the far side of the net across from the puck carrier ready to receive a pass and shoot. Defend against this pass first. If there is no attacker on the far side of the net, then attempt to break up any pass to the slot (No. 2). If the puck carrier has his head down, the defenseman can make an initial move toward him as he cuts toward the net to try and force him to shoot, while covering any pass across the slot. In some situations, you may have to confront the puck carrier (No. 3) if it appears that he has gained good scoring position.
- Make sure that any rebounds are covered up or can be cleared if the puck carrier shoots. If you gain control of the puck, begin a counterattack, clear the puck out of the defensive zone using a flip pass or freeze it along the boards if nothing else works. Communicate with your goaltender so there is no confusion about loose pucks or possible rebounds.

In the second scenario, the defenseman (XD) has read the oncoming play and determined that there is an immediate threat posed by the two attackers (OF and OF), and help is on the way from a backchecking teammate (XD), as shown in Figure 7-11. This scenario requires the defenseman to:

- Play the man as long as the backchecking teammate is in close proximity to the non-puck carrying attacker. This scenario will initially start out with the defenseman playing the pass until his teammate has closed the distance on the non-puck carrying attacker.
- Concentrate on the puck carrier once the trailing teammate is close, attempt to angle him toward the boards and knock the puck off his stick with a stick check. If he cuts toward the net, execute a body block while the backchecking teammate covers the other attacker. At this point, you are attempting to force a turnover (either by a shot or a stick check) so that you can gain possession of the puck.
- Make sure that you aren't screening the goaltender if the puck carrier shoots. Make sure that any rebounds are covered up or can be cleared.
- Ensure that if a pass is made to the trailer, your trailing teammate covers him.

A **two-on-two** scenario is defined as two attackers against two defenders and usually consists of two opposing forwards against two defensemen. As the defensemen move with the attackers into the defensive zone, there are two scenarios that will be addressed — a two-on-two scenario with a trailing attacker and a two-on-two scenario with either no trailers or a trailing teammate. In the first scenario, the defensive unit (XD and XD) has read the oncoming play and determined that both attackers (the

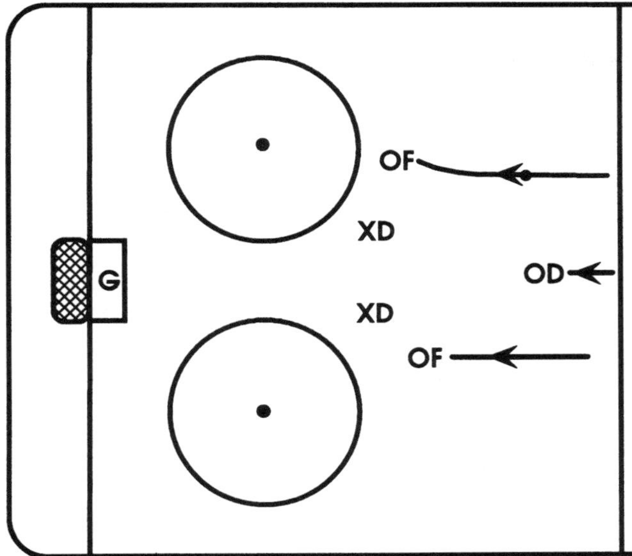

Figure 7-12; Two-On-Two With A Trailing Attacker

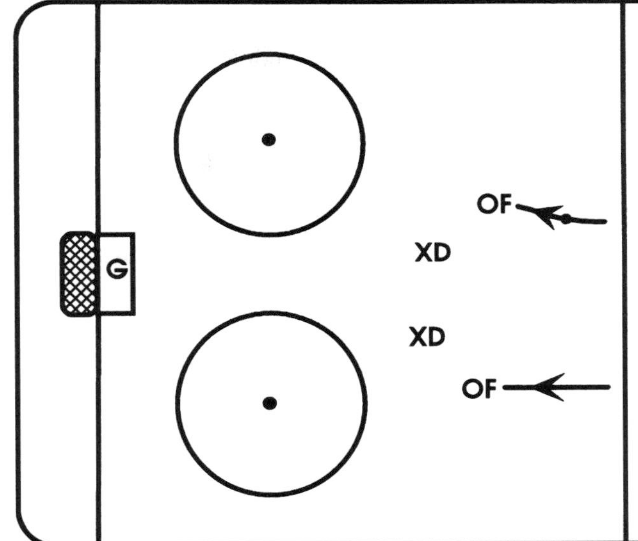

Figure 7-13; Two-On-Two With No Trailer

puck carrier OF and the non-puck carrier OF) pose immediate threats, while the trailing attacker (OD) poses a potential threat, as shown in Figure 7-12. This scenario is similar to a two-on-one situation for each defenseman with each defenseman covering his respective attacking forward as well as considering the trailing attacker. The defensemen will generally play the attackers from the left and right defensive zones. This scenario requires the defensive unit to:

- Play the pass as the first priority. If the puck carrier passes back to the trailer, the closest defenseman should force him to the outside while the other defenseman plays the pass to the most dangerous attacker. The most dangerous attacker would be positioned on the far side of the net. If there is no attacker on the far side of the net, then the defenseman should attempt to break up any pass to the slot.
- Utilize the **strongside defenseman** (the defenseman who is on the side of the playing surface that the puck is on and, in this case, is covering the shooter) to slow the shooter down after the shot has been taken and keep him from getting a rebound while the **weakside defenseman** (the defenseman who is on the opposite side of the playing surface that the puck is on and is the strongside defenseman's partner) makes sure that the puck is covered up by the goaltender or can be cleared.
- Attempt to angle the puck carrier toward the boards, forcing a low-percentage shot or a turnover. If the puck carrier cuts to the outside of the defenseman and toward the net, the strongside defenseman should angle him off to the side of the playing surface while the weakside defenseman plays the pass to the most dangerous attacker.
- Utilize the strongside defenseman to body block the puck carrier out of the play while the weakside defenseman picks up the loose puck if the puck carrier tries to split the defense.
- Stay in their original zone and pick up the new coverage after the cross is complete if the attackers cross zones (reverse or weave play).
- Communicate with your partner and signal your coverage if two of the attackers stay on one side of the rink. A good approach is to stay in your own defensive zone and do not cross unless there is a definite scoring threat.

In the second scenario, the defensive unit (XD and XD) has read the oncoming play and has determined that both attackers (the puck carrier OF and the non-puck carrier OF) pose immediate threats, and there is either a teammate trailing (backchecker) or no trailers, as shown in Figure 7-13. This scenario is similar to a one-on-one situation with each defenseman covering his respective attacker. This scenario requires the defensive unit to:

- Play the man as the only priority. Attempt to angle the puck carrier toward the boards forcing a low-percentage shot or turnover, while the

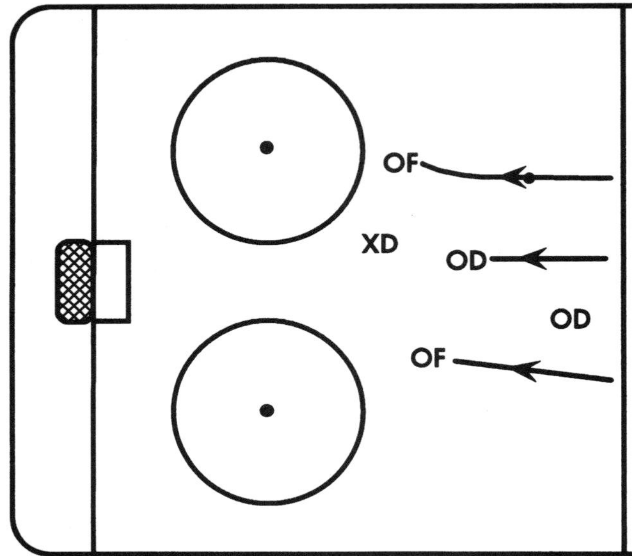

Figure 7-14; Three-On-One With A Trailing Attacker

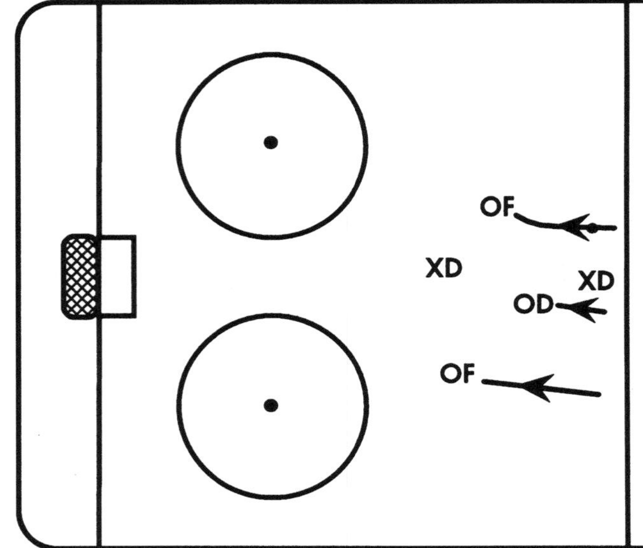

Figure 7-15; Three-On-One With A Trailing Teammate

other defenseman reads the play for a possible pass or rebound (if a shot is taken). The defenseman can be more aggressive in covering the attackers in this scenario and the use of a stick check and body block is important. If the defenseman suceeds, either he or his partner can retrieve the puck and begin an offensive play.

- Utilize the strongside defenseman to body block the puck carrier out of the play while the weakside defenseman picks up the loose puck if the puck carrier tries to split the defense.
- Stay in their original zone and pick up the new coverage after the cross is complete if the attackers cross zones (reverse or weave play).
- Communicate with your partner and signal your coverage if both attackers stay on one side of the rink.

A **three-on-one** scenario is defined as three attackers against one defender and usually consists of two opposing forwards and one opposing defenseman against one defenseman. The three-on-one usually occurs following an aggressive offensive attack (with two or three teammates still deep in the offensive zone) with the defending team eventually gaining control of the puck and moving it out of the offensive zone. As the defenseman moves with the attackers into the defensive zone, there are two scenarios that will be addressed — a three-on-one scenario with a trailing attacker and a three-on-one scenario with either no trailer or a trailing teammate. In the first scenario, the defenseman (XD) has read the oncoming play and determined that the three attackers (the puck carrier OF and the two non-puck carriers OF and OD) pose immediate threats, while the trailing attacker (OD) poses a potential threat, as shown in Figure 7-14. This scenario requires the defenseman to:

- Play the pass as the first priority, maintaining a position in the central defensive zone. If the puck carrier passes back to the trailer, contain any further passes to the most dangerous attacker. The most dangerous attacker would be positioned on the far side of the net across from the puck carrier ready to receive a pass and shoot. If there is no attacker on the far side of the net, then the defenseman should break up any pass to the slot.
- Angle the puck carrier toward the boards as the defenseman's second priority, forcing a low-percentage shot or a turnover while constantly reading and reacting to the non-puck carrier's positioning. If the puck carrier cuts toward the net you should attempt to play the pass to the most dangerous attacker. If the puck carrier has his head down, the defenseman can make an initial move toward him as he cuts to the net to try and force him to shoot, while covering any pass across or to the slot.
- Make sure that any rebounds are covered up or can be cleared if the puck carrier shoots. Communicate with your goaltender so there is no

confusion about loose pucks or possible rebounds. The best outcome is to freeze the puck and not give out any rebounds.

- Stay in the central defensive zone if the attackers cross zones and constantly read the play while playing the pass.

In the second scenario, the defenseman (XD) has read the oncoming play and determined that there is an immediate threat posed by the three attackers (OF, OF and OD), and there are either no additional threats or there is a backchecking teammate (XD), as shown in Figure 7-15. This scenario requires the defenseman to:

- Play the pass as the first priority, maintaining a position in the central defensive zone. The backchecking teammate can play the pass to an attacker who remains in the *high slot* (an area in the slot farthest from the net. The low or deep slot is an area in the slot closest to the net).
- Angle the puck carrier toward the boards, forcing a low-percentage shot or a turnover as his second priority. If the puck carrier cuts toward the net, you should play the pass to the most dangerous attacker. If the puck carrier has his head down, make an initial move toward him as you cut toward the net to try and force him to shoot while covering any pass across or to the slot. In some situations, you may have to confront the puck carrier if it appears that he has gained good scoring position. In this case, the trailing teammate should cover a pass to the most dangerous attacker.
- Make sure that any rebounds are covered up or can be cleared if the puck carrier shoots. Communicate with your goaltender so there is no confusion about loose pucks or possible rebounds. The best outcome is to freeze the puck and not give out any rebounds.
- Stay in the central defensive zone if the attackers cross zones and constantly read the play while you and your trailing teammate play the pass.

A **three-on-two** scenario is defined as three attackers against two defenders and usually consists of two opposing forwards and one opposing defenseman against two defensemen. As the defensive unit moves with the attackers into the defensive zone, there are two scenarios that will be addressed — a three-on-two scenario with a trailing attacker or no trailers and a three-on-two scenario with a trailing teammate. In the first scenario, the defensive unit (XD and XD) has read the oncoming play and determined that the three attackers (the puck carrier OF and the two non-puck carriers OF and OD) pose immediate threats, while a trailing attacker (OD) poses a potential threat, as shown in Figure 7-16. This scenario requires the defensive unit to:

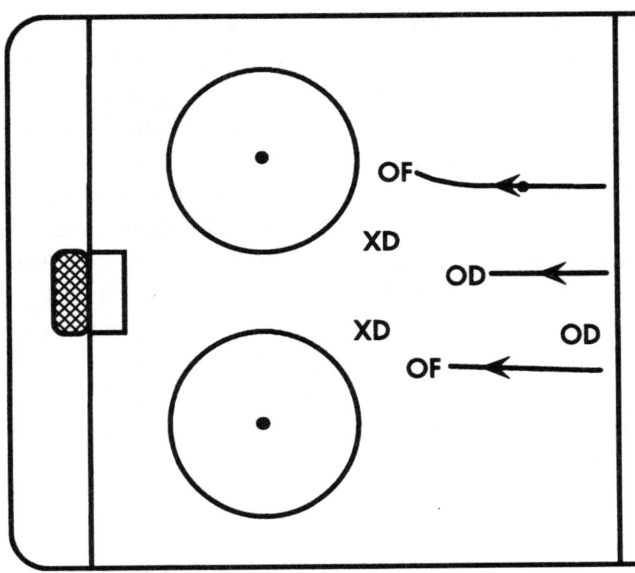

Figure 7-16; Three-On-Two With A Trailing Attacker

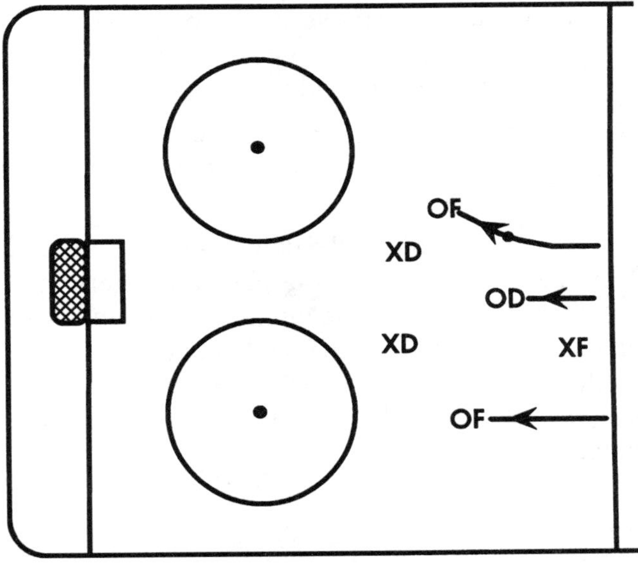

Figure 7-17; Three-On-Two With A Trailing Teammate

- Play the pass as the first priority, maintaining a position in the left and right defensive zones. If the puck carrier passes back to the trailer, contain any further passes to the most dangerous attacker. The most dangerous attacker would be positioned on the far side of the net, across from the puck carrier, ready to receive a pass and shoot. If there is no attacker on the far side of the net, then the defensemen should attempt to break up any pass to the slot.
- Angle the puck carrier toward the boards as their second priority, forcing a low-percentage shot or a turnover while constantly reading and reacting to the non-puck carrier's positioning. If the puck carrier cuts toward the net, play the pass to the most dangerous attacker. If the puck carrier has his head down, the strongside defenseman makes an initial move toward him while cutting toward the net to try and force him to shoot, while the weakside defenseman covers any pass across or to the slot. In some situations, you may have to confront the puck carrier if it appears that he has gained good scoring position.
- Utilize the strongside defenseman to body block the puck carrier out of the play while the weakside defenseman picks up the loose puck if the puck carrier tries to split the defense.
- Make sure that any rebounds are covered up or can be cleared if the puck carrier shoots. Communicate with your goaltender so there is no confusion about loose pucks or possible rebounds. The best outcome is to freeze the puck and not give out any rebounds.
- Stay in your defensive zones if the attackers cross zones and constantly read the play while playing the pass.

In the second scenario, the defensive unit (XD and XD) has read the oncoming play and determined that there is an immediate threat posed by the three attackers (OF, OF and OD) and help is on the way in the form of a backchecking teammate (XF), shown in Figure 7-17. This scenario requires the defensive unit to:

- Start out playing the pass until the backchecking teammate has closed the distance on one of the non-puck carrying attackers. At that point, this scenario becomes a one-on-one, with each defender playing the man. Once the backchecking teammate is close to the attacker, the strongside defenseman can concentrate on the puck carrier, angling him toward the boards or forcing a low-percentage shot or turnover, while the weakside defenseman and the backchecking teammate cover the other attackers. If the puck carrier cuts toward the net, the strongside defenseman can use the stick check and body block techniques. If the defenseman is successful, either he or his partner can retrieve the puck and begin an offensive play.
- Make sure that any rebounds are covered up or can be cleared if the puck carrier shoots. Communicate with your goaltender so there is no confusion about loose pucks or possible rebounds. The best outcome is to freeze the puck and not give out any rebounds.
- Utilize the strongside defenseman to body block the puck carrier out of the play while the weakside defenseman picks up the loose puck if the puck carrier tries to split the defense.
- Stay in your defensive zones if the attackers cross zones and constantly read the play while continuing to play the man.

Remembering that the objective of a team in a defensive or transitional role is to gain control of the puck, the defensive unit can effectively defend against this oncoming attack by using the information in Table 7-2 and the sections above. The section that you have just completed contains a lot of information and you won't have time to review any of it during a game. The role of the individual defenseman and the defensive unit is to become knowledgeable on this information prior to stepping onto the playing surface, while the role of the coach is to ensure that each defenseman and the defensive unit understand the information and have ample opportunity to practice what they have learned in real or simulated situations.

Siller Player And Team Evaluation Profile©
Defensive Player Checklist

Evaluator: The Coach | **Date**: 1/5/95 | **Location**: The Arena

	Player Name											
Notes: The one/two/three-on-two drills were not performed and were not used in the evaluation of any of the players.	**RYAN**		**TOMMY**		**KATY**		**MIKE**					
Fundamental Defensive Techniques												
Communicating	8		8		8		8					
Reading And Reacting	7		6		7		7					
Poke Check	8		8		8		8					
Sweep Check	8		8		8		8					
Diving Sweep/Poke Check	8		5		5		5					
Stick Lift/Press	8		8		8		8					
Body Blocking	6		7		7		8					
Riding A Player Out Of A Play	6		9		7		8					
Covering In Front Of The Net	8		6		7		8					
One/Two/Three-On-One	6		8		7		6					
One/Two/Three-On-Two	**0**		**0**		**0**		**0**					
Advanced Defensive Techniques												
Learning Opponents Patterns	7		7		7		7					
Blocking Shots With Your Body	6		6		7		6					
Fake Shot	5		5		6		4					
One-Time Shot	7		5		6		8					
Rushing	6		**3**		5		4					
TOTAL SCORE	**104**		**99**		**103**		**103**					
AVERAGE SCORE	**6.9**		**6.6**		**6.9**		**6.9**					

Comments: Ryan, Tommy, Katy and Mike have all demonstrated medium overall defensive proficiency with total scores of 104, 99, 103 and 103, respectively, and average scores of 6.9, 6.6, 6.9, and 6.9 respectively. All techniques were performed except the one/two/three-on-twos. Tommy needs to improve on rushing.

Scale: 0 = Not Performed, 1 - 3 = Low Proficiency, 4 - 6 = Medium Proficiency, 7 - 9 = High Proficiency, 10 = Excellent Proficiency

Table 7-3; Defensive Player Checklist

Advanced Techniques

The five advanced defensive techniques consist of learning the opponents' patterns, blocking shots with your body, fake shots, one-time shots and rushing.

Learning the opponent's patterns. To progress to the next level of roller hockey, it is imperative that each defenseman makes a point of learning the various moves and play patterns of his opponents, including the forwards, defense and goaltender(s). A lot of players just try to *do their job* without attempting to understand why or how a player gets by them. Don't leave it only up to the coach to tell you what is working and what is not; **think and evaluate!** If you are playing a team for the first time, you should begin **keeping a book** (mental notes) on the favorite moves and plays of the opposing players, various line combinations and goaltending styles. Determine the opponents' best playmakers, best shooters, how they react to certain circumstances, and exchange this information with your coach and teammates. Watch how the other team's defensemen play your forwards. Determine if this information will help you with how you play your opponents and also share this information with your forwards. By the second half of the game, you should at least have a decent book on the team. If you have played a team before, you should recall the information from your book and use it so that you can be in a position to recognize moves and plays when they are initiated. The defenseman should not guess the move or play of the opponents, but wait until it starts. If you guess, and commit too early, a good attacker will have you for dinner. By being ready for a certain play or occasionally forcing a play, the percentages will be on your side; but you must be alert for any play to occur.

Blocking shots with your body. There is no doubt that when used properly, this play can be a goal saver. Blocking a shot at the right time can also have a positive impact on momentum and could result in an offensive break for your team if possession of the puck is regained. Since this technique requires a player to slide along the playing surface and be out of the play for a few seconds, and since there are certain playing surfaces that this technique is not recommended (such as asphalt or cement), blocking a shot with your body should only be attempted on forgiving playing surfaces during situations where a goal-scoring opportunity is great. This could occur when the shooter is within 25 feet of the net and in a good position or during a *scramble* (period of transition where each team is trying to gain control of the puck) near the net. To be effective, the defenseman should move toward the shooter, waiting until the shooter's stick starts forward in the shooting action, and then slide his legs (and body) in a path perpendicular to the path of the puck. The defenseman should try and get as close to the puck as possible, using his shin pads as the equipment that actually blocks the shot. After the shot has been taken, do not stay down on the playing surface unless the puck is under you; otherwise, get up immediately and get back into the play. If you commit too early, the shooter will have an opportunity to go around you. Do not go down until you feel confident that the shooter is actually going to shoot.

Fake shot. The fake shot is an excellent deceptive move to use on any team once or twice a game and can provide the defenseman with an opportunity to move in closer to the net for a real shot. The fake slap shot is the most effective due to the large windup required. As the defenseman takes his stick back and then forward, he stops it just before it contacts the puck. The defenseman moves the puck around the defender and toward the net for a better scoring opportunity.

One-time shot. Although the one-time shot was described in Chapter 6, I want to reiterate its importance as a tool from the defenseman's viewpoint. The one-time shot is used with a snap or slap shot and relies on exact timing to be executed. When the defenseman has signaled to a forward that he is open, and a pass is made to the defenseman, he needs to prepare himself. Instead of receiving the pass, draw your stick back and time the travel of the pass so that your follow-through with the blade of the stick coincides exactly with the arrival of the puck. When the puck reaches you, execute the one-time shot. This type of shot is very deceptive because as a goaltender attempts to follow the puck on the playing surface, it is moved from the passer to the defenseman to the net, usually before the goaltender has a chance to prepare himself for the shot. This shot requires a lot of practice to perfect and should only be used occasionally so that the goaltender does not expect it.

Rushing. In getting an offensive move started, remember that passing is the safest and quickest way to get the puck moving. However, do not neglect the capability of the defenseman to *rush* (carry the puck up the playing surface). The game of roller hockey is designed for the defense to become involved in the offense; with the four-on-four style of play creating more room to maneuver with the puck than the five-on-five style of play used in ice hockey. The difference between a good roller hockey team and an excellent roller hockey team, all other factors being equal, lies in the defensemen contributing on offense. A rush can occur either in the offensive or defensive zones. Deep in the defensive zone, the rush is started with a breakout play, which moves the puck out of that zone and into the offensive zone. Anywhere else on the playing surface, a rush can be initiated by gaining control of the puck and moving it toward the net for a scoring opportunity. Defensemen who have good skating and stickhandling skills will be better prepared to rush than those who don't. In roller hockey, it is important for defensemen to be as effective as the forwards at skating with and handling the puck.

Drills

Defensive drills should be selected to enable players to adjust to as many defensive situations as possible. Defensive proficiency comes with knowledge and practice. By learning the material in this chapter, the coach and players will become familiar with the particular skills and strategies required to play solid defense, allowing the defensemen to become better overall roller hockey players. As the coach discovers the particular needs of his players, he can select the drills required for the players to improve. The drills in this chapter include the components of skating, stickhandling and puck control, passing and receiving, shooting and scoring, and individual and unit defensive skills. Drills from Chapters 3 through 6 that should become part of a defenseman's fundamentals include Drills 3-3 (Starting Efficiency), 3-4 (Developing Powerful Starts), 3-5 (Backward Starting), 3-6 (Stopping), 3-14 (Sprint Skating), 4-3 (Developing Soft Hands), 4-7 (Puck Control and Turns), 5-4 (Around The Boards Pass), 5-5 (Peripheral Vision Drill), 5-6 (Give-And-Go) and 6-11 (Race For The Puck).

Drill 7-1; Transitions. Position the players into two lines starting on the goal line so that they will start out skating backward. At the whistle, each player skates backward toward the other end of the rink. At the next whistle, the players should transition to skating forward. The transitions should all be made in a counterclockwise direction. The players should continue transitioning at each whistle as they skate

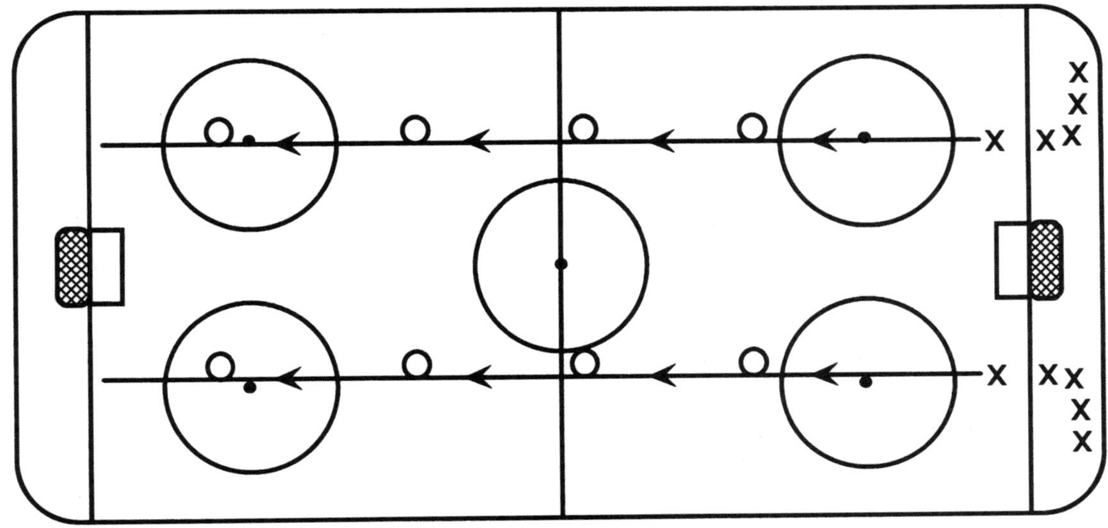

Drill 7-1; Transitions

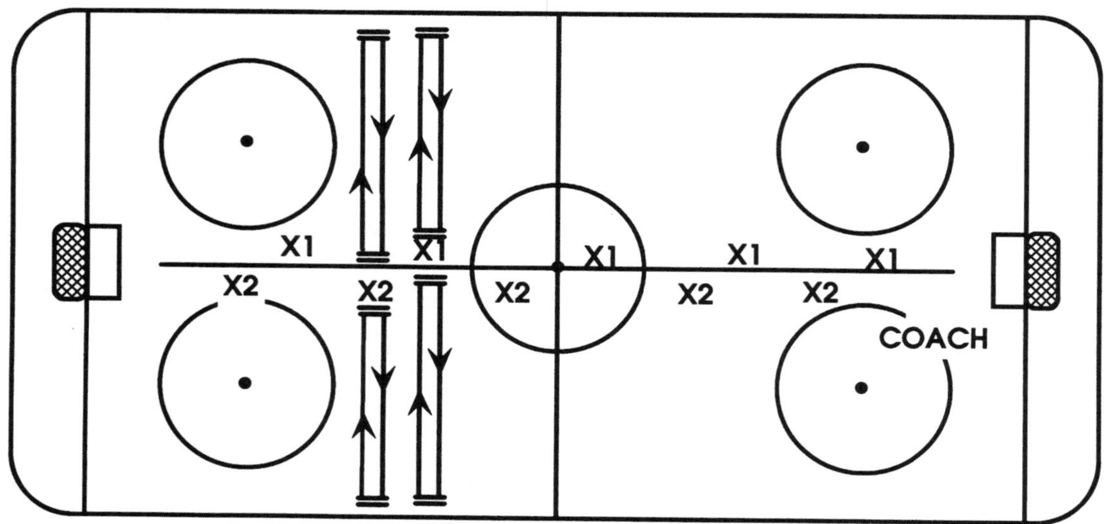

Drill 7-2; Side-To-Side Sprints

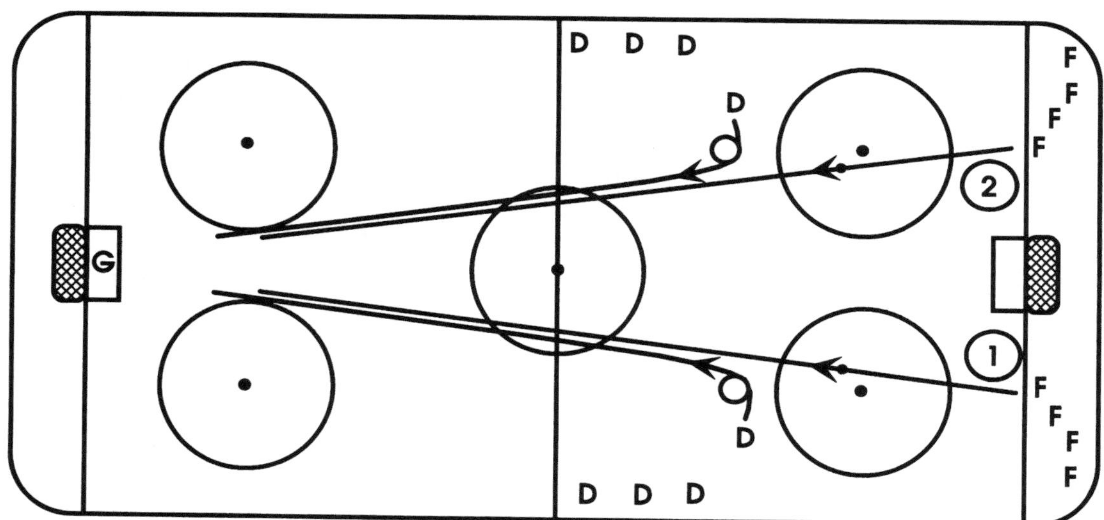

Drill 7-3; Using The Stick

to the far goal line. A minimum of four transitions should be performed by each player (seven or eight is ideal). Repeat this drill so that each player has skated the length of the rink a minimum of three times.

Variations:

- Transition in a clockwise direction.
- Transition using both clockwise and counter-clockwise movement.

Drill 7-2; Side-To-Side Sprints. This drill simulates the skating demands of a defenseman in the defensive zone. Position the players (X1 and X2) on a line between the two goals spaced about 10 feet apart, as shown in the corresponding diagram. At the whistle, have the X1 players skate, at three-quarter speed, toward the boards and stop. All players should be facing the coach when they stop. At the second whistle, have the same X1 players skate toward their original starting location. All players should be facing the coach when they stop. At the next whistle, have the X1 players skate toward the other boards and stop, again facing the coach. At the fourth whistle, the X1 players should skate back to their original starting position and stop, facing the coach. Repeat the drill with the X2 players. Complete the cycle one more time for both X1 and X2 players. A variation could be simultaneously working the X1 players on one half of the playing surface and the X2 players on the other half.

Drill 7-3; Using The Stick. Line up the defensemen in two groups just inside the center red line on each side of the boards as shown in the corresponding diagram. Line up the forwards in two groups behind the goal line, between the net and the boards. At the whistle, the first forward and defenseman from side No. 1 begin skating toward the far goal. As the defenseman curls in his pattern, he transitions to skating backward. As the forward approaches the defenseman, the defenseman executes a poke check, attempting to knock the puck off the forward's stick. If the poke check is successful, the defenseman should try to gain control of the puck and skate back to his starting location. If the poke check is unsuccessful, the forward should attempt to take a shot on net. After the first defenseman/forward pair from side 1 complete the drill, the first pair from side 2 should execute the drill at the whistle. The two sides alternate until all players have gone. After the drill is completed, players should switch sides and repeat the drill.

Variations:

- Employ the sweep check.
- Employ the diving sweep check.
- Employ the diving poke check.
- Employ the stick lift.
- Employ the stick press.

Drill 7-4; Body Blocking. This drill teaches defensemen to use their bodies to play the man. Line up the players in the same pattern as described in Drill 7-3, except the defensemen will not be allowed to use their sticks. Have the defensemen place their sticks along the boards. At the whistle, the first forward and defenseman from side 1 begin skating. As the forward approaches the defenseman, the defenseman should focus on the forward's chest. The defenseman should move backward, laterally, and at the proper speed so that the forward moves into him. The body block should only be continued for a second or two. If the forward gets by, the defenseman should skate back to the net as if to retrieve a rebound. After the first defenseman/forward pair from side 1 complete the drill, the first pair from side 2 should execute the drill. The two sides alternate until all players have gone. After the drill is completed, players should switch sides and repeat the drill.

Drill 7-5; Riding A Puck Carrier Out Of The Play. This drill is designed to teach defensemen to physically contain a player along the boards and retrieve the puck. Line up the players as shown in the corresponding diagram. At the whistle, the first forward and defenseman in each line begin skating down the boards. As the forward moves into the defensive zone, the defenseman moves to force him toward, and then along, the boards. The defenseman should make body contact with the puck carrier or his stick, using his hip and shoulder, retrieve the puck, and begin skating with the puck toward the far end. After the first defenseman/forward pair from each side complete the drill, the next pair from each side should execute the drill. After the drill is

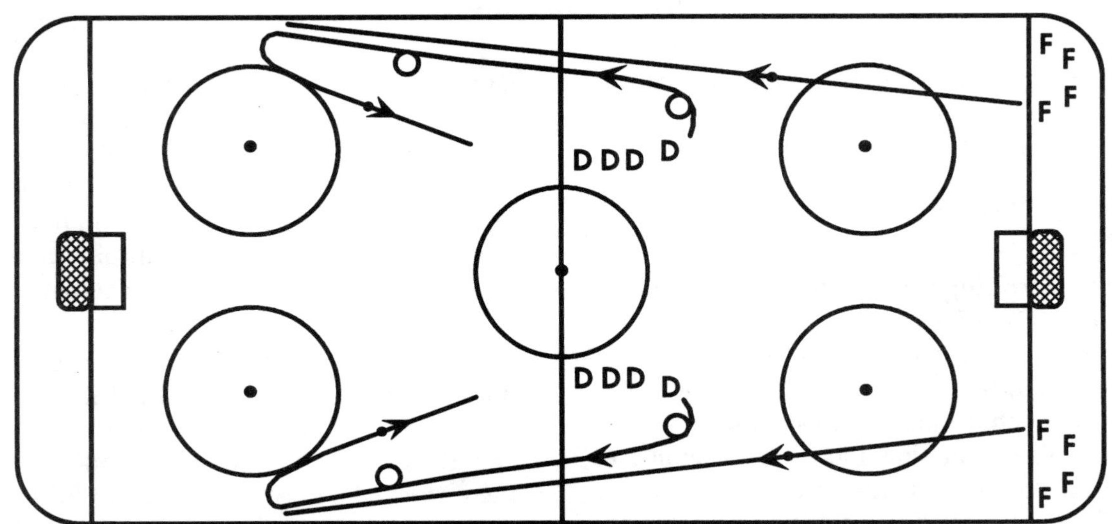

Drill 7-5; Riding A Player Out Of The Play

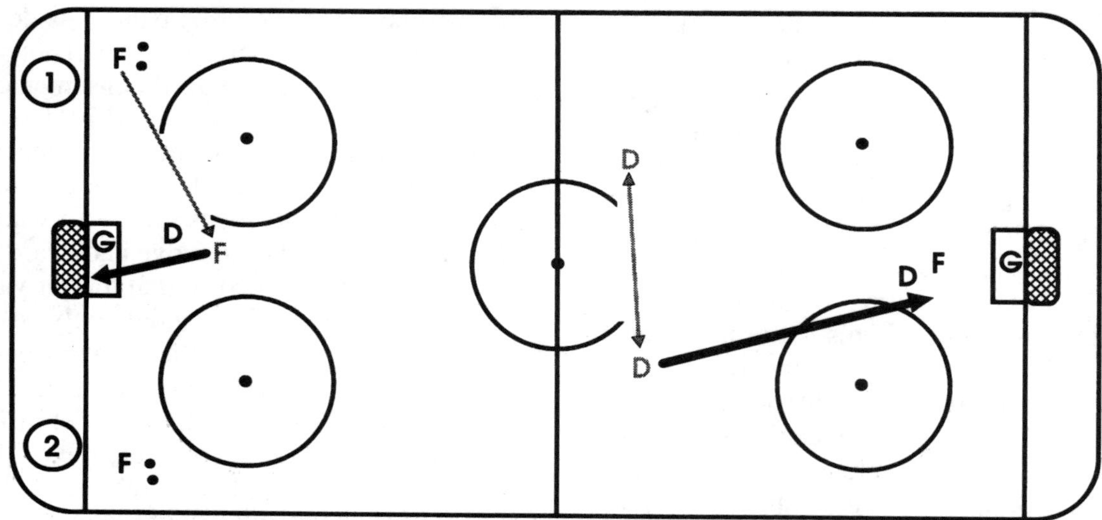

Drill 7-6; Controlling the Man in Front of the Net

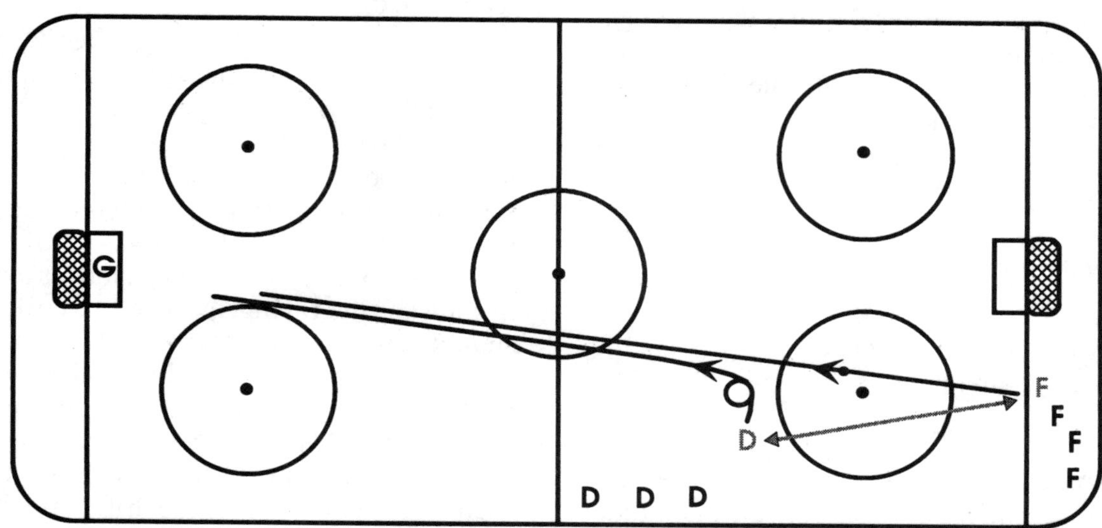

Drill 7-7; One-On-One

completed, players should switch sides and repeat the drill.

Variation:

■ Have the defensemen execute the drill without using a stick.

Drill 7-6; Controlling Opponents in Front of the Net. This drill combines two drills and can be run simultaneously. In the first drill (shown on the left of the corresponding diagram), two players are positioned in each corner with two pucks. At the whistle, the player on side 1 has five seconds to pass the first puck to the forward in front of the net. The forward moves around the low slot area to get open for a shot on goal while the defenseman attempts to cover him. The defenseman should stay close to the opponent (within a stick's length) and position himself between the opponent and the puck or to the side of the opponent. The defenseman practices controlling the opponent, in a legal manner, by angling, blocking, bumping and using his stick. Repeat the drill with the second puck from side 1 and then again for side 2.

After both sides have completed the drill, four new players are brought in and the drill is repeated. In the second drill (shown on the right of the corresponding diagram), two defensemen are placed at the **points** (the normal position of the defensemen in the offensive zone) and pass the puck back and forth, while a third defenseman attempts to cover the moving forward in the slot. After the point men have made three or four passes to each other, one of the point men should shoot the puck on net. The defenseman in the slot should attempt to move the forward so that the goaltender has a clear view of the puck while the forward attempts to deflect the puck, screen the goaltender or capitalize on a rebound.

Note: For Drills 7-7 through 7-12, assume there is no trailing support. These drills can be easily modified, however, to include a trailing attacker or a trailing teammate based on specific needs.

Drill 7-7; One-On-One. This is one of the fundamental defensive drills upon which many other defensive drills and strategies are built. This drill forces the defenseman to stretch his backward skating speed to its maximum level while playing the one-on-one situation. Line the players up as shown in the corresponding diagram. At the whistle, the forward passes the puck to the defenseman, who passes it back to the forward. After the forward receives the pass, both skaters move toward the far goal at three-quarter speed. The objective of this drill is for the defenseman to play the man, attempting to angle the puck carrier toward the boards, forcing a low-percentage shot, or stripping him of the puck using one of the stick check techniques. If the puck carrier cuts toward the net, the defenseman should use the body blocking technique to contain him. If the forward takes a shot, the defenseman should make sure that he isn't screening the goaltender, and that any rebounds are covered up or can be cleared. The coach should provide feedback to the defenseman based on the above criteria and the end result. After the first forward/defenseman pair have completed the drill, the next forward/defenseman pair should execute the drill. All players perform the drill at least three times.

Drill 7-8; Two-On-One. The objective of this drill is to teach the defenseman to play the pass as the first priority for any two-on-one. The second priority should be to angle the puck carrier toward the boards, force a low-percentage shot or strip the forward of the puck. If the puck carrier cuts toward the net, the defenseman should use the body blocking technique to contain him. If the forward takes a shot, the defenseman should make sure that he isn't screening the goaltender, and that any rebounds are covered up or can be cleared. If you gain control of the puck, skate it out of the defensive zone, use a flip pass or freeze it along the boards if nothing else works. Communicate with your goaltender so there is no confusion about a loose puck or possible rebound. To start the drill, position the players as shown in the corresponding diagram. At the whistle, the two forwards and the defenseman start skating toward the far end, with the forwards passing the puck back and forth as they move down the playing surface. As the forwards cross the center red line, the defenseman should position himself so that he is between the two forwards. The forwards should pass, skate the puck in or shoot, depending on the position of the defenseman. The coach should provide feedback to the defenseman based on his position with respect to the forwards, the above criteria, as well as

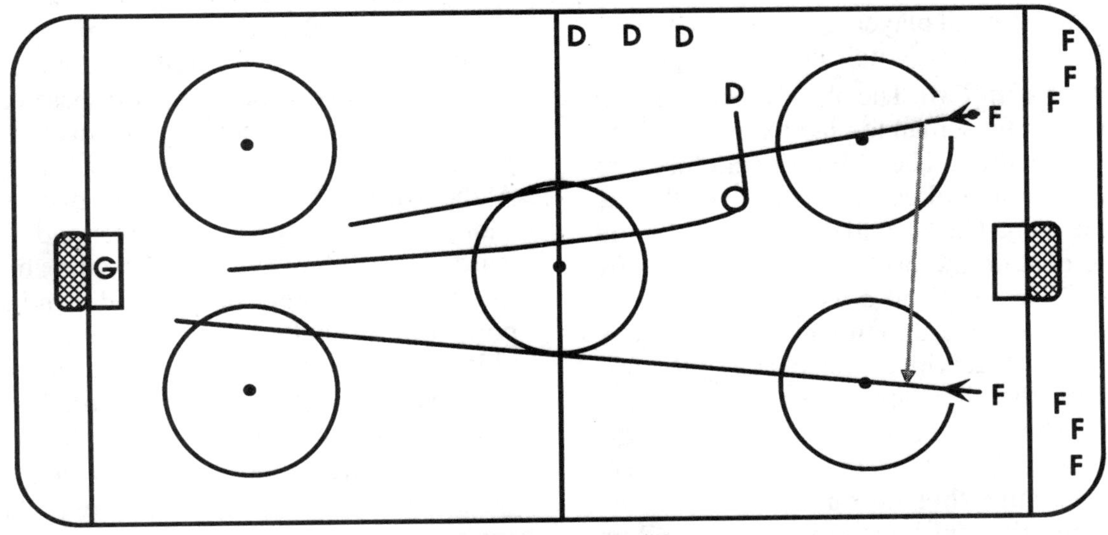

Drill 7-8; Two-On-One

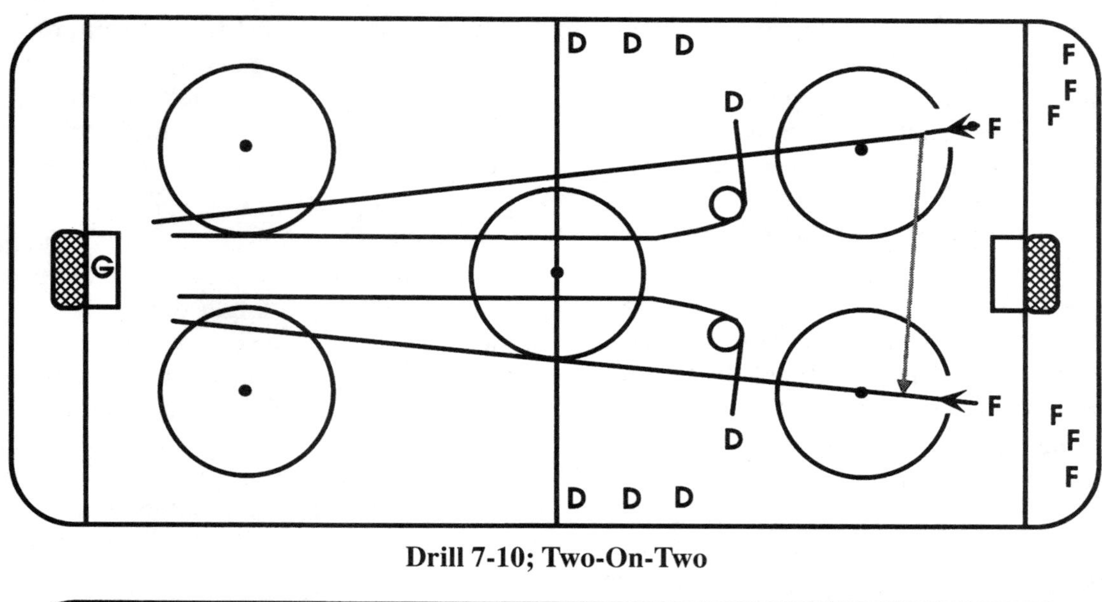

Drill 7-10; Two-On-Two

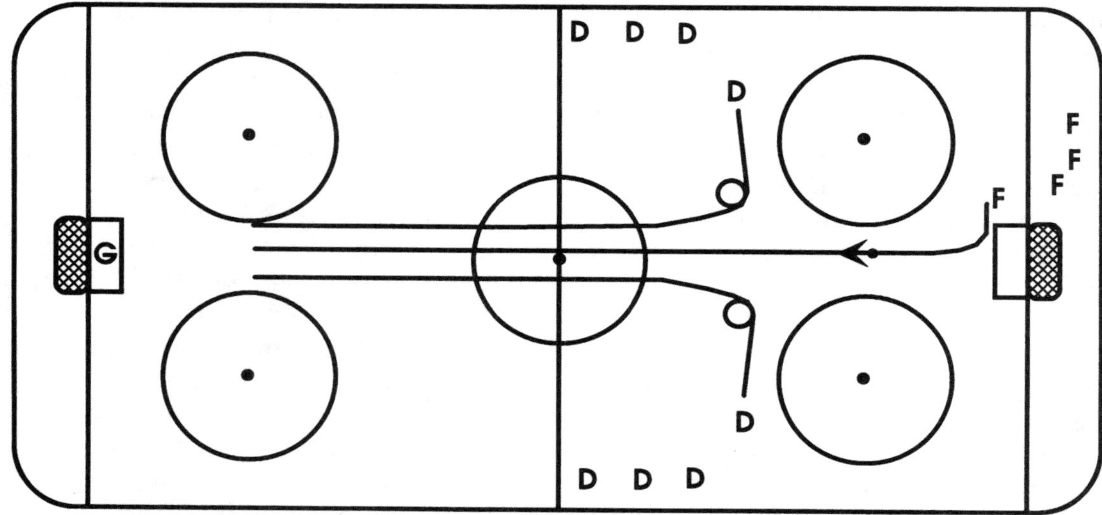

Drill 7-9; One-On-Two

the end result. After all players have completed the drill, have the forwards switch sides and repeat.

Drill 7-9; One-On-Two. The objective of this drill is to teach the defenseman to play the man for any one-on-two situation. The defenseman closest to the puck carrier should call to his partner that he will play the man. The second defenseman should be ready to contain the puck carrier if he gets by the first defenseman. The covering defenseman should force the forward to the outside and knock the puck off his stick with a stick check. If the forward gets by the first defenseman, the second defenseman should execute a body block. If the forward takes a shot, the covering defenseman should make sure that he isn't screening the goaltender and that any rebounds are covered up or can be cleared by the second defenseman. If the defenseman gains control of the puck, skate it out of the defensive zone, use a flip pass or freeze it along the boards if nothing else works. Line the players up as shown in the corresponding diagram. At the whistle, the forward and the two defensemen should start skating toward the far end. As the forward crosses the center red line, he should skate the puck in on goal or shoot, depending on the position of the defensemen. The coach should provide feedback to the defensemen based on their position with respect to the forward, the above criteria and the end result.

Drill 7-10; Two-On-Two. The objective of this drill is for the defenseman to learn to play the man for any two-on-two situation. While playing the man, the defenseman should attempt to angle the puck carrier toward the boards, forcing a low-percentage shot or a turnover, while his partner watches for a possible pass or rebound (if a shot is taken). The defenseman uses a stick check and body block when appropriate. If the defenseman is successful, either he or his partner can retrieve the puck and begin to move the puck out of the defensive zone. Line the players up as shown in the corresponding diagram. At the whistle, the two forwards and the two defensemen should start skating toward the far end, with the two forwards passing as they go. As the forwards cross the center red line, they can skate the puck in on goal or shoot, depending on the position of the defensemen. The coach should provide feedback to the defensemen based on their position with respect to the forwards, the above criteria and the end result.

Drill 7-11; Three-On-One. A three-on-one scenario is usually defined as two forwards and one trailing defenseman against one defenseman. The objective of this drill is for the defenseman to learn to play the pass as his first priority for any three-on-one situation. The second priority should be to angle the puck carrier toward the boards and force a low-percentage shot or strip the puck carrier of the puck. If the forward takes a shot, the defenseman should make sure that he isn't screening the goaltender and that any rebounds are covered up or can be cleared. If control of the puck is gained, skate with the puck out of the defensive zone, use a flip pass or freeze it along the boards if

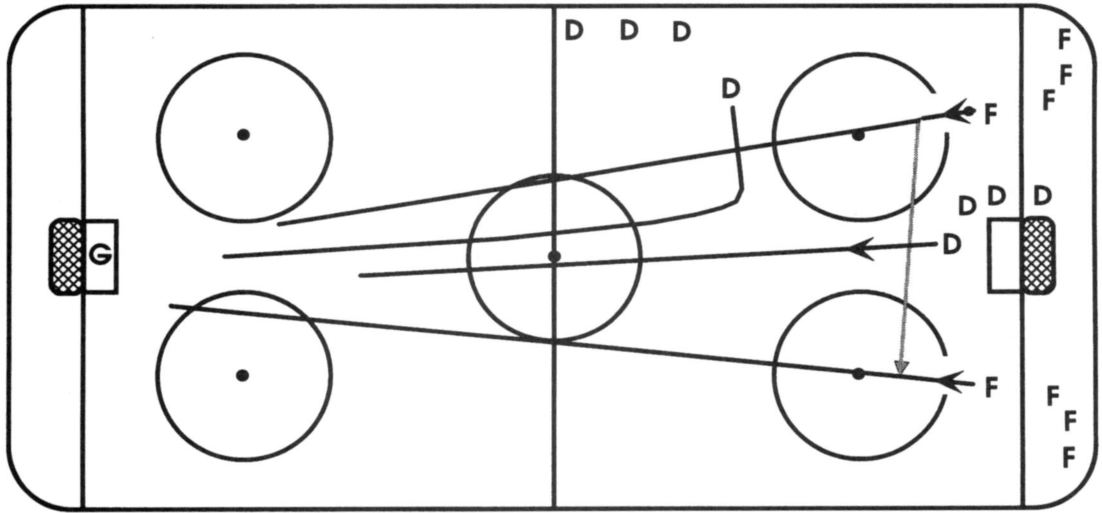

Drill 7-11; Three-On-One

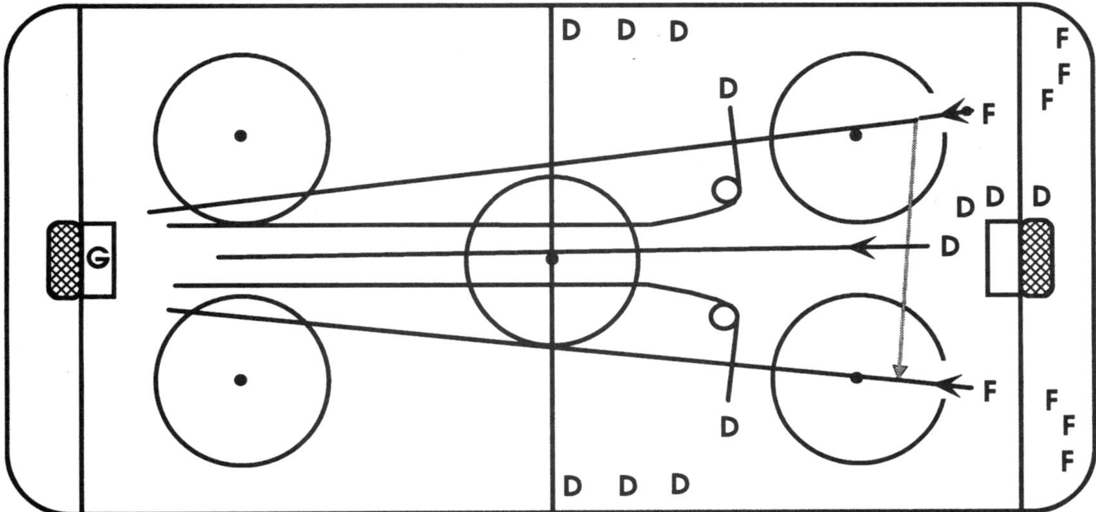

Drill 7-12; Three-On-Two

nothing else works. Communicate with your goaltender so there is no confusion about a loose puck or possible rebound. Line the players up as shown below. At the whistle, the two forwards and the defenseman start skating toward the far end, with the forwards passing the puck back and forth as they move down the playing surface. The trailing defenseman should stay about 15 feet behind the play. As the forwards cross the center red line, the defenseman should position himself so that he is between the two forwards without giving the puck carrier too much room to maneuver. The forwards can pass, skate the puck in or shoot, depending on the position of the defenseman. If the puck carrier cuts toward the net, the defenseman should attempt to play the pass to the most dangerous attacker. If the puck carrier has his head down, the defenseman can make an initial move toward him as he cuts toward the net to try and force a shot while covering any pass across or to the slot. The coach should provide feedback to the defenseman based on his position with respect to the forwards, the above criteria and the end result. After the entire drill is completed, have the forwards switch sides and the attacking and defending defensemen switch roles and repeat the drill.

Drill 7-12; Three-On-Two. The objective of this drill is for the defensemen to learn to play the pass as their first priority for any three-on-two situation. The second priority should be to angle the puck carrier toward the boards and force a low-percentage shot or strip the puck carrier of the puck. If the puck carrier has his head down, the strongside defenseman makes an initial move toward him while cutting toward the net to try and force him to shoot, while the weakside defenseman covers any pass across or to the slot. In some situations, the defenseman may have to confront the puck carrier if he has gained good scoring position. If the forward takes a shot, the defenseman should make sure that he isn't screening the goaltender and that any rebounds are covered up or can be cleared. If control of the puck is gained, skate with the puck out of the defensive zone, use a flip pass or freeze it along the boards if nothing else works. Communicate with your goaltender so there is no confusion about a loose puck or possible rebound. Line the players up as shown in the corresponding diagram. At the whistle, the two forwards and the defensemen start skating toward the far end with the forwards passing the puck back and forth as they move down the playing surface. The trailing defenseman should stay about 15 feet behind the play. As the forwards cross the center red line, they should pass, skate the puck in on goal or shoot, depending on the position of the defensemen. The coach should provide feedback to the defensemen based on their position with respect to the attackers, the above criteria and the end result. After the entire drill is completed, have the forwards switch sides and the attacking and defending defensemen switch roles and repeat the drill.

Advanced Drills

Drills from Chapters 3 through 6 that should become part of a defenseman's advanced techniques include Drills 3-16 (Power Slide), 4-12 (One-Handed Puck Control), 5-11 (Bank Passes While Skating), 5-12 (Touch Pass), 6-13 (Slap Shots), 6-18 (Screen Shots), 6-19 (One-Time Shots) and 6-20 (Deflections).

Drill 7-13; Blocking Shots With Your Body. This drill is designed to teach defensemen to block shots and to develop confidence in their blocking abilities. Set up the players as shown in the corresponding diagram. At the whistle, have the forward pass the puck from the corner to the point man (shooter). The blocking defenseman should skate toward the shooter, who will execute a low and moderate speed wrist shot toward the net while the defenseman moves as close to the puck as possible, slides and uses his shin pads to block the shot. After the shot has been taken, the defenseman should get up immediately. Work with various shots and speeds.

Variations:

- Use the snap shot and slap shot.
- Increase the speed of the shots.

Drill 7-14; Backward Stickhandling and Passing. Transitioning with the puck is a skill that will give any defenseman an extra edge in setting up an offensive attack. Line up the players as shown in the corresponding diagram. At the whistle, the forwards will pass the puck to the top of the face-off

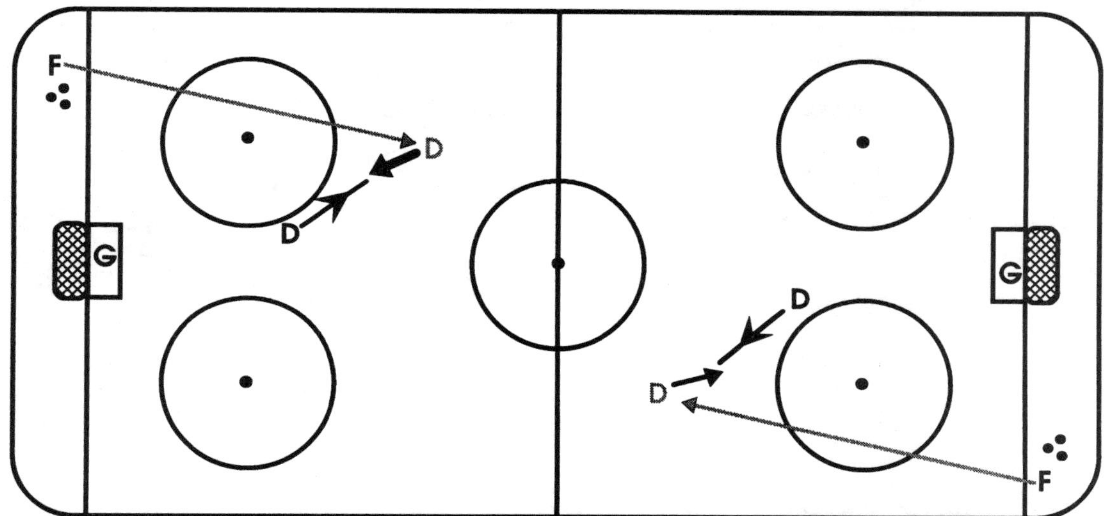

Drill 7-13; Blocking Shots With Your Body

circle and the defensemen will skate forward from the center red line at half- to three-quarter speed and pick up the puck. At the pylon, the defensemen transition to skating backward with the puck to the next pylon, where they transition to skating forward, and then pass the puck back to the forward at the center face-off circle. The defensemen should perform this drill skating both in a clockwise and counterclockwise direction.

Drill 7-15; Fake Shot. The fake shot is an advanced technique that should be used at least one time per game because it provides an opportunity for the defenseman to move in closer to the net to execute a higher percentage shot. The drill is set up as shown in the corresponding diagram. At the whistle, the forward on side 1 passes the puck to the defenseman, who takes his stick back and then forward as if to execute a slap shot, but stops just before it contacts the puck. The defenseman moves with the puck around the defender (XF) and toward the net for a real shot. Alternate the drill from side 1 to side 2 and back again until all players have performed the drill three times.

Variations:

- Use a snap shot with the fake.
- Practice alternating a fake shot and real shot in conjunction with Drill 7-13.

Drill 7-16; Rushing. This drill is designed to develop a defenseman's confidence in moving the puck up the playing surface. Line up the players as shown in the corresponding diagram. At the whistle, the

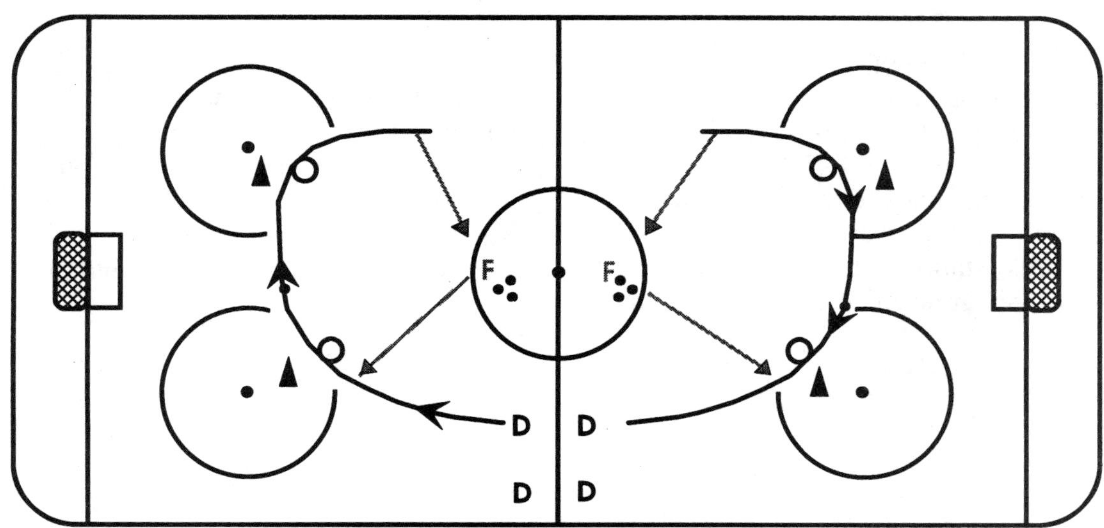

Drill 7-14; Backward Stickhandling and Passing

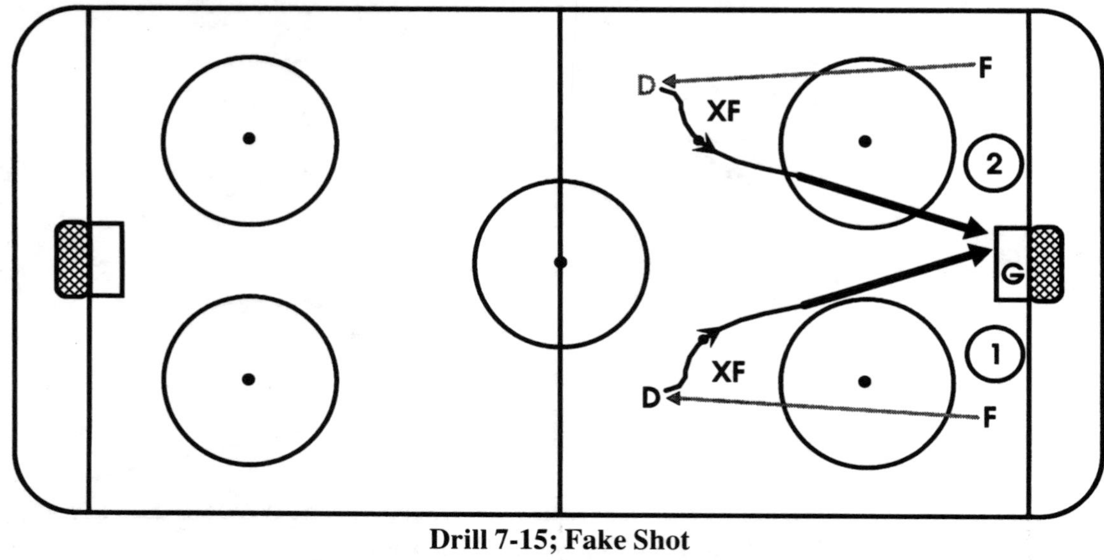

Drill 7-15; Fake Shot

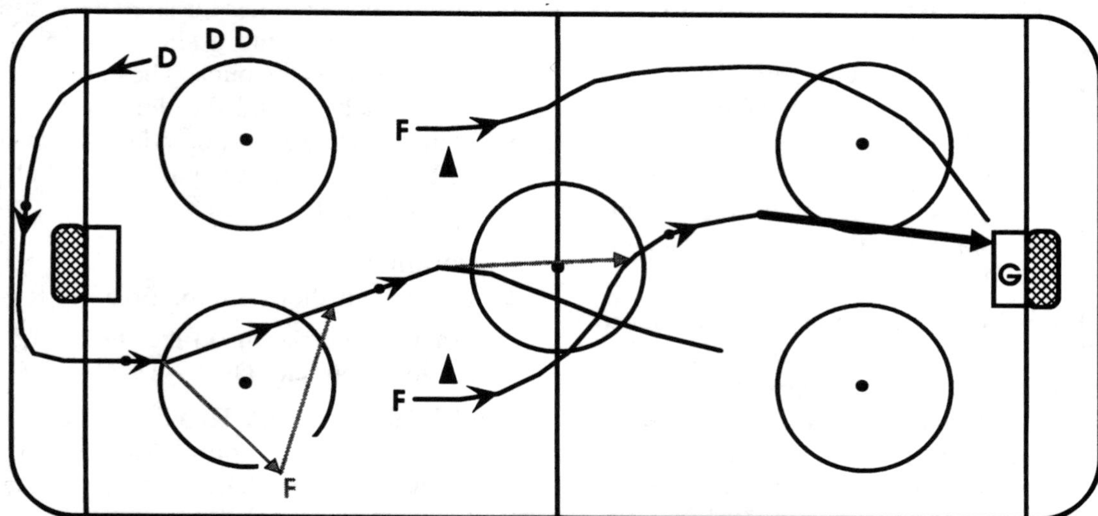

Drill 7-16; Rushing

defenseman retrieves the puck, skates behind the net and begins moving the puck up the playing surface. Once he reaches the face-off circle, he executes a give-and-go play with the stationary forward, who returns the puck to the defenseman. As soon as the stationary forward receives the pass, the two forwards (stationed by the pylons) begin skating toward the far net. The defenseman skates with the puck to the pylons and passes the puck to one of the forwards, who moves in toward the net and executes a shot on net. The other forward moves in on the net to deflect the puck, screen the goaltender or retrieve a rebound.

Variation:

- Add a defenseman in the far end to create a two-on-one scenario.

Recap

After reading and studying the material in this chapter, you should be able to answer the following questions:

1. What is the primary role of the defense?
2. Define a defensive unit. What are the requirements of a defensive unit?
3. How does communication benefit the defensive unit?
4. Define defensive reading and reacting.
5. Define four phases of full-strength roller hockey. What are the objectives of each phase?
6. List five stick checking techniques. How are each of these techniques used?
7. Where are the body blocking and riding the puck carrier out of the play techniques best used? What are the benefits of each?
8. What is the role of the defenseman in front of the defensive net?
9. Describe the zone and man-to-man defenses.
10. What are the prioritized roles of the defenseman during the One-on-One/Two-on-One/Three-on-One scenarios? For this question, assume that there is no trailing support for the one-on-one or two-on-one scenarios, and there is trailing support from a backchecking teammate for the three-on-one scenario.
11. What are the prioritized roles of the defensemen during the One-on-Two/Two-on-Two/Three-on-Two scenarios? For this question, assume that there is no trailing support for the one-on-two or two-on-two scenarios and that there is trailing support from a backchecking teammate for the three-on-two scenario. Why is it important to communicate between the two defensemen and the goaltender during the above scenarios?
12. Why is it important to learn your opponent's patterns?
13. How does a defenseman block shots with his body? What should the defenseman watch out for when performing this technique?
14. What is the benefit of a fake shot? How is it used?
15. How will you use the Defensive Player Checklist and the drills provided in this chapter to help improve individual defenseman and defensive team performance and correct existing deficiencies?

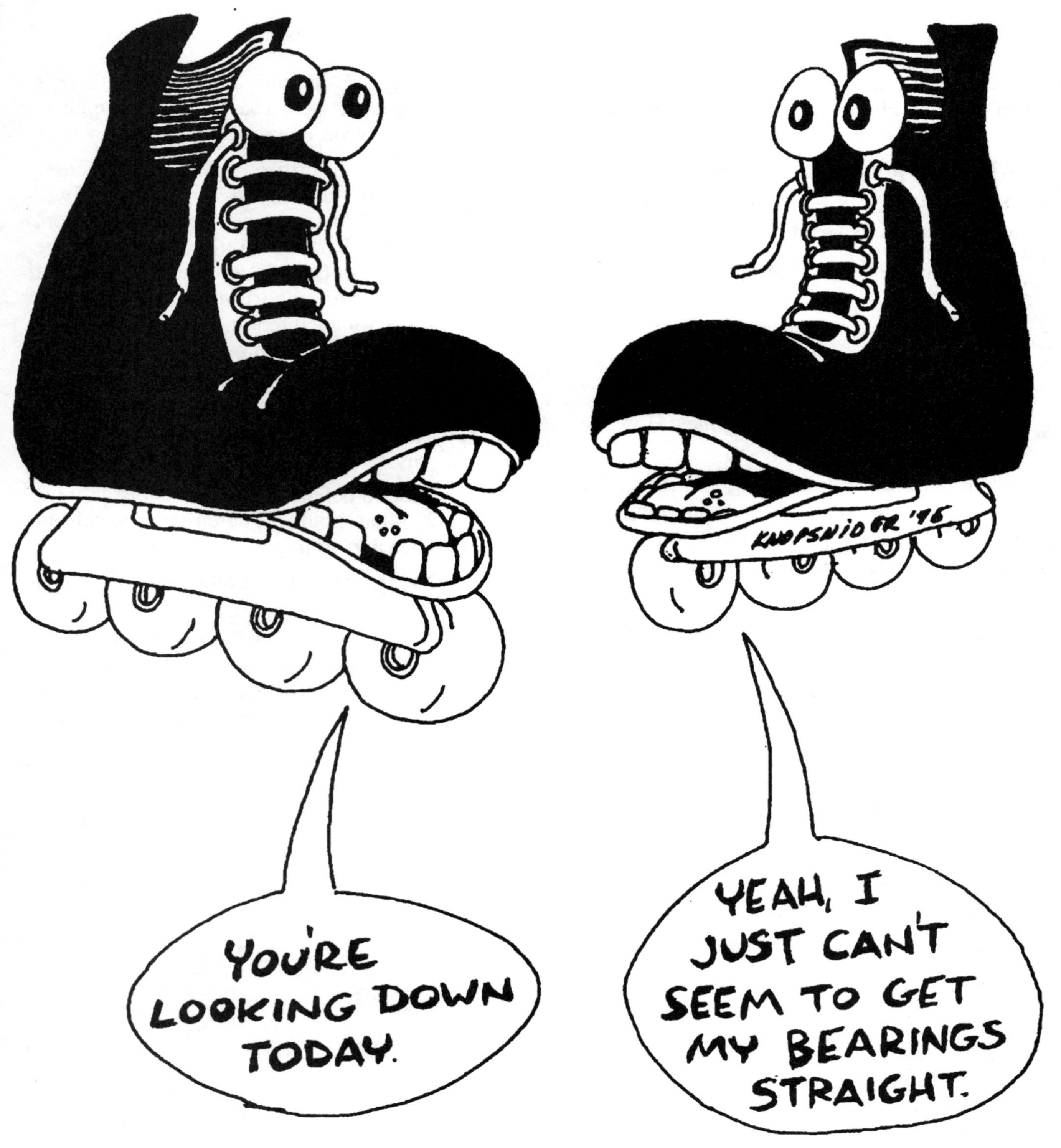
YOU'RE LOOKING DOWN TODAY.
YEAH, I JUST CAN'T SEEM TO GET MY BEARINGS STRAIGHT.

8

The Forward Faction

Highlights

This chapter addresses the role of the forwards and the integrated individual and positional skills required of this position. Chapter 8 presents the following information:

Discussion

Fundamentals

- *skating*
- *stickhandling and puck control*
- *passing and receiving*
- *shooting*
- *communicating with your partner(s)*
- *offensive reading and reacting*
- *puck fakes and body deception*
- *body blocking*
- *moving the puck into the offensive zone*
- *forechecking*
- *backchecking*

Advanced Techniques

- *learning the opponents patterns*
- *rebounds*
- *screen shot*
- *deflections*
- *one-time shot*
- *fake shot*
- *spin-o-rama*

Siller Player and Team Evaluation Profile — Offensive Player Checklist

Drills

Advanced Drills

Recap

There aren't any great men. There are just great challenges that ordinary men like you and me are forced by circumstances to meet.
— William F. Halsey —

You can do nothing about the past — but you can learn from it. Worrying about what might have been, what could have been, locks us in the past. Nothing can be done to change the past. However, the past can be a great teacher — if we learn from it.
— Roger Kirkham —

Discussion

The play of the forwards is an important factor in the success of any roller hockey team. The **primary role of the forwards** is to create offensive opportunities by setting up and scoring goals. However, successful forwards are also adept at the defensive side of the game by working hard to regain possession of the puck after a turnover in the offensive zone and to break up any attack that the opposing team has initiated. These roles define the skilled forward as a two-way player. To be a two-way player, the forward has to be proficient at reading each play and reacting correctly. By being aware of the play around you and understanding what patterns exist, the forward has the information required to make a good judgment about his participation in any offensive or defensive play.

Offensively, the forward should strive to play hard and aggressively while maintaining discipline and control; it is a double-edged sword, but it is the best way to create scoring chances. An important attribute of the forward's role is the ability to control the game. By controlling the puck, a forward can control the speed, positioning and intensity of the game. Physically, a forward should be a fluent skater since he will probably do more end-to-end skating in the course of a game than any other position. Mentally, the forward should know when to pass, shoot, execute a puck fake/body deception and how to get open when he doesn't have the puck.

What a forward does without the puck is just as important as what he does with it. When another player on your team is shooting, the forward should move to the net and get into position for a rebound, since many goals are scored off rebounds in roller hockey.

Defensively, a forward needs to think about preventing goals and creating turnovers. It's not only the defenseman's and goaltender's job to play defensively, it's everyone's job. Playing in a defensive role, a forward is required to forecheck and backcheck. A key to successful defensive play in the offensive zone starts with effective forechecking. Forechecking can create some of the most exciting action in roller hockey and, if executed effectively, can quickly transition a team from a defensive to an offensive role. To beat a good offensive team you have to do an excellent job of forechecking, because effective forechecking will have a neutralizing effect on an opposing team's offense and provide many opportunities to regain control of the puck. When the opposing team does gain control of the puck and is moving it toward your defensive end, forwards need to backcheck. Good backchecking is initiated from a determination to regain control of the puck. A good two-way roller hockey forward knows that if he does hustle back, he may get there just in time to save a goal, pick up a rebound or cover the open man.

Fundamentals

The 11 fundamental offensive techniques consist of the topics discussed in chapters three through seven — skating, stickhandling and puck control, passing and receiving, shooting, and communicating with your partner(s), as well as:

- Offensive reading and reacting.
- Fakes and body deception.
- Body blocking.
- Moving the puck into the offensive zone.
- Forechecking.
- Backchecking.

Skating. Skating is a crucial skill for all forwards to master. A forward whose skating is technically sound will skate fast, be hard to move off the puck, and tire less rapidly. The skating techniques described in Chapter 3 should be practiced so that each forward develops confidence in his ability to expertly execute each technique. The skating motion is effectively maintained using the stride-then-glide technique. Mastering the stride-then-glide technique will make any forward a very efficient skater, allow him to maintain speed and allow him to beat opponents to the puck. One or two extra steps on most defenders will allow an efficient forward to create many exciting opportunities.

Turning and crossovers should be practiced to quickly change direction. Agility is a key factor in a forward's ability to change direction. Turning is used to avoid a defender or when moving into the offensive zone for a scoring opportunity. The power turn is an effective way for a forward to beat a defender to the outside in a one-on-one situation. Making use of the crossover turn allows the forward to increase his speed and move laterally as he changes direction. Practicing drills 3-9 (Two-Skate Turning), 3-10 (Power Turns) and 3-13 (Snake) will help the forward perfect these skills.

Stickhandling and Puck Control. Stickhandling and puck control skills help the forward maintain possession of the puck while moving around the playing surface. The stickhandling and puck control techniques described in Chapter 4 should be practiced so that the forward develops confidence in his ability to move and control the puck with precision. Stickhandling skills are used by the forward while moving the puck into the offensive zone with the eventual goal of setting up a scoring opportunity. Stickhandling skills should be practiced while keeping the head and eyes looking up and around. A forward should also develop soft hands so that he has the ability to control and manipulate the puck quickly, accurately and consistently by feel. Review Drill 4-3 (Developing Soft Hands) to perfect this skill.

Puck control consists of maintaining possession of the puck while skating in close proximity to an opponent. Puck control can also allow a forward additional time to execute a play. While moving around a defenseman, the forward can control the stick and puck with one arm while keeping the defender away with his other arm. When confronting a defender for possession, control of the puck can be obtained using the skates. Once the puck is free, the forward can break away from the defender to advance the puck. Occasionally, incidental body contact will occur when a forward is carrying the puck. The forward should be strong enough on his skates to withstand the effect of the incidental body contact while still being able to control the puck. Drills 4-7 (Puck Control And Turns), 4-13 (One-Handed Puck Control Past A Defender) and 4-14 (Puck Control Using The Skates) will help the forward become proficient at puck control.

Passing and Receiving. Passing and receiving, used in conjunction with stickhandling and puck control, are essential to moving the puck into and around the offensive zone. The passing and receiving techniques described in Chapter 5 should be practiced so that the forward develops confidence in his ability to expertly pass the puck to a teammate or receive a pass from a teammate. Passing is the quickest and most effective way for a forward to move the puck up the playing surface. By using peripheral vision, the forward can avoid telegraphing his intentions to the defenders and will have a better chance for passing success. After the forward makes the pass, he should get into position for a return pass or decoy a defender away from the play.

There are a variety of passes for the forward to choose from:

- The sweep pass is the most commonly used and most accurate pass.
- The snap pass is used in conjunction with stickhandling to quickly and deceptively move the puck to a teammate.
- The flip pass can be used to pass the puck to a teammate over a stick or fallen defender.
- The around-the-boards pass allows the forward to quickly move the puck to an open forward who is positioned along the boards.
- The give-and-go pass can be used when entering the offensive zone or to move around a defender.
- The bank pass can be used to pass the puck off the boards to another forward or back to the passing forward as a solo give-and-go.
- The open area pass moves the puck to an unoccupied area of the playing surface when a teammate anticipates the pass.
- The drop pass is used to deceive an opponent or used in conjunction with a goaltender screen play.
- The touch pass can be used to quickly redirect the puck to another player.
- The reverse pass is a deceptive pass used to confuse an opponent into the wrong coverage.
- The weave pass is used in the same manner as the reverse pass.
- The skate pass can be used to move the puck to a teammate when the forward's stick is tied up.

When receiving a pass, the forward should read the defensive coverage and react by getting into an open area and communicating to the passer that he is available. Forwards communicate with their teammates by pointing their stick in the direction that they want the pass to go, tapping it on the playing surface, raising it in the air, or calling a teammate's name or call sign. The forwards should receive the pass by correctly angling their stick blade and using soft hands, described earlier. In some cases, passes will not be on target and the forward will have to turn or reach to receive it. Other times, he will have to receive it with his skates or with his glove (if it is the air).

Shooting. An effective shooting technique is the main ingredient for scoring goals. A forward can develop effective shooting and scoring skills by utilizing the techniques described in Chapter 6. The ability of a forward to get off a good shot is crucial to the offensive game of roller hockey. When a forward is shooting, he should shoot quickly and accurately from a location that has a high-percentage opportunity of scoring (refer to Figures 6-2 and 6-3). Unless the forward is playing against a goaltender who remains low in the crease, such as a butterfly goaltender, has a clear opening up top, or knows that the goaltender has a weak glove, he should keep his shots low. Low shots have a greater chance of being deflected, provide better rebounds and work more effectively when the goaltender is screened by a teammate or an opponent.

The moment the forward gets the puck and has a chance to score, his first thought should be to get into the best possible scoring position. If the forward is not able to get into a good scoring position, he should look around for a teammate who may be open and pass the puck to create a better scoring opportunity. Many beginning roller hockey forwards have a habit of moving in too close to the net before they shoot because they believe that they need to be as close to the net as possible to score. This habit is the main reason they miss many scoring opportunities. Moving too close to the net gives the goaltender added time to react and allows him to take advantage of the decreased shooting area.

The type of shot used by a forward has a great deal to do with creating the element of surprise, noting the position of the goaltender at the time of the shot and how far you are in front of the net.

- The wrist shot is the most accurate shot in roller hockey and should be chosen when the forward is close to the goaltender (generally between 5 and 25 feet) or just needs to get a quick shot on net. Since this shot does not require a back swing, you can release the puck quickly. This shot is effective using both the forehand and backhand techniques.
- The snap shot allows the forward to get a quick, hard shot on net. When stickhandling in on a goaltender, this shot can be used effectively to catch a goaltender off guard, since it can be executed in-stride. The snap shot is a valuable weapon because it is quick and accurate up to 30 feet from the net.
- The flip shot is generally used when the forward is close to the goaltender (within 10 feet), such as when he has skated in to retrieve a rebound, and is most effective when the goaltender or a covering defenseman is flat on the playing surface in front of the net. Like the wrist shot, the flip shot can be executed quickly due to the lack of a backswing and is effective using both the forehand and backhand techniques.
- The slap shot is valuable when the forward is forced to shoot from far out because the puck can be shot with greater speed and from greater distances than with any other shot. This shot should only be used when the forward has enough time for a backswing. Also, since the slap shot requires a fair amount of upper body strength, it is not recommended for players under 10 years old.

Communicating With Your Partner(s). An **offensive unit** is defined as two players operating in an offensive role. Other players can be included depending upon the circumstances of the game (such as a trailing defenseman acting as the third man in on an offensive attack), but for the purpose of this chapter, two forwards are considered an offensive unit. Working effectively as an offensive unit requires:

- Each forward to be knowledgeable of and be able to execute the individual skills described above.
- The desire to perform as a team by complementing each other's skills.
- Experience — gained from playing with several offensive partners over time.

- Making mistakes — and learning from those mistakes.
- Most importantly, constructive communication between the members of the offensive unit as well as feedback from the coach, other teammates and practice/game videos.

Can you think of some other factors required of an effective offensive unit?

Communication is the exchange of information and is dependent upon the personnel involved. Verbal communication is very important, but you shouldn't rely on it too much while on the playing surface. There are so many things happening so fast that it is impossible to tell your partner everything you are thinking. Spend time after each shift discussing the effectiveness of your offensive strategies and sharing information about opposing players. Knowledge of your partner's tendencies will often be the deciding factor as to who will initiate an offensive play or who will cover a particular attacker. Get to know your partner, but just as important, be realistic about your own abilities. Knowing your own strengths and weaknesses, and developing your game around them, is critical.

Offensive Reading and Reacting refers to the ability of the offensive unit's players to perceive the play of the opponents around them and to respond appropriately. As with defensive reading and reacting, total situational awareness and accurate perception form the basis upon which effective offensive reading and reacting occur. An example of offensive reading and reacting occurs when the offensive unit reads that the defensemen have gained control of the puck, the offensive unit normally reacts by getting into an open area to receive a pass to start a breakout play. Another example of offensive reading and reacting could occur when the opponent's defenseman gains control of the puck in the offensive zone. The forward, in this case, could begin to aggressively forecheck the defenseman with the puck, while the other forward skates in to gain control of the puck. In both cases, the offensive unit gathers information from the players around it and responds to this information based upon its ability, experience, and knowledge to coordinate actions for a successful end result. Quick reaction to a specific situation won't come from careful planning, but from plenty of practice. Many smart offensive moves can be implemented if the offensive unit uses an analytical approach while playing and finds out what kind of moves are most effective.

Table 7-1 provides some simplified, yet effective, underlying information with respect to reading and reacting and should help the coach and players in determining the proper overall reaction for a particular read. In roller hockey, there are four phases of the full strength game. The first phase occurs when you are in your defensive zone and are in an offensive role (i.e., you have control of the puck). Your objective should be to break out of your defensive zone. When you are in the transition zone and are in an offensive role, your objective should be to move the puck into the offensive zone. The third phase of the game occurs when you are in the offensive zone and in an offensive role. Your objective should be to score. The fourth phase occurs when you are operating in a defensive or transitional role. A transitional role is neither offensive nor defensive and occurs when neither team has definite control of the puck, such as when each team is trying to gain control of the puck immediately following a face-off. This could happen in any of the three zones and your only objective should be to gain control of the puck.

Puck Fakes and Body Deception

These skills have many similarities to the discussion on deking the goaltender, described in Chapter 6. In both cases, the intent is to defeat the opponent. In the case of deking, the forward is attempting to get the puck past the goaltender and into the net and in the case of a puck fake or body deception, the forward is attempting to get both the puck and player past the defender(s) to eventually move the puck and/or player into a scoring position. The player who develops a good variety of effective puck fakes and combines these with convincing body deception moves will present a real challenge to the best of defenders.

Puck fakes are used to deceive a defender and to create offensive opportunities from anywhere on the playing surface. A successful puck fake makes the defender read that the puck is going in one direction when it will actually move in another direction. Puck faking essentially boosts a stick handler's power with the ability to deceive an opponent. Puck fakes are not roller hockey's nirvana, and they should not be used every time a player wants to get around a defender. It is important that a player knows when to use a puck fake and when to pass the puck to beat a man. Many plays are broken up by the defending team when a player attempts to execute a puck fake instead of passing. Generally, **a player should use a puck fake** when he does not have a teammate in a position for a pass, when the player is in close proximity and a pass cannot be made, or in a one-on-one situation with no trailing teammate. A cardinal sin in roller hockey is to execute a puck fake deep in your own end of the rink when you are the last man out since this could lead to a breakaway if you lose the puck to a defender. To effectively utilize a puck fake, determine the defender's speed, direction, whether he is sweeping his stick, looking up or down at the puck, or off balance; all are factors that can be taken advantage of. Don't use the same move all the time (i.e., going to the forehand side), as overused fakes *will* result in turnovers. Puck fakes can provide spectacular results, but don't forget when to pass or shoot.

Before you can begin building a reserve of effective puck fakes, it is imperative that you:

- Become a better-than-average stick handler, which includes carrying the puck with your head and eyes up.
- Learn to read the eyes and body action of defenders.
- Become very agile on your skates to be able to change direction quickly.
- Develop an effective wrist, snap and flip shot.

A classic example of a puck fake is as follows: The puck carrier approaches the defender straight on, and as he gets close to the defender, takes a stride to the left side and moves the puck over at the same time. Then the puck carrier quickly moves back to the right side, going around the defender who has covered the first move. To be most effective, a puck carrier must go right though with his first move occasionally so that he will not develop a definite pattern to which the defenders will soon catch on.

The **secrets of successful faking** are timing the move properly so as not to be either too soon or too late, making the puck fake convincingly, and perhaps most important, taking advantage of the fake by putting on added speed at the end of the move. If the fake is started too soon, the defender will have time to recover and cover the final movement. If it is started too late, the puck carrier will be so close to the defender that, when he moves back to his original position, he may get stick checked or run into a body block. The exact time to fake is difficult to determine as it depends upon the speed the puck carrier is traveling and whether the defender is stationary, moving toward the puck carrier, or backing up. As a general rule, the puck fake should be started just outside the stick checking range of the defender (about five or six feet away). This is a point, however, that the puck carrier should figure out for himself by experimenting. If he analyzes his play intelligently, he will soon find out for himself when he should fake a little later or a little sooner against certain types of players. The hardest type of man to beat with a fake is a defender backing up in front of the puck carrier.

Body deception refers to those body movements a player, puck carrier or non-puck carrier, makes to deceive a defender into reacting incorrectly or making the wrong read regarding which move the player is going to use or in which direction he has decided to go. Included are maneuvers such as shifting, body weaving, head faking and shoulder dipping. Body deception does not depend on any special talent inherited by the player and it can be developed by any player willing to work on it. There are some players who will learn it easier than others because they have better coordination, flexibility and agility. However, any player can become skillful regardless of body type. Each player, after he learns the fundamentals of deception will develop certain personal variations and styles that will make his shift or weave a little different from those of any other player. The secret is to train the muscles of the body (primarily the upper body) so that they will react quickly to any direction the mind dictates. For example, if the player is skating down the playing surface, comes to a defender, and then thinks *I will shift to the left and then go to the right*, his body will react smoothly and efficiently if his muscles have been trained in that type of movement. If he has never performed the movement before, the response to his mental thought will not be as efficient. This is one reason why top level results can rarely be gained when a player just tries new moves in a game without first practicing them.

Head and shoulder moves are **generally the most effective** against good defenders. Good defenders focus the majority of their attention on your chest. Because your head and shoulders are closest to your chest, their movement has the greatest chance of fooling the defender into thinking the rest of your body will move in the same direction. The lower half of the body moves very little from side-to-side during a head and shoulder move. Also, subtle movements of the head and shoulders are more effective than large ones, and several may be required to *sell* the move to the defender. **Selling** is the ability of a player to make a puck fake or body deception move believable to a defender. Once sold, look for the defender to move his stick or body as this will tell you that the deception worked. If his body or stick moves noticeably in one direction, your next move should be your final move in the opposite direction. If the movement of the defender is slight, your next move should be the in-between move, with the final move to follow in the same direction as the defender's slight movement.

Fourteen types of puck fakes, body deception moves and combinations are presented in this section. Experiment with this list, and then vary some of the tactics to create some of your own. This tailoring process allows each player to incorporate specific moves at which he is proficient. If the player is to develop top-level skill at performing these various moves, he must do them over and over again. As with puck fakes, just trying them in games is not enough. The player must work on them during practice. Variations of these moves can be developed by the player according to each situation. Every player should learn each of these basic moves because he will then avoid being in the position of being stick checked time and time again because his opponents have him tagged as always going one way when using a puck fake or body deception move. The more a player experiments and practices with the various possibilities, the more situations he will find use for them. The thing to do is to learn the basic fake to either side and then work on developing variations. The techniques presented here include the fake pass, fake against the boards, flip out, forehand shift, backhand shift, backhand-to-forehand shift, forehand-to-backhand shift, slip-through, slip across, change of pace, the weave, shoulder turn, shoulder drop and the flip through.

- **Fake pass.** This can be a very effective fake which will frequently draw the defender out of position. It is most effective when there is a teammate moving up the playing surface with you, but it can be used even when you are alone, because the defender will often act involuntarily to cover the fake pass, even though he may *know* that there is no one there. As the puck carrier gets to a spot about five or six feet away from the defender (or the distance found to be ideal through experimentation by the player), he turns his head to either side as if he is looking at a teammate in order to aim the pass, and actually starts a pass. However, as the puck gets well to that side, he stops it, and then moves the puck quickly back to the other side and goes past the defender. This move is most effective against a defender who is good at intercepting passes because he is always looking for a chance to intercept the pass. The puck carrier should make sure, as with all moves, that he can fake equally well to either side. Selling the fake pass is actually not accomplished with much puck movement, but rather with a tensing of the arms and shoulders toward the direction of the fake pass. Once you've faked the pass, your next action must be quick, or your fake was simply a waste of time.
- **Against the boards.** This type of fake is used when the play is at the side of the rink, and is especially effective if the defender is moving slowly or standing still. A good time to use this fake is just as you are leaving your defensive zone. Approach the defender, then, just before you get within stick checking distance, shoot the puck against the boards at a forward angle, shift around the defender, and then pick the puck up again and continue skating. By using this fake, the puck carrier can often get the defender to move in toward the boards, giving the puck carrier room to get around him quickly.
- **Flipout.** This play is particularly effective when used by a puck carrier who can break quickly. It is mainly for use when the puck is recovered in a scramble or if a defender has the puck carrier cut off; for example, if the defender is in front of the puck carrier when the puck carrier is in the corner. The idea is to flip the puck quickly into open area and then break after it immediately. When the puck carrier flips the puck, the defender will also move and go after it, even though his best play is to block you with his body. The puck carrier has the advantage because he knows what he is going to do and will

probably beat the defender to the puck because he starts sooner. The puck carrier will also be facing the direction in which he will go after the puck, while the defender will have to make at least a half turn before he can go after the puck. The average player, when he gets the puck after a scramble or when he is cut off, tries to stick handle out of trouble and is frequently stick checked or body blocked. The best plan is usually to flip the puck into an open area and break after it.

- **Forehand shift.** This fake is performed by skating directly toward the defender with the puck in front of you. When you are about six feet from him, move quickly to your forehand and move the puck around him. Use your arm and body to keep the defender from successfully stick checking you.
- **Backhand shift.** This fake is performed like the forehand shift except you move to your backhand and then move around the defender. Again, use your arm and body to keep the defender from successfully stick checking you.
- **Backhand-to-forehand shift.** The puck carrier skates toward the defender and when he is about six or seven feet away from him, shifts the puck to his backhand, moves it quickly back to his forehand side, and then moves around the defender. This fake requires above average puck control skills to master.
- **Forehand-to-backhand shift**. This is the opposite of the backhand-to-forehand shift described above. Move the puck to your forehand side, move it quickly back to your backhand side and then move around the defender.
- **Slip-through.** This is a fake in which the puck carrier slips the puck through the defender's legs and then goes quickly around him to pick it up again. This fake is effective when the defender has slowed down, has his head down and has a large enough space between the legs. Though straightforward, this is one of the most effective fakes when properly timed. The move is most effective when prefaced by a couple of fakes to lead the defender to believe that you are going to carry the puck around him. The puck carrier should make sure he does not always go around the same side to pick up the puck.
- **Slip across.** With the slip across, as opposed to the slip-through, the puck travels across and under the defender's stick instead of between his skates. Set this move up using a shift to one side to get the defender to shift his weight to that side, and then slip the puck across and between the defender's skates and the heel of the stick. The player shifts directions and then picks up the puck on the other side of the defender.
- **Change of pace.** As with many other sports, the ability to change pace is a valuable skill. By using pace changes it is possible to get free from a defender, deceive him while carrying the puck, and be very difficult to cover. A combination of pace and direction changes can often make a defenseman look bad. To change pace, decrease or increase the stride length on the back foot, since it is one of the main factors that governs speed. The most common change of pace move has the player closing in on a defender at about three quarter speed. When he gets about a sticks length away, he bursts into full speed. The defender will probably try to time his move according to the speed of your approach and when you suddenly change your pace it will throw him off. This move is especially useful when a defenseman is skating backward slowly and there is room to move on either side. You must possess excellent agility to be successful with this fake.
- **The weave** is an effective move to use when there isn't much room to maneuver or when you are trying to beat a defender who is easily faked. When the puck carrier is about five or six feet away from a defender, he bends his upper body to one side and then goes quickly in the opposite direction. Alternatively, he can move the upper body to the left, come part way back, and then go back to the left and around the defender. Another variation is when the puck carrier gets nine or 10 feet from the defender, he starts his upper body weaving back and forth to try and unsettle the defender, and tries to force the defender into making the first move. If the defender moves one way, the puck carrier goes around the other way.
- **Shoulder turn.** This is another type of upper body move that can be used to deceive the defender and is a variation of the weave. Instead of bending to the side as in the weave, the puck

carrier turns his shoulders, as if he were going to head in that direction. Then he quickly moves his shoulders around in the opposite direction and goes around that side. As with the weave, there are many variations that can be effectively used to defeat a defender.

- The **shoulder drop** is another variation of upper body deception. Just as the puck carrier gets to within stick checking distance of the defender, the puck carrier leans his head to one side and drops the shoulder to the same side. He then moves with the puck back to the other side and goes around the defender. As with all body deception moves, the puck carrier should often try the shoulder drop and then occasionally go in that direction to keep the defenders guessing.
- **Flip through.** This is an excellent move to use when you are the lone forward against two defensemen. The idea behind this technique is to move as if you are going to try to split the defensemen, then if the defensive pair comes together to body block you, flip the puck in between them and shift around to one side and pick up the puck behind them. Timed just right, this move is very effective, especially if you are agile and the defensive pair are on the slow side. This play is often spoiled because the puck carrier flips the puck too fast, causing it to slide too close to the goaltender or the puck is flipped too soon, giving away your intention. Once the player has done this move a few times, the defensive pair will be set up for it, and the next time the forward can actually move in between the two defensemen (split the defense).

Here are some additional guidelines to follow when deciding on which type of puck fake or body deception technique to use and when to use them:

- If the defenseman plays the puck, then use a puck fake on him.
- If the defenseman plays the man, head straight for the defenseman, and then use change of direction and change of pace moves to disrupt his timing. Puck fakes are less effective against a defenseman who plays the man.
- If the defenseman is strong on one side (for example, the stick side), fake to that side, since he will probably be more eager to try and use his stick, and then move quickly to the other side.
- If the defenseman is slow, make him skate fast and then make your play. Use skating moves such as change of pace and direction or moving to open playing surface to beat slow opponents. The more you make him move the better your chances are.
- If the defenseman backs up, slow down and let him back up. Try to force him into making a play, or use the defenseman as a screen for a shot on goal.
- Try to head for the defender you are most confident in beating.

Body blocking is a technique used by a forward to slow the speed of an opponent while providing a teammate the opportunity to gain or keep possession of the puck without being challenged. The approach to body blocking is to minimize the opponent's progress in a particular direction (toward your teammate) without interfering with it. A body block used by a forward is similar to a basketball player setting a pick against an opponent. To execute an effective body block, the forward must intercept the opponent by crossing in front of his path and maintain this posture for a second or two. This will force the opponent to take evasive action or run into you. Either way, you have succeeded in rerouting the opponent and allowing your teammate a second or two of uninterrupted puck control. If an official views the body block as interfering with the forward progress of the opponent, a warning or penalty could result.

Moving the puck into the offensive zone. Forcing the opposition into making bad plays is good offensive roller hockey and is critical in the offensive end. The assets of quickness and correctly reading a play will allow you to win many battles in the offensive zone. As you move into the offensive zone, the individual forward or the offensive unit has to consider just how to play the attack. Some general guidelines to consider when deciding **how to structure an attack** are as follows:

- Always skate with the puck to draw the individual defenseman or defensive unit out of position. By forcing the defensive unit to move, you have a better chance to create offensive opportunities by forcing the defense into making mistakes.
- Pass the puck if a teammate is available and is in a better scoring position than you are.

- Shoot the puck if you are in a good scoring position, have a screen shot or want to force a rebound.
- Use a puck fake/body deception move if there is no one to pass to, you are far enough out from the goaltender to make this move effective (about 25 feet) or you aren't in a good shooting location.

Many forwards tend to head for the defense and then improvise at the last moment, *hoping* to get by. They will be more successful if they practice the various plays since they will react more effectively using instinct rather than improvisation. When the puck carrier has either one or two teammates along, whether they are well-guarded or not, the situation is a great deal different. He can then use his teammates as decoys or start a maneuver designed to set up an actual play, which one of his teammates can finish. Non-puck carrier(s) should take their cues from the puck carrier. They should try to maneuver themselves into an open position, and they should base the moves they make on the puck carrier, the defenders and the open playing surface available. Forwards should avoid the kind of mental attitude that causes them to wait for opportunities to develop. The player who is always working to get into position will be able to set up many opportunities whereas the player who just waits for an opportunity to come his way may wait a long time. The wise coach will give his players plenty of practice at beating the defense. During practice the coach should make sure that his players are trying definite plays and not just ad-libbing. Though roller hockey is a game in which the player must do a lot of improvising because of the ever changing play patterns, he will be able to select the right move more often if he has learned as many basic maneuvers as possible during practice.

All of the information gained by reading the play is used in many scenarios. Nine scenarios are defined in Table 8-1. The table defines the situational scenario; whether there is offensive, defensive, or trailing support; and the priority plays that the offensive player or unit utilize.

A **one-on-one** scenario is defined as one attacker against one defender and usually consists of a forward against an opposing defenseman. As the forward moves into the offensive zone, there are two scenarios that will be addressed; a one-on-one scenario with either an opponent trailing or no trailer and a one-on-one scenario with a trailing teammate (refer to Table 8-1). In the first scenario, the forward (OF) has read the play and determined that there is only one defender to beat (XD), as shown in Figure 8-1. This requires the forward to:

- Execute a puck fake/body deception move if the forward is confident in his faking and deception skills or the defenseman is more than 25 feet from the goaltender.

Scenario	Trailing Support	Priority Plays
1-on-1	Opponent or None	Fake or Shoot
1-on-1	Teammate	Pass or Shoot
1-on-2	Opponent or None	Fake or Shoot
1-on-2	Teammate	Pass or Fake
2-on-1	Opponent, Teammate or None	Pass or Shoot
2-on-2	Opponent or None	Pass or Fake
2-on-2	Teammate	Pass or Shoot
3-on-1	Opponent, Teammate or None	Pass or Shoot
3-on-2	Opponent, Teammate or None	Pass or Shoot

Table 8-1; Fundamental Offensive Zone Scenarios

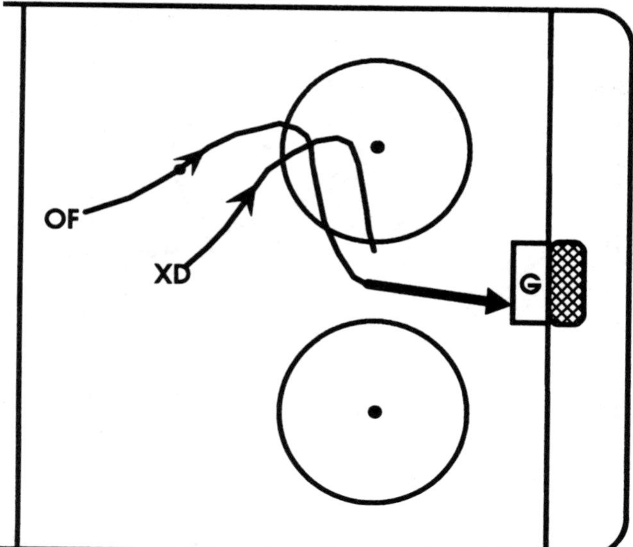

Figure 8-1; One-On-One With No Trailer

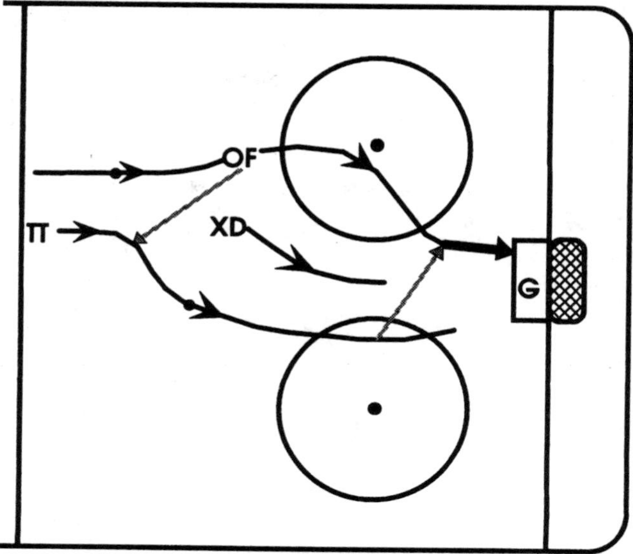

Figure 8-2; One-On-One With A Trailing Teammate

- Utilize the defenseman as a screen, shoot the puck toward an open area on net, and move in for a possible rebound if the forward is not confident in his faking and deception skills or the defenseman is less than 25 feet from the goaltender.

In the second scenario, the forward (OF) has read the play and determined that he has one defender to beat (XD) and that he has support in the form of a trailing teammate (TT), as shown in Figure 8-2. This requires the forward to:

- Pass the puck to TT if he is open and head to the net for a return pass, rebound or deflection. TT should pass the puck back to OF if the defenseman has left him open or shoot the puck if OF is covered.
- Carry the puck to the outside of the defenseman, trying to draw XD away from the central defensive zone (see Figure 8-2). If XD moves toward OF, then OF should pass the puck to TT for a quick shot or deke. If XD stays between the two attackers, then OF should shoot the puck and have TT move in for a rebound.

One-on-two. The fundamental principle that should govern the puck carrier's choice of plays during a one-on-two scenario is knowing that the defensive unit is always easier to beat when it has to move. If they can stay in position, the defensemen are tough to beat because they can operate as one effective unit, covering a lot of playing surface. If the puck carrier can maneuver so that he can take the defensive unit on one-by-one, the situation becomes obviously better. A one-on-two scenario is defined as one attacker against two defenders and usually consists of a forward against a defensive unit. As the forward moves into the offensive zone, there are two scenarios that will be addressed: a one-on-two scenario with either an opponent trailing or no trailer and a one-on-two scenario with a trailing teammate (refer to Table 8-1). In the first scenario, the forward (OF) has read the play and determined that there are two defenders to beat (LD and RD), as shown in Figure 8-3. This scenario requires the forward to:

- Execute a puck fake/body deception move if the forward is confident in his faking and deception skills or the defensive unit is more than 25 feet from the goaltender. A good play to use is for the puck carrier to fake a shot between the defensemen or between the legs of one defenseman and then shift out and around. The fake shot between the defensemen may cause the defensive pair to stiffen momentarily in order to protect themselves or to attempt to block the shot, which will give the puck carrier that all important fraction of a second to move around them. A fake shot aimed at one defenseman is often successful because it can neutralize both defensemen. The defenseman at whom the shot is aimed

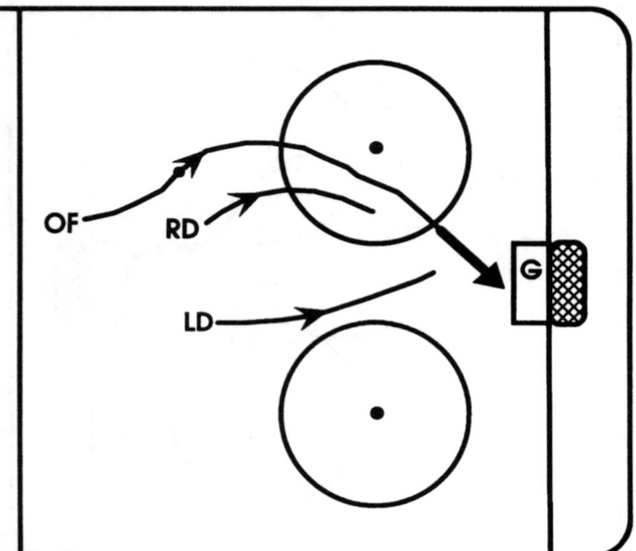

Figure 8-3; One-On-Two With No Trailer

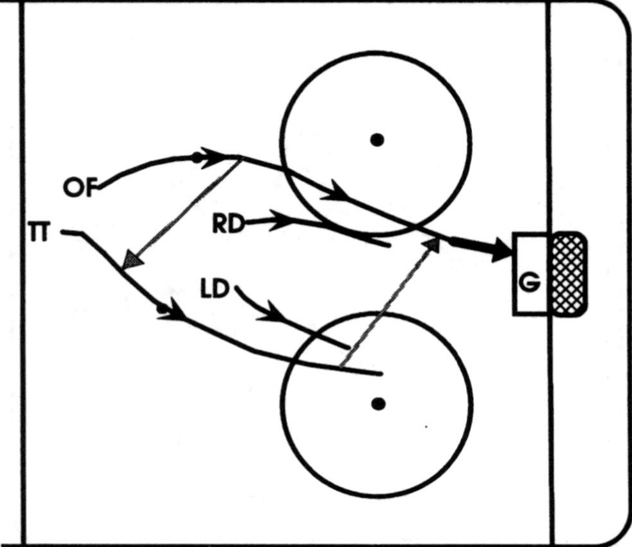

Figure 8-4; One-On-Two With A Teammate Trailing

is likely to tense up in preparation to block the shot, and the other defenseman is likely to go in toward the net to clear any possible rebound.

- Utilize one of the defensemen as a screen, shoot the puck toward an open area on net, and move in for a possible rebound if the forward is not confident in his faking and deception skills or the defensemen is less than 25 feet from the goaltender.

In the second scenario, the forward (OF) has read the play and determined that there are two defenders to beat (LD and RD) and that he has support in the form of a trailing teammate (TT), as shown in Figure 8-4. This scenario requires the forward to:

- Pass the puck to TT if he is open and head to the net for a return pass, rebound or deflection. TT should pass the puck back to OF if the defenseman has left him open, or shoot the puck if OF is covered.
- Execute a puck fake/body deception move if the forward is confident in his faking and deception skills or the defensive unit is more than 25 feet from the goaltender. A good play to use is the fake shot.

Two-on-one. In this situation, the offensive unit *should* win out every time. Even if the defenseman plays the two-on-one well, the offensive unit should at least end up with a shot on goal. One of the main reasons that this type of attack fails is due to the poor position in which the offensive unit approaches the defenseman, giving the defenseman a chance to cover both attackers. The attackers should always approach this scenario in such a way as to force the defender into making a move that will place the non-puck carrier in an open position from which he can quickly go in on goal. Another reason for failure is that the timing of the play is faulty because a pass is made too soon or too late. This is the result of an incorrect read of the play by either or both the puck carrier and the non-puck carrier. A two-on-one scenario is defined as two attackers against one defender and usually consists of an offensive unit against a defenseman. As the forwards move into the offensive zone, there are two scenarios that will be addressed: a two-on-one scenario with either an opponent trailing or no trailer and a two-on-one scenario with a trailing teammate. In both cases, the pass should be the first priority with the shot being the second. In the first scenario, the offensive unit (LF and RF) have read the play and determined that there is one defender to beat (XD), as shown in Figure 8-5. This scenario requires the forwards to:

- Utilize LF by putting on a burst of speed and move to the outside of XD. This causes XD to concentrate on LF, leaving RF to head straight for the net. Once RF is near the net and open, LF passes the puck to RF who puts a shot on net. If XD does not move back to cover LF, LF should continue toward the net heading for the

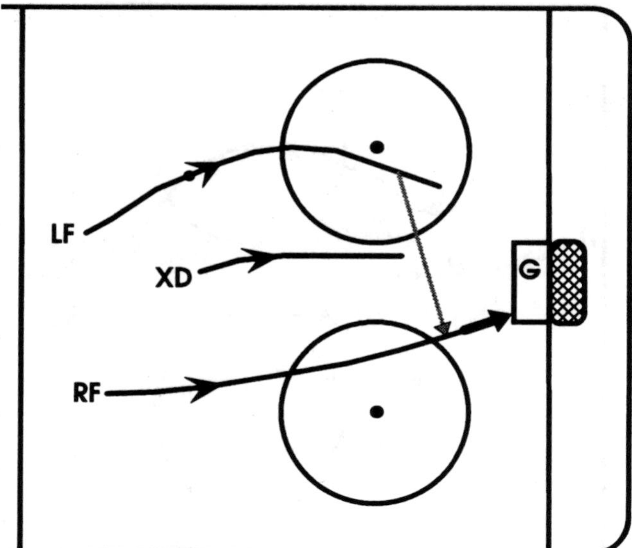

Figure 8-5; Two-On-One With No Trailer

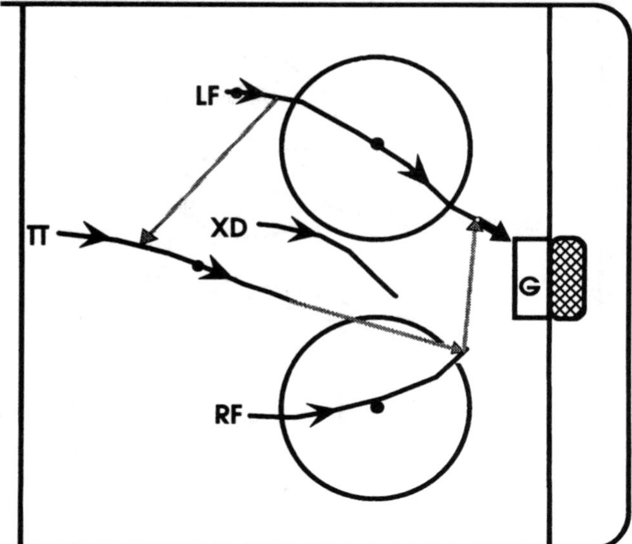

Figure 8-6; Two-On-One With A Teammate Trailing

slot, and put a shot on goal, with RF moving in for a rebound.

- Utilize the defenseman as a screen (if he is in such a position), shoot the puck (generally a low shot) toward an open area on net, and have the other forward move in for a possible rebound. This would occur when the defenseman is blocking a pass to the non-puck carrier, while leaving the puck carrier with an open shot on net.

In the second scenario, the forwards have read the play and determined that there is one defender to beat (XD) and that they have support in the form of a trailing teammate (TT), as shown in Figure 8-6. This should provide at least one excellent scoring opportunity and requires the forwards to:

- Utilize LF to put on a burst of speed and move to the outside of XD. LF can then pass the puck to TT (if he is open) and head to the net for a return pass, rebound, or deflection. As this is occurring, RF can head for the net, receive a pass from TT and either shoot or pass to LF, who can shoot. In either case, the action is occurring at a rapid pace, and each player needs to quickly and correctly read the play.
- Utilize the defenseman as a screen (if he is in such a position), shoot the puck (generally a low shot) toward an open area on net, and have the other attackers move in for a possible rebound.

Two-on-two. In many ways, this scenario can be viewed similarly to the one-on-one, with each defenseman attempting to cover one forward. A two-on-two scenario is defined as two attackers against two defenders and usually consists of an offensive unit against a defensive unit. As the forwards move into the offensive zone, there are two scenarios that will be addressed: a two-on-two scenario with either an opponent trailing or no trailer and a two-on-two scenario with a trailing teammate. In the first scenario, the offensive unit (LF and RF) have read the play and determined that there are two defenders to beat (LD and RD), as shown in Figure 8-7. This scenario requires the forwards to:

- Utilize LF to carry the puck between RD and the boards, trying to outskate RD as he cuts in toward the goal. In the meantime, RF moves to the inside of LD and heads straight for the net. Once RF is open, LF should make a pass to RF who can put a shot on net.
- Utilize LF to head right at the defensive pair as if he is going to try to go through them. Just before he reaches them, he passes to RF and then bursts between the defense trying to draw both defensemen with him. If he is successful, RF should have a clear shot on net and LF can move in for a rebound. If LF is not successful, RF should attempt to return the pass back to LF, who is on the inside of RD, and can move in for a shot on net. If the defensive pair are backing in on their goaltender, the puck carrier should prepare to execute a screen shot.

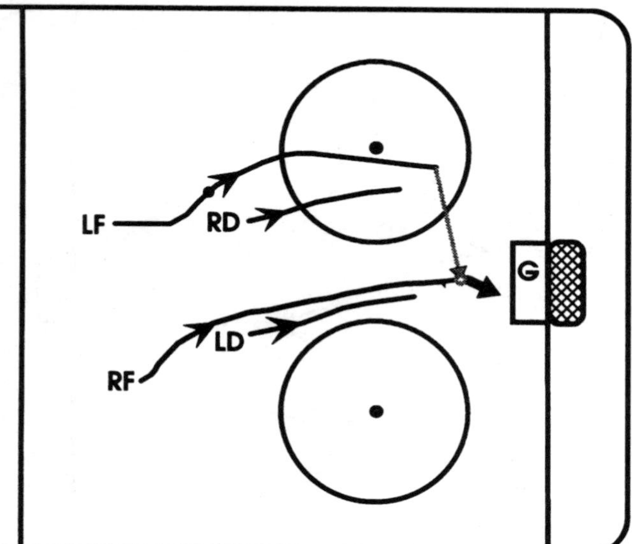

Figure 8-7; Two-On-Two With No Trailer

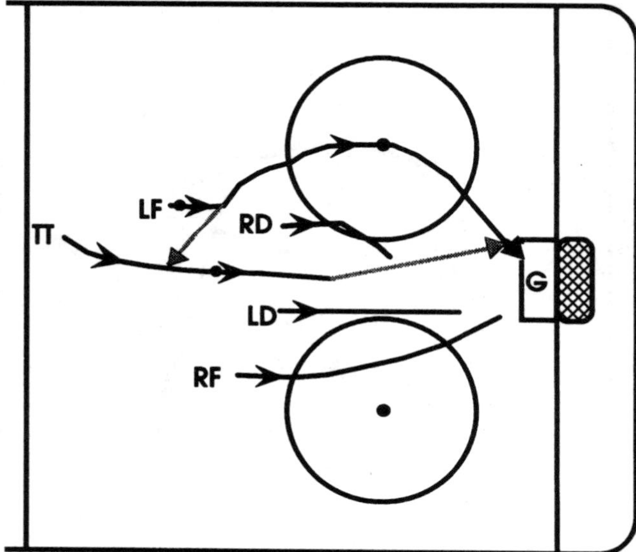

Figure 8-8; Two-On-Two With A Teammate Trailing

In the second scenario, the forwards have read the play and determined that there are two defenders to beat (LD and RD) and that they have support in the form of a trailing teammate (TT), as shown in Figure 8-8. This scenario requires the forwards to:

- Utilize LF to move to the outside of RD and pass the puck to TT, who is skating down the middle of the playing surface. TT skates at a moderate pace while both LF and RF move quickly around the outside of their respective defensemen for the net. If either LF or RF are open, a pass should be made followed by a shot on net. If both defensemen follow LF and RF toward the net leaving TT open, TT should execute a low shot on net and either LF or RF should capitalize on any rebound or deflection opportunity.

Three-on-one. The basic strategy behind this scenario is to force the single defender to move out of the central defensive zone, from where he can force the offensive players to shoot from an angle. What must be avoided is carrying the puck close enough to the defenseman or passing it close enough to him to give him a chance to break up the play. This

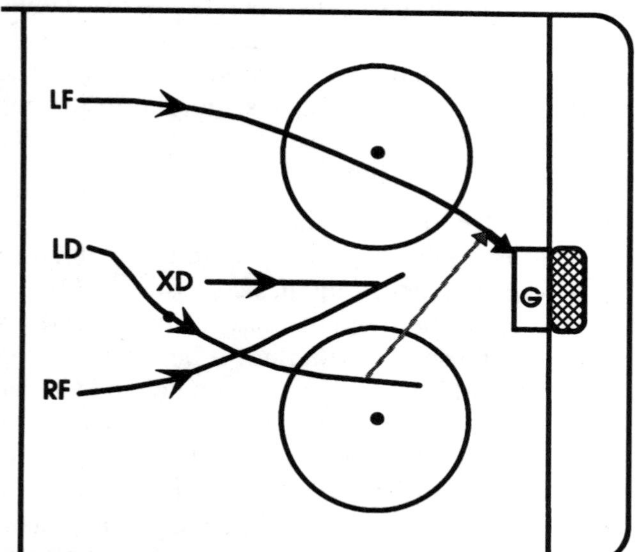

Figure 8-9; Three-On-One With No Trailer — 1

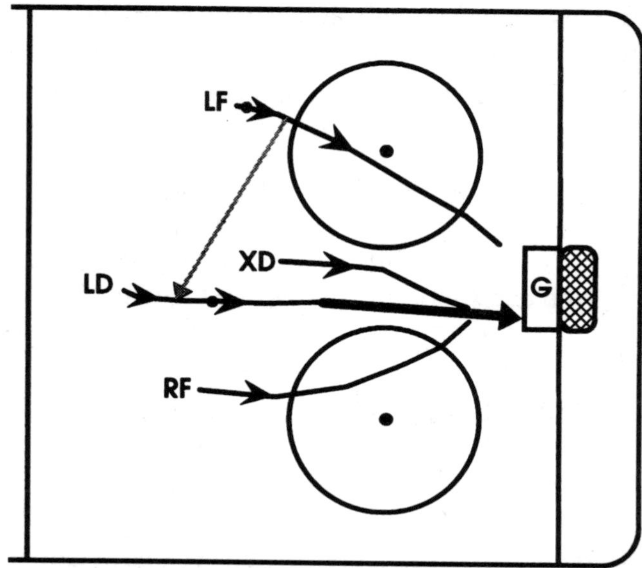

Figure 8-10; Three-On-One With No Trailer — 2

occurs more often than it should. A three-on-one scenario is defined as three attackers against one defender and usually consists of two forwards and an offensive defenseman against a defenseman. This scenario has the offensive unit (LF and RF and LD) reading the play and determining that there is one defender to beat (XD), as shown in Figure 8-9, and requires the offensive trio to:

- Utilize RF to quickly break on a path to block XD out of the play. As this is occurring, LD (puck carrier) cuts behind RF and moves toward the net while LF also moves to the net. As soon as RF has (legally) contained XD, LD passes the puck to LF who executes a shot on net, with LD available for any rebound.
- Utilize LF (puck carrier) to pass the puck to LD, and then have LF and RF head for the net, attempting to draw XD with them. As XD backs in on the goaltender, LD should hold the puck until XD backs up far enough for a screen shot to be used, as shown in Figure 8-10. LF and RF should be available for a rebound or deflection.

Three-on-two. This is another good goal-scoring situation which should end up in at least a shot on net from a high-percentage scoring location. The specific play used should be selected according to the type of defensive unit to beat and how they react to the specific player and puck movement. A three-on-two scenario is defined as three attackers against two defenders and usually consists of two forwards and an offensive defenseman against a defensive unit. This scenario has the offensive unit (LF, RF and OD) reading the play and determining that there are two defenders to beat (LD and RD), as shown in Figure 8-11, and requires the offensive trio to:

- Utilize OD to carry the puck straight for the defensemen. As he approaches the defensive unit, he passes the puck to LF who slowly moves to the outside of RD. As LF is skating, OD heads straight for the high slot while RF moves quickly around behind the net to a point about six feet from the net. LF passes the puck to RF, who passes the puck to OD for a quick shot on net. The intent of this play is to cause the defensive unit to move out of its normal zone coverage through the use of moves designed to confuse them. A lot of quick and accurate offensive reading needs to be performed with this play, but the reward is worth it.
- OD takes the puck into the offensive zone and moves to the left side of RD, as if he is going to move around him. After moving about 10 feet with the puck, OD leaves a drop pass for LF and continues skating toward the net. As RD starts to move with OD to try and stop him, LF moves with the puck toward the net using the open area vacated by RD. This situation has now turned into a two-on-one with the options being to shoot the puck on net or pass to RF if he is open and in a better scoring position.

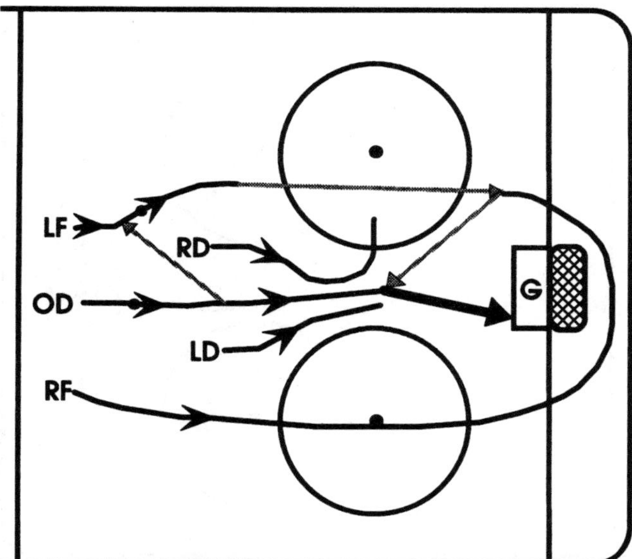

Figure 8-11; Three-On-Two With No Trailer — 1

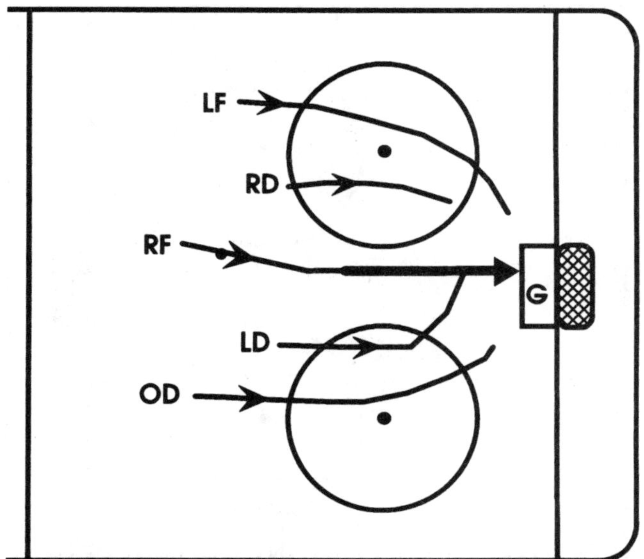

Figure 8-12; Three-On-Two With No Trailer — 2

- Utilize RF to carry the puck in slowly. LF and OD should quickly head for the net, attempting to draw RD and LD with them. As RD and LD back in on the goaltender, RF should hold the puck until a screen shot can be used, as shown in Figure 8-12. LF and OD should be available for a rebound or deflection.

Forechecking. Forechecking is a tactic used to gain or regain possession of the puck in the offensive zone and to eventually set up a scoring opportunity. When the offensive team loses possession of the puck or neither team has definite possession in the offensive zone, Table 7-1 states that the only role is to gain control of the puck. Forechecking is an important technique that is used to gain control of the puck in the offensive zone. This is because when a team successfully forechecks an opponent (gaining or regaining control of the puck), an offensive play can immediately be set up inside the offensive zone.

The area closest to the goal (area 1 in Figure 8-13) represents the ideal area to forecheck because it is the area where the puck carrier (generally a defenseman) has the smallest amount of open playing surface in which to maneuver. The net blocks the middle portion of area 1 and if the forechecker plays the angles right, he can force the puck carrier to stay between him and the boards. A good move when forechecking in area 1 is to leave a spot *apparently open* right beside the net for the puck carrier to skate through. This is important because if the puck carrier perceives that the area near the goal is the only place that he can maneuver in, he may try to skate with the puck and give you a chance to stick check him right in front of the net or he may make a poor pass in front of the net which could be intercepted and lead to a scoring opportunity (see Figure 8-14). Area 2 is the next best forechecking zone, because the puck carrier is hemmed in by the angle of the boards. When forechecking in area 2, go after the puck carrier at an angle, so that you can force him along the boards and stick check or body block him, possibly resulting in a turnover. The best approach in area 2 is to try and force the puck carrier into area 1, where your forechecking task will be more effective. Area 3 is included because the forechecker can maneuver in this area, about 10 feet from the boards, and force the puck-carrier to move toward the boards, where he can body block him and retrieve the puck, as shown in the top portion of Figure 8-14.

Some general guidelines for forechecking are:

- The forward closest to the puck carrier should move in to forecheck, with the other forward reading the offensive forwards and the puck carrier carefully in order to intercept any passes.
- For example, if the right forward is the closest man to the puck, he should go in with the other forward covering for a pass. By following this system, you can keep your opponent covered and prevent a quick breakout play that may catch the forecheckers out of position.

Figure 8-13; Prioritized Forechecking Areas

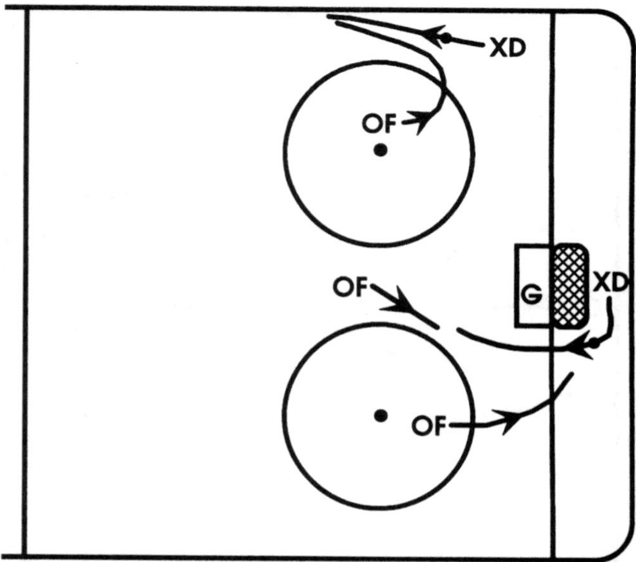

Figure 8-14; Forechecking Examples

- The average forechecker makes an error by skating in at top speed to forecheck, trying to make energy and effort take the place of controlled play and strategy. A good forechecker goes in under full skating control at about three-quarter speed. In this way he can force the puck carrier to commit himself, and he will be set and ready to change position quickly to counteract any move made by the puck carrier. Another point to remember when forechecking is to use short strides at all times so that you will always be ready to change direction quickly.
- The forechecker should always keep his head up and play the man, then go for the puck. If you play the puck, you can be beaten with one deceptive stickhandling maneuver. To play the man, angle him toward the boards to cut off his skating space. Do not approach the puck carrier straight on and do not chase him behind the net unless you are very close to him. After you have him between you and the boards, execute a stick check to gain possession of the puck.
- Finally, remember that the most important fundamental of good forechecking is spirit and determination. Good coaches never forget that a team that makes hard, persistent, well-organized and planned forechecking an important part of its system can disorganize and beat many teams that might otherwise be the winner. A well forechecked team will soon get frustrated which will affect morale and cohesion, and cause it to make mistakes.

Backchecking is the second part of the forward's responsibility to be a two-way player and is an important component of a team's success. Backchecking is a tactic used to regain possession of the puck when the opposing team has control and is moving toward your defensive zone or is in your defensive zone. This tactic assists the defensemen by allowing them to force a play, since they have read that their teammates will eventually be available to cover some of the attackers. Backchecking requires the forwards to quickly skate back toward their defensive zone to help contain an attack by the opposition; in most cases that requires the forwards to come back and cover any attacker in the high slot.

Backchecking incorporates many attributes; two of the most important are conditioning and attitude. If a player is not in shape, he will not be inclined to make the effort to backcheck. He may tend to save his strength for the offensive work. A well-conditioned player will rarely be a lazy player, mentally or physically. The other attribute is the attitude of the player when he sees he is behind the play. A good backchecking attitude translates into a determination to regain control of the puck. Some forwards think that it will not do any good to hustle back when they believe that they are too far out of the play. A good two-way roller hockey forward knows that if he does hustle back, he may get there just in time to save a goal, pick up a rebound or cover the open man.

Advanced Techniques

The seven advanced offensive techniques consist of learning the opponent's patterns, rebounds, screen shot, deflections, one-time shot, fake shot and the spin-o-rama.

Learning the opponent's patterns. To progress to the next level of roller hockey, it is imperative that each forward makes a point of learning the various moves and play patterns of his opponents, including the forwards, defense and goaltender(s). A lot of players just try to *do their* job without attempting to understand why they can't get past a certain defender. Don't leave it only to the coach to tell you what is working and what is not; **think and evaluate!** If you are playing a team for the first time, you should begin keeping a book (mental notes) on the favorite moves and plays of the opposing players, various line combinations and goaltending styles. Determine the opponent's best playmakers, best defensemen, how they react to certain circumstances, and exchange this information with your coach and teammates. Watch how the other team's forwards move past your defensemen. Determine if this information will help you with how you play your opponents and also share this information with your defensemen. By the second half of the game, you should at least have a decent book on the team. If you have played a team before, you should recall the information from your book and use it so that you can be in a position to get past the defenseman and goaltender.

Rebounds. Another way to pick up more goals is to get into the habit of following in on your initial shot as quickly as possible to take advantage of any rebounds. The average goaltender allows many rebounds, especially from low shots. If you follow in quickly, these rebounds can be turned into additional scoring opportunities. Study the goaltender to see how the rebounds come out from his pads, stick, blocker or skates. This information is important because it gives you clues regarding just where to follow up. If you are not in position for a shot and have no one to pass to, keep your shot low so that you or a teammate can get any rebounds. Avoid the bad habit of shooting and then watching to see what happens. Another good play, when you are at a bad angle or blocked off, is to flip the puck so that it will land at the goaltender's feet and then follow in quickly. This may result in picking up a rebound or may unsettle the goaltender.

Timing, quickness and strength to move into position in front of the net are essential factors in obtaining rebounds. With limited space and defensive coverage by the opponents in the slot, you must be strong on your skates, work your way to the puck, anticipate a shot from your teammate (if your teammate is the shooter), obtain the rebound and shoot the puck. Three keys to obtaining rebounds are to position aggressively in the scoring area, concentrate on the puck and keep your stick on the playing surface. The determination to drive the rebound home is the mark of a good scorer and should be a main feature in all rebound drills.

Screen shot. During the average roller hockey game there are many opportunities to shoot on goal using a screen created by either opponents or teammates. A screen shot can be a particularly effective play in a one-on-one or one-on-two situation. This occurs when the player skates up to the defense on one side and then cuts across. Just as he starts across, he fires a shot on goal between the defense. If this technique is well timed it will often catch a goaltender unprepared for the shot, and a goal or a rebound could result. It can also be used whenever the defensive unit has backed up fairly close to the goal. When playing against such opponents, the puck carrier should slow down, let the defense back up as far as possible, and then shoot through their legs or between them. The forward should always be alert for this situation to develop, firing the puck carefully through an open spot. When the goaltender is being screened, it is best to shoot low since there is a better chance of the puck getting through.

Deflections. Many goals are scored by a player changing the direction of a shot using the blade of his stick. To deflect or redirect a puck, it is important to get in a good scoring position. There are three locations in which deflections work effectively; directly in front of the net, or off to either side of the net and a couple feet away from the goal line. When in front of the net, the player should attempt to block the goaltender's view of the shot (screen shot) and be available to redirect a straight-on shot to the corner of the net. When off to the side of the net, the player should be watching the shooter with his body turned slightly toward the shooter for a forehand deflection and with his back turned slightly toward the shooter for a backhand deflection. Keep a tight grip on the stick for all deflections.

One-time shot. Although the one-time shot was described in Chapter 6, it is an important tool from the forward's viewpoint. The one-time shot is used with a snap or slap shot and relies on one factor to be executed — timing. When the forward signals to a teammate that he is open, and a pass is made, he needs to be prepared. Instead of receiving the pass, draw the stick back and time the travel of the pass so that the follow-through with the blade of the stick coincides exactly with the arrival of the puck. When the puck is close, execute the one-time shot. This type of shot is very deceptive because as a goaltender attempts to follow the puck on the playing surface, it is moved from the passer, to the forward, to the net usually before the goaltender has a chance to prepare himself for the shot. This shot requires a lot of practice to perfect and should only be used occasionally so that the goaltender does not get accustomed to it.

Fake shot. Of all the fakes, this is probably the one that will bring the most consistent results, if properly performed. The secret is to make the fake convincing by actually starting the shot. The player who has a hard shot will find this move especially effective because the defender will be even more anxious to get out of the way or protect himself from the shot. This fake is most effective when the fake shot is the slap or snap shot, due to the backswing required. The player assumes a shooting position and starts the puck forward fairly quickly until the moment when the shot would normally be made.

Siller Player And Team Evaluation Profile© Offensive Player Checklist												
Evaluator: The Coach	**Date**: 3/22/95				**Location**: The Pond							
	Player Name											
Notes:	**DAVID**		**PAUL**		**JASON**		**JOSH**					
Fundamental Offensive Techniques												
Communicating	7		8		6		6					
Reading and Reacting	9		8		9		9					
Fake Pass	8		8		8		8					
Against the Boards	**10**		**10**		**10**		**10**					
Flip Out	0		0		0		0					
Forehand and Backhand Shifts	8		8		8		8					
Backhand-To-Forehand Shift	7		6		8		7					
Forehand-To-Backhand Shift	7		8		6		7					
Slip-Through	8		8		8		8					
Slip Across	8		8		8		8					
Change of Pace	8		7		8		7					
The Weave	7		6		5		6					
Shoulder Turn/Drop	6		5		6		7					
Flip Through	6		6		6		6					
Body Blocking	8		8		8		8					
One/Two/Three-On-One	7		8		8		7					
One/Two/Three-On-Two	8		7		7		8					
Forechecking	7		7		7		7					
Backchecking	5		6		5		6					
Advanced Offensive Techniques												
Learning Opponents Patterns	7		7		6		6					
Rebounds	7		7		8		6					
Screen Shot	7		7		5		6					
Deflections	7		7		7		7					
One-time Shot	7		5		6		8					
Fake Shot	7		7		7		7					
Spin-O-Rama	5		**3**		4		4					
TOTAL SCORE	**181**		**175**		**174**		**177**					
AVERAGE SCORE	**7.2**		**7.0**		**7.0**		**7.1**					
Comments: David, Paul, Jason and Josh have all demonstrated high overall offensive proficiency with total scores of 181, 175, 174, and 177 respectively and average scores of 7.2, 7.0, 7.0 and 7.1, respectively. All players scored excellent on the against-the-boards move. The flip out technique was not performed. Paul needs to improve on the spin-o-rama.												
Scale: 0 = Not Performed, 1 - 3 = Low Proficiency, 4 - 6 = Medium Proficiency, 7 - 9 = High Proficiency, 10 = Excellent Proficiency												

Table 8-2; Offensive Player Checklist

Then the stick is lifted quickly and placed in front of the puck to stop it in its forward motion and the puck is moved well out to the side as the player moves to go around the defender.

The **Spin-o-rama** is probably the ultimate puck control and body deception move available to a forward and is used to get around a defender, generally in a one-on-one scenario. Very few forwards can effectively perform this move and even fewer use it in a game. The spin-o-rama demands a high degree of timing, balance and agility but can be learned with frequent practice. To execute this move, the forward skates toward the defender and then begins to move to the outside of him. Just as the defender thinks that he has to cover the forward going outside, the forward pivots on his front wheels so that he ends up skating backward toward the net and to the inside of the defender, and then transitions to skating forward toward the net. The knees must be well bent and a good forward body lean must be kept. The speed of the pivot is governed by the quickness of the body turn, especially the hips. The upper body must be leaned to the inside during the pivot for balance. Once the forward is heading straight for a shot on net, the goaltender and beaten defenseman can watch in amazement as the forward completes this move with a goal. All of this action happens in about one second, and the most difficult task is keeping the puck on your stick as all of the spinning is taking place.

Drills

Offensive drills should be selected to enable players to adjust to as many offensive situations as possible. Offensive proficiency comes with knowledge and practice. By learning the material in this chapter, the coach and players will become familiar with the particular skills and strategies required to play the many levels of offense, allowing the forwards to become better overall roller hockey players. As the coach discovers the particular needs of his players, he can select the drills required for the players to improve. The drills in this chapter include the components of skating, stickhandling and puck control, passing and receiving, shooting and scoring, and stick checking. Drills from chapters 3 through 7 that should become part of a forward's fundamentals include Drills 3-7 (End-To-End), 3-10 (Power Turns), 3-12 (Zigzag), 3-13 (Snake), 3-14 (Sprint Skating), 4-1 (Stationary Puck Control - Part 1), 4-2 (Stationary Puck Control - Part 2), 4-3 (Developing Soft Hands), 4-7 (Puck Control and Turns), 4-8 (Puck Control and Circles), 4-10 (Puck Control and The Coach), 4-11 (Zigzag), 5-5 (Peripheral Vision Drill), 5-7 (Keep Away), 6-11 (Race for the Puck), 7-3 (Using the Stick), 7-4 (Body Blocking) and 7-5 (Riding a Puck Carrier Out of the Play).

Drill 8-1; Under the Defender's Stick. This drill provides practice moving the puck near a defender while you and the defender are stationary. Divide the team into pairs and designate one player in each pair as the defender and the other player as the puck carrier. Space each pair about four or five feet apart and at the whistle, have the puck carrier begin side-to-side stationary stickhandling, with the puck moving under the defender's stick. Practice for about one minute and then have the players switch roles. The puck carrier should be given feedback on keeping his head up and on using soft hands.

Drill 8-2; Puck Fakes and Body Deception. This drill is really a collection of individual drills that are designed to provide practice on the 14 puck fake and body deception moves described earlier in this chapter. Both types of these moves strive for the same end result — to deceive and defeat (move past) a defender using specific puck and/or body movement. To begin this drill, divide the team into three lines and place them on the goal line. Pucks will not be required for the first portion of the drill. Place three pylons in the path of each of the lines, about 30 feet apart, as shown in the corresponding diagram. At the whistle, the first player in each line skates, at half speed, toward the pylon and executes a forehand shift puck fake (without the puck). The coach should provide feedback to each player on the timing of each fake and whether the player had his head up none, some or most of the time. The puck fake should be started about six feet away from the pylon to provide the player the most realistic practice. If the fake is started too soon, a defender will have time to recover and cover the final

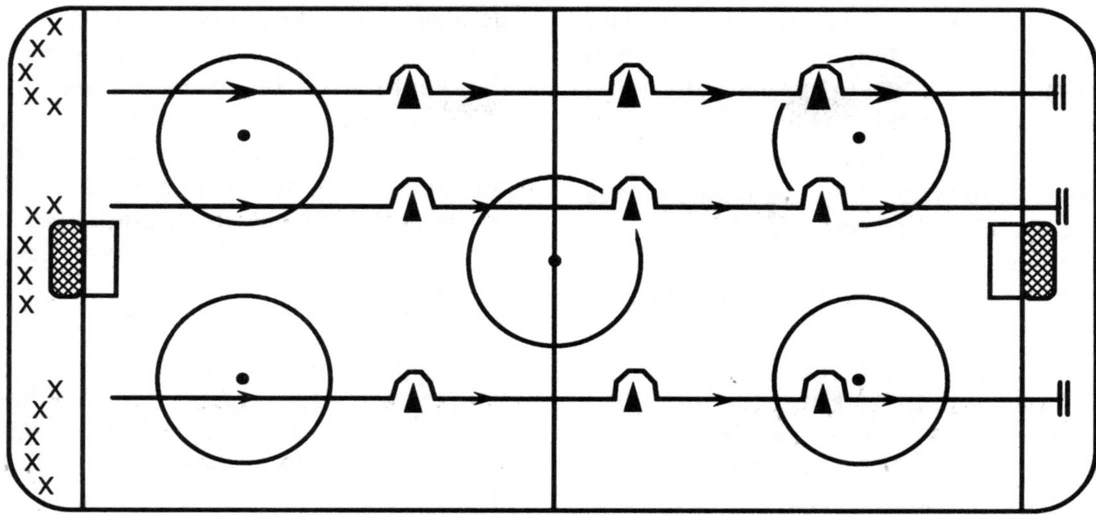

Drill 8-2; Puck Fakes And Body Deception

movement. If the move is started too late, the puck carrier will be so close to a defender that he may get stick checked or run into a body block. At the second whistle, the second players in each line perform the same move, with the coach providing feedback to each individual. After all three lines have completed the drill in one direction, the coach can introduce the puck. The drill should be repeated at least three times using the puck. Introducing the puck into the drill will probably produce a less effective execution initially, but that only fortifies the reason to practice this drill: the players need to practice puck fakes and body deception moves to perfect them and confidently execute them during a game! To move to the next level of this drill, remove the pylons and replace them with stationary players. The players should not try and stick check the puck carrier, but are in the position to allow each puck carrier practice moving around an actual player. Once a high skill level has been developed, variations as well as a competitive approach should be developed. The more a player experiments and practices with the various possibilities, the more he will find use for them. The point is to learn the basic fake to either side and then work on developing variations.

Variations. Set up pylon/player configurations to practice the following puck fake and body deception moves:

- Fake pass.
- Against the boards.
- Flip out.
- Backhand shift.
- Backhand-to-forehand shift.
- Forehand-to-backhand shift.
- Slip-through.
- Slip across.
- Change of pace.
- The weave.
- Shoulder turn.
- Shoulder drop.
- Flip through.
- Increase the speed of the drill.
- Use a combination of puck fake and body deception moves at each pylon/defender.

For the next series of drills, players will have the opportunity to put into practice their skill at puck fakes and body deception. Some guidelines to follow when deciding on which type of puck fake or body deception technique to use and when to use each include the information listed in Table 8-1 and the following:

- If the defenseman plays the puck, then use a puck fake.
- If the defenseman plays the man, head straight for the defenseman, and then use body deception moves such as change of direction and change of pace to interrupt his timing. Puck fakes are less effective against a defenseman who plays the man.

- If the defenseman is strong on one side (i.e., the stick side), fake to that side, since he will probably be more eager to try and use his stick, and then move quickly to the other side.
- If the defenseman is slow, make him skate fast and then make your play. Use skating moves such as change of pace and direction or moving to open playing surface to beat slow opponents. The more you make him move the better your chances are.
- If the defenseman backs up, slow down and let him continue to back up. Try to use the defenseman as a screen for a shot on goal and then go in for a possible rebound.
- Head for the defender you are most confident in beating.
- When there is one or more non-puck carrying forwards in a play, their roles are to get open to receive a pass, set up for a rebound, or to move so that the puck carrier has additional time and space to maneuver.

Drill 8-3; One-on-One. This drill is one of the fundamental offensive drills upon which many other offensive drills are built. This drill forces the forward to test his skill at executing a specific puck fake/body deception move or using the defenseman as a screen. Line the players up as shown in the corresponding diagram. At the whistle, the forward passes the puck to the defenseman, who passes it back to the forward. After the forward receives the pass, both skaters move toward the far goal at three-quarter speed. If the forward reads that the defenseman is staying out from the net, he should execute a puck fake or body deception move on the defenseman. If the defenseman continues to move toward the net, the forward should set up and execute a screen shot and go in for a possible rebound. The coach should provide feedback to the forward based on the above guidelines and the end result. After the first pair have completed the drill, the next pair should begin. All players should perform the drill at least three times.

Drill 8-4; Two-on-One. The objective of this drill is to teach the forwards to force the defender into making a move that will place the non-puck carrier in an open position. Line the players up as shown in the corresponding diagram. At the whistle, the forward pair and the defenseman move toward the far goal at three-quarter speed, with the forwards passing as they go. As they move toward the top of the far face-off circle, the puck carrier needs to decide whether to pass or to shoot. This decision will be based on the puck carrier's ability to make the defender move out of the central defensive zone and whether the non-puck carrier can get open. If the defenseman stays out from the net, pass to the other forward, who should be open. If the defenseman moves in toward the net, set up and execute a screen shot, with the other forward moving in for a possible rebound. The coach should provide feedback to the forwards based on the above guidelines and the end result. After the first trio have completed the drill, the next trio should begin. All players perform the drill at least three times.

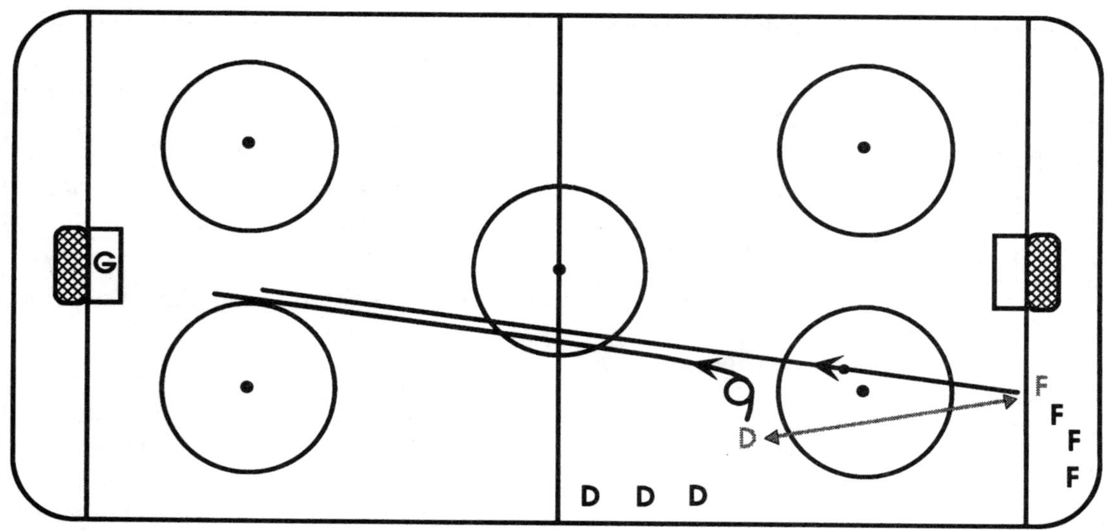

Drill 8-3; One-On-One

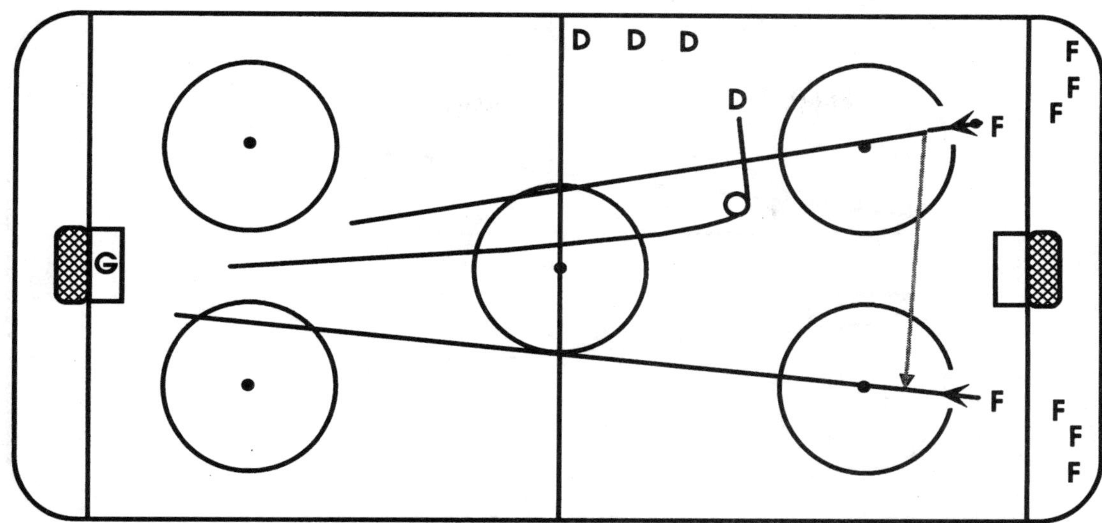

Drill 8-4; Two-On-One

Drill 8-5; One-on-Two. The objective of this drill is to teach the forward that the defensive unit is always easier to beat if he can force it to move. If the puck carrier can maneuver so that he can take the defensive unit on one-by-one, the situation becomes better. Line the players up as shown in the corresponding diagram. At the whistle, the forward and the two defensemen start skating toward the far end. As the forward crosses the center red line, his priority plays are to execute a puck fake/body deception move or to shoot, depending on the position of the defensemen. If the defensemen stay out from the net, then a good play to use is to fake a shot between the defensemen or between the legs of one defenseman, and then shift out and around. If the defensemen move in toward the net, set up and execute a screen shot and then go in for a possible rebound. The coach should provide feedback to the forward based on his position with respect to the defensemen, the above guidelines and the end result.

Drill 8-6; Two-on-Two. Since the defensemen will probably be playing each forward using a one-on-one approach (i.e., playing the man), the objective of this drill is to teach the forwards to create a situation in which the non-puck carrier either executes a move on his defenseman or draws his coverage off to the side. In either case, the role of the non-puck carrier is crucial to the successful execution of this play. At the whistle, the two forwards and the two defensemen start skating toward the far end, with the forwards passing as they go. If the

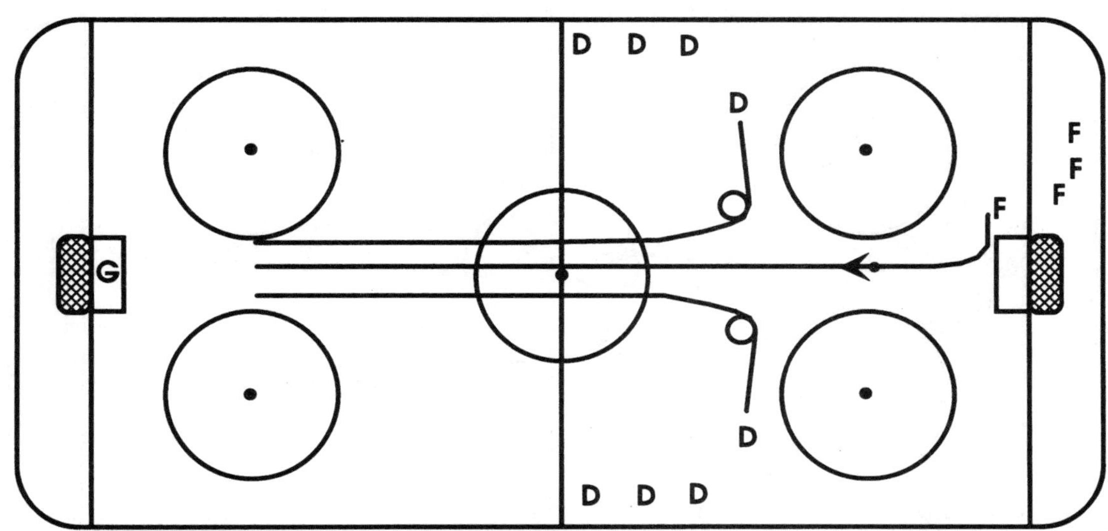

Drill 8-5; One-On-Two

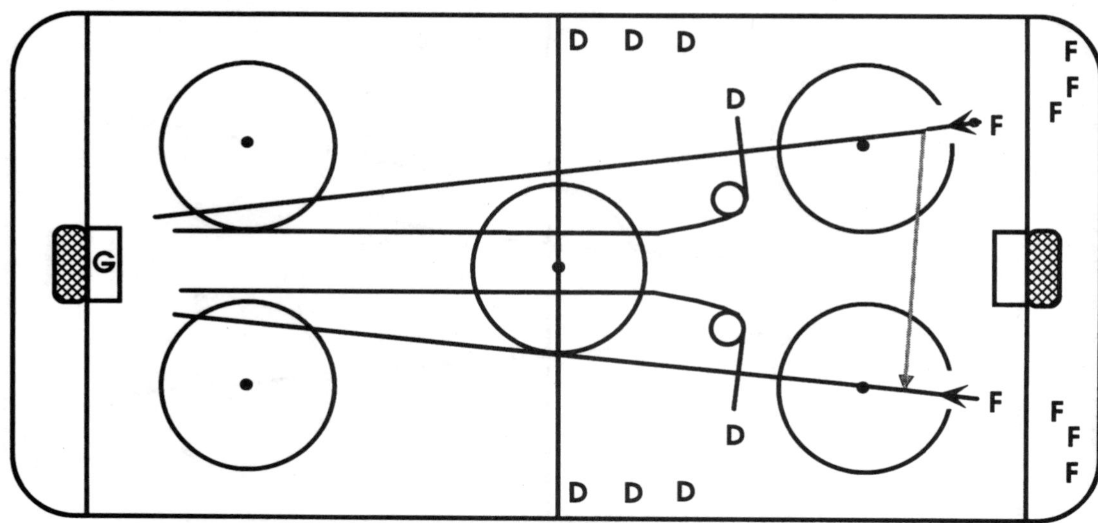

Drill 8-6; Two-On-Two

non-puck carrier is moving to get open or drawing his defenseman off to the side, then a pass or puck fake/body deception is in order. If the non-puck carrier is unable to perform either of these roles, then the puck carrier should head right at the defensive pair as if he is going to go through them. Just before he reaches them, he passes to his partner and then bursts between the defense trying to draw both defensemen with him. The new puck carrier can now return the pass or shoot. The coach should provide feedback to the forwards based on their position with respect to the defensemen, the above guidelines and the end result.

Drill 8-7; Three-on-One. The objective of this drill is for the offensive trio to pass the puck to an open man and set up for a shot on the goaltender. This drill also teaches the attackers not to stick handle too much when teammates are open, and not to carry or pass the puck too close to the defenseman to give him an opportunity to break up the play. Line the players up as shown in the corresponding diagram. At the whistle, the offensive trio and the defenseman move toward the far goal at three-quarter speed. Keep the two non-puck carrying attackers open so that they can receive a pass, shoot and then follow in for a possible rebound. If one of the non-puck carrying attackers can decoy the defenseman, then the puck carrier can move in on net unchallenged, pass to his other teammate for a one-time shot or use the defenseman as a screen. The coach should provide feedback to the offensive trio based on their position with respect to the

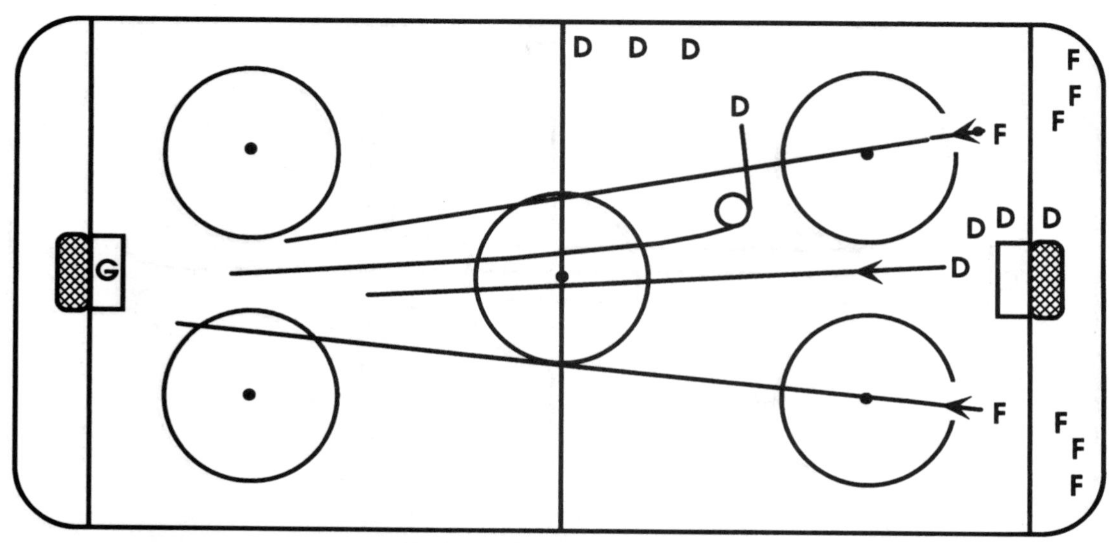

Drill 8-7; Three-On-One

defenseman, the above guidelines and the end result.

Drill 8-8; Three-on-Two. The objective of this drill is for the offensive unit to set up positioning to pass the puck to an open man and/or shoot. The specific play used should be selected according to the type of defensive unit to beat and the reaction to the specific player and puck movement. Line the players up as shown in the corresponding diagram. At the whistle, the offensive trio and the defensemen start skating toward the far end. Have the puck carrier control the play by either lagging back behind the two non-puck carriers or speeding ahead of them. The non-puck carriers should take their cues from the puck carrier and get open to receive a pass or head for the net for a possible deflection or rebound. If one of the non-puck carrying forwards can decoy the defensemen, then the puck carrier can move in on net unchallenged or pass to his other teammate for a one-time shot. The coach should provide feedback to the offensive trio based on their position with respect to the defensemen, the above guidelines and the end result.

Drill 8-9; Forechecking. This drill is designed to provide forwards with practice gaining possession of the puck in their offensive zone and setting up a scoring opportunity. Select four players as the forechecking team and two defensemen as the team being forechecked. The defensemen that are being forechecked should be instructed that they can only carry the puck, not shoot it out of the zone. This gives the forechecking team every opportunity to

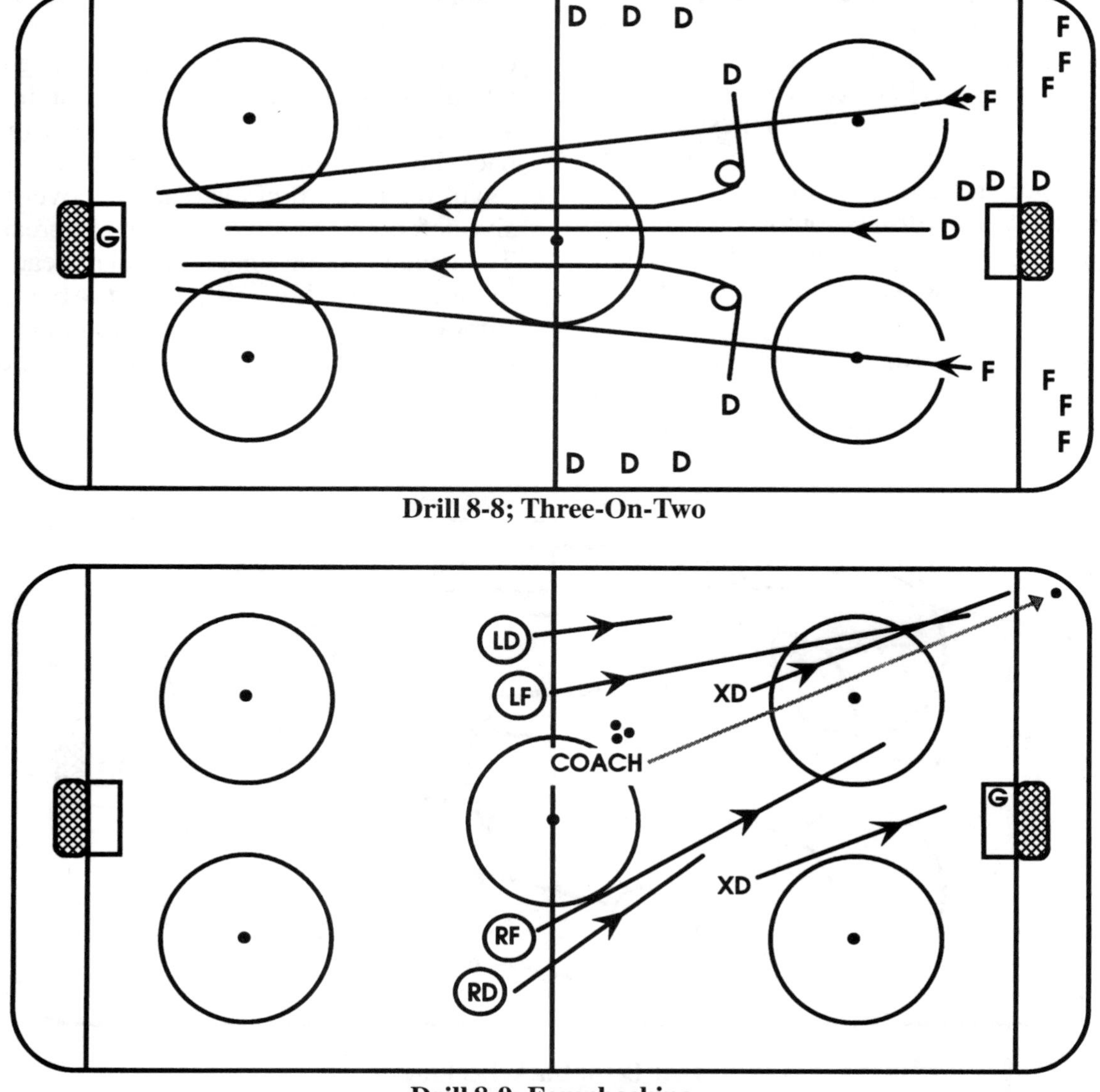

Drill 8-8; Three-On-Two

Drill 8-9; Forechecking

practice forechecking techniques. Position the forecheckers at the center red line and the two defensemen at the top of the circle as shown in the corresponding diagram. At the whistle, the coach or a player shoots the puck into a corner. The strongside defenseman skates into the corner to pick up the puck, the weakside defenseman positions himself in front of the net and the forechecking team heads into the zone with the strongside forward (LF) attempting to gain control of the puck from the defenseman in zone 1. The second forward (RF) should be positioned in zone 2, on the inside of the face-off circle, ready to prevent the defenseman from skating up the middle. RF moves into the slot for a pass if LF gains control of the puck. LF should try to force the defenseman behind the net. If the defenseman carries the puck behind the net, LF and RF should switch roles. If the forechecking team gains control of the puck, it should pass the puck to the slot or the point to get a shot on net. **The coach should provide feedback to the forechecking forwards** based on their position with respect to the puck, their quickness in the zone, their determination to gain control of the puck and the end result. After the drill is completed, have the defensemen who are being forechecked switch positions with the forechecking defensemen and repeat the drill.

Drill 8-10; Backchecking. This drill is designed to provide forwards with practice backchecking. The objective of this drill is to regain possession of the puck when the opposing team has control and is moving toward your defensive zone or is in your defensive zone. Since backchecking is the second part of the forward's responsibility to be a two-way player and is an important component of a team's success, it should become incorporated into most practices. Position the players as shown in the corresponding diagram. At the first whistle, the offensive defenseman (D) will move the puck up to one of his corresponding forwards (F), and both forwards will begin moving the puck toward the far goal, as the defensive defensemen (LD and RD) play the two-on-two scenario. At the second whistle, the backchecking forwards (RF and LF) skate quickly back toward their defensive zone to regain possession of the puck. If the backchecking forwards can get to the attacking forwards, they should take the puck and begin moving toward their offensive zone. If the backchecking forwards read that they cannot catch up to the attacking forwards, one of them should move toward the high slot to stop any activity in that area while the second backchecking forward positions himself near the top of the face-off circle ready to cover the offensive defensemen or to move out on a breakout play. The coach should whistle the play dead after one minute and **provide feedback to the backchecking forwards** on hustle, determination to gain control of the puck, reading and reacting, and defensive zone positioning.

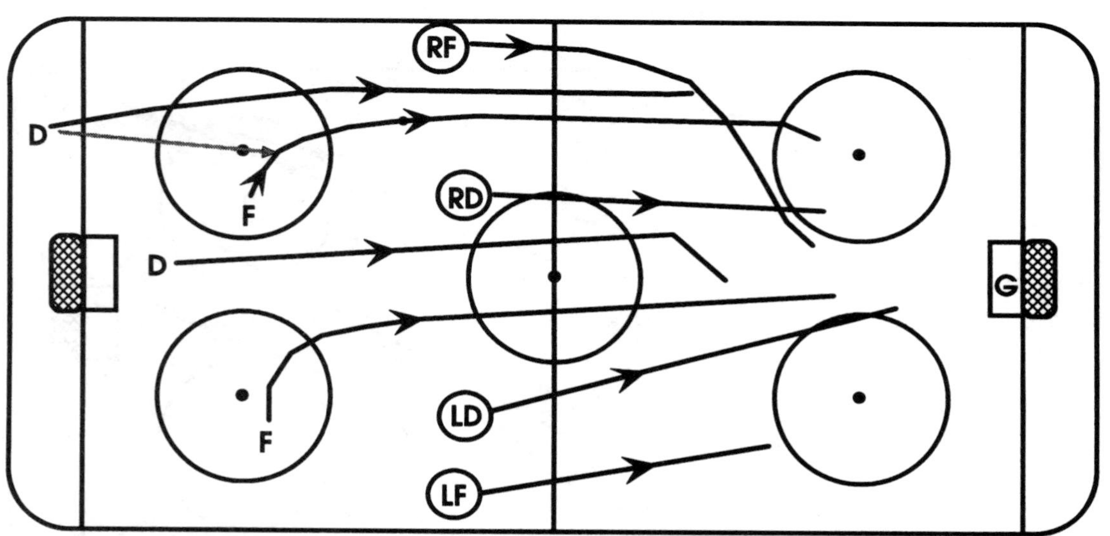

Drill 8-10; Backchecking

Advanced Drills

Drills from chapters 4 through 7 that should become part of a forward's advanced techniques include Drills 4-13 (One-Handed Puck Control Past a Defender), 4-14 (Puck Control Using the Skates), 5-12 (Touch Pass), 5-13 (Reverse), 5-14 (Weave), 6-15 (Shooting Off the Back Leg), 6-16 (Deking the Goaltender), 6-17 (Breakaways), 6-21 (Incidental Body Contact While Shooting), and 7-13 (Blocking Shots With Your Body).

Drill 8-11; Rebounds. Divide the team into two groups and place them at the center red line near the boards. Select one player from each group (X1) and position him in the corner as shown in the corresponding diagram. Player X1 will be the shooter for this drill and the first player in the line will be the trailer, following X1 in for a rebound. At the whistle, player X1 skates toward the center red line and around the pylons. As he passes the second pylon, the first player in line passes the puck to him, and both players skate in on net while X1 executes a snap shot at the pads of the goaltender from about 15 feet out. As X1 peels away from the net, the trailer retrieves any rebound and executes a forehand wrist shot on net. The trailer becomes the shooter (X1) for the next cycle and the shooter goes to the end of the line. This drill gets the players used to following in after a shot so that if a rebound becomes available, a second scoring chance is created.

Drill 8-12; Screen Shot. This drill is designed to provide practice shooting on a goaltender who is screened by a teammate. The role of the player in front of the net is to block the view of the goaltender or at least create a certain amount of commotion to distract him. This screener should also be looking for any rebounds. To perform this drill, divide the team into two groups, and place five players from each group in a semicircle about 20 to 25 feet from the net as shown in the corresponding diagram. The remainder of each group should move to the corner, with one player from this group playing the first screener (X). The screener should stand on a path between the net and the shooter, about three feet from the goaltender. At the whistle, player X1 executes a low forehand wrist or snap shot toward the net. The screener should screen the goaltender and not block the shot. The coach should stress to the shooters that the intent of the drill is not to shoot the puck as hard as they can or to shoot without aim. The shooters should keep the puck low, shoot with medium speed, and aim for a location in either corner or between the legs of the screener. This will allow the screener to develop confidence in the shooter's ability to control the location and speed of the puck. At the next whistle, player X2 executes the same shot. After the first five shots have been taken, the screener moves to X1, the next player in line moves to the screener

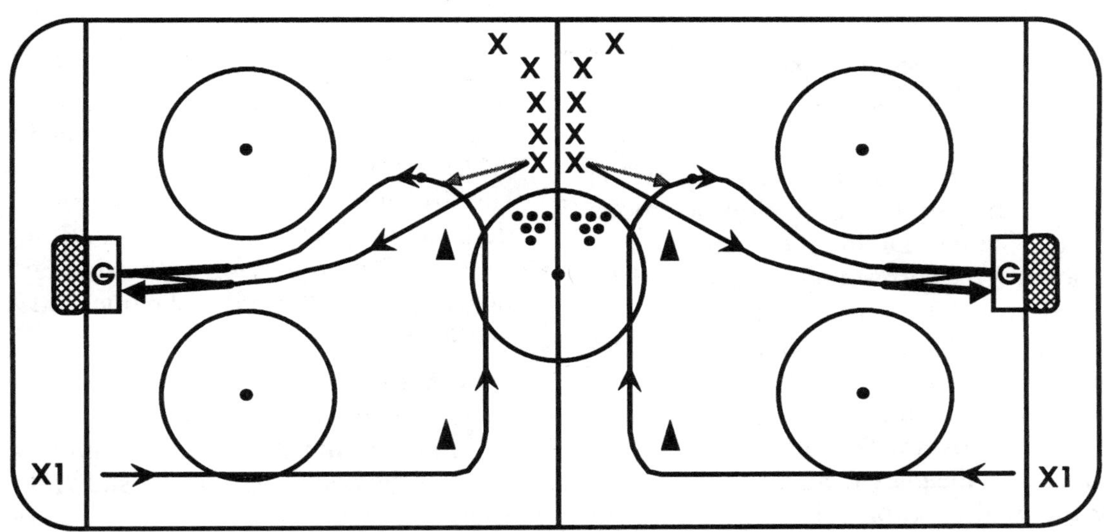

Drill 8-11; Rebounds

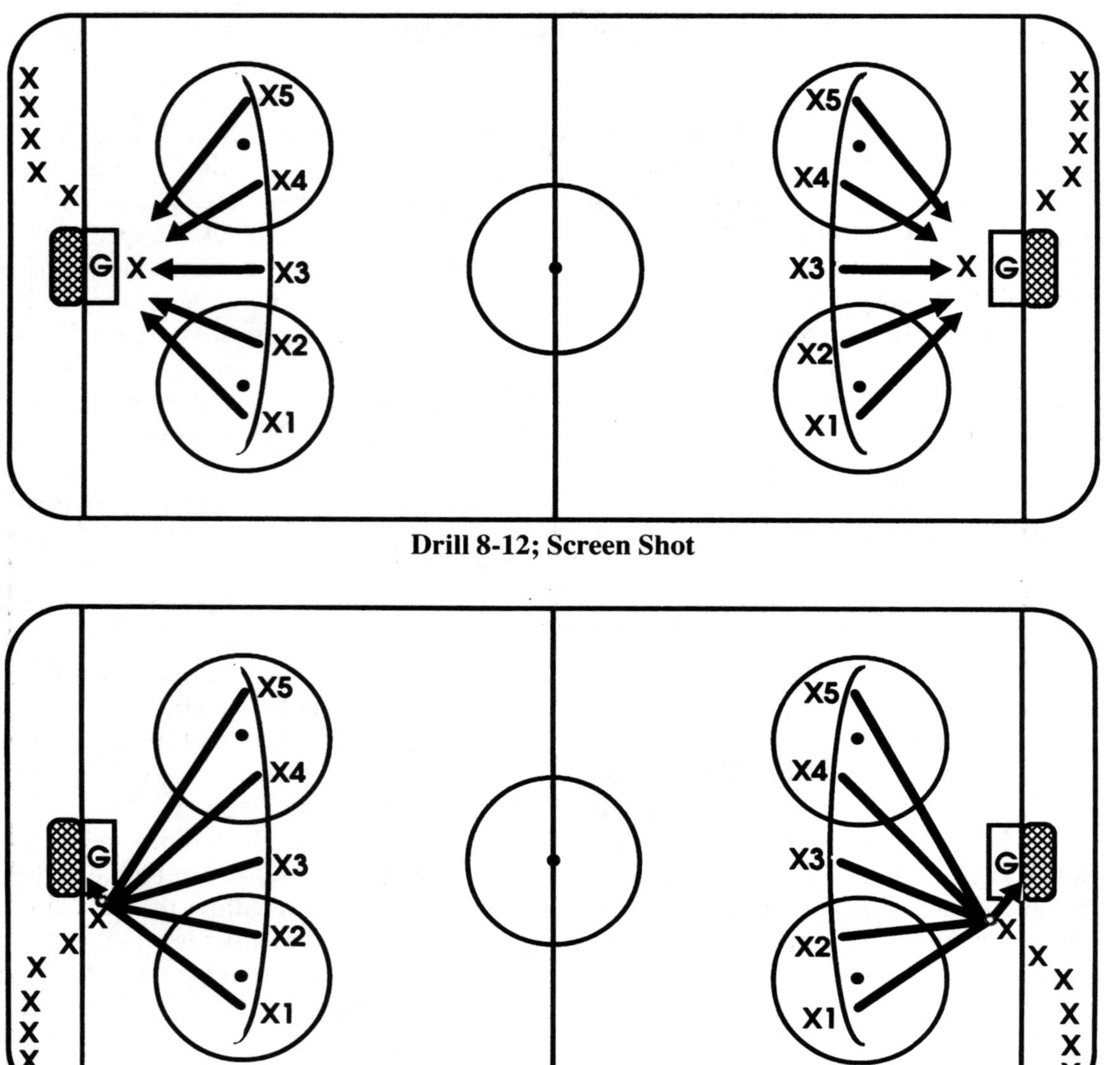

Drill 8-12; Screen Shot

Drill 8-13; Deflections

position in front of the net, X5 takes a place at the end of the line, and X1, X2, X3 and X4 shift one position.

Drill 8-13; Deflections. The purpose of this drill is to practice deflecting shots from various locations and angles into the net. Divide the team into two groups as shown in the corresponding diagram. The role of the deflector (X) is to redirect the puck from its original path into the net. The deflector should stand about three feet from the goal post and just outside the goal line. At the whistle, player X1 executes a low shot toward the net. The deflector attempts to redirect the puck from its original path, just inside the goal post, past the goaltender and into the net. The shooters should keep the puck low and shoot with medium speed. This will allow the deflector to develop confidence in the shooter's ability to control the location and speed of the puck. At the next whistle, player X2 executes the same shot. After the first five shots have been taken, the deflector moves to X1, the next player in line moves to the deflector position at the side of the net, X5 takes a place at the end of the line, and X1, X2, X3 and X4 shift one position.

Drill 8-14; One-time Shot. This drill is actually two drills in one, both variations of the one-time shot. Divide the team into two groups and place them at the center red line as shown in the corresponding diagram. The group on the right will be divided into two lines (X1 and X2) and placed near

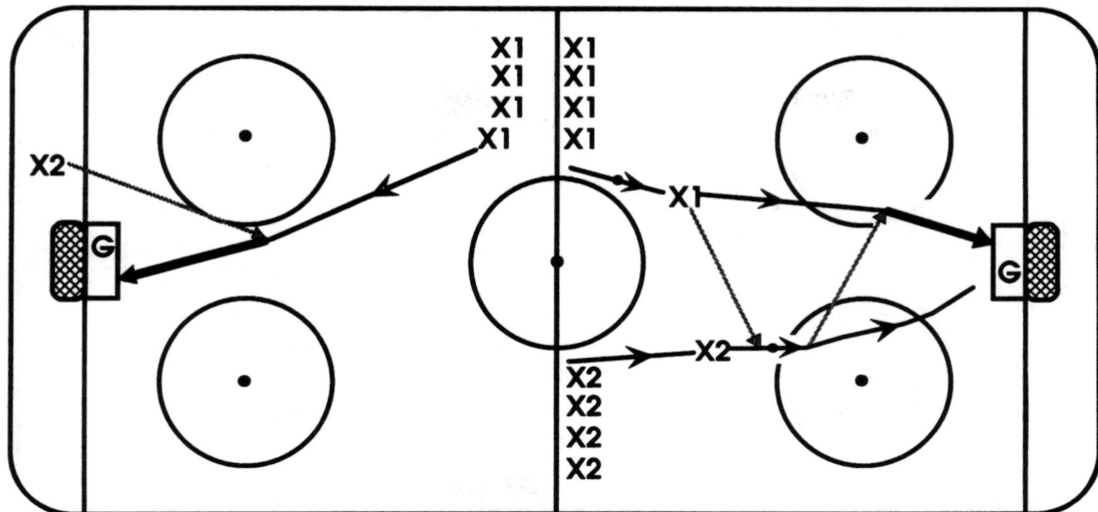

Drill 8-14; One-Time Shot

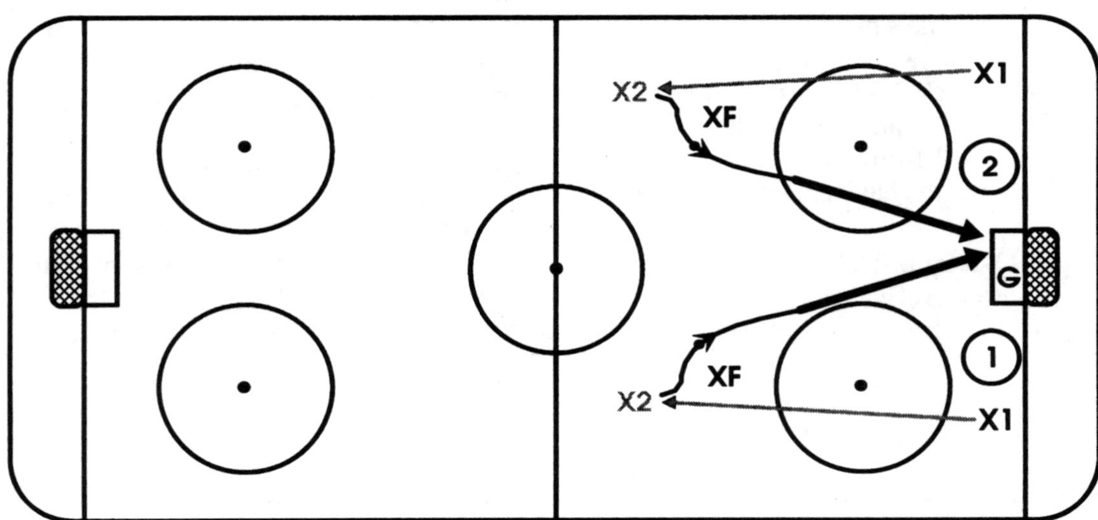

Drill 8-15; Fake Shot

the boards at each end of the center red line. Start the drill by having the first player in X1 and X2 skate three or four strides and then have X1 pass the puck to X2 who will return the puck to X1. As the puck nears X1, he one-times it toward an open area in the net. Players in X1 and X2 should alternate lines once each player has completed the cycle. The group on the left will also line up along the center red line (X1). Choose one player from that group (X2) and position him about five feet from the net and behind the goal line. Start this drill by having the first player from X1 skate toward the net, with X2 passing the puck to X1 when X1 enters the slot. As the puck nears X1, he one-times it toward an open area in the net. Players in X1 and X2 should also alternate once each player has completed his cycle. After both the left and right groups have completed their cycles, have them switch sides. This drill relies on timing to be executed properly. Perfecting this shot requires a lot of practice. If you practice this drill, you will see the results from the surprised goaltenders who rarely have time to move across the crease to stop this quick shot.

Drill 8-15; Fake Shot. The fake shot is an advanced technique that should be used at least one time per game because it provides an opportunity for the forward to move in closer to the net to execute a higher percentage shot. The drill is set up as shown in the corresponding diagram. At the whistle, the low zone player (X1) passes the puck to the high

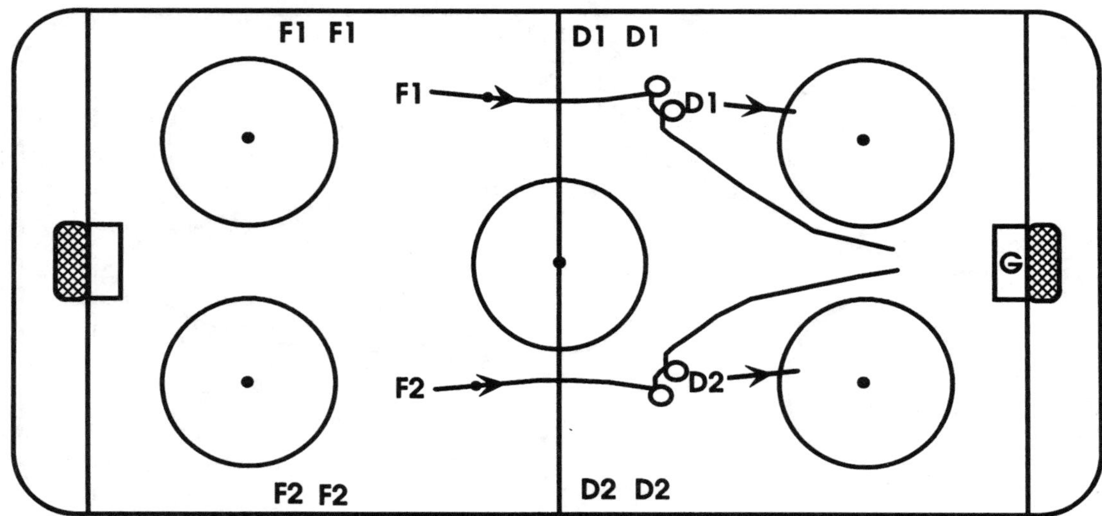

Drill 8-16; Spin-O-Rama

zone player (X2), who takes his stick back and then forward, as if to execute a slap shot, but stops just before it contacts the puck. X2 moves with the puck, around the defender (XF) and toward the net for a shot. Alternate the drill from side 1 to side 2 and back again until all players have performed the drill three times.

Drill 8-16; Spin-O-Rama. The spin-o-rama move is a difficult yet effective way to get free from a defender. It demands a high degree of timing, balance and agility but can be learned with frequent practice. The drill is set up as shown in the diagram above. At the whistle, the first player in line F1 skates toward the defenseman D1. When he gets within about six feet of the defenseman, F1 should begin to move to the outside. After he has taken about two strides to the outside, F1 executes a spin-o-rama move, rotating, cutting back to the inside and then skating forward toward the net for a shot. After side 1 completes the drill, side 2 begins.

Recap

After reading and studying the material in this chapter, you should be able to answer the following questions:

1. Define a forward's offensive and defensive responsibilities.
2. Define an offensive unit. What are the requirements of an offensive unit?
3. How does communication benefit the offensive unit?
4. Define offensive reading and reacting.
5. What are puck fakes and how are they used? What skills need to be perfected before you can be effective at puck fakes?
6. What is body deception and how is it used? What is meant by *selling* when used in conjunction with body deception?
7. List three of the fourteen puck fake/body deception moves and briefly describe each of them.
8. Describe how a forward would employ the body blocking technique. What does the forward need to be careful of when using this technique?
9. When moving into the offensive zone, how should the average attack be structured?
10. What are the priority plays that a forward or offensive unit should use during the one-on-one, two-on-one, and three-on-one scenarios? For this question, assume that there is no trailing support for the scenarios.
11. What are the priority plays that a forward or offensive unit should use during the one-on-two, two-on-two and three-on-two scenarios? For this question, assume that there is a teammate trailing for the one-on-two scenario and that there is no trailing support for the two-on-two or three-on-two scenarios.
12. Where are the three prioritized forechecking areas? How does a forward forecheck in each area? What four forechecking items should the coach monitor and provide feedback on?
13. What is backchecking and how does it benefit a team? What four backchecking items should the coach monitor and provide feedback on?
14. Why is it important to learn your opponent's patterns?
15. What is the benefit of a fake shot? How is it used?
16. How will you use the Offensive Player Checklist and the drills provided in this chapter to help improve individual forwards and offensive team performance, and correct existing deficiencies?

9

Goaltending at Ground Zero

Highlights

This chapter addresses the role of the goaltender and the integrated individual and positional skills required of this position. Chapter 9 presents the following information:

Discussion

Fundamentals

- *stance*
- *knowing where you are in net*
- *crease movement*
- *playing the angles*
- *types of saves*
- *controlling the puck after a shot*
- *handling an offensive attack*

Advanced Techniques

- *learning the opponent's patterns*
- *handling the puck*
- *stopping the puck behind the net*
- *using the stick for active deflections*
- *stick checking*

Siller Player and Team Evaluation Profile — Goaltender Checklist

Drills

Advanced Drills

Recap

Speak softly, and carry a big stick; you will go far.
— Theodore Roosevelt —

The only sure thing about luck is that it will change.
— Wilson Mizner —

Discussion

The position of goaltender is quite possibly the most difficult to play in roller hockey. Faced with a large number of shots, a goaltender is the one player who has a direct impact on the outcome of each game. This is because he has the final opportunity to stop the puck from entering the net. **The role of the goaltender is to defend the net**. He won't stop everything but must try and maximize his potential to stop everything. A goaltender's potential increases when he is in proper position. Positional play is the most important aspect of goaltending.

Unlike other members of a roller hockey team who can rest between shifts, a goaltender is usually on the playing surface for the entire game. He must be able to maintain his workload over a 40- to 50-minute game in a highly efficient manner. Because of this, stamina is crucial. A goaltender must be one of the best-conditioned players on the team, as well as an efficient and powerful skater. The ideal goaltender is also physically strong and able to work at top speed while wearing about 25 pounds of protective equipment. A goaltender must have good balance and reflexes so he can react quickly to high-speed shots which can unpredictably change direction through a deflection. He must have excellent eyesight, combining depth perception, peripheral vision and the ability to focus quickly. He must be extremely agile so he can move quickly near the net and must also be flexible so he can stretch and contort himself in any way required to block or trap the puck. Although goaltending equipment continues to become lighter and more protective than just a few years ago, the lightness has been obtained through the use of plastic, nylon and foam. This combination of materials hinders the skin's ability to breathe and creates body heat buildup and water loss. This loss of water results in an easily fatigued goaltender, so it is very important that a goaltender have access to plenty of water.

A sound basis in fundamental skills is the only way a goaltender can ensure that he will be prepared for the quick pace of roller hockey. Fundamentals are developed through the constant repetition during practice until they become second nature. Practice also develops the confidence and mental toughness required of this position. Goaltenders should be included in all practice planning, as they need instruction just like any other player on the team.

Finally, the forwards can look to the defensemen for help. The defensemen can look to the goaltender for help. The goaltender knows that the puck must stop with him. Roller hockey is a team game, but in the end, the greatest pressure is on one position, the goaltender, at ground zero.

Fundamentals

The **seven fundamental goaltender techniques** covered in this section include stance, knowing where you are in net, crease movement, playing the angles, types of saves, controlling the puck after a shot and handling an offensive attack.

Stance refers to the way a goaltender positions his body in preparation for a shot. An effective stance allows the goaltender to maintain proper balance, cover the maximum net area, move as efficiently as possible and feel comfortable.

- To **maintain proper balance**, the goaltender should lean forward slightly and get into a crouched position with the stomach comfortably drawn in and the chest held high. The body should be positioned so that the weight flows in a line from the shoulders, through the bent knees to the skates. An ideally balanced goaltender has his weight directly over the balls of the feet. A goaltender who puts most of his weight on the toes of the skates is leaning too far forward and is off balance. A goaltender who puts most of his weight on the heels of the skates is either leaning too far back or standing too straight. In either case, balance and mobility will suffer.

- To **cover the maximum net area**, the goaltender needs to properly position his upper body, lower body, glove and blocker, and stick.

  The upper body leans forward at the waist to maintain proper balance, not too upright or bent over, and always faces the play (puck). As the

Goaltender's Stance

goaltender crouches closer to the playing surface, the line between the ankles, knees and shoulders will be forward leaning with respect to the playing surface. This forward lean can be used when there is traffic in front of the net and the goaltender needs to get low to see the play. The head should be held up slightly to allow the goaltender to view the playing surface fully.

Leg pads should be angled away from the body's midline by pointing the toes slightly outward. When viewed from above, the angling of the pads resembles a wedge, which is pointed toward the shooter. This will provide the goaltender with the ability to direct the puck away from the front of the net. The knees should be together and slightly bent, with the skates apart. This produces an inverted V or ***lambda*** (the Greek letter Ë) pad positioning. By using the lambda positioning, the goaltender creates an opening called the *five-hole* (the space between the goaltender's legs). The five-hole is the most vulnerable spot on a goaltender; but with this vulnerability comes benefits. Lambda positioning allows greater protection of the two lower corners, with less protection for only one location, the five-hole. Using a more standup style of goaltending, with the pads close together, the five-hole is covered but the two corners are left open. Lambda pad positioning also makes it easier for goaltenders to go down to their knees and to get back up on their skates again.

The glove and blocker should be positioned off to the sides, slightly ahead and above the knees. The glove should be open and ready to catch the puck at all times. Sometimes young players become so involved in the play that they forget about the glove hand and let it drop in front of them. A glove that is closed or resting on the knee will rarely stop a puck. The blocker should be angled to deflect shots toward the corner of the rink.

The stick is held by the blocker hand on the thin part of the shaft next to the paddle. The hand fits snugly over the arch of the shaft of the stick, with the index finger on the front side and the rest of the fingers wrapped around the shaft. The stick is positioned with the blade flat on the playing surface. Sometimes only the heel or toe of the stick blade is in contact with the playing surface. This is not proper technique. The goaltender may have an incorrect stick lie or the heel of his stick may be worn down. Check the stick and if either problem exists, replace it. The stick blade should be angled slightly toward the corner of the rink, ensuring that any puck that strikes the blade will deflect into the corner and not bounce back out in front of the net. The blade should be positioned about four inches in front of the skates. This will guarantee that the puck strikes a flexible blade which can cup the puck and better control it. A stick resting too closely against the toes of the skates will cause the puck to bounce off the blade, possibly right back to the opposition.

- A goaltender **moves efficiently** by learning, practicing and improving the proper techniques and overall system described in the remainder of this chapter. Moving efficiently allows a goaltender to save, deflect and control the puck with minimum effort.
- **Feeling comfortable** while wearing 25 pounds of protective equipment can be trying at best. But to be the most effective goaltender possible, comfort must enter the picture. This fourth facet of stance is a way to incorporate a part of the individual into the game in the form of style and uniqueness. Feeling comfortable should not only be employed with the stance, but with each of the techniques described in this chapter to produce results that are both effective as well as best suited for the individual. A cardinal rule for

instructors is that you don't try to change a goaltender's style, you try to improve it. As a player matures and gains more experience in the net, he will begin to adjust and adapt his skills to his particular likes and dislikes. As long as the adaptation is in the direction of improvement, it is acceptable.

Knowing where you are in net. A goaltender needs to know where he is in relation to his net at all times. Unfortunately, he rarely has time to look behind to see where the net is and where he is in relation to it. Awareness of position near the net must become second nature for the goaltender and is the kind of skill that is only developed through constant practice. There are **two methods** a goaltender can use to determine where he is in relation to the net without turning the head: tapping the posts and using reference points.

Tapping the posts means just what it says. By using the stick, blocker or glove to tap the post periodically, a goaltender can quickly assess where he is in relation to the net. This technique should be done with the least possible disruption to the goaltender's stance. This method works when the goaltender is close to a post, but is not effective if the goaltender has moved out more than a couple feet away from the net. When he is out and away from the net, a goaltender should use reference points, such as the far net, the center red line and the two near face-off circles, to gauge his location. By lining up the far net, the center face-off circle and the halfway point between the two near face-off circles, the goaltender can locate position P3, which is the center of his net. To locate the right/left post, the goaltender can:

- Line up the point where the center red line meets the right/left boards and the inside of the right/left face-off dots. This point is P2/P4.
- Connect a line between the two near face-off dots and the boards. Where this line meets the right/left boards, connect another line between that point and the lower inside edge of the face-off circle. This point is P1/P5.

If these cues are used properly, there should be no need for the goaltender to touch the posts with his stick, blocker or glove, or to look back at the net.

***Note*:** Some roller hockey rinks may not have many markings on their playing surface. To get around this problem, one of the first things a goaltender should do when he moves into the crease before a game is to find some reference points on the boards or on the walls that will help him. Tap the posts when you can, but you will need to use reference points to help you when you are out and away from the net.

Crease Movement. Moving around the crease requires quickness, efficiency, agility and the discipline to maintain all of this while remaining in the basic stance. Goaltenders are constantly starting, moving and stopping when the play is in their end in an effort to maintain proper position. Since most goaltenders are on their skates about 90 percent of the game, they must develop strong legs and be very effective at moving around the crease. Being a good skater is by far the biggest asset in goaltending. In order to move from side to side and

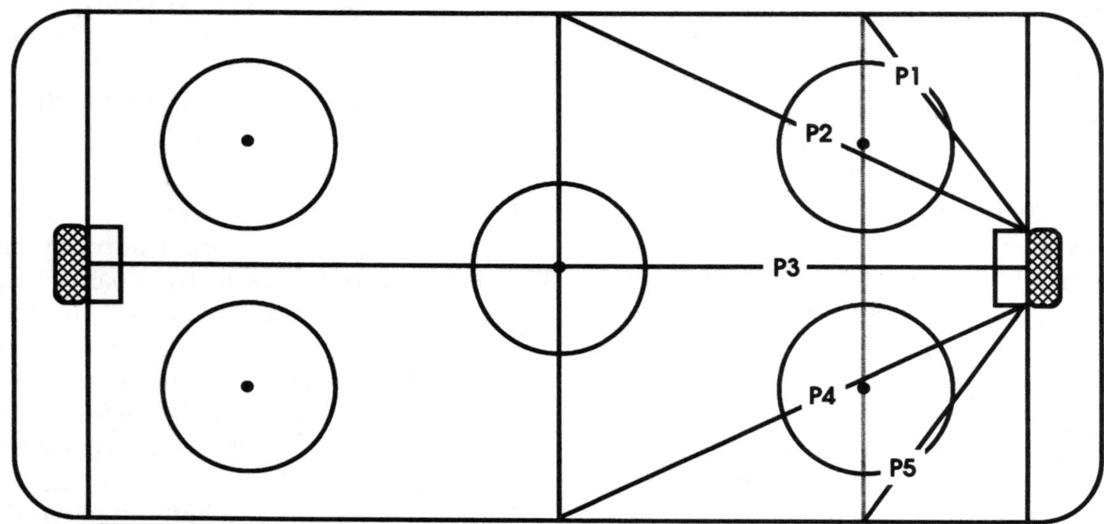

Figure 9-1; Net References

cover all parts of the net, a goaltender must be confident on his wheels. Crease movement consists of **three basic kinds of motion** — forward and backward, left and right, and down and up.

- **Forward and backward** motion allows the goaltender to move toward and away from the shooter to better challenge him. When the goaltender moves forward or backward to cover the play, he must do so with a minimum of extra movement. This motion should be smooth because too much movement from the leg, knee or shoulder disrupts the stance. Moving forward and backward consists of starting and moving, and stopping, and in both cases, the goaltender must maintain his ready stance so that he can effectively face the shooter at all times. A goaltender has three options to initiate and maintain forward motion — the figure-eight, the T-push and the V-push. The figure eight (or double-C) begins with the toes of the skates about shoulder width apart and pointed outward. The goaltender leans slightly forward to begin moving. When the skates move apart about 2½ feet, the goaltender points the toes of his skates inward. This type of movement is used to slowly move out of the crease about six feet. The T-push requires the goaltender to rotate the drive (pushing) skate so that it is at a 90-degree angle with the glide skate, with the glide skate pointed in the intended direction of travel. Extend the drive leg moderately or fully to move. A moderate leg extension will move the goaltender out about six to eight feet at a moderate pace, while the full leg extension will move the goaltender out beyond eight feet at a quicker pace. Once the drive leg has extended, it must be brought back into the lambda position and glides forward to face the shooter. This technique can be repeated a couple of times to move the necessary distance and is a good technique to use when the goaltender needs to quickly move toward the shooter or when moving around to the side or back of the net to retrieve the puck. The V-push combines attributes of the figure-eight and T-push to allow the goaltender to move quickly to any destination. To begin, both skates are turned slightly outward (to a V position) and the drive leg extends in the same manner as with the T-push, and then returns to the lambda position. The other leg then acts as the drive leg and the cycle is repeated. This technique is similar to the V-start described in Chapter 3 and is used when the goaltender wants to skate more than two or three strides out from the crease to intercept a loose puck before an attacker can retrieve it.

  Once the shooter gets close, the goaltender has to move backward to avoid being caught too far out from the net. A goaltender has two options to initiate and maintain backward motion; the figure-eight and the C-push. The figure-eight is executed in the same manner described above except that the toes are pointed inward at the beginning and outward at the end. The C-push (similar to the C-start described in Chapter 3) requires the goaltender to rotate the drive (pushing) skate so that it is at a 45-degree angle with the glide skate, with the glide skate pointed in the intended direction of travel. Extend the drive leg out and then bring it around in the shape of a C to move. The drive leg must be brought back into the lambda position while gliding backward so that the goaltender can track the shooter toward the net. This technique can be repeated to move the necessary distance back to the crease.

  To stop while skating either forward or backward and still maintain proper stance, the goaltender has to employ a snowplow, also called the V-stop. Beginning goaltenders should start out using both skates to stop, since this a more comfortable and balanced technique. As they progress, goaltenders should only use one skate to stop. This allows the other leg pad to remain squarely to the play and allows the goaltender to quickly transition from forward-to-backward movement (or vice versa) since the drive leg is already in position. To perform this stop, position both skates (for the two skate V-stop) so that the point of the V is in the direction of travel (i.e., if you want to stop while moving backward, the heels will be brought together so that the V is pointing behind you). Crouch and lean slightly away from the direction of travel as the skates are brought together to form a V (lean forward if you are moving backward) and put pressure on the inside edge of the wheels. The goaltender should eventually be able to stop using either the left or right skate. The best stop is made by using the farside skate (the skate farthest away from the shooter), whenever possible. This will give the goaltender a chance to react using the shortside skate and leg pad if shots are directed to his short side.

- **Left and right** motion allows the goaltender to move to the left and right of his current position to better challenge a shooter or to protect the crease near either post. Moving laterally consists of starting and moving, and stopping, and in both cases, the goaltender must maintain his ready stance so that he can effectively face the shooter at all times. Goaltenders use two methods for moving laterally: the shuffle and the T-push. The shuffle is the slower of the two methods and is only used when the puck is more than 35 feet from the net. If the goaltender wants to move to the right he moves the right skate about one foot to the right, then brings the left skate over to the right skate, and repeats this process one or two more times to cover the desired distance. The reverse happens when he wants to move left. With each step of the shuffle, the five-hole opens wider than with the T-push. This, plus the lack of speed, are two reasons why the shuffle shouldn't be used when the puck is in close. The faster and more efficient lateral move is the T-push. The T-push is utilized the same way as described earlier, with the glide leg pointed either to the left or right instead of forward. Be sure the shoulders lean into the intended direction and do not pop upward, since this may cause imbalance. The stick blade should be kept on the playing surface at all times to protect the five hole during this move. When using either of these lateral moves it is important to move efficiently. Any movement in any direction other than the one intended prevents the goaltender from moving as quickly as he should and compromises balance. To stop, the lead skate is rotated back until it is parallel with the drive skate. Weight is then placed over the inside edge of the wheels of the lead skate.
- **Down and up** movement is required by the goaltender to block low shots, deflections, screen shots and lateral plays. With newer goaltenders, the coach should concentrate on one item — making sure that when a goaltender goes down he can get back up again. Down and up movement is covered in more detail in the sections below.

Playing the angles is a technique used to position a goaltender in the correct shooting line to cover the largest area of the net. The angles being referred to are the surface angle and the aerial angle. The **surface angle** is created by drawing a line from the center of the goal line to the puck (see figures 9-2 and 9-3) and the **aerial angle** is created by drawing a line from the crossbar to the puck (see Figure 9-4). By drawing these lines, angles are created (with respect to the net) that are used by the goaltender to **guide his body and glove/blocker to the most effective placement**. Angles are classified into three general categories: slight, moderate and extreme.

- Slight surface angles occur when the goaltender plays a shot which is coming at him from a point between the two near face-off circles (upper angle in Figure 9-2). A moderate surface angle is played by a goaltender when the puck is between the inside edge of either near face-off circle and the face-off dot (lower angle in Figure 9-2). An extreme surface angle is played by a goaltender when the puck is between either of the nearest face-off dots and the left or right portion of the goal line where it meets the boards (Figure 9-3). By centering themselves on the surface angle, goaltenders increase the amount of net they cover (as opposed to standing in the middle of the net facing directly ahead). Positioning the body at this optimal angle to reduce the openings in the net is one of the key areas for successful goaltending. A goaltender can stop many shots just by playing the proper angle, even if the puck is moving faster than the goaltender can physically move. Many times, when the shot is coming from the side of the rink, especially if the shooter is on his off-wing (i.e., left-handed shooter coming down the right side), goaltenders will mistakenly line up their angle with the player rather than the puck. By playing the shooter instead of **playing the puck**, a goaltender is incorrectly positioning himself and will not be centered at the optimal angle, allowing additional open net area to shoot at. **Goaltenders *must* align themselves with the puck** to stay in the best position. It is also important that beginning goaltenders play the surface angles evenly and do not over- or under-cover the short or far side (called cheating). Experienced goaltenders can utilize cheating to

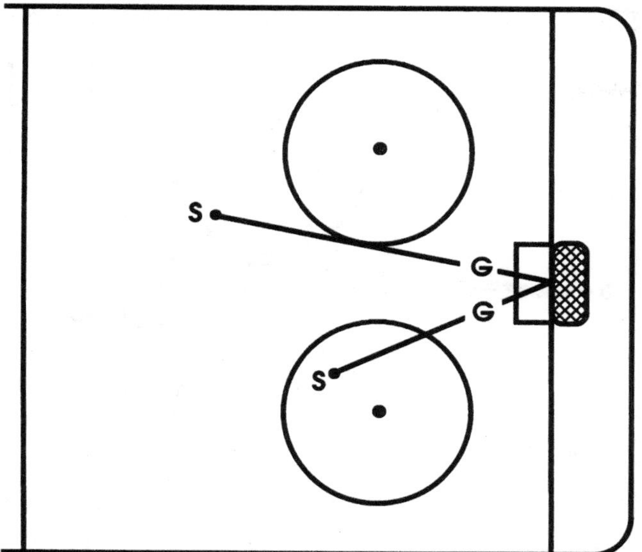

Figure 9-2; Slight/Moderate Surface Angles

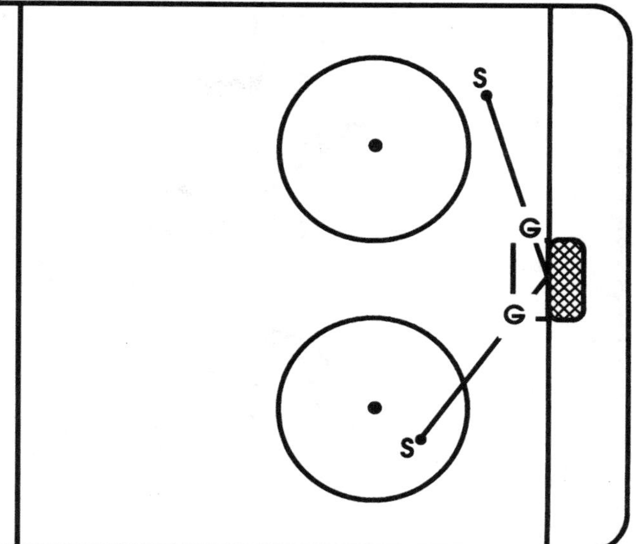

Figure 9-3; Extreme Surface Angles

provide a shooter with a false opening, which can be covered up by a quick goaltender.

- Aerial angles are important because they determine the maximum height that the puck can be placed to go into the net. By reading this height (angle), the goaltender knows that his glove and blocker must be kept at or below this height. If the glove/blocker are placed above this height, the goaltender is covering an area above the net. Slight aerial angles occur when the puck is between the bottom of the face-off circle and the goal line (Figure 9-4). Moderate aerial angles occur when the puck is between the top and bottom of the face-off circle, and extreme aerial angles occur when the puck is beyond the top of the face-off circle. As the goaltender moves to face the shooter and play the proper surface and aerial angles, he must remember to maintain his stance so that he can cover the most net area.

Once the goaltender understands how to play the angles, he must determine how far to move toward the shooter to cover the most net area without getting too far out of position. This balance is developed with lots of experience, understanding what is meant by the goaltender's alley and a technique called telescoping. The **goaltender's alley** is the area formed by drawing lines from each goal post to the puck. In Figure 9-5, the surface angle is shown as the gray line and the goaltender's alley is shown as the area within the solid black lines. The puck, when shot, must remain inside the alley to be on goal (barring a redirection of the puck). The goaltender should always stay in the alley when facing the shooter. If he goes outside the alley, he is covering an area outside of the net.

To understand how the concept of **telescoping** works, look at an object on the wall, like a clock or small picture. Extend your finger toward it, and close one eye. Now, move your finger back toward

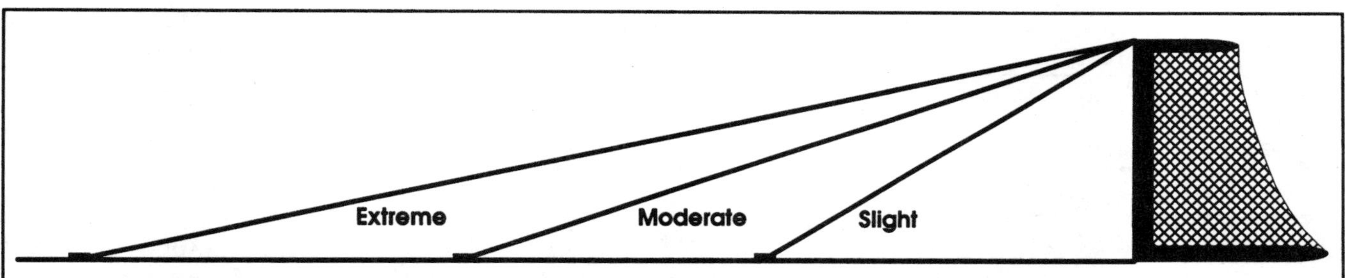

Figure 9-4; Aerial Angles

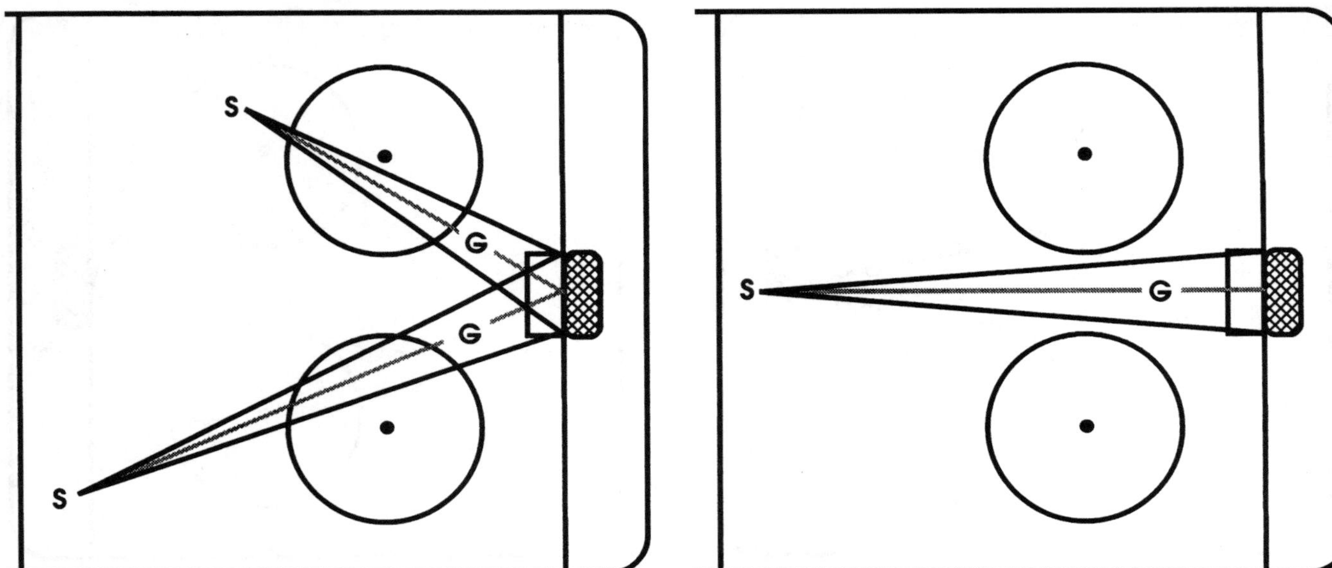

Figure 9-5; Goaltender's Alley

your open eye. As you move your finger toward that eye, the object is covered more and more by your finger, and at some point, your finger will totally block your view of the object. This same principle is used by a goaltender when trying to find that point where his body most effectively blocks the shooter's open net area. For example, let's say that a shooter has the puck and is 20 feet out directly in front of the net. If the goaltender is positioned directly on the goal line, how far out should he move toward the shooter (telescope) on the surface angle to reduce the available net area by 50 percent? By telescoping, the goaltender will reduce the available net area every foot he moves out from the goal line. Table 9-1 shows that a *reduction in shooting area of more than 50 percent* can be achieved by having the goaltender move out six feet from the goal line (when the shooter is 20 feet from the goal line, as compared to having the goaltender on the goal line). This also translates into the fact that for every foot the goaltender moves out past the goal line to cover the shooter, *the available net area decreases by approximately one square foot!* The following two pictures provide visual proof that there is more available net area when the goaltender is on to the goal line (left photo) than when he is out six feet from the goal line (right photo).

To cover 100 percent of the available net area (blocking the net completely from the shooter), the

Distance a Goaltender Moves Out From The Goal Line	**Shooting Area** (square feet)	**Reduction in Shooting Area** (compared to 0 feet)
0 feet	24 - 10 = 14	0.0%
1 foot	12.8	8.5%
2 feet	11.6	17.0%
3 feet	10.4	25.5%
4 feet	9.2	34.0%
5 feet	8.0	42.5%
6 feet	6.8	**51.0%**

Table 9-1; Shooting Area Versus Goaltender Distance

Note: This table was developed using the following assumptions: the net size is 6 feet by 4 feet (24 square feet), the goaltender covers 10 square feet and the shooter/puck is 20 feet from the goal line directly in front of the net.

In The Crease

Six Feet Out

goaltender has to move out from the net approximately 12 feet. In that case he would be closer to the shooter than the net and this creates a situation where the shooter could easily move around the goaltender and score. Although telescoping is an effective technique, a goaltender needs to balance the distance from the shooter with the distance from the net. To maximize the effectiveness of telescoping, the goaltender should be aware of the **front door/back door** concept. The front door refers to the area between the shooter and the goaltender and the back door refers to the area between the goaltender and the net. If the goaltender comes out when the puck and shooter are near the boards, he is always involved in a tradeoff between how much area to allow for both the front door and back door. The farther a goaltender comes out to take away the front door, the more the back door is left vulnerable to a passing play. The goaltender must read the situation and use experience developed during practice and game situations to react appropriately. If there is no one on the back door (no opponent to the side or behind the goaltender), he can come out farther and cover more of the front door. If an opponent is near the back door, the goaltender must give up a bit of the front door to cover the back door. The goaltender's positioning is based on the location of all players — not just the puck. Therefore, playing the angles is based on the situation and how you read it.

Types of saves. The coach who understands the dynamics of a save can help goaltenders dramatically improve their save percentage. The **four factors required to make a save** are proper stance, being square to the shooter, moving along the surface angle with respect to the shooter within the goaltender's alley, and keeping your blocker and glove at or below the aerial angle. All of these factors are designed to cut down the available net area. In addition, the goaltender needs to be aware of all potential attackers, not just the shooter. Peripheral vision is used to keep track of the potential attackers. Peripheral vision allows the goaltender to keep an attacker in view while watching the puck. It also allows him to see a large percentage of the playing surface in the direction his head is turned. By being aware of other players, the goaltender has that additional information required to play the puck while being able to anticipate the options that the attacking team has. After a shot has been taken, the goaltender must follow it from the moment it leaves the shooter's stick to the moment it strikes the goaltender's equipment. The goaltender must be able to react quickly to the movement of the puck and move accordingly. Reaction time and movement time are improved through constant practice.

To be able to save the puck, a goaltender must understand the mechanics of each type save. The **six types of saves** covered in this section consist of using the glove, blocker, pads, skates, upper body and stick. Once the goaltender understands the individual type of saves, he can begin to combine one or more to stop multiple shots. A special type of save situation also described in this section occurs when the puck is to the side or behind the net. Remember that a goaltender is not alone; the posts and crossbar can always be counted on to come up with a couple of additional saves each game.

- **The glove** hand is usually a goaltender's strong point. The glove allows the goaltender to do what no other player can do — hold onto the puck. The glove also provides for some of the most spectacular saves in roller hockey. Excellent hand-eye coordination is essential to perfect the glove save. Cross-training in other sports, such as racquetball, tennis and pingpong is one way to improve a goaltender's hand-eye coordination. The catching or grasping action is perhaps the most instinctive of all goaltending moves. The goaltender should not attempt to stop every shot with his glove. Reaching over to the blocker side or down to the playing surface can compromise the goaltender's balance. The glove should be used to stop shots directed at the glove side of the goaltender from the midline of the body out to the arm's full extension and above the knees. The glove arm should be relaxed. This allows the arm to give, like a shock absorber, when the puck reaches it, making the shot easier to hold and control. The glove should be positioned at knee height, just above the leg pad and open in preparation of a shot. During practice, beginning goaltenders should catch and hold onto every puck. Later, they can be coached to continue play, if their team is under no pressure. The glove is also used to trap or smother the puck against any portion of his body or when it is lying on the playing surface. To smother the puck effectively, the goaltender must lower his center of gravity as he moves the glove to the puck. This can be done by dropping to one or both knees or by diving onto his stomach. Once the glove has firmly trapped the puck, the goaltender should ensure it is not dislodged by an opponent by putting his body weight into the glove and by protecting the glove with his stick. The goaltender can use the stick blade to cover the back of his glove, making sure he leaves a cushioning space between the blade and the glove.

- **The blocker** is used most effectively to deflect pucks into the corner. The blocker is positioned at knee level, just above the leg pads. The blocker should not be moved across the body to cover shots on the glove side or shots that are much below the waist. The blocker move should involve a rotation of the wrist toward the corner. This angles the blocker and directs the puck away from the shooter. Move the blocker backward slightly as the puck approaches. This cushions the shot, reducing the chance of a fast rebound. Some goaltenders like to bend their blockers, giving them a banana shape. This can also help cushion shots and allow the goaltender better control of rebounds. However, it does slightly reduce the blocking area as compared to a flat blocker.

Butterfly Position

- **Pads.** Three pad saves discussed in this section include the wedge, the butterfly and stacking the pads. The **wedge pad save** involves the goaltender using the leg pads to direct the puck away from the net while maintaining the basic stance. The pads are angled slightly toward the sides of the rink, allowing the puck to hit the pads and deflect away from the front of the net. If the knees are pushed forward, this stance allows the goaltender to direct the puck down to the playing surface where it can be trapped.

  With low shots, a goaltender can choose to extend his pad or stick, or go down to the playing surface using the **butterfly** position. The butterfly position requires the goaltender to drop to his (or in this example, her) knees and push the skates and leg pads to the sides so that both pads are parallel to the playing surface and facing out toward the shooter to cover the lower corners. The butterfly position can extend into the splits as a last resort to stop a low shot. When in the butterfly position, goaltenders have their stick in front of the five-hole and keep their knees fairly close together. The upper body must be erect and the center of gravity must be forward over the knees. The glove is open and out to the side and in front of the upper body. If the goaltender does not stop play after the save, she must get back to her skates right away. The move requires flexibility at the hips, excellent leg strength and a refined level of balance. When the goaltender uses both legs simultaneously to raise herself, this allows movement to either left or right in reaction to the direction of the next shot.

As a last resort, the goaltender can **stack the pads** to stop the puck. Use this move to block the puck as it moves across the front of the net and close to the goaltender. This will occur with point shots which are deflected from the side of the crease, on quick shots from an extreme angle, shots made from passes from behind the net and on breakaways. This pad save utilizes the entire body, like a wall, to minimize open net area. The goaltender has to ensure that no holes are created in this wall through improper technique. The save begins with the T-push, followed by a sliding motion of the body in the direction of puck travel along the playing surface. Both leg pads are extended and stacked, one on top of the other. The arm on the top of the wall covers open area above the wall (the goaltender needs to watch the puck to determine where to move this arm) while the lower arm stretches outward to cover any open space along the playing surface.

- **Skates.** Goaltenders usually make skate saves on shots to the low corners. The goaltender uses the T-push to initiate the skate save. Turn the save skate in the direction the rebound should go, bend the drive leg slightly and push toward the puck with the drive leg. The wheels are kept on the playing surface as the leg continues to move sideways to deflect the puck. The bent knee should drop to the playing surface to maximize lateral distance of the save skate and for goaltender comfort. Skate saves leave goaltenders very vulnerable; they wind up out of position and out of proper stance. Once the skate save is made, the goaltender must quickly resume proper stance.
- The **upper body** save is made using the chest, arms, shoulders or stomach to block the puck. This type of save is one that does not require any special movement for the chest and stomach save, and little special movement for the arm and shoulder save. The goaltender can deflect the puck over the net if it is shot at the arms or shoulders. When the puck is shot at the chest or stomach, control the puck using the glove if you are standing on your wheels, or use either the glove or blocker if you are down on the playing surface.
- **The goaltender's stick** is a multipurpose tool

Stacking The Pads

and should be used to:

- Stop shots with the blade, paddle or shaft.
- Direct pucks into the corner.
- Shoot pucks away.
- Pass pucks.
- Scoop the puck into the goaltender's body or glove.
- Trap the puck.
- Protect the goaltender from attacking players (legally).
- Bat the puck out of the air and away from the net.
- Push opposing players who may be screening the goaltender's vision.
- Stick check pucks away from opponents.

The stick is usually the best means of stopping shots along the playing surface. The stick can deflect the puck at any desired angle or can cushion the puck with a little give of the blade. When the stick is held at the optimum angle and at the proper location on the shaft, the blade is perfectly balanced on the pivot point of the wrist. If the goaltender is having difficulty controlling the stick, more than likely the stick is either too long or too heavy for the player. The stick blade should be positioned flat on the playing surface, slightly ahead of the toes of the skates. Make sure that the stick has the proper lie for the goaltender (the lie is the angle between the shaft of the stick and the playing surface). If a goaltender seems to have a lot of trouble with low shots, there is a good chance that he has the wrong lie on the stick or that the stick is not kept flat on the playing surface. Goaltenders should not hold onto the stick too tightly. They should allow the momentum of the shot to move the stick back to the toes of the skates or in the case of a butterfly save, against the leg pads. Pucks shot at the stick should be steered to a teammate or to the corner by angling the blade to that area on the playing surface, or trapped.

- **Play coming from behind the net.** When the puck is to the side or behind the net, the goaltender is required to position himself differently than when the play is coming from in front. The goaltender needs to move to the post nearest the puck with the skate hugging that post. The stance should be fairly tight, with his body coming out on a 45-degree angle from the goal line. The goaltender should be ready to use his stick to block a centering pass. At all times, the goaltender should watch the puck, but never fully turn around to face it, since he would not be facing the shooter if the puck was moved out front. The head may have to be rotated back over the other shoulder, *but only if the puck moves in that direction.* The goaltender should keep the puck in view and not assume that it is somewhere without seeing it.

Play Coming from Behind the Net

If the blocker arm is nearest the post, that elbow or upper arm should hold the post tightly. The stick should be extended outside the net with the end of the shaft just behind the goal line. The stick blade must be able to pull the puck against the net to freeze it. If the glove arm is the closest one to the post, the entire arm holds the post tightly as the stick blade is extended parallel to the goal line. The blade should be ready to either poke check or deflect the puck if it is carried or passed near the post. If the puck comes free, the stick blade can sweep across and trap the puck on the net. In either case, the stick blade should be ready to protect the space between the skate and the post.

When the puck moves out from behind the net or from the corner toward the side of the net, the goaltender must hold his ground and prevent the puck from being pushed into the net between the post and his leg. The goaltender moves to the post and assumes the proper stance. The leg closest to the post should be tightly held against the post. This will prevent the puck from being squeezed into the goal. An important point to remember is that the goaltender should stay on his skates and in the proper stance, ready to move to the center of the net at any time. If the goaltender drops down to trap the puck, he could open up a space which could allow the puck to slip under a pad or in off the post.

Controlling the puck after a shot requires the goaltender to have a plan, and that plan involves effectively reading the play. Reading and reacting refers to the ability of the goaltender to perceive the play of opponents around him and to respond appropriately. Total situational awareness and accurate perception form the basis upon which effective goaltender reading and reacting occur. How the goaltender controls the puck should be a team decision. **The rule is,** if the team is under pressure, the goaltender should stop play. If the team is not under pressure, the goaltender can keep the play going. Pressure occurs when:

- There are attackers near the net.
- The goaltender is tired, or a teammate is tired from a long shift.
- The goaltender or another player has lost a stick.
- The opposition has taken several shots in a short period of time and the goaltender wants to halt the momentum.

When there is pressure, the goaltender can stop play by catching the puck and holding on to it, covering up the puck on the playing surface or deflecting the puck out of play. If there is no pressure, the goaltender can continue play by deflecting the puck into the corner or move the puck to a teammate. The complete goaltender needs to practice puck control skills to set up or move the puck to a teammate. Even though the glove and blocker take some getting used to, make sure that the goaltender participates in puck control drills, and expect the same level of commitment from him that you expect from every other player. The goaltender must be quick to clear any pucks in front of the net to a teammate or to the corner.

Handling an offensive attack is what it all comes down to for a goaltender. This job combines all of the material previously presented in this chapter to maximize the potential to stop the puck from entering the net. Patience is crucial to handling the attack. By being patient, you can read the play develop and not overcommit yourself. Having confidence is not only important, it is also fundamental to playing the attack. Coaches must constantly instill confidence in their goaltenders. If a goaltender is going to stop shots, he must have confidence in himself and believe that he can stop the shots. A player's negative thoughts and self-doubts are often a shooter's best friend. Two types of offensive attacks will be covered in this section. The first occurs when the goaltender has no immediate defensive support, such as a breakaway, shoot-out or penalty shot. The second type of attack occurs when the goaltender has immediate defensive support in the form of one or two defensemen and/or backchecking forward.

During the first type of offensive attack, the goaltender reads the developing play and determines that he is the only defender immediately available to stop the oncoming attack. To effectively play this situation, the goaltender needs to continue to read the play and quickly answer the following questions:

- How many attackers are in the play? Where are they positioned?
- Are there any trailing attackers?
- Is the puck carrier/shooter coming down the middle of the playing surface or to the side? If he is on the side, is he on his off-wing (left-handed shooter on the right side) or on his normal side?
- Is the puck carrier/shooter a good skater? Is he able to confidently control the puck?
- Are any teammates available to protect rebounds?
- Which attacker is in the best position to score?

The goaltender can use this information to develop an appropriate strategy to maximize his potential to stop the puck. The strategy for this first type of offensive attack is a six-step process as follows:

1. **Maintain the proper stance.** This consists of maintaining balance; covering the maximum net area; positioning the upper body, lower body and pads, glove and blocker, and stick properly; moving efficiently; and feeling comfortable.
2. **Know where you are in net** by tapping the posts and using reference points.

3. **Play the surface and aerial angles** to cover the maximum net area.
4. **Read the play** using the goaltender's alley and telescoping as guides, and move toward the puck carrier/shooter. Come out at least six to 10 feet beyond the goal line initially. This leaves little open net area, and should force the player to deke. Stay out from the crease until the player is about 30 feet away. Always be aware of how much space is available at the front door and back door. Use peripheral vision to watch any non-puck carriers and prepare and anticipate to move if a pass is made. When the player is near the top of the face-off circles, the goaltender begins his backward motion. This backward motion also provides the necessary momentum to move laterally. The gap between the goaltender and the shooter should close slowly. Don't back in too slowly or the player will go around you. But don't back in too fast, either, because a shooter just has to wait until the goaltender is on the goal line and then shoot into an open corner. Experience and lots of practice will determine the proper flow for a particular play. Don't get any deeper than the top of the crease, and don't stop your backward motion or plant your skates. Stay on your skates as long as you can. It is better to let the shooter make the first move and anticipate a second move rather than guess what is going to happen next (anticipation is planning based on proper reading of the play and a goaltender's experience level; guessing is planning based upon random and incomplete reading of the play and a goaltender's experience level). **When a player decides to deke**, the puck is usually in front of him and **when he intends to shoot**, it is usually on his side.
5. **Decide how to control the puck after the shot.** Is it better to stop play or keep it going?
6. **Choose the appropriate save for the situation.** These saves include using the glove, blocker, pads (wedge, butterfly, stacking the pads), skates, upper body and stick. During this type of offensive attack, the puck carrier/shooter is almost always going to go to the deke versus the shot. This is because when the goaltender is positioned in his proper stance, he is harder to beat than when he has to move and is in a transition phase. During this transition phase, the moving goaltender opens up areas which become the targets for the player executing the deke. Remember to play the puck, not the shooter. Make sure that the two low corners and five-hole are protected. Use pad saves on dekes, since they cover more net, more quickly. When stacking the pads or using the butterfly on a deke, the goaltender's motion should be at a diagonal from the top of the crease toward the outside of the goal post. This minimizes the chance of the player going around the goaltender and having a large area of open net to shoot at. **After the save**, cover the puck or get back into position if the puck is still in play.

The second type of attack occurs when the goaltender reads the play and determines that he has immediate defensive support in the form of one or two defensemen and/or backchecking forwards. During this offensive attack, the goaltender needs to continue to read the play and answer the following questions:

- How many attackers are in the play? Where are they positioned?
- How many defenders are in the play? Where are they positioned?
- Are there any trailing attackers?
- Is the puck carrier/shooter coming down the middle of the playing surface or to the side? If he is on the side, is he on his off-wing (left-handed shooter on the right side) or on his normal side?
- Is the puck carrier/shooter a good skater? Is he able to confidently control the puck?
- Are any teammates in a position to potentially screen you?
- Which attacker is in the best position to score?

The goaltender can use this information to develop an appropriate strategy to maximize his potential to stop the puck. The strategy for this second type of offensive attack consists of the six steps described in the first type of offensive attack in addition to the following two steps:

1. **The defense must play the man on an even or advantaged attack and play the pass on an outnumbered attack.** In both cases, the goaltender must concentrate on the puck and rely on the defense to do its job with the open attacker(s). On an even or advantaged attack,

the goaltender can come out a little farther to cut down the angle, knowing the defense will prevent the player from moving across the slot. The defense should play the attacker wide to an extreme angle, forcing a bad-angle shot (as shown in Figure 7-13), or poke check the puck away. On an outnumbered attack, the defensive strategy should focus on the pass. The goaltender should play conservatively and be ready to move across the crease in case of a pass. If a shot is executed, the defense should immediately move to neutralize any open attackers. If a pass is executed, the goaltender needs to be aware of the most dangerous potential attacker. Figure 7-10 shows the prioritized locations to cover. With the puck carrier coming down the right side, the most dangerous potential attacker (No. 1) would be positioned on the far side of the net across from the puck carrier, ready to receive a pass and shoot. If there is no attacker on the far side of the net, then the most dangerous potential attacker (No. 2) would be in the slot. In some situations, the defense may have to confront the puck carrier (No. 3) if he has gained good scoring position. This system breaks down when the defense or goaltender forgets his role.

2. **The goaltender must communicate with his teammates** by calling out that an opposing player is open in the slot, a potential deflector should be cleared from the line of fire, or to inform a defenseman not to back in too close or screen the goaltender. If the goaltender is being screened, he should crouch down a little more than in a normal stance to gain sight of the puck. Once the puck has been located, the goaltender should move toward the puck to cover the angle. This movement should not get him caught up in traffic or out of position in case of a pass. If the goaltender gains control of the puck, he should stop play immediately or deflect the puck to the corner. The goaltender and defense must communicate to ensure that the puck is covered or cleared after a shot.

Advanced Techniques

The five advanced goaltender techniques covered in this section include learning the opponent's patterns, handling the puck, stopping the puck behind the net, using the stick for active deflections and stick checking.

Learning the opponent's patterns. To progress to the next level of roller hockey, it is imperative that each goaltender make a point of learning the various moves and play patterns of his opponents, including the forwards, defense and goaltender(s). A lot of players just try to *do their* job without attempting to understand why or how a player moves the puck by them. Don't leave it only up to the coach to tell you what is working and what is not; **think and evaluate!** If you are playing a team for the first time, you should begin keeping a book (mental notes) on the favorite moves and plays of the opposing players, various line combinations and overall offensive patterns. Determine the opponent's best playmakers, best shooters, how they react to certain situations and exchange this information with your coach and teammates. Watch how the other team's goaltender plays your forwards. Watch how the other team's forwards move past your defensemen. Determine if this information will help you with how you play your opponents and also share this information with your teammates between periods. By the second half of the game, you should at least have a decent book on the team. If you have played a team before, you should recall the information from your book and use it so that you can be in a position to recognize moves and plays when they are initiated. The goaltender should not guess the play of the opponents, but wait until it starts. If you guess and commit too early, a good attacker will put the puck in the net. By correctly reading the play, or occasionally forcing a play, the percentages will be on your side; but you must be alert for any play to occur and anticipate potential plays.

Handling the puck. Goaltending has quickly evolved to the point where a roller hockey goaltender cannot excel without being able to handle and move the puck effectively. Roller hockey goaltenders are becoming more integrated team players due to the pace and style of the game. Communication and reading are essential skills for a goaltender to effectively handle the puck. Goaltenders need to handle the puck as part of the transition game; the phase in which a team transitions from defense to offense. The problem with handling the puck is that most goaltenders do not know how or where to move it. Once the goaltender gains possession of the puck, he can leave the puck or pass it. The first and best choice is to leave the puck for a teammate (usually a defenseman). Ideally, this would be away from the front of the net or behind the goal line and away from the boards. These two locations help prevent the puck from entering the net in case either the defenseman or goaltender mishandle it. When **handling the puck, the goaltender usually has four choices**:

- First, the goaltender can pass to a teammate. Passing the puck requires the goaltender to be a confident stick handler. The goaltender should be able to control the puck with one or two hands. The blocker hand should be strong enough to backhand the puck away from the net. This is done by cupping the puck in the middle of the stick blade, well off to the blocker side. The wrist is rotated as the stick is drawn quickly across in front of the goaltender. The puck is passed to the target with the stick blade following through in the open position. With a two-handed forward pass, the hand position is considerably different from that used by forwards or defensemen. The top glove holds the stick well out from the body so that the stick blade is fully on the playing surface. The upper hand is at the end of the stick shaft and the lower glove is positioned at the top of the paddle. Whether the goaltender chooses a direct pass or chooses to move the puck around the boards, the puck should not be sent too hard. Often, in order to assist the goaltender, the defenseman peels off to avoid a forechecker and gets into a passing lane to wait for the goaltender's pass.
- A second objective would be to clear the puck into the transition zone (Figure 7-1). When clearing, always avoid the middle of the playing surface, and clear the puck toward the boards, between the top of the near face-off circle and the center redline. Remember, do not just aimlessly fire the puck up the boards. Do that and odds are it will wind up on an opponent's stick, and then quite possibly in your net!
- There are times when no teammate is open for a pass and no open lanes exist to clear the puck. In this case, the goaltender must simply move the puck to the corner. This option is better than a direct turnover.
- The fourth option is to appear ready to move the puck, and when an opponent comes within 10 to 15 feet of the goaltender, cover the puck to set up a face-off.

Stopping the puck behind the net. If the opposing team chooses not to carry the puck into the zone but instead dumps the puck into your zone around the boards, the experienced goaltender can gain control of the puck and either leave it there for a teammate or pass it. The goaltender must move quickly out behind the net, gain control of the puck and then return to the net. If the puck is shot around the boards off to the goaltender's blocker side, the goaltender must push off to the glove side and move behind the net to stop the puck using his backhand, one hand on the stick. The stick blade is jammed into, and at right angles to, the boards. The blade should be cupped to help trap the puck. The leg must be ready to be pushed against the boards to block and trap those high shots. If the puck is shot around the boards off to the goaltender's glove side, the goaltender must push off to the blocker side and move behind the net to stop the puck using his forehand with two hands on the stick in the passing position. Again, the stick blade should be jammed into the boards and cupped. The blade should be at a 45-degree angle to help trap the puck and the leg pads must be ready to be pushed against the boards to block and trap high shots. In both cases, if the puck is to be left for a teammate, the puck should be placed out from the boards about six to 12 inches. Too close to the boards and the player may have difficulty picking up the puck. If rushed by the attacking players, the puck should be shot back to the corner it came from.

Using the stick for active deflections

Passive deflections require only an angled stick blade and are described in the fundamental section of this chapter. **Active deflections** are used to clear pucks into corners or to the side boards after a shot when an attacker is rapidly approaching for a rebound. As the shot is taken, the goaltender decides in which direction he wants the rebound to go. The goaltender rotates the stick blade toward the intended direction of the rebound. As the puck hits the blade of the stick, the goaltender uses his skate to kick the stick, either with a small or large kick,

Siller Player And Team Evaluation Profile©
Goaltending Checklist

Evaluator: The Coach **Date**: 4/3/95 **Location**: The Palace

	Player Name									
Notes:	**JAY**		**AMANDA**		**CURTISS**					
Fundamental Goaltending Techniques										
Stance										
• maintain proper balance	9		8		8					
• cover maximum area of net	8		8		8					
• move efficiently	6		5		5					
Knowing Where You Are In Net	6		5		5					
Crease Movement										
• forward and backward	8		8		8					
• left and right	7		8		7					
• down and up	6		8		6					
Playing The Angles	8		8		8					
Glove Saves	9		9		8					
Blocker Saves	8		8		8					
Pad Saves	7		8		7					
Skate Saves	7		7		7					
Upper Body Saves	**10**		**10**		**10**					
Stick Saves	8		8		8					
Plays From Behind The Net	8		8		8					
Controlling The Puck After A Shot	8		8		7					
Handling An Offensive Attack	8		8		6					
Advanced Goaltending Techniques										
Learning Opponent's Patterns	8		7		6					
Handling The Puck	8		7		6					
Stopping The Puck Behind The Net	0		0		0					
Active Deflections	8		8		6					
Stick Checking	6		6		6					
TOTAL SCORE	**161**		**160**		**148**					
AVERAGE SCORE	**7.7**		**7.7**		**7.0**					

Comments: Jay, Amanda and Curtiss have all demonstrated high overall goaltending proficiency with total scores of 161, 160, and 148 respectively, and average scores of 7.7, 7.7, and 7.0 respectively. All three goaltenders scored excellent on the upper body saves. The stopping the puck behind the net technique was not performed during this evaluation session.

Scale: 0 = Not Performed, 1 - 3 = Low Proficiency, 4 - 6 = Medium Proficiency, 7 - 9 = High Proficiency, 10 = Excellent Proficiency

Table 9-1; Goaltending Checklist

to direct the puck away. By adding the velocity of the kicking skate to that of the oncoming puck, the goaltender can actually redirect the puck off to the side at a greater speed than the puck had when it approached the stick blade.

Stick checking can be used as an effective tool to strip opponents of the puck and prevent them from scoring. Stick checking is a technique whereby a goaltender uses his stick (legally) to prevent an opponent from maintaining or acquiring control of the puck. Two stick checking techniques are discussed below, the poke check and the sweep check:

- The **poke check** allows the goaltender to knock the puck off an opponent's stick blade or to intercept a pass. The poke check can be used either when the offensive player cuts across the net or moves straight in close to the goaltender. The action requires the goaltender to let the shaft of the stick slide through his blocker hand until it reaches the knob with the arm fully extended. When the attacker cuts across in front of the net, the goaltender should execute the poke check with the bottom of the blade as the puck carrier draws even to the net. When the player comes straight in, wait until he reaches within an extended stick length. The front knee should be on the playing surface and the back leg is extended. Timing and the element of surprise are very important. If the poke check is done too soon, the attacking player can draw the puck back out of the goaltender's reach and move around the committed goaltender.
- The **sweep check** is used to clear the puck from a wide area. The goaltender extends his blocker up the shaft of the stick, as with the poke check. The glove grasps the stick just below the blocker and the entire length of the stick is pressed down onto the playing surface. The goaltender should drop down on his glove side leg pad to assist the stick in meeting the playing surface. The stick is then swept across the front of the goaltender into the path of the oncoming puck. This check can clear an area of the puck *and any opposing players* quickly. As with the poke check, the goaltender must be sure that the puck is in range before executing the sweep check.

Drills

Goaltending drills should be selected to enable players to adjust to as many situations as possible. Proficiency and confidence come with knowledge and practice. By learning the material in this chapter, the coach and players will become familiar with the particular skills and strategies required to play the unique position of goaltender. As the coach discovers each goaltender's particular needs, he can select the drills required for specific improvement. Drills from chapters 3, 6 and 8 that should be used to improve a goaltender's fundamentals include 3-2 (Starting), 3-5 (Backward Starting) and 3-14 (Sprint Skating), 6-9 (Box Passing and Shoot), 6-14 (Rebounds), 6-16 (Deking The Goaltender), 6-17 (Breakaways) 6-18 (Screen Shots), 6-19 (One-Time Shots), 6-20 (Deflections) and 8-2 (Puck Fakes And Body Deception). Use the Goaltender Checklist to monitor performance and plan improvements for each goaltender.

Prior and subsequent to any of the drills listed in this chapter (and book), goaltenders should warm up and cool down by performing **stretching** techniques designed to lengthen and loosen the muscles associated with the feet, legs, back, arms and shoulders. These techniques will help prevent injuries during practices and games and will prevent some of the muscular tightness that follows the day after a practice or game.

For each drill, the coach should monitor proper technique and provide feedback. The most important fundamental that should be practiced by a goaltender is the stance. The coach should provide feedback to the goaltender on the **nine factors that produce an effective stance:**

- Balance — weight flows in a line from shoulders through the knees to the feet.
- Head up.
- Leg pads angled away from the body's midline (toes pointing slightly outward).
- Knees together and slightly bent, skates apart to produce lambda (inverted V) pad positioning.
- Glove and blocker positioned off to side, slightly ahead and just above knees.

- Glove open and ready to catch the puck at all times.
- Blocker angled to deflect shots toward the corner.
- Stick blade flat on the playing surface, angled slightly toward the corner, positioned about four inches in front of the skates.
- Feel comfortable.

It is important that coaches help prevent bad habits at an early stage. Try not to let the goaltender assume a bad stance or get lazy in the stance. Look for warning signs that the goaltender is getting tired, lazy or sloppy. Usually he begins to let the glove hang at his side with no upward extension. He may begin to sit back on his heels or lean too far forward. Watch for the arms resting on the leg pads or the head held down with only the eyes facing the play.

Drill 9-1; Crease Movement. This drill teaches the goaltender the three basic forms of crease movement — forward (figure-eight, T-push and V-push) and backward (figure-eight and C-push), laterally left and right (shuffle and T-push), and down and up (butterfly). Position the goaltender in the center of the crease just in front of the goal line. The coach calls out one type of crease movement (such as forward T-push) and observes the goaltender action and provides feedback on the move. Lateral movement should be post-to-post and forward/backward movement should be six to eight feet out. Start slowly and then increase the pace. Work the goaltender for 60 seconds, then have him rest for 30 seconds. As the pace increases, work the goaltender for 60 seconds and rest for 45 seconds. Provide feedback to the goaltender on his motion, stance and positioning of the stick blade, making sure that when a goaltender goes down he can quickly get back up again, and symmetry of movement (doesn't favor one side). A variation of this drill is to add four players and a puck, in a box formation around the net. As the players move the puck around the box, the goaltender executes the proper crease movement.

Drill 9-2; Knowing Where You Are In Net. This drill teaches the goaltender how to determine where he is in net. Position the goaltender in the center of the crease, just in front of the goal line. At the whistle, have the goaltender move to the left post and then back to the center of the crease. At the next whistle, have the goaltender move to the right post and then back to the center of the crease. Provide feedback to the goaltender on his positioning. Repeat the process four more times.

The second part of this drill teaches the goaltender how to determine where he is in net when he is out from the crease. Prior to this drill, the coach should help the goaltender identify appropriate reference points around the rink (see corresponding diagram) that will help him determine the location of the left and right posts and the center of the net. Position the goaltender two feet out from the goal line along P3. At the whistle, have the goaltender move along P5 and then back to P3. At the next whistle, have

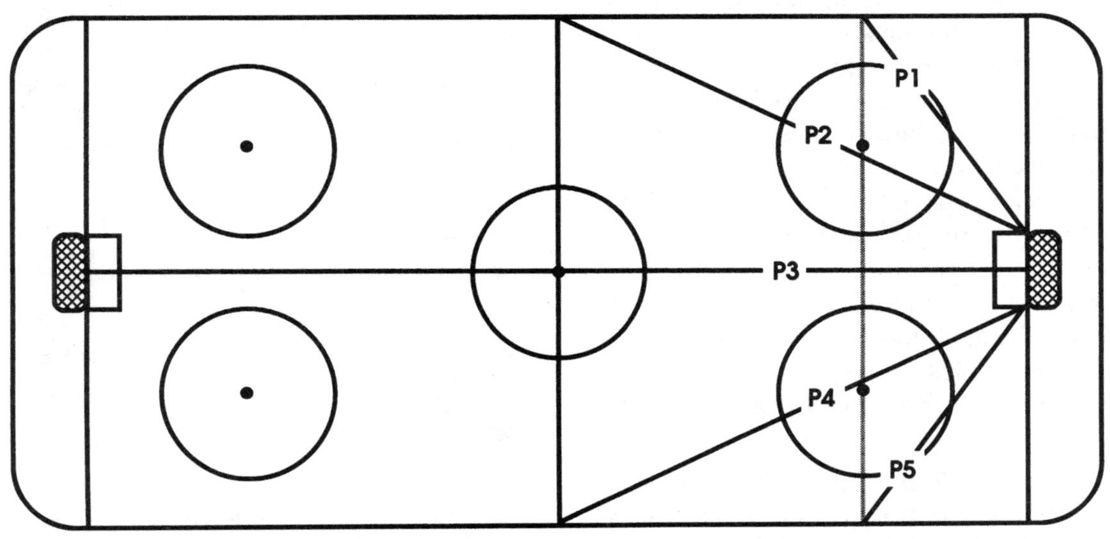

Drill 9-2; Knowing Where You Are In Net

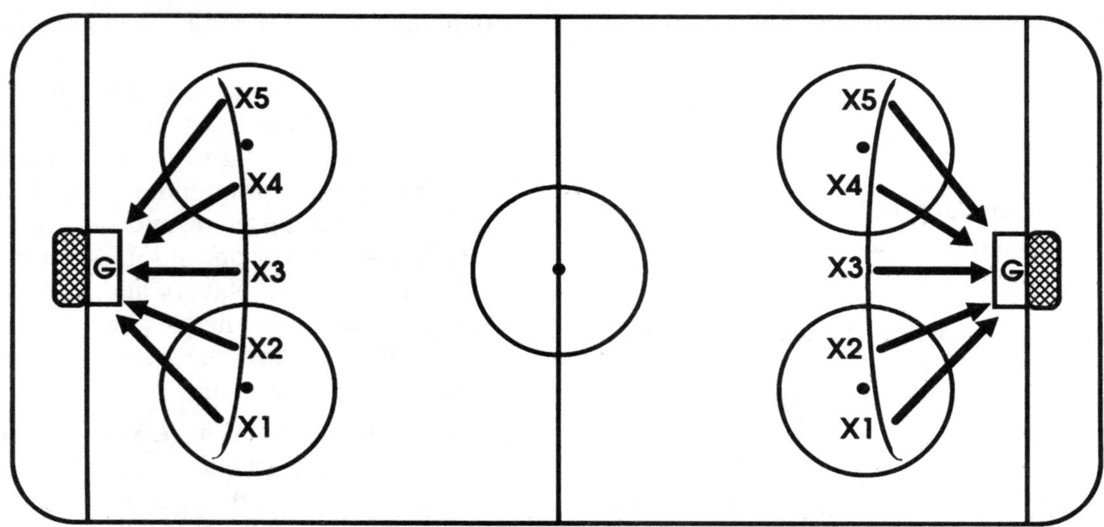

Drill 9-4; Saves *du jour*

the goaltender move along P1 and then back to P3. At the third whistle, have the goaltender move along P4 and then back to P3. At the final whistle, have the goaltender move along P2 and then back to P3. Provide feedback to the goaltender on his positioning. Repeat the process with the goaltender moving out to a point five feet from the goal line and then 10 feet from the goal line.

Drill 9-3; Playing the Angles. Playing the angles (both surface and aerial) is a technique used to position a goaltender in the correct shooting line to cover the most area of the net (refer to Figures 9-4 and 9-5). To start this drill, position the goaltender in the center of the crease a couple of feet out from the goal line. The coach should begin to move a puck around, slowly at first, and have the goaltender move to play the appropriate surface and aerial angles. Provide feedback to the goaltender on his positioning, glove and blocker placement, stance, and making sure that he remains within the goaltender's alley as he moves. The second part of this drill adds four players, spread out in a semicircle about 25 feet from the net. At the whistle, have the players pass the puck around, slowly at first, and have the goaltender move to play the surface and aerial angles as well as staying in the goaltender's alley. Provide feedback to the goaltender.

Drill 9-4; Saves *du jour*. This drill provides the goaltender the opportunity to practice making saves using his six tools; the glove, blocker, pads (wedge, butterfly and stack), skates, upper body and stick. In addition, it provides the goaltender the opportunity to improve hand-eye coordination, reaction time and movement time. Position five shooters in a semicircle about 15 feet from the net. At the whistle, player X1 executes a forehand wrist shot at the glove. At the next whistle, player X2 performs the same shot also at the glove. Continue until all five players have shot. The players should wait to shoot until the coach blows the whistle so that the goaltender has a chance to get set for each shot. Repeat the drill executing shots at the blocker, pads, skates, upper body and stick. The coach should provide feedback to the goaltender on proper stance, making sure that he is square to the shooter, moving along the surface angle within the goaltender's alley, keeping the blocker and glove at or below the aerial angle, keeping the stick flat on the playing surface, following the puck from the moment it leaves the shooter's stick to the moment it strikes the goaltender's equipment, and noting where the rebounds are directed.

Variations:

- Alternate shooting (i.e., X5-X4-X3-X2-X1, X1-X5-X2-X4-X3, or X5-X1-X4-X2-X3).
- Vary the distance of the shots from 10 feet to 30 feet.
- Use slap shots, flip shots, backhand shots, snap shots.
- Have the goaltender lie on his side in front of the net (in a stacking-the-pads position), and have players shoot both low and high.

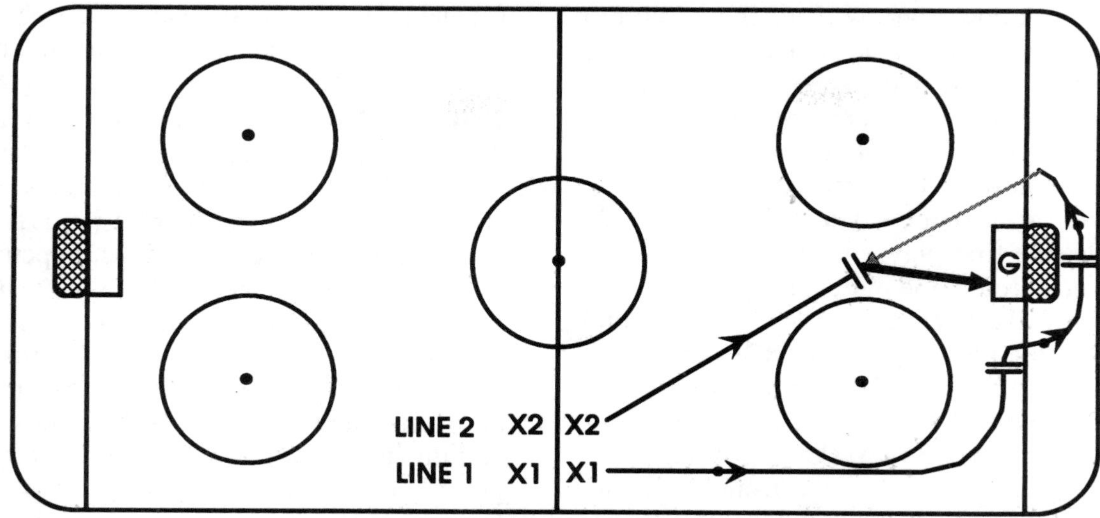

Drill 9-5; Play Coming From Behind The Net

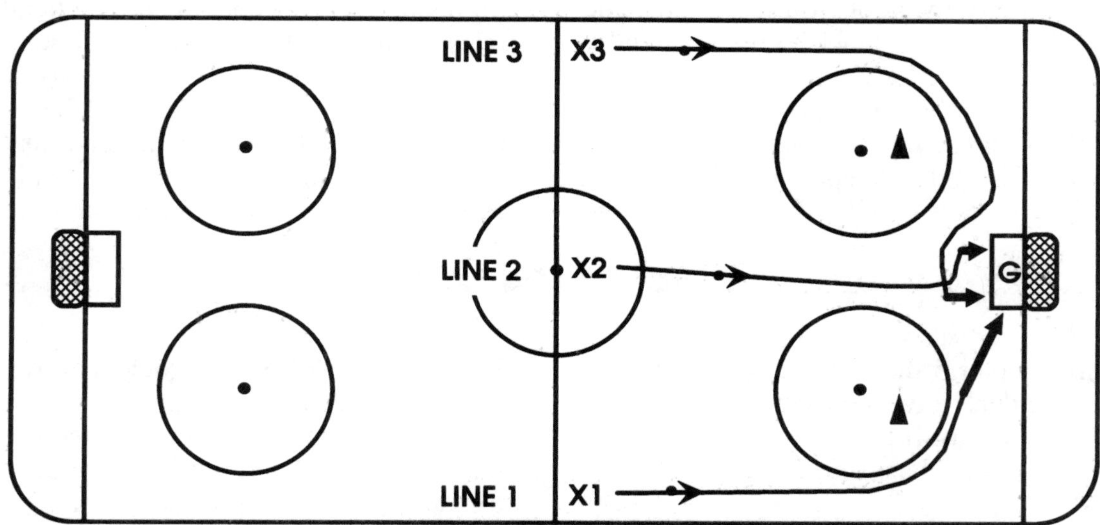

Drill 9-6; Telescoping

Drill 9-5; Play Coming From Behind The Net. This drill teaches the goaltender how to position himself as the puck is moved to the side of the net, behind the net and then to the slot. Place the players in two lines as shown in the corresponding diagram. At the whistle, the first player in line 1 (X1) skates with the puck around toward the side of net and stops. At the same time, the first player in line 2 (X2) skates to the slot and stops about 15 feet in front of the net. The goaltender should move from the center of the crease to the left post to cover the angle of the puck carrier. The coach should provide feedback to the goaltender on his positioning and stance. At the second whistle, X1 skates with the puck behind the net and stops. The coach should again provide feedback to the goaltender on his positioning and stance making sure that the goaltender is not turned around facing the back of the net. At the third whistle, X1 brings the puck around from behind the net (going either left or right) and passes to X2, who shoots on net. If the goaltender has the opportunity, he should use his stick to block the pass to the slot. If the pass is not blocked, the goaltender should move to the shooter and play the corresponding surface and aerial angles. The coach should provide feedback to the goaltender on his positioning, stance, crease movement and save selection or rebound (if any).

Drill 9-6; Telescoping. This drill provides the goaltender with the opportunity to determine how far he should come out (telescope) from the net when playing the angle and to put into practice the front door/back door concept. By coming out too far, the goaltender allows the puck carrier room to move around the goaltender, while staying too close to the crease allows the shooter additional available net area at which to shoot. Set the players in three lines as shown in the corresponding diagram. Place a pylon at each of the two areas indicated. At the whistle, the first player in line 1 (X1) skates with the puck around the pylon and shoots on net. X1 returns to the back of line 2. At the second whistle, the first player in line 2 (X2) skates with the puck and executes a deke on the goaltender. X2 returns to the back of line 3. At the third whistle, the first player in line 3 (X3) skates with the puck around the pylon and across the front of the net and then shoots. X3 returns to the back of line 1. The drill should be repeated until each player has had the opportunity to shoot from each line. The coach should provide feedback to the goaltender following each shot based on the amount of front door/back door area, stance, positioning, being square to the shooter, playing the corresponding surface and aerial angles, keeping the stick flat on the playing surface, following the puck from the moment it leaves the shooter's stick to the moment it strikes the goaltender's equipment, type of save, and noting where the rebounds are directed (if any).

Drill 9-7; Handling an Offensive Attack. This drill is excellent preparation for gamelike situations for both the goaltender and teammates. During the approach to the net, the puck carrier is faced with a decision to shoot, pass or deke, depending upon the coach's scenario, and consists of the breakaway, one-on-one, one-on-two, two-on-one, two-on-two, three-on-one and three-on-two as described in chapters 7 and 8. The goaltender can put into practice all of his knowledge gained from this chapter in addition to previous experience. The coach should provide feedback to the goaltender on his stance; knowing where he is in net; properly playing the surface and aerial angles; reading the play and moving using the concepts of the goaltender's alley, telescoping and front door/back door; peripheral vision; and type of save or rebound (if any). When the goaltender has defensive help, the coach should make sure that the goaltender and his teammates are communicating to ensure proper player coverage and puck control if a rebound is created.

Advanced Drills

Drills from Chapter 5 that should be used to improve a goaltender's advanced techniques include 5-1 (Stationary Passing and Receiving), 5-4 (Around-the-Boards Pass) and 5-9 (Stationary Bank Pass).

Drill 9-8; Handling the Puck. This drill provides the goaltender with the opportunity to handle the puck under various gamelike situations. The five goaltender puck handling situations included in this drill are; the setup (right side of corresponding dia-

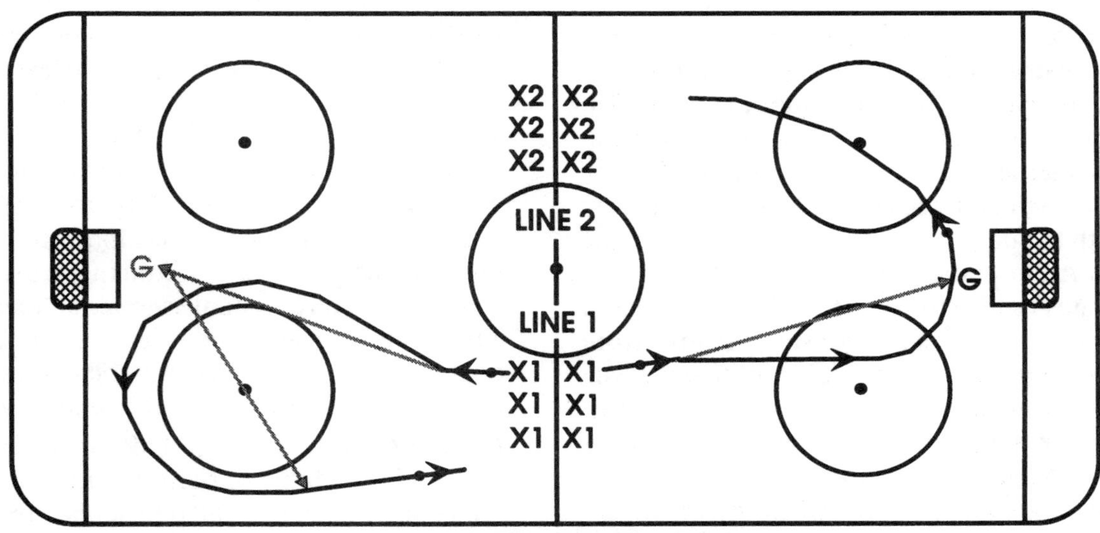

Drill 9-8; Handling The Puck

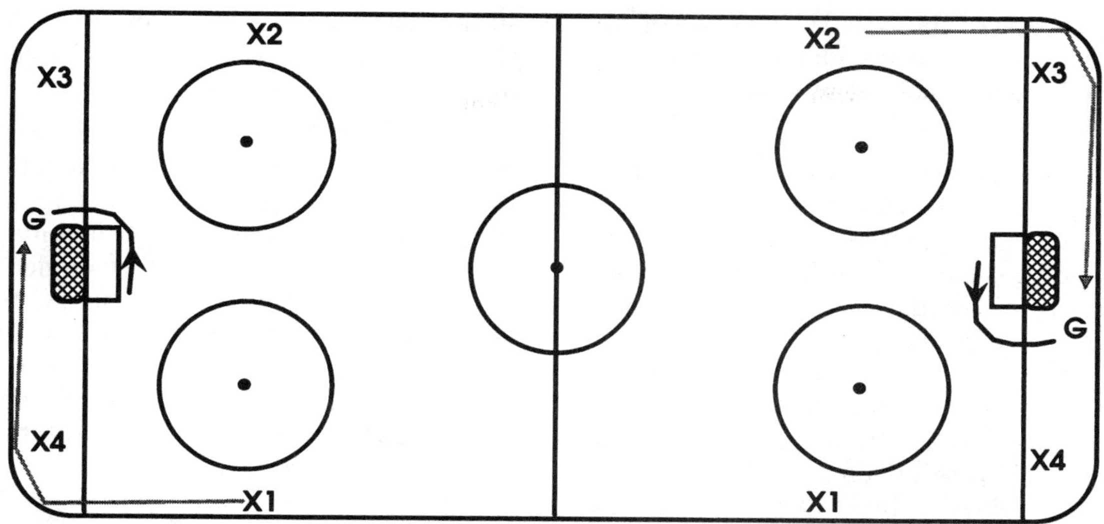

Drill 9-9; Stopping The Puck Behind The Net

gram), direct pass (left side of corresponding diagram), bank pass, clearing pass and puck-to-the-corner. Divide the team into lines and position them to perform the setup first (right side of the corresponding diagram). At the whistle, the first player in line 1 (X1) takes two strides and then passes the puck to the goaltender. X1 continues skating toward the net as the goaltender stops the puck and sets it up for him. X1 retrieves the puck and skates back out to the center red line. At the second whistle, the first player in line 2 (X2) performs the same play. The coach should provide the goaltender feedback on how he handles the puck and on not keeping his eyes solely on the puck. Once all players have executed this play, the coach should move to the direct pass (left side of diagram).

At the whistle, X1 takes two strides and then passes the puck to the goaltender. X1 continues skating, moves around the face-off circle and receives a pass from the goaltender before he reaches the top of the circle. At the second whistle, X2 performs the same play. The coach should provide the goaltender feedback on how he initially handles the puck, the positioning of the glove and blocker on the stick, and the location of the pass. Work with the goaltender to instill confidence in his passing ability. Only through practice will his confidence improve. With younger goaltenders, have them pass the puck the way they shoot (i.e., for a left-handed shooter, place the glove at the paddle and the blocker at the top of the shaft). For more experienced goaltenders, have them practice passing using both the left-handed and right-handed styles.

Once all players have executed this play, the coach should move to the bank pass, clearing pass and puck-to-the-corner pass (these last three passes are not shown in the corresponding figure).

Drill 9-9; Stopping the Puck Behind the Net. Position four players as shown in the corresponding diagram. At the whistle, X1 executes an around-the-boards pass to X3. As X1 passes the puck, the goaltender should move in the same direction as the puck from the crease to behind the net to stop the puck. At the second whistle, X2 executes an around-the-boards pass to X4, with the goaltender moving behind the net as X2 passes the puck. The goaltender should stop the puck using the blocker hand backhand approach if the puck is shot around the boards to the goaltender's blocker side. When the puck is shot around the boards to the goaltender's glove side, the goaltender should use the two-handed forehand approach. Once the puck is stopped, the coach should instruct the goaltender to either leave the puck (place it out from the boards about six inches) for X3 or X4 to retrieve, or execute a puck-to-the-corner pass to X3 or X4.

Drill 9-10; Using the Stick for Active Deflections. Position the team as shown in Drill 9-4. At the whistle, the first shooter executes a low (on the playing surface) wrist shot at the goaltender. As the puck hits his stick, the goaltender actively deflects the puck to the side boards. For each series of shots, the goaltender should alternate to which side of the boards he actively deflects the puck (i.e., left, right, left...). The coach should provide feedback to the goaltender, making sure that he rotates the stick blade toward the intended direction of the rebound and kicks the stick with the correct skate (left skate moves the puck to the right boards and vice versa).

Drill 9-11; Stick Checking. This is one technique that is underutilized in all levels of roller hockey. Stick checking is an aggressive goaltending technique, and most goaltenders have learned to be more reactive than aggressive during their training. When it comes time to strip an opponent of the puck and save a goal, a stick check can be the goaltender's best weapon. This drill focuses on the poke check and sweep check. Position the team into two lines, as shown in the corresponding diagram. At the whistle, the first player in line 1 (X1) stick handles toward the pylon at a slow to moderate pace. As X1 moves past the pylon and across the front of the net, the goaltender executes a poke check. At the second whistle, the first player in line 2 (X2) stick handles past the pylon and across the front of the net, and the goaltender executes a poke check. The coach should monitor and provide feedback to the goaltender on his timing of the poke check (too late, too soon), making sure that the shaft of the stick slides through the blocker hand quickly, position of the legs (blocker side knee on the playing surface and the other leg extended back), overall effectiveness of the poke check and the goaltender's reaction time to get back into position.

Have all of the players participate in the poke check portion of this drill at least once, and then restart the drill with the goaltender executing a sweep check. The coach should again monitor and provide feedback to the goaltender on his timing of the sweep check (too late, too soon), position of the glove and blocker hands, position of the legs (glove side knee on the playing surface and the other leg extended back), overall effectiveness of the sweep check and the goaltender's reaction time to get back into position.

A variation that will bring in gamelike situations is to have the goaltender read the play and either allow the puck carrier to shoot (not execute a stick check) or execute the poke check or sweep check. This variation allows the goaltender to begin to experience the most appropriate situations to execute a stick check.

Since this drill can be very tiring for a goaltender, the coach should alternate goaltenders (if this option is available) or make sure that proper rest time is built into the drill.

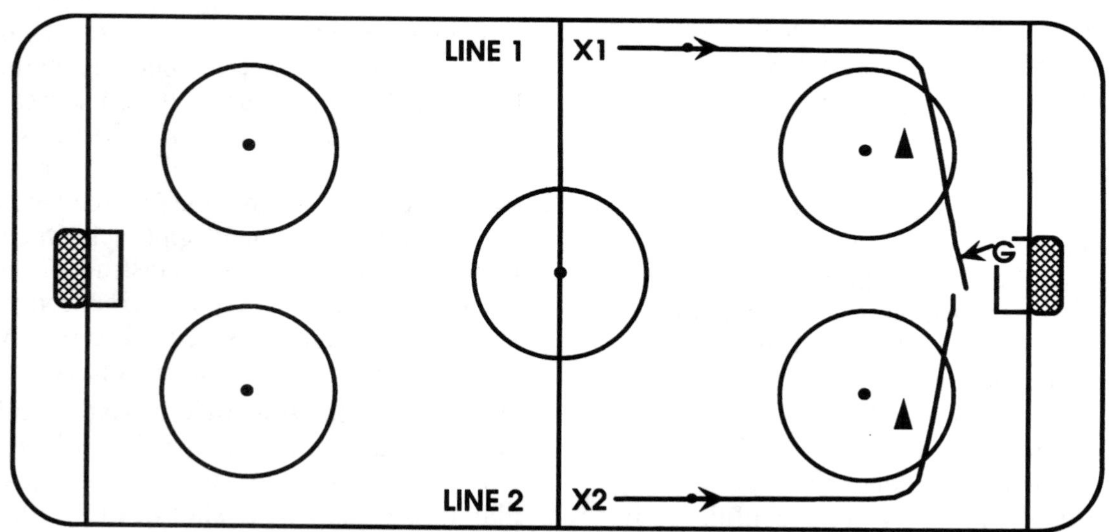

Drill 9-11; Stick Checking

Recap

After reading and studying the material in this chapter, you should be able to answer the following questions:

1. Define the role of the goaltender.
2. List the seven fundamental goaltender techniques.
3. Define stance. What are the four main components that make up an effective stance? Describe each of them in terms of what a coach should watch for.
4. Describe the two methods that a goaltender can use to determine where he is in relation to the net without turning the head.
5. Describe the three types of movement a goaltender uses in the crease.
6. When playing the angles, how does the goaltender use the information gained from reading the surface and aerial angles? Why is it important to play the puck versus the shooter?
7. What is a goaltender's alley? Why is it important to stay within this alley when getting ready for a shot?
8. How do the concepts of telescoping and front door/back door relate to goaltender positioning?
9. What four factors are required to make a save? List the six types of saves covered in this chapter. Define how to use each of them.
10. When deciding how to control the puck after a shot, what is the rule?
11. What clues can a puck carrier provide that indicate whether he will shoot or deke?
12. What should a goaltender do after a save?
13. When should a goaltender communicate with a teammate? Why?
14. Why is it important to learn your opponent's patterns?
15. What options does a goaltender have while handling the puck?
16. What are active deflections? How do they work?
17. Describe the two stick checking techniques.
18. How will you use the Goaltending Checklist and the drills provided in this chapter to monitor and improve goaltending performance?
19. Why is stretching so important to a goaltender prior and subsequent to a practice or game?

THE #1 REASON OFFICIALS WEAR STRIPED SHIRTS— THE SKATE MARKS DON'T SHOW.

10

Defensive Zone Team Play

Highlights

This chapter addresses the role of team play in the defensive zone. Chapter 10 presents the following information:

Discussion

Fundamentals

- *covering the opposing team in the defensive zone*
- *zone defense*
- *man-to-man defense*
- *breakout techniques*
- *strongside breakout*
- *weakside breakout*
- *defenseman skating breakout*
- *around-the-boards breakout*
- *fast breakout*
- *face-off techniques*
- *3-0-1, 2-1-1 and 2-0-2 alignments*
- *assignments*
- *how to win face-offs*

Advanced Techniques

- *overload defense*
- *defense-to-defense breakout*
- *behind-the-net breakout*
- *defense reverse breakout*
- *goaltender breakout*

Siller Player and Team Evaluation Profile — Defensive Zone Team Play

Drills

Advanced Drills

Recap

A hero is no braver than an ordinary man, but he is braver five minutes longer.
— Ralph Waldo Emerson —

They can conquer who believe they can.
— Vergil —

Discussion

The **primary role of a team in its defensive zone** is to prevent the opponent from scoring goals. All successful teams make it a priority to be dominant in their defensive zone because if you give up more goals than you score, you will lose. Preventing goals is accomplished through hard work and discipline by breaking up any offensive attack, regaining possession of the puck and moving it out of your defensive zone. To execute these three responsibilities, a team must have an overall defensive zone team strategy.

Defensive zone team strategies are situational by nature and based on the attacking offensive scenario and on playing the percentages because it is very difficult to execute specific plays when your team does not have control of the puck. When your team is in your defensive zone and operating in a defensive or transitional role, the only objective should be to gain control of the puck. One important objective of this chapter is to teach each coach and player that **Puck Possession Provides Opportunities**. This is known as the ***3PO Principle***. With possession of the puck, you can transition from defense to offense and create potential scoring opportunities as well as control the overall flow of the game.

Three components of a defensive zone team strategy that should remain constant during any situation are that the defensive team should:

- Become effective at **reading, reacting and anticipating (roller hockey's tactical triad)**. The key to gaining an edge over your opponent in your defensive zone is the ability to read what the other team is doing, anticipate what it may be going to do and respond with an appropriate series of actions. To make this happen, it is imperative that the defensive team learn the various play patterns that the opponents use in your defensive zone. This is accomplished by determining the opponent's best playmakers, shooters and the strategies they employ in your defensive zone, and incorporate this information into your defensive zone strategy. The assets of quickness, correctly reading, reacting and anticipating a play will help prevent the attacking team from consistently maintaining control of the puck in your defensive zone.
- Keep the opposition from controlling the puck in the slot because of the high percentage of scoring opportunities from this area. The defensive team accomplishes this by using its bodies, arms and sticks (legally) to contain or angle opponents away from the slot who are looking for a shot, pass, rebound or deflection.
- Always pressure the attacking team and force it into making bad plays. By pressuring, you can interrupt timing, force the opponent to release control of the puck or create a turnover in which your team regains control of the puck.

By being ready for certain plays, or occasionally forcing a play, the percentages of breaking up an opponent's offensive attack, regaining control of the puck and initiating your own offensive attack will be on your side.

Fundamentals

Three fundamental defensive zone team skills covered in this section include covering the opposing team in the defensive zone, breakout techniques and face-off techniques.

Covering the opposing team in the defensive zone is a team skill that is designed to prevent the opposing team from scoring goals with the intent of minimizing high-percentage scoring opportunities (see Figure 6-3). This is accomplished through proper team positioning, controlling the slot, reading, anticipating, reacting, communicating, breaking up any offensive attack and regaining possession of the puck through defensive pressure and hustle. An offensive team is going to get some scoring chances during each game, but it's up to the coach (with his defensive strategy) and the players (with their execution of the strategy) to ensure that these opportunities occur only from low-percentage scoring locations.

Two strategies used to cover the opposing team in the defensive zone consist of the zone and man-to-man defenses. Both of these approaches have advantages and disadvantages and must be evaluated by the coach to determine which strategy will work during any given situation.

- **Zone defense** is normally used as a basic defensive zone strategy when the opponents are not using an aggressive offensive attack. **It is the best strategy to teach beginning roller hockey players** because of its basic design and set of responsibilities. This strategy also allows for a more balanced transition to offense when your team gains control of the puck. Figure 10-1 shows the three zones that both teams operate in and are defined as the left, central and right defensive zones. The zone defense utilizes the defensive players in a boxlike formation to cover the opponents with the objective of gaining control of the puck or at least neutralizing the opponent's attack. The defensive team generally positions one forward and one defenseman on the strong side, one defenseman in the central zone (controlling the slot) and one forward on the weak side. The distance between the defensive player and the player he is covering should be between five and 15 feet depending upon where the puck carrier is. If the puck carrier is close, maintain close coverage; if the puck carrier is away from the player you are covering, you can extend the distance up to 15 feet. The forward's job is to cover the opponent's point men (defensemen in the offensive zone) and the defensemen's job is to cover the opponent's forwards. Use your stick to check any puck-carrying opponent, block any pass or shot, and use your body to angle opponents away from the slot.

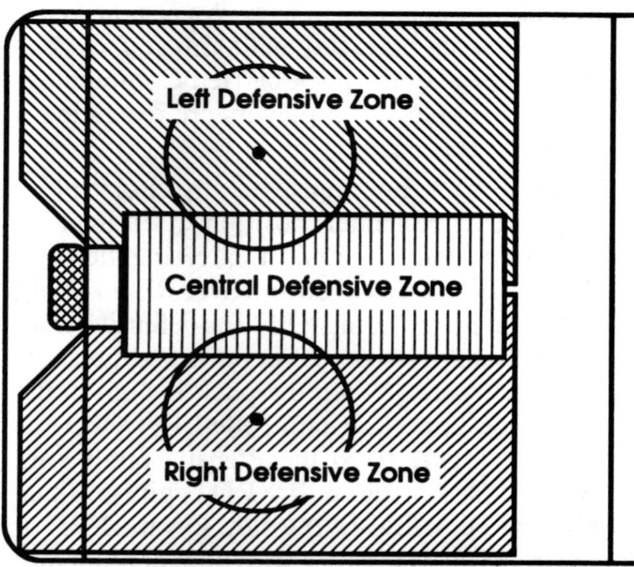

Figure 10-1; Three Defensive Zones

The defensive team should always favor the middle of the defensive playing surface, especially the slot area, and approach scrambles for the puck from this defensive side, pressuring from the inside out. During all of this, the goaltender should have the best overall view of the playing surface and the developing play. His responsibility is to inform his teammates where coverage may be deficient or if he is being screened. When executing the zone defense, the defensive players are not free to skate all over the playing surface to retrieve the puck. They should only maintain a position in their normal zone and the adjacent zone; not all three. **Discipline** is a key element in the defensive zone because the success of an offensive attack is attributed to both the determination and skill of the offensive team as well as the lack of discipline by the defensive team.

One disadvantage of the zone defense strategy occurs when more than two opponents converge into one location within a zone. This generally causes confusion on the part of the defensive players and can create an open attacker in that zone due to a missed assignment. Communication is essential during those situations.

In Figure 10-2, the defensive team (circled players plus the goaltender operating using a zone defense) positions one forward (LF) and one defenseman (LD) on the strong side (left zone in this example), the second forward (RF) is placed on the weak side (right zone) and the second defenseman (RD) is placed in the central zone in the slot. The defensive players move quickly in the zones to cover, control and pressure their counterparts. When the puck is deep in the defensive zone and controlled by XRF (Figure 10-2), the offensive options are to skate, pass or shoot. If XRF begins to skate with the puck toward the slot, behind the net or toward XRD, LD moves with him, angling him away from the slot and toward the boards while executing a stick check or body block. If XRF passes the puck to any of the attackers, both LD and the corresponding defender maneuver to intercept the pass while the corresponding defender covers the opponent. If XRF passes

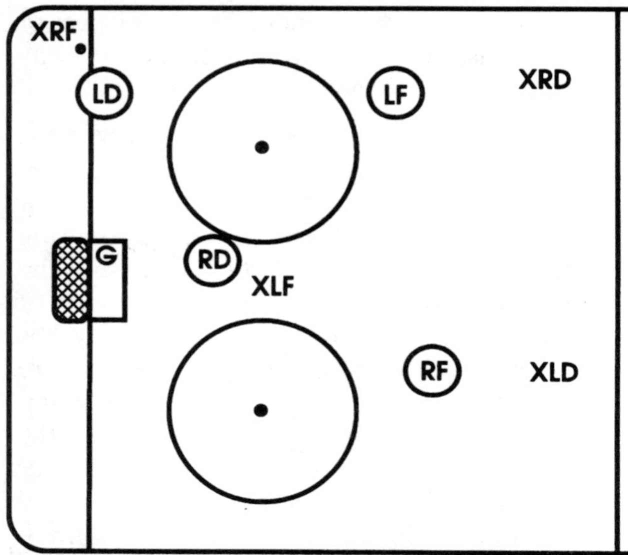

Figure 10-2; Zone Coverage

the puck behind the net (open area pass) to XLF, LD moves to the central defensive zone while RD controls XLF and gains control of the puck. If XRF takes a shot, RD covers XLF, making sure that the goaltender is not being screened, and secures or clears any rebounds. If XRF has possession of the puck behind the net, LD and RD position themselves near the two posts while either LF or RF covers XLF in the slot. When the offensive team has control of the puck deep in the defensive zone, the defensive team should cover any players in the slot at the expense of the point men.

The defensive players (including the goaltender) need to be constantly reading the play, positioning themselves appropriately, and reacting to movement by the puck carrier and the player they are covering to eventually gain control of the puck. Once puck control is gained, the defensive team transitions to the offensive team and has three options: establish an offensive attack, clear the puck out of the defensive zone or freeze the puck. The goaltender can also help during certain situations by clearing the puck to the corner or freezing it. When clearing the puck, the defensive team should quickly move the puck away from the slot by skating it to the side or behind the net. The defensive team should think defense first and offense only when it has full control of the puck.

- **Man-to-man defense** is a defensive zone strategy that can best be used when your team is fast and agile and playing an aggressive offensive team. This strategy is best suited for a more experienced team that can skate well, has a high endurance level and can keep up with the opponents. The man-to-man approach is essentially a series of one-on-one battles with the objective of gaining control of the puck by preventing the opposition from creating any odd-man attacks (i.e., two-on-ones). Each defensive player is responsible for covering one opponent and staying with him as long as the opposing team has control of the puck. The advantage of this strategy is that, since each player is continuously covered, it is very difficult for the offensive team to set up a strong attack. When executed perfectly, man-to-man defense is one of the most aggravating styles of defense that a team can play. Problems occur when any of the defensive players cannot keep up with the opponent, but even if the other team's puck carrier beats the man covering him, your goaltender should only have to stop one shot because all the other players will be covered. When you read that one of your teammates has been beaten by the puck carrier, you have to determine whether exchanging defensive coverage with that teammate will do more harm than good. **Defensive exchanging** is a transfer or exchange of coverage in the defensive zone from one defender to another. If your teammate has been beaten by the puck carrier and the puck carrier is the most dangerous attacker, then execute a defensive exchange. But if leaving your man places him in a situation where he can receive a pass and easily make a big play, stay with him and let your goaltender play the puck carrier. Communication is essential when players are executing a defensive exchange.

In Figure 10-3, the defensive team (circled players plus the goaltender) positions itself in proximity to its counterparts; LF covering the puck carrier XRD, LD covering XRF, RF covering XLD, and RD covering XLF. The defensive team moves quickly to cover, control and pressure its counterparts. When the puck is high in the defensive zone and controlled by XRD (as shown in Figure 10-3), the offensive options are to skate, pass or shoot. If XRD begins to skate with the puck toward the slot, toward XRF or toward XLD, LF moves with him, angling him away from the slot or toward the boards while

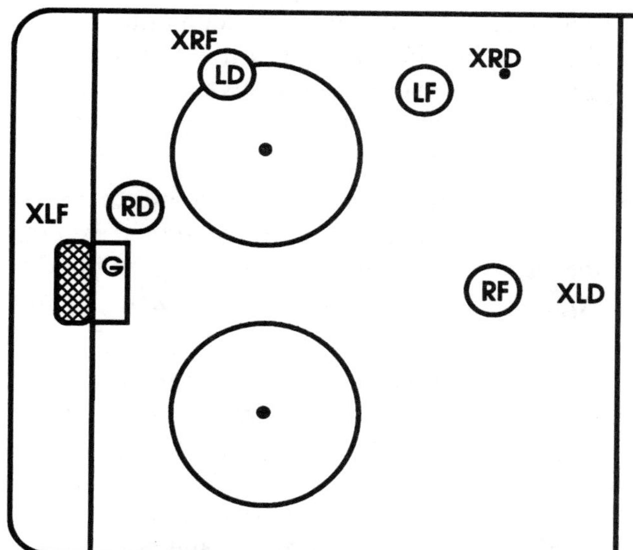

Figure 10-3; Man-to-Man Coverage

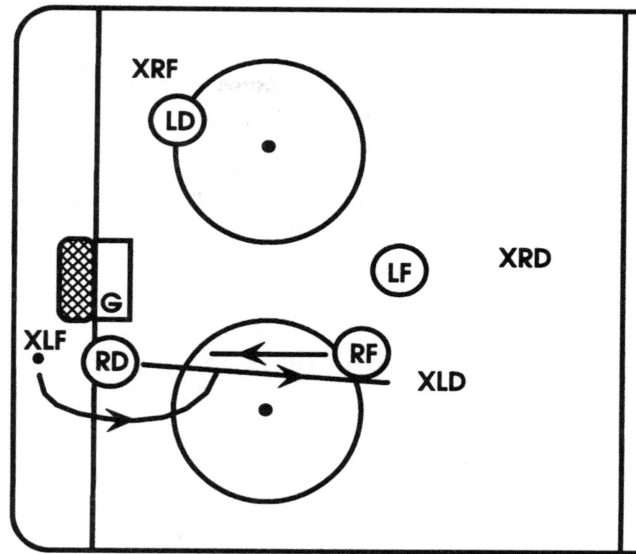

Figure 10-4; Man-to-Man Part 2

executing a stick check or body block. If XRD passes the puck directly to one of the attackers, both LF and the corresponding defender maneuver to intercept the pass while the corresponding defender pressures the opponent. If XRD passes the puck to the lower left corner (open area pass) to XLF, RD moves to control XLF and gain control of the puck while the other three defenders read the play and react by moving with their coverage. If XRD takes a shot, LF maneuvers to block the shot while RD covers XLF, making sure that the goaltender is not being screened, and helps secure or clear any rebounds. If XLF gains possession of the puck behind the net (as shown in Figure 10-4) and moves to the outside of and past RD, RF leaves his coverage (XLD) to cover XLF while RD moves to cover XLD (defensive exchanging).

Defensive players need to be moving constantly, reading, anticipating the play, positioning themselves appropriately, pressuring the opponents, communicating (especially if there is a defensive exchange) and reacting to opponents to eventually gain control of the puck. Once puck control is gained, the defensive team transitions to the offensive team and can establish an offensive attack, clear the puck out of the defensive zone or freeze the puck. Again, the defensive team should think defense first and offense only when it has full control of the puck.

Breakout techniques are used by a team to move the puck out of its defensive zone on an offensive attack. The ability to effectively move the puck out of your own end is important both defensively and offensively. Defensively it means that you have eliminated the offensive threat from your opponent. Offensively it means that you have possession of the puck, and from the *3PO principle* described earlier, we know that you now have an opportunity for an offensive attack. The saying *the best defense is a sound offense* is particularly meaningful in the context of breakouts. Every coach should establish some fundamental breakout plays early in the season.

A good breakout play will move the puck out of the defensive zone quickly and trap some of the opposing team's forecheckers deep in that zone. Trapping puts the forecheckers in position to be late in their backchecking duties. To trap the forecheckers, the breakout players must position themselves to be able to break out quickly, as well as to play defensively if puck possession is lost. If the forwards are properly positioned in the defensive zone, they will be ready for a quick pass, can trap some of the forecheckers, or provide good protection if puck possession is lost. However, by being too deep, players may have difficulty breaking out of their defensive zone and will be easier to cover and forecheck by the opposing team.

Three keys to an effective breakout:

1. Initial control of the puck. The players must not move to their breakout positions until the team has control of the puck. All players need to read, anticipate and react to know when to drop their

defensive coverage and get into position for a breakout. If players move prematurely, they may be leaving their opponents open for a quick scoring opportunity if the opposition gains control of the puck.

2. Creating space. Space is needed for the breakout play to develop. The positioning of the forwards and defensemen depends upon puck position, forechecking intensity, team abilities and how aggressive, conservative or creative the coach is with the breakout plays. Although many breakouts appear to involve only one or two players in the execution of the play, all players need to assume a role to enhance the likelihood of success. The perfect pass to an open forward is what seems most evident and important; however, the players *away* from the puck also play a significant role. This point reflects the necessity for team play during a breakout; by creating space as a team, you create options for the team.
3. Maintaining puck control. No turnover is more dangerous than one that occurs in your defensive zone. That is why I emphasized in Chapter 5 (Passing and Receiving) drills that the first pass must be accurate. If it isn't, players should start the drill over. It is essential that all receivers need to make sure that they control the puck after receiving a pass.

A few additional points to consider when executing a breakout play are:

- All players should be in motion, even if this is a relatively confined area. Movement should be incorporated into all breakout plays.
- One or two players should position themselves to be available to receive a pass during any effective breakout play (this creates options).
- Crossing, circular and curvilinear patterns should prevail over strictly linear movement.
- One player, generally a defenseman, should provide close support to the puck carrier. This player can be ready for a quick pass if the puck carrier becomes pressured.
- One defenseman should assume a more defensive role, remaining behind the play, while the two forwards (and possibly the second defenseman) move on the offensive attack.
- Be *very* careful about passing the puck rinkwide or across the front of your own net. For beginning players, this technique should definitely not be taught. For more experienced players, make sure that the reward (the successfully executed pass) is worth the risk (having the puck intercepted).
- When moving the puck up the boards or across the playing surface, look first and then execute the pass. Do not attempt to pass the puck blindly. Again, a turnover in your own zone means trouble.

Five fundamental breakout techniques presented in this section consist of the strongside breakout, weakside breakout, defenseman skating breakout, around-the-boards breakout and the fast breakout. Variations of these five techniques can be devised depending upon the creativity and specific strategy of the coach and the ability of the team.

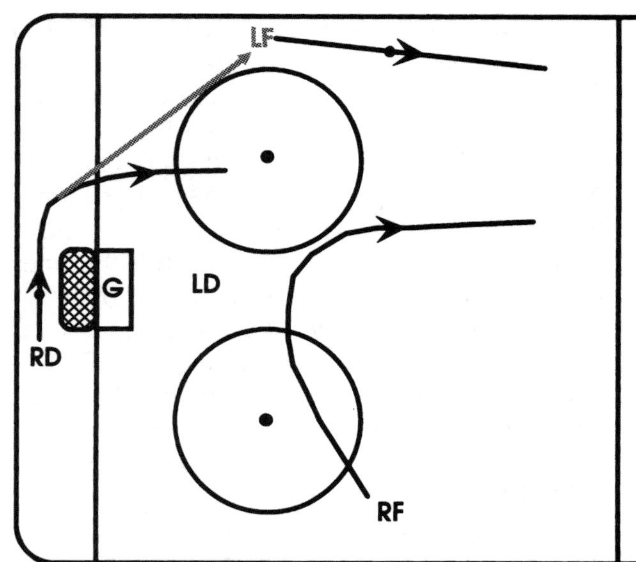

Figure 10-5; Strongside Breakout

- **Strongside breakout** is the most fundamental breakout in roller hockey. The objective of this play is to move the puck up the playing surface using the strongside forward. The advantage of the strongside breakout is that it affords the team a low risk way in which to move the puck out of the defensive zone. In Figure 10-5, RD gains control of the puck deep in the defensive zone, reads that there is minimal coverage on the left side of the playing surface, and skates behind the net to the left side. As he moves out from behind the net, he passes the puck to LF, who begins skating out of the defensive zone with it. This first pass is the most critical one in the breakout; RD must be accurate and LF must maintain control of the pass. While this is occurring, RF is moving to get open so that LF has the option to pass the puck (remember, a breakout play should be designed so that one or two players are open). By moving toward the center of the playing surface, RF is also creating space, forcing at least one of the opponent's defensemen to retreat toward his defensive zone and away from LF. LD maintains a position in front of the net and plays in a defensive role in case of a turnover. RD moves with LF and becomes a relief valve if LF becomes pressured by an opponent. If the opponent's strongside defenseman moves in from his normal position to cover LF (pinching), LF has four options. He can execute a bank pass (to himself) and move around the defender, pass the puck to RF or he can execute a give-and-go pass back to RD, who can move the puck out of the defensive zone. As a last resort, LF can just shoot the puck out of the defensive zone.

- **Weakside breakout** is another fundamental breakout play. The objective of this play is to move the puck up the playing surface using the weakside forward. The advantage of the weakside breakout is that it moves the flow of the play from the strong side of the playing surface to the weak side, creating space for the receiver to maneuver. In Figure 10-6, RD gains control of the puck deep in the defensive zone, reads that there is minimal coverage on the left side of the playing surface, and skates behind the net to the left side. As he moves out from behind the net, he reads that the opponent's defenseman has moved in to cover LF. Instead of executing a low probability pass to LF, RD reads that the weakside forward (RF) is open and passes the puck to him. This play offers an excellent offensive opportunity because you have now trapped the opponent's defenseman in your zone while your team is moving out; it can easily turn into a 2-on-1. LD again maintains a position in front of the net and plays in a defensive role in case of a turnover. RD moves with RF and LF and becomes a trailing attacker.

  If, during the initial breakout, both LF and RF are covered and RD is pressured by an opponent, RD could pass the puck to LD. LD would read the play, move away from the slot, curl up the playing surface, and receive the pass. LD should pass the puck to either RF or LF as soon as possible to create a 2-on-2 situation.

- **Defenseman skating breakout** is another fundamental breakout play and can be used just after a scramble for the puck deep in your defensive zone in which your defenseman has regained control of the puck. This requires your defenseman (LD as shown in Figure 10-7) to quickly break out of your zone by skating up the middle of the playing surface (or an area that is not congested). As he skates with the puck, both forwards exchange positions so that RF is moving to the left side of the playing surface

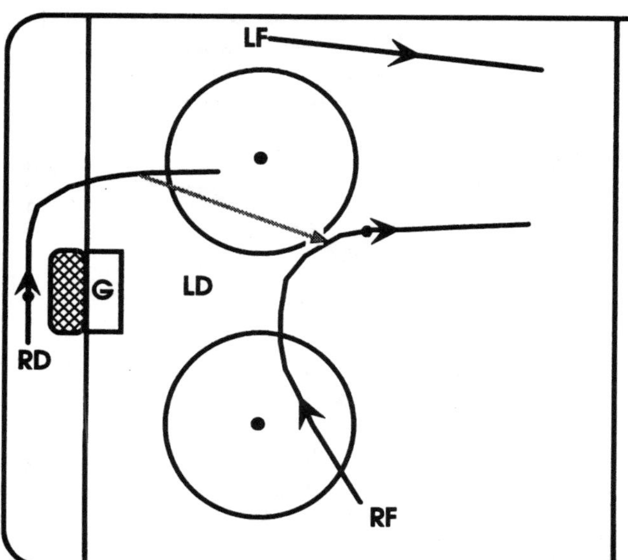

Figure 10-6; Weakside Breakout

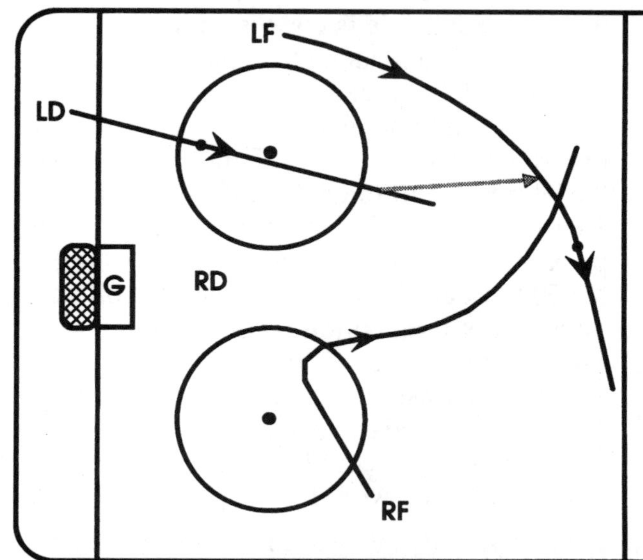

Figure 10-7; Defenseman Skating Breakout

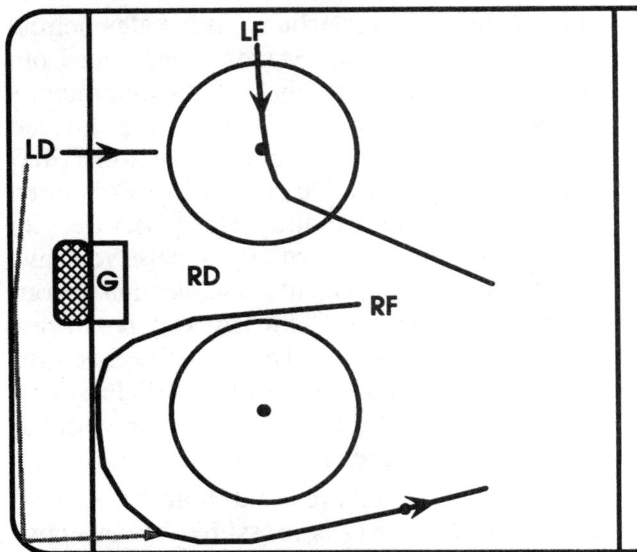

Figure 10-8; Around-The-Boards Breakout — 1

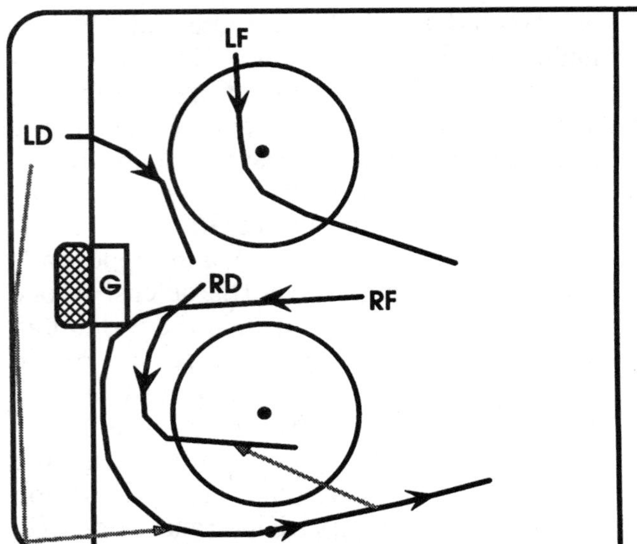

Figure 10-9; Around-The-Boards Breakout — 2

and LF is moving to the right. This gives LD two passing options and may confuse the opponent's defensemen. If LD passes the puck, he should continue skating with the play and become a trailing attacker. RD maintains a position in front of the net and plays in a defensive role in case of a turnover.

If the opponent's defensemen have both LF and RF covered, LD should continue skating with the puck and move it into the offensive zone.

- **Around-the-boards breakout** play is used when your team must play the puck deep in the defensive zone while the opposition has flooded the strong side of the playing surface. Seeing that the strong side is congested, RF moves to the weak side and along the boards in anticipation of a pass. LD reads this move and executes an around-the-boards pass to RF (as shown in Figure 10-8). During this, LF moves away from the boards and through the high slot to become a passing option. RF can either skate with the puck or pass it to LF. Another option would be for RD to curl down and out and become another outlet pass option for RF (Figure 10-9). Since RD moves away from the slot, LD now has the responsibility to cover the slot. If RF became pressured by an opponent while skating with the puck, he could execute a pass to RD, who could skate with it or pass.
- **Fast breakout**, a play used to catch the defenders off-guard, is excellent to use when the opposing team is forechecking heavily. Once your team has control of the puck, the strongside forward (LF as shown in Figure 10-10) should start skating toward the center red line. In most cases, at least one of the opponent's defensemen moves out of the zone to cover him, which opens up the playing surface. As this occurs, RF begins skating out of the defensive zone. LD passes the puck to RF who quickly passes the puck to LF. In many cases this type of breakout can create a 2-on-1 scenario by catching two or even three opponents deep in your defensive zone. This will also make your opponents think twice about their deep forechecking strategy.

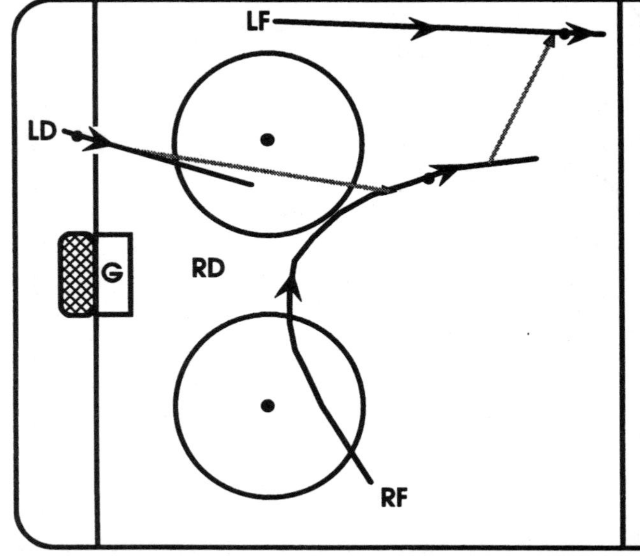

Figure 10-10; Fast Breakout

If a pass to RF is not a viable option, then LD can execute a bank pass to LF. Even if the pass is not successfully received by LF, the puck will be moved out of the defensive zone and LF will be available to forecheck the new puck carrier.

- **Face-off techniques** are used by a team to optimize its chances of gaining control of the puck following a face-off. Consistently gaining control of the puck following a face-off, especially in your defensive zone, forces the opposing team to immediately go on the defensive and allows your team the opportunity to move the puck into the offensive zone for a scoring opportunity (3PO Principle). Successful roller hockey teams take face-offs seriously. Realizing face-offs are a vital part of the game is an important first step for any good coach and team. Roller hockey's speed does not allow a coach much time to implement specific strategy during the game. However, face-offs are opportunities where the coach can set up a specific strategy before the play begins. Therefore, it is necessary that every coach establish some fundamental face-off strategies early in the season. In the **defensive zone, the face-off strategy** should be built around winning the face-off and gaining control of the puck first, preventing a scoring opportunity by the opponents second and initiating a breakout play or offensive attack third. After understanding these three elements of the strategy, the team should work on **two tactical components of the face-off — alignments and assignments**.

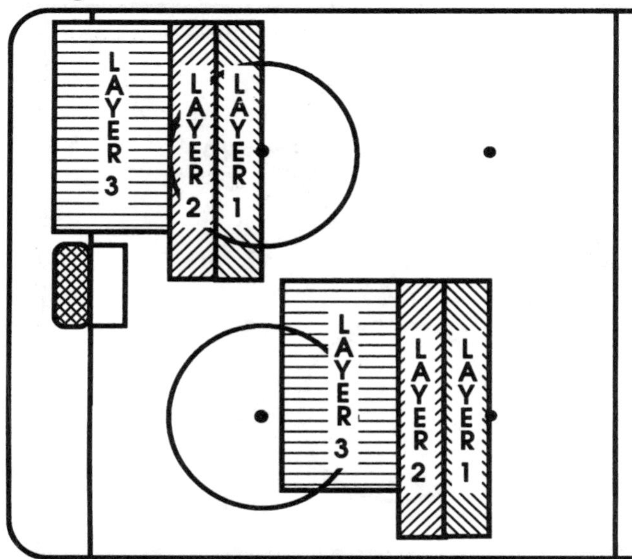

Figure 10-11; Face-off Layers

- **Alignments** are defined as the placement of players to most effectively implement the face-off strategy. Since the strategy should be built around winning the face-off and gaining control of the puck first and foremost, player alignments should reflect this. **Three face-off alignments** described in this section consist of the 3-0-1, 2-1-1 and 2-0-2 alignments; the numbers refer to the number of players in each of the three face-off layers. 3-0-1 and 2-1-1 are the most used alignments, while 2-0-2 is used with beginning players and teams as this is a basic roller hockey face-off alignment. As shown in Figure 10-11, Layer 1 refers to the area from the face-off dot to a point about seven feet back from the face-off dot. Layer 2 starts where Layer 1 leaves off and continues an additional seven feet back from Layer 1, and Layer 3 starts where Layer 2 leaves off and continues back about 15 more feet. These layers occur anywhere there is a face-off, whether in the defensive, transition or offensive zones.

How a team aligns itself for a face-off in the defensive zone depends upon where the face-off occurs and how the other team aligns itself. When the face-off is deep in the defensive zone (as shown in the upper left portion of Figure 10-12), the players should align themselves using the 3-0-1 alignment. The center (the player taking the face-off and LF in this example) positions himself at the face-off dot in Layer 1. The other forward (RF in this example) plays on the edge of the face-off circle and one of the

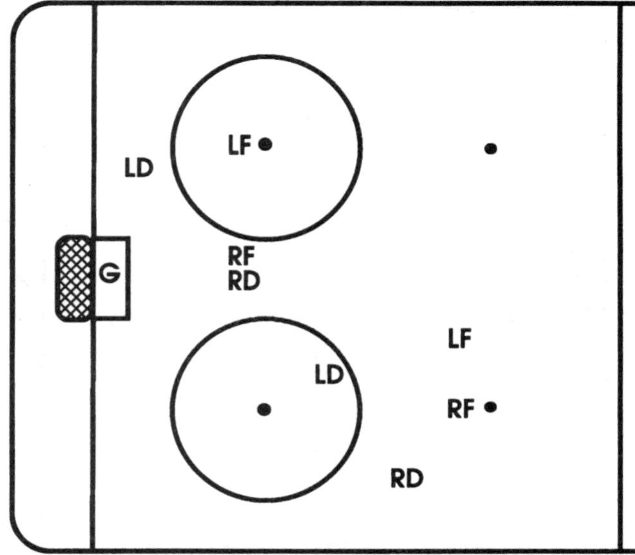

Figure 10-12; Defensive Zone Alignments

defensemen (RD in this example) plays just outside of RF, both also in Layer 1. The other defenseman (LD in this example) positions himself behind the center in Layer 3. This alignment puts the most pressure on the opposing team if it wins the face-off (using the three Layer 1 players) and allows your team to control the puck if you win the face-off (using the one Layer 3 player).

When the face-off is near the transition zone (as shown in the lower right portion of Figure 10-12), the players should align themselves using either the 3-0-1, 2-1-1 or 2-0-2 configurations, and should also take into account how the other team lines up for the face-off. Players must be taught to read what the opposition is trying to do with the face-off and then align themselves accordingly. For instance, if the opposing team lines up using a 3-0-1 alignment, your team should read this alignment and also line up using the 3-0-1 alignment. If the opposing team lines up in either a 2-1-1 (as shown in the lower right portion of Figure 10-12) or 2-0-2 alignment, align your players accordingly. These alignments allow your team to maintain balance during face-offs near the transition zone.

- **Assignments** are defined as each player's responsibilities during and subsequent to each face-off. These assignments must be carried out to perfection for a successful face-off strategy. The center is your quarterback for the face-off, and it is his job to position the players based on what he is planning to do with the puck. On every face-off, each player must have a primary assignment that he will carry out once the puck is dropped. After the puck has been dropped, his assignment may change depending upon whether the draw is won, lost or undetermined (both centers continue to battle for the puck). **Three essential assignments** that each team should understand and employ during and subsequent to every face-off depend upon whether your team wins, loses or neutralizes a face-off.

  When the face-off is deep in your defensive zone and your team (circled players plus the goaltender as shown in Figure 10-13) wins the face-off, get the puck back to your defenseman (LD) so that he can maneuver away from traffic and give the rest of the team time to set up for a breakout play. Following the face-off win, LF contains XRF, RF moves to his breakout position, RD contains XLF, and the goaltender reads the overall play and provides information to LD in terms of whether one of the opponents is coming. Once LD has the puck away from traffic, LF moves to his breakout position in anticipation of one of the breakout plays described earlier in this chapter. When the face-off is near the transition zone and your team wins the face-off, you can either move on an offensive attack immediately by moving the puck toward the offensive zone or execute a delayed attack by getting the puck back to a defenseman, having players move into open space and then moving the puck toward the offensive zone.

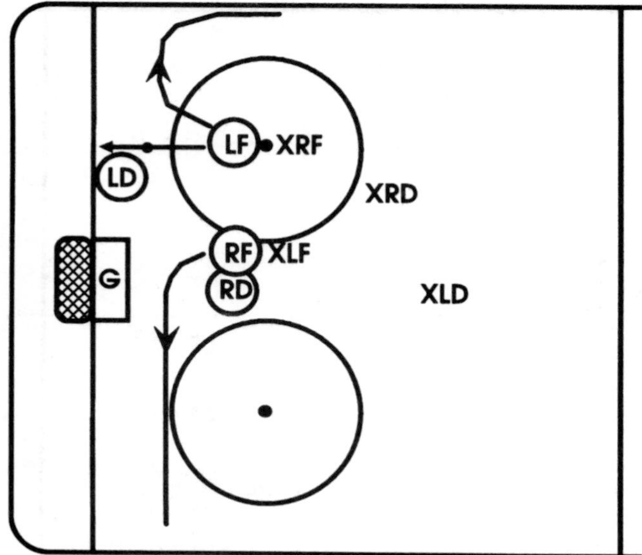

Figure 10-13; Face-off Win

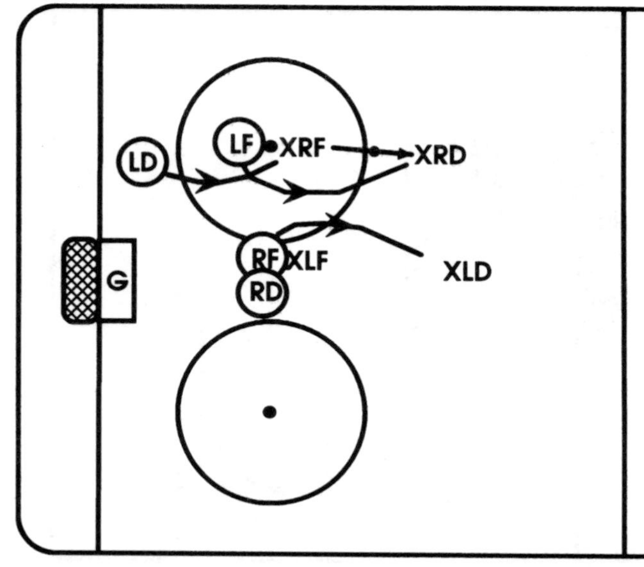

Figure 10-14; Face-off Loss

When the face-off is deep in your defensive zone and your team loses the draw, then LF moves out to cover XRD and RF moves out to cover XLD (as shown in Figure 10-14). LF and RF move out toward their coverage from the inside out, forcing the play to the outside of the playing surface. LD moves to cover XRF and RD contains XLF. Both LD and RD keep their coverage out of the slot area or at least ensure that they are not screening the goaltender. The goaltender needs to let RD and LD know if he is being screened and if any opponent is not being covered in the slot. When the face-off is near the transition zone and your team loses the face-off, set up the zone or man-to-man defense to contain the opponent's offensive attack.

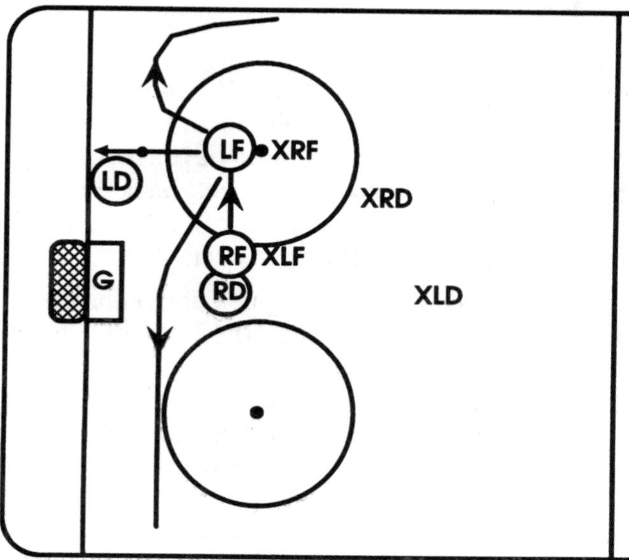

Figure 10-15; Face-off Draw

When the face-off is anywhere in your defensive zone, neither team immediately wins the face-off, and the puck remains in the area of the two centers, your center (LF) needs to contain the opposing center while the second forward (RF) moves in to get the puck back to the strongside defenseman (LD as shown in Figure 10-15). The weakside defenseman (RD) maintains his position in or near the slot area to cover any opponent who may move into the slot. Players should maintain movement during the struggle for puck control. While some players are battling for the puck, supporting players should maintain movement close to the play so they can ensure that they are not caught standing still when a play is initiated. If RF gets the puck back to LD (as shown in Figure 10-15), then LD moves the puck away from traffic, LF moves to an open area on the strong side of the playing surface, RF moves to the weak side, RD positions himself in front of the net, while the goaltender reads the overall play and provides information to LD in terms of whether one of the opponents is coming. LD now has the opportunity to execute a breakout play. If both teams are battling for the puck after the face-off and your team does not gain control of the puck, immediately begin pressuring the opponents through the execution of your zone or man-to-man coverage.

How to win face-offs. Now that you know how to line up for a face-off and who to cover during and subsequent to each face-off, your center needs to know exactly how to win a face-off. Basically, there are **three ways of winning a face-off**. First, be quicker and stronger than your opponent and move the puck back to a defenseman or push it through the opposing center's legs and then skate around him to retrieve it. Second, concentrate on playing the opposing center's stick. This requires you to employ the stick press or stick lift techniques described in Chapter 7 to first control the center's stick and then play the puck. The third option is to use your stick and body to tie up the opposing center's stick and body, then use your skate to direct the puck back to your defensemen or have your other forward come in and move the puck back to your defensemen. Each method requires plenty of practice in both drills and scrimmages. Practice specific face-off plays with the specific left or right-handed centers. For instance, deep in your defensive zone, it is more effective to have a left-handed center for face-offs in the left defensive zone and a right-handed center for face-offs in the right defensive zone. The reason for this is that in the left defensive zone, a left-handed center will take a backhand draw toward the left side of the playing surface and away from the slot and the right-handed center (taking a face-off in the right defensive zone) will take a backhand draw toward the right side of the playing surface and away from the slot. You should prefer the opposite for the offensive zone where your team wants to win the draw and move the puck toward the slot.

To win face-offs, centers should master the following four points:

1. Never approach a face-off until you check your opponent's alignment, your team's alignment and your goaltender's readiness. Set up your team before you step into the face-off, not while you're waiting for the puck to be dropped.
2. Position your hands effectively to defeat your opponent. Move your lower hand down on the shaft of the stick for a face-off. This provides maximum strength, lowers your center of gravity and increases stability. Next, position your skates in the most balanced position, which is wider than shoulder width apart. Use your whole body during the face-off, not just your arms, in order to control as much of the playing surface as possible.
3. Get a good jump. Watch for the official's hand — not the puck — to get the best possible jump. Play starts as soon as the official releases the puck, not when it hits the playing surface. If you wait until the puck has been dropped, you will lose time.
4. Practice. By practicing the correct face-off techniques, you will learn how effective you are as a center and as a team. This knowledge can then be applied during a game to improve your winning percentage against any opponent.

Advanced Techniques

Two defensive zone team skills covered in this section include advanced defensive zone coverage and advanced breakout techniques.

Overload defense is an advanced defensive zone strategy that combines elements of the zone and man-to-man fundamental defensive strategies while adding a third element to the execution: defensive overloading. **Defensive overloading** is the tactic of employing two defenders to pressure any puck carrier when the puck is deep in the defensive zone. One defender slows the puck carrier's progress or contains him along the boards while the second defender gains control of the puck. This type of strategy requires the defensive team to quickly read or anticipate an offensive play and time its reaction precisely. The defensive team wants to prevent the offense any time or opportunity to set up a play deep in the defensive zone and accomplishes this by covering the slot and employing a series of two-on-one battles on the puck carrier when the puck is below the overload line.

The **overload line** is an imaginary line drawn between the boards and the deep face-off dots, as shown in Figure 10-16. Anywhere below the line, the overload defense is put in place; anywhere above the line, a zone or man-to-man defense is put in place. The advantage of this strategy is that it reduces the deep offensive attack by overloading that area as well as controlling the slot. The disadvantage is that since two players are deep when the puck is below the overload line, one player has to cover two opposing point men. When the puck is passed back to one of the point men, however, the normal zone or man-to-man defense can be reinitiated if the second forward gets back quickly. When executed perfectly, the overload defense is very frustrating and difficult to beat.

When the opposition has the puck above the overload line, as shown in Figure 10-17, the defensive team (circled players plus the goaltender) positions itself in proximity to its counterparts and moves quickly to cover, control and pressure the opponents as with the zone or man-to-man defense.

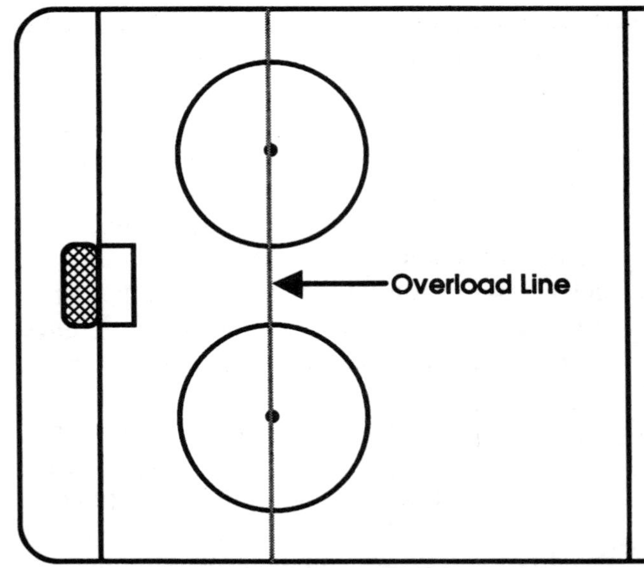

Figure 10-16; Overload Line

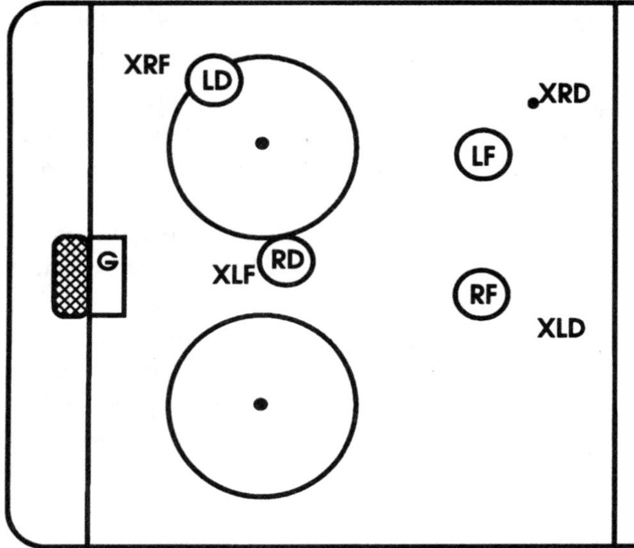

Figure 10-17; Overload Coverage — 1

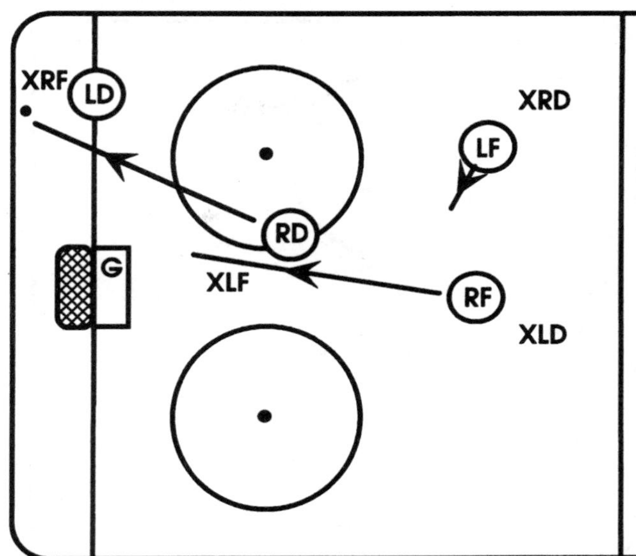

Figure 10-18; Overload Coverage — 2

When the puck is moved below the overload line, as shown in Figure 10-18, the weakside defenseman (RD) reads the play and reacts by supporting the strongside defenseman (LD) to overload that zone, pressuring the puck carrier and gaining control of the puck. The weakside forward (RF) leaves his coverage at this point and moves to cover any opponent in the slot while the strongside forward (LF) positions himself between both point men. If the puck is moved back out past the overload line, coverage returns to positions shown in Figure 10-17. The transition from overload defense to zone/man-to-man defense should take about three seconds.

Defensive players need to be moving constantly, reading, anticipating the play, positioning themselves appropriately, pressuring the opponents, communicating if there is a defensive exchange and reacting to opponents' movement to eventually gain control of the puck. Once puck control is gained, the defensive team transitions to the offensive team and can establish an offensive attack, clear the puck out of the defensive zone, or freeze it. Again, the defensive team should think defense first and offense only when it has full control of the puck.

Four **advanced breakout techniques** presented in this section consist of the defense-to-defense breakout, behind-the-net breakout, defense reverse breakout and goaltender breakout. Variations of these four techniques can be devised depending upon the creativity and specific strategy of the coach and the ability of the team.

- The **defense-to-defense breakout** play is used when a defenseman has the puck in the corner, has no room to maneuver and neither forward can get open to receive a pass. Reading this, the weakside defenseman (RD) moves from his position in the slot to the weak corner, as shown in Figure 10-19. The strongside defenseman (LD) executes a bank pass to RD who has the option of skating or passing the puck. This type of breakout alleviates forechecking pressure on the strong side through the execution of a low-risk pass behind the net to the weak side.

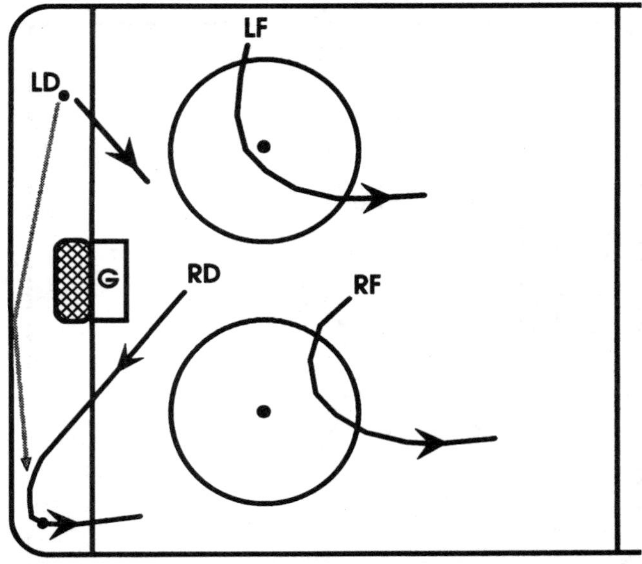

Figure 10-19; Defense-to-Defense Breakout

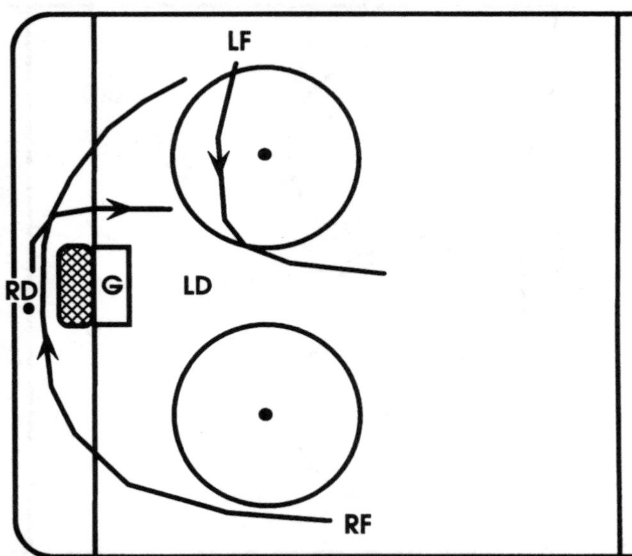

Figure 10-20; Behind-The-Net Breakout

- **Behind-the-net breakout** is another good play to use when a defenseman has the puck behind the net, has no room to maneuver and neither forward can get open to receive a pass. Reading the play, RF skates behind the net, as shown in Figure 10-20. As he moves behind the net, RF reads the area around the net for forecheckers so he can decide whether to take or leave the puck. If RF takes the puck, he should move toward the middle of the playing surface and out of the defensive zone. If RF becomes pressured, he can execute a drop pass to RD or pass to LF. If RF leaves the puck for RD, RF should proceed wide to the corner for a pass from RD as LF moves toward the weak side of the playing surface to become another passing option.
- **Defense reverse breakout** is a good play to use when both forwards are being covered. The play is initiated by the strongside defenseman (LD) bringing the puck up the playing surface as shown in Figure 10-21. Once he moves toward the face-off circle, the weakside defenseman (RD) crosses behind LD (reverse) and is available to receive a drop pass if LD gets pressured. As this occurs, both LF and RF move toward the center red line to create space for LD to maneuver with the puck. This play allows both defensemen to get into the offensive attack and provides LD with the options to skate or pass.
- The **goaltender breakout** is used when the goaltender has control of the puck, either in the crease, behind or to the side of the net. A play designed for the goaltender to pass the puck to a defenseman or forward to initiate a breakout play will, on many occasions, fool the opponents and allow your team to progress on a quick offensive attack. When the goaltender retrieves the puck, as shown in Figure 10-22, the strongside defenseman (LD) positions himself along the boards while the weakside defenseman (RD) covers the slot. The two forwards should read that the goaltender is going to pass the puck and react by executing curvilinear patterns, as shown in Figure 10-22. The goaltender can pass the puck to LD who can quickly pass the puck to either forward, RF in this example.

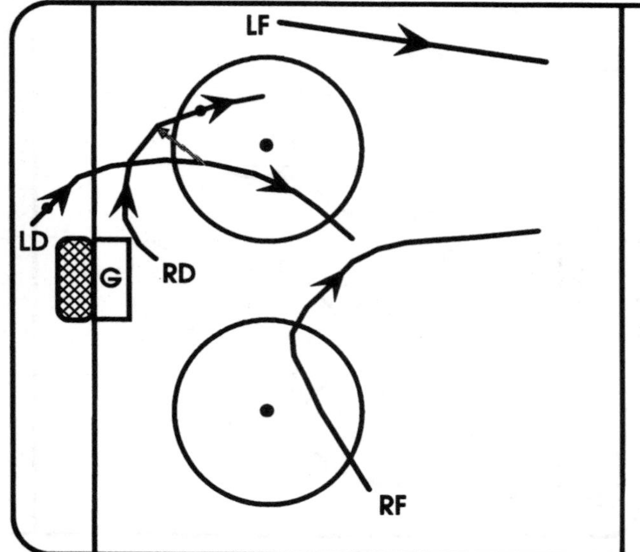

Figure 10-21; Defense Reverse Breakout

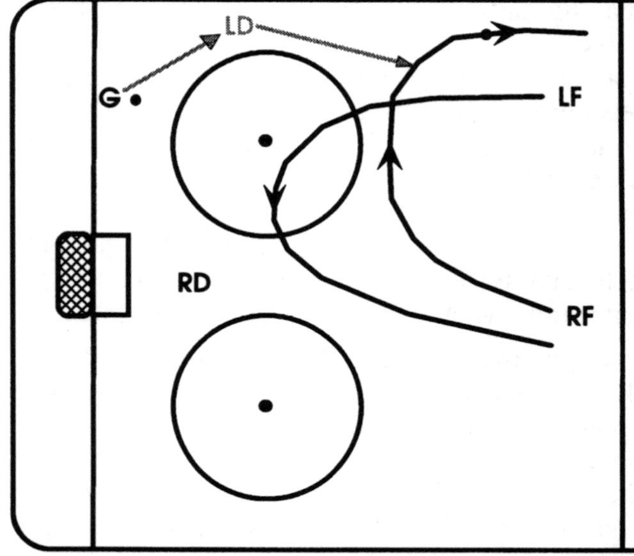

Figure 10-22; Goaltender Breakout

Siller Player And Team Evaluation Profile©
Defensive Zone Team Play Checklist

Evaluator: The Coach | **Date**: 6/10/95 | **Location**: Thunderdome

	Line Number									
Notes: Line 1 - Bill/Elliot/Mike/Benny Line 2 - Jason/Ken/Greg/Doug Line 3 - John/Travis/Tom/David Goaltenders - Amanda/Jay	**LINE 1**		**LINE 2**		**LINE 3**					
Fundamental Defensive Zone Team Techniques										
Zone Defense	8		8		8					
Man-to-Man Defense	7		6		6					
Strongside Breakout	8		8		8					
Weakside Breakout	8		8		8					
Defenseman Skating Breakout	8		5		5					
Around-the-Boards Breakout	8		8		8					
Fast Breakout	6		7		7					
3-0-1 Face-off Alignment	8		7		7					
2-1-1 Face-off Alignment	8		6		7					
2-0-2 Face-off Alignment	0		0		0					
Advanced Defensive Zone Team Techniques										
Overload Defense	7		5		4					
Defense-to-Defense Breakout	6		6		5					
Behind-the-Net Breakout	7		6		6					
Defense Reverse Breakout	7		5		6					
Goaltender Breakout	6		6		5					
TOTAL SCORE	**102**		**91**		**90**					
AVERAGE SCORE	**7.3**		**6.5**		**6.4**					

Comments: Line 1 demonstrated high overall defensive proficiency with a total score of 102 and an average score of 7.3. Lines 2 and 3 demonstrated medium overall proficiency with total scores of 91 and 90, respectively, and average scores of 6.5 and 6.4, respectively. All techniques were performed except the 2-0-2 Face-off alignment. I am pleased with the results from Line 1. Lines 2 and 3 defensemen need to improve on the defenseman skating breakout. At this point in the season, I will only employ the overload defense using line 1. Lines 2 and 3 need additional practice in this area and they may not be ready to use this technique until next season. Line 3 needs to work on the defense-to-defense and goaltender breakouts. Line 3 forwards did not read the play correctly when the goaltender retrieved the puck during the goaltender breakout.

Scale: 0 = Not Performed, 1 - 3 = Low Proficiency, 4 - 6 = Medium Proficiency, 7 - 9 = High Proficiency, 10 = Excellent Proficiency

Table 10-1; Defensive Zone Team Play Checklist

Drills

Defensive zone team drills should be selected to enable players to adjust to as many defensive zone situations as possible. Defensive zone proficiency comes with knowledge and practice. By learning the material in this chapter, the coach and players will become familiar with the particular skills and strategies required to play the many styles in the defensive zone, allowing the individual players and units to become a better overall roller hockey team. As the coach discovers the particular needs of his team, he can select the drills required for the team to improve. The coach should employ the Defensive Zone Team Play Checklist to monitor performance and plan improvements for each player and line throughout the season.

Drill 10-1; Zone Defense. This drill provides the team with practice operating in the defensive zone in a defensive role using the zone defense. The defensive players should be instructed to move in a boxlike formation covering the opponents with the objective of gaining control of the puck or at least neutralizing the offensive attack. Position the players as shown in the corresponding diagram. Continue the drill for one minute or until the defensive team gains control of the puck. It does not matter if the offensive team gets a shot on net during the drill; what is important is how the defensive team reacts to the attacker's movement. Ensure that the offensive team moves the puck to the point men along the boards, below the goal line, behind the net and to the slot. This provides the defensive team with maximum learning potential.

The coach should monitor and provide feedback to the defensive team after the allotted time on the following **eight defensive zone coverage criteria**:

- Positioning
- Controlling the slot
- Reading, anticipating and reacting
- Communicating
- Hustling and putting pressure on the offense
- Ensuring that the goaltender is not being screened during a shot
- Breaking up the offensive attack
- Regaining possession of the puck

Drill 10-2; Man-To-Man Defense. This drill provides the team with practice employing the man-to-man defense. Defensive players should move with their counterparts in a series of one-on-one encounters for one minute or until they gain control of the puck. Position the players as shown in the corresponding diagram. Again, it does not matter if the offensive team gets a shot on net during the drill; what is important is how the defensive team reacts to the various offensive maneuvers. At the whistle, have the offensive team move the puck

XRF
XRD
LD
LF
RD
XLF
G
RF
XLD

Drill 10-1; Zone Defense

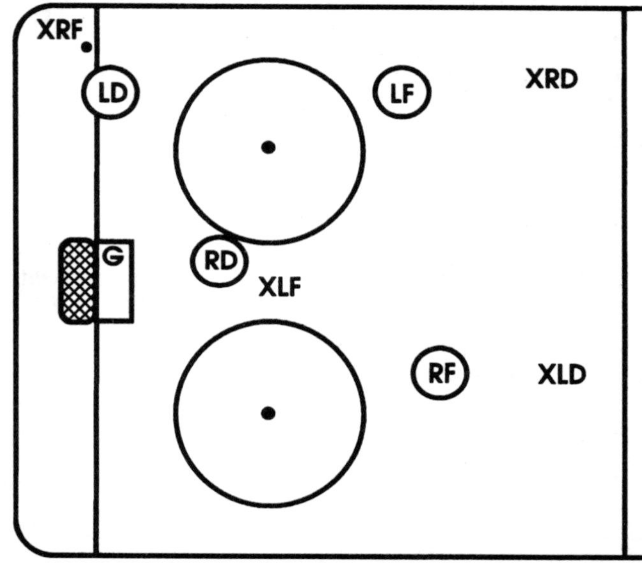

Drill 10-2; Man-To-Man Defense

around in the zone. Monitor and provide feedback to the defensive team after the allotted time on the eight criteria cited above as well as on defensive exchanging (if it occurred).

Drill 10-3; Strongside Breakout. Line up the four members of the breakout team (two defensemen and two forwards) on the center red line. This drill begins with no defenders (4-on-0). Once the breakout team has mastered the drill with no defenders, introduce two defenders (4-on-2). **Note**: Do not add all four defenders until the breakout team has had the opportunity to learn at least three breakout plays. Once the breakout team has some additional options for moving the puck out of its zone, set up any of the breakout drills using a 4-on-4 configuration. As the coach shoots the puck into one of the corners, the breakout team skates into its defensive zone and takes its breakout position according to the corresponding diagram. The strongside defenseman retrieves the puck in the corner, either skates behind the net or turns up the playing surface, and executes a pass to the strongside forward. The strongside forward should then either skate with the puck to the center red line, pass the puck to the weakside forward, execute a drop pass to the strongside defenseman or dump the puck out of the zone. Ensure that all options are practiced. Execute the drill at half speed initially and move to full speed.

Note: Use a volleyball or soccer ball to initially present any of the breakout drills since this will allow the less experienced players an opportunity to read the movement of the other breakout team members (i.e., keeping their heads up) instead of trying to control the puck and read the play around them at the same time. Work both sides of the playing surface so that all four players become accustomed to their proper positioning and movement.

The coach should monitor and provide feedback to the breakout team on the following **five breakout criteria:**

- Accuracy of the first and subsequent passes
- Receipt and control of the puck following a pass
- Positioning and movement of all players — creating space
- Reading, anticipating and reacting
- Communicating

Drill 10-4; Weakside Breakout. Line up the breakout team on the center red line. Initiate the drill with no defenders (4-on-0) and then after the team has mastered the drill, introduce two defenders (4-on-2). As the coach shoots the puck into one of the corners, the breakout team skates into its defensive zone and takes its breakout position according to the corresponding diagram. The strongside defenseman retrieves the puck in the corner, either skates behind the net or turns and skates up the playing surface to the lower portion of the face-off circle, and executes a pass to the weakside forward. The weakside forward (after receiving the puck will now be the strongside forward) should then either skate with the puck to the

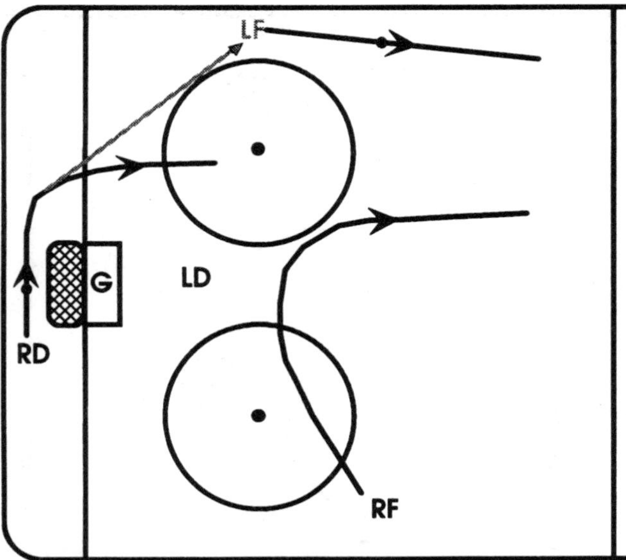

Drill 10-3; Strongside Breakout

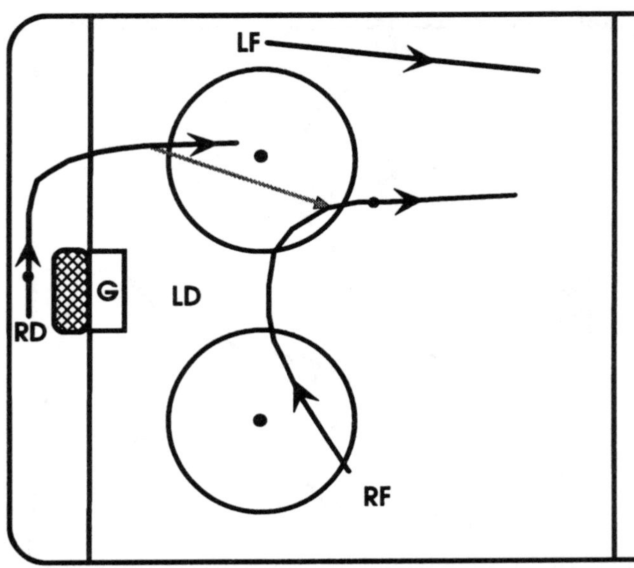

Drill 10-4; Weakside Breakout

center red line, pass the puck to the other forward, execute a drop pass to the original defenseman or dump the puck out of the zone. Ensure that all options are practiced. Another option would be to have the weakside defenseman move away from his position in the slot as the strongside defenseman moves the puck toward the lower portion of the face-off circle. The strongside defenseman could then execute a pass to the weakside defenseman and he could skate, pass or dump the puck. Execute the drill at half speed initially and then move to full speed. Work both sides of the playing surface so that all four players become accustomed to their proper positioning and movement. Monitor and provide feedback to the breakout team on the five criteria described in Drill 10-3.

Drill 10-5; Defenseman Skating Breakout. Line up the breakout team on the center red line. Initiate the drill with no defenders (4-on-0) and then after the team has mastered the drill, introduce two defenders (4-on-2). As the coach shoots the puck into one of the corners, the breakout team skates into its defensive zone and takes the breakout position according to the corresponding diagram. The strongside defenseman retrieves the puck in the corner, either skates behind the net or turns and skates up the middle of the playing surface (or an area that is not congested). As he skates with the puck, both forwards should exchange positions so that the right forward is moving to the left side of the playing surface and the left forward is moving to the right. This gives the puck carrier two passing options and confuses the opponents. Practice all options. Execute the drill at half speed initially and then move to full speed. Work both sides of the playing surface so that all four players become accustomed to their proper positioning and movement. Monitor and provide feedback to the breakout team on the five criteria described in Drill 10-3.

Drill 10-6; Around-the-Boards Breakout. Line up the breakout team on the center red line. Initiate the drill with no defenders (4-on-0) and then after the team has mastered the drill, introduce two defenders (4-on-2). As the coach shoots the puck into one of the corners, the breakout team skates into its defensive zone and takes the breakout position according to the corresponding diagram. The strongside defenseman retrieves the puck in the corner and executes an around-the-boards pass to the circling weakside forward. The weakside forward (after receiving the puck will now be the strongside forward) picks up the puck and begins skating with it. Options are to continue skating with the puck to the center red line, pass the puck to the other forward, execute a drop pass to the defenseman or dump the puck out of the zone. Practice all options. Execute at half speed initially and gradually move to full speed. Work both sides of the playing surface so that all four players become accustomed to their proper positioning and movement. Monitor and provide feedback to the breakout team on the five criteria described in Drill 10-3.

Drill 10-7; Fast Breakout. Line up the breakout team on the center red line. Initiate the drill with no

LF
LD
G
RD
RF

Drill 10-5; Defenseman Skating Breakout

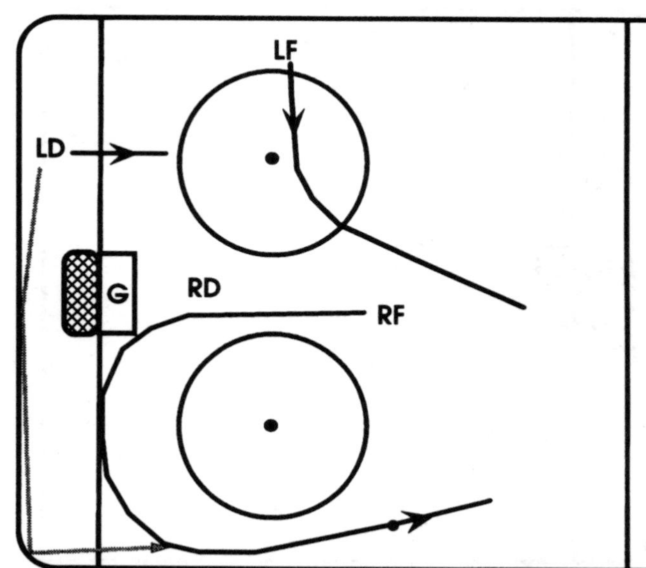

Drill 10-6; Around-the-Boards Breakout

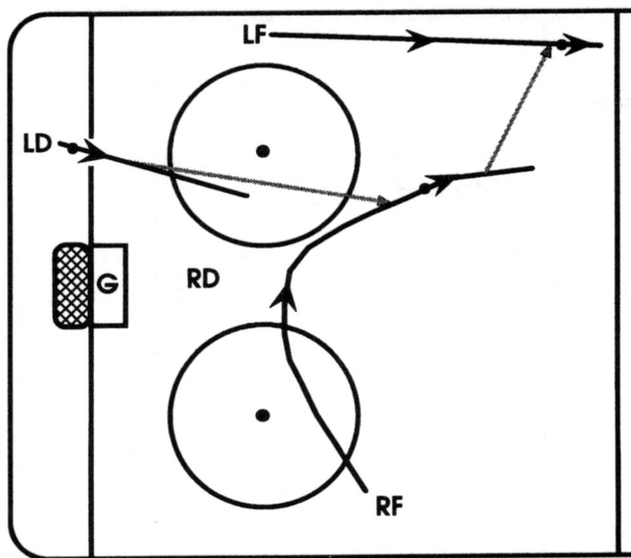

Drill 10-7A; Fast Breakout — 1

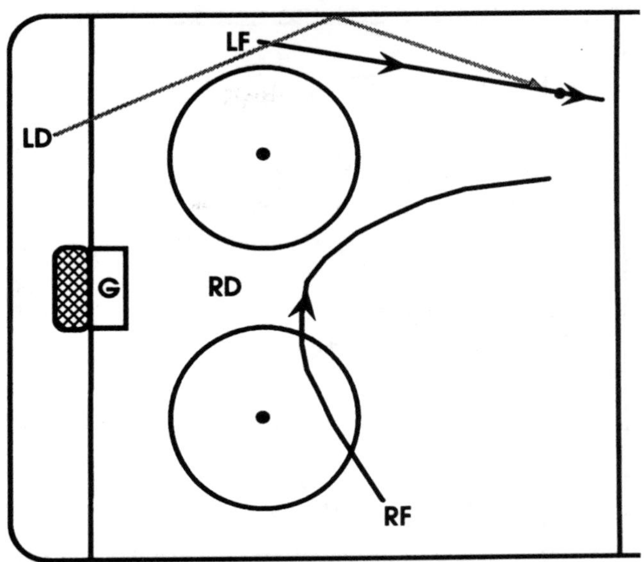

Drill 10-7B; Fast Breakout — 2

defenders (4-on-0) and then after the team has mastered the drill, introduce two defenders (4-on-2). As the coach shoots the puck into one of the corners, the breakout team skates into its defensive zone and takes the breakout position according to the corresponding diagram. Once the strongside defenseman gains control of the puck, the strongside forward skates toward the center red line. The strongside defenseman should pass the puck to the circling weakside forward, who quickly passes the puck to the other forward as shown in Drill 10-7A. Another option would be for the strongside defenseman to execute a bank pass to the strongside forward as shown in Drill 10-7B. Ensure that both of these options are practiced using both sides of the playing surface so that all four players become accustomed to their proper positioning and movement. Execute at half speed initially and then move to full speed. Monitor and provide feedback to the breakout team on the five criteria described in Drill 10-3.

Drill 10-8; Deep Zone Face-offs. Line up the team in the defensive zone using the 3-0-1 face-off alignment at either of the deep face-off circles, as shown in the corresponding diagram. Rotate the attacking team's face-off alignments (using the 3-0-1, 2-1-1 and 2-0-2) so that the defending team will be comfortable with any opponent alignment. Get both centers in the habit of checking out the opponent's alignment and their own team's alignment before preparing for the face-off. The defensive team should also make sure that its goaltender is ready. The defensive team's strategy should be to win the face-off and gain control of the puck first, prevent a scoring opportunity by the opponents second and initiate a breakout play or offensive attack third. Instruct both teams on positioning if the face-off is won, lost or drawn. If the defensive team wins the face-off (as shown in Drill 10-8A), it should move to break out of the defensive zone. If it loses the face-off (as shown in Drill 10-8B), it should begin a zone or man-to-man defense. If neither team clearly wins the face-off, the defensive center should tie up his counterpart while the other defensive forward moves in to get the puck back to the defenseman. Once everyone is ready, the coach should drop the puck. Immediately after the puck is dropped and the outcome of the face-off is known, the coach should stop the play and provide feedback to both teams on the proper positioning of each player. Continue stopping the play immediately after the face-off for four more times (for a total of five face-offs). On the sixth face-off, instruct the players that after the puck is dropped, they should continue playing until the whistle is sounded.

The coach should monitor and provide feedback to the defensive team on the following **six face-off criteria:**

- Positioning and movement of all players — creating space
- Zone or man-to-man defense if the face-off is lost
- Breakout if the face-off is won

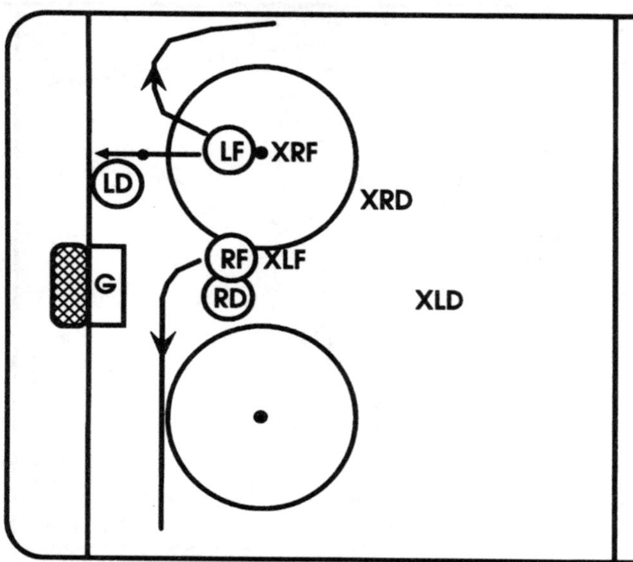

Drill 10-8A; Deep Zone Face-off — Win

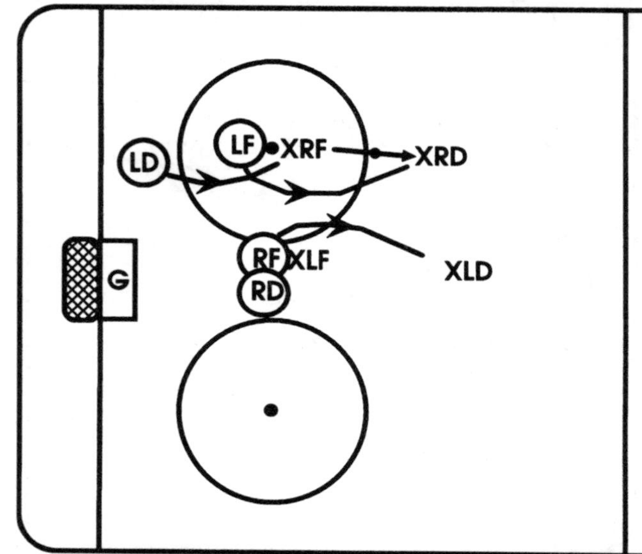

Drill 10-8B; Deep Zone Face-off — Loss

- Forward moving to retrieve the puck if the face-off is neither won or lost
- Reading, anticipating and reacting
- Communicating

Provide feedback to the centers on their quickness, strength, face-off strategy, how they used their stick, skates and body against the opposing center, and how effective both the right and left centers were in right and left defensive zone face-offs.

Drill 10-9; High Zone Face-offs. Line up the team in its defensive zone, initially using the 2-1-1 face-off alignment, at either of the high face-off dots as shown in the corresponding diagram. The coach should rotate the attacking team's face-off alignments (using the 3-0-1, 2-1-1 and 2-0-2) so that the defending team will be comfortable with any opponent alignment. Both centers should check out the opponent's alignment and their own team's alignment before preparing for the face-off. Both teams should be instructed on positioning if the face-off is won, lost or drawn. If the defending team wins the face-off (as shown in Drill 10-9A), it should move on an offensive attack. If they lose the face-off (as shown in Drill 10-9B), they should begin a zone or man-to-man defense. If neither team clearly wins the face-off, the defending center should tie up his counterpart while the other defending for-

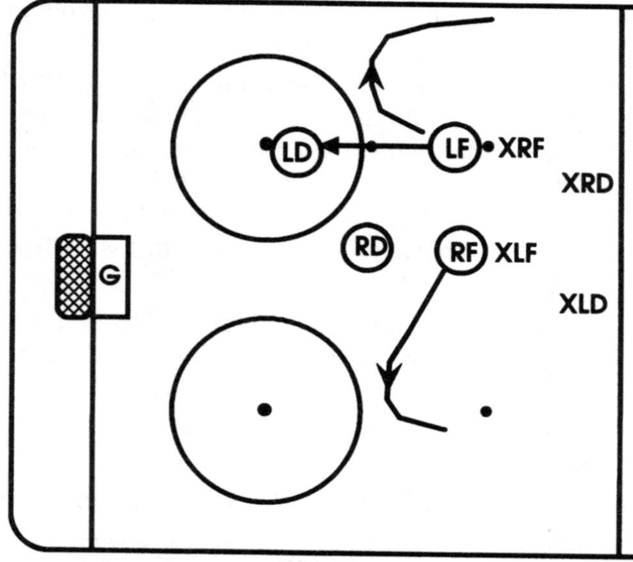

Drill 10-9A; High Zone Face-off — Win

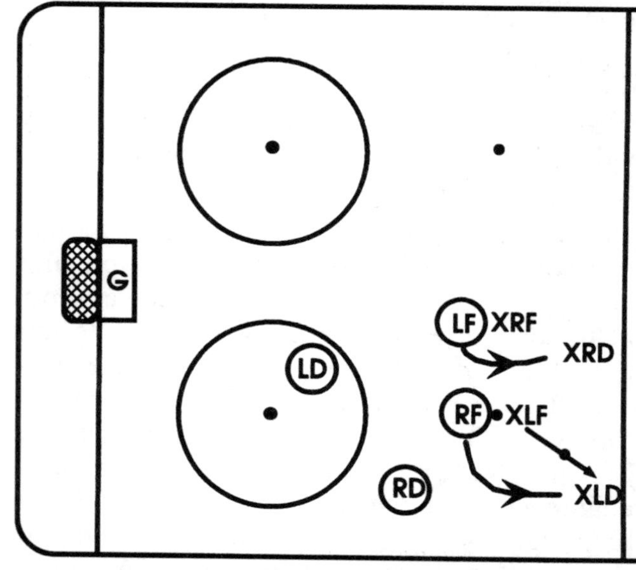

Drill 10-9B; High Zone Face-off — Loss

ward moves in to get the puck back to the defenseman. Once everyone is ready, the coach should drop the puck. Immediately after the puck is dropped and the outcome of the face-off is known, the coach should stop play and provide feedback to both teams on the proper positioning of each player. Continue stopping the play immediately after the face-off four more times. On the sixth face-off, instruct the players that after the puck is dropped, they should continue playing until the whistle is sounded.

Advanced Drills

Drill 10-10; Overload Defense. This drill provides the team with practice employing the overload defense. Defensive players should be instructed to employ the overload defense when the puck is below the overload line (as shown in Drill 10-10A) and move with their counterpart, using a zone or man-to-man defense when the puck is above the overload line (Drill 10-10B). Initially position the players as shown in Drill 10-1. It does not matter if the offensive team gets a shot on net during the drill; what is important is how the defensive team reacts to the various offensive maneuvers. At the whistle, have the offensive team move the puck around in the defensive zone, both above and below the overload line, while the defensive team executes its coverage. If the defensive team gains control of the puck, it can establish an offensive attack, clear the puck out of the defensive zone or freeze the puck. The defensive team should think defense first and offense only when it has full puck control. Monitor and provide feedback to the defensive team on the eight defensive zone coverage criteria cited in Drill 10-1 as well as defensive exchanging (if it occurred).

Drill 10-11; Defense-to-Defense Breakout. Line up the breakout team on the center red line. Initiate the drill with no defenders (4-on-0) and then after the team has mastered the drill, introduce two defenders (4-on-2) and finally four defenders (4-on-4). As the coach shoots the puck into one of the corners, the breakout team skates into the defensive zone and takes the breakout position according to the corresponding diagram. The strongside defenseman retrieves the puck in the corner and executes a bank pass behind the net to the weakside defenseman. The weakside defenseman (after receiving the puck will now be the strongside forward) has the option of skating with the puck, passing it back to the other defenseman or passing it ahead to one of the forwards. Practice all options. Execute the drill at half speed initially and move to full speed. Work both sides of the playing surface so that all four players become accustomed to their proper positioning and movement. Monitor and

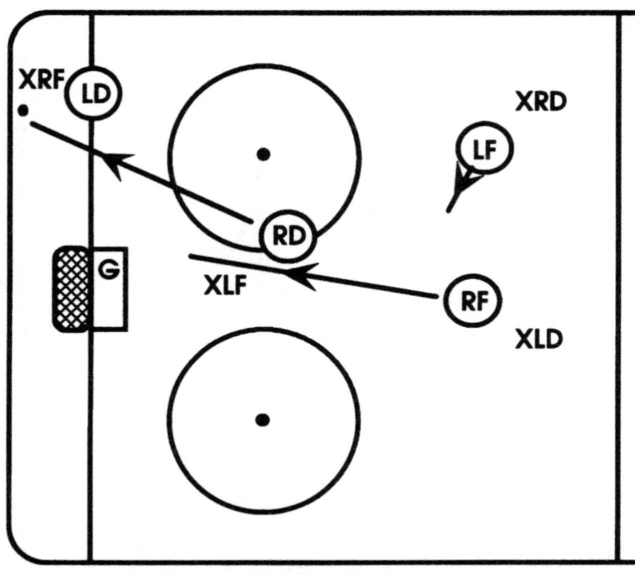

Drill 10-10A; Overload Coverage — 1

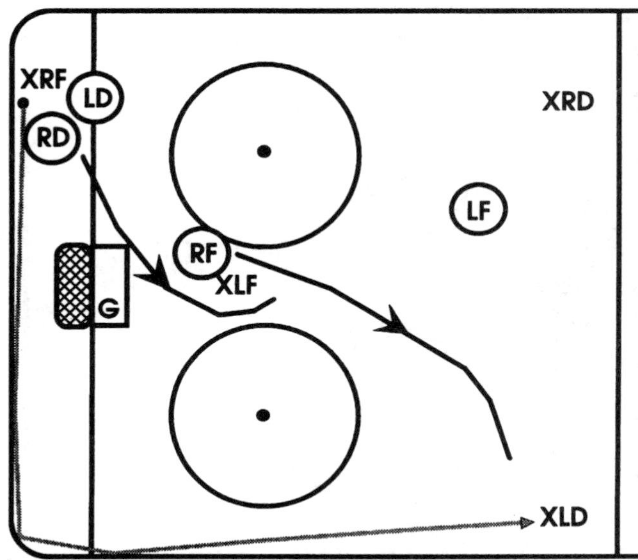

Drill 10-10B; Overload Coverage — 2

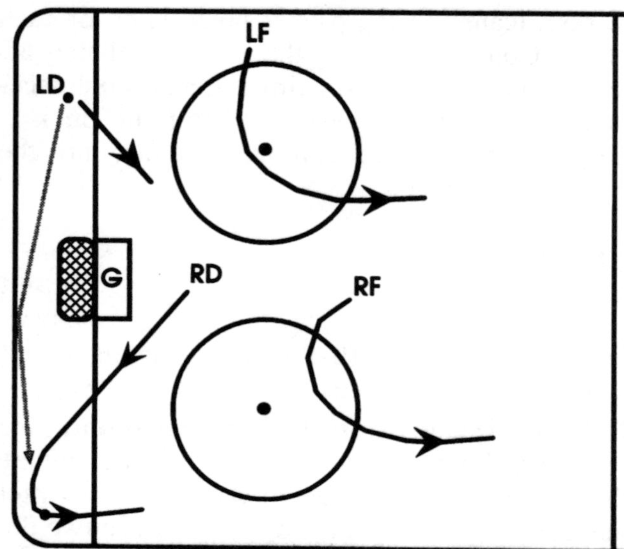

Drill 10-11; Defense-to-Defense Breakout

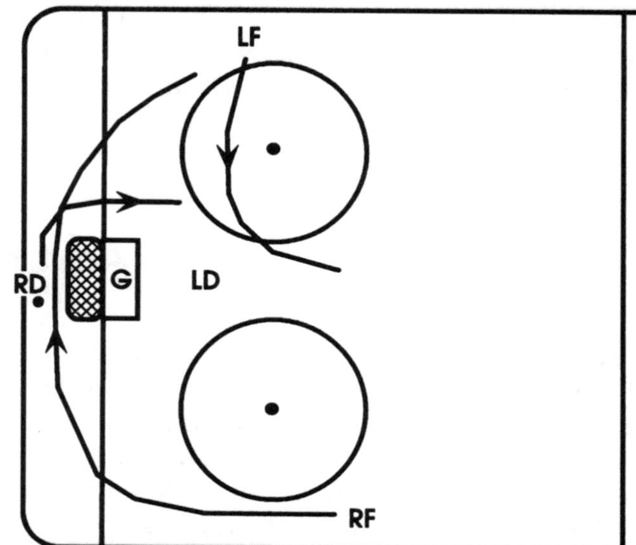

Drill 10-12; Behind-the-Net Breakout

provide feedback to the breakout team on the five breakout criteria described in Drill 10-3.

Drill 10-12; Behind-the-Net Breakout. Line up the breakout team on the center red line. Initiate the drill with no defenders (4-on-0) and after the team has mastered the drill, introduce two defenders (4-on-2), and finally four defenders (4-on-4). As the coach shoots the puck into one of the corners, the breakout team skates into the defensive zone and takes the breakout position according to the corresponding diagram. The strongside defenseman retrieves the puck in the corner and skates behind the net and stops. One of the forwards then skates behind the net and has the option of taking the puck or leaving it. If the forward takes the puck, he can skate with it, pass it to the other forward or pass it back to the original defenseman. If he leaves it, the defenseman can skate with it or pass it to one of the forwards. Practice all options. Execute at half speed initially and move to full speed. Work both sides of the playing surface so that all four players become accustomed to their proper positioning and movement. Monitor and provide feedback to the breakout team on the five breakout criteria described in Drill 10-3.

Drill 10-13; Defense Reverse Breakout. Line up the breakout team on the center red line. Initiate the drill with no defenders (4-on-0) and then after

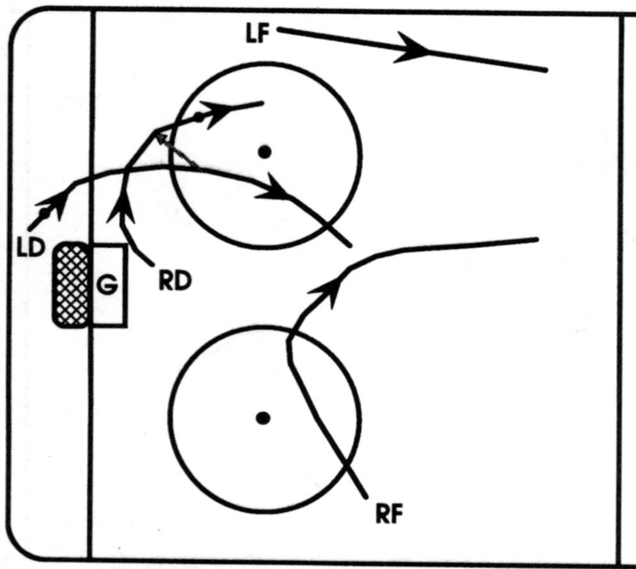

Drill 10-13; Defense Reverse Breakout

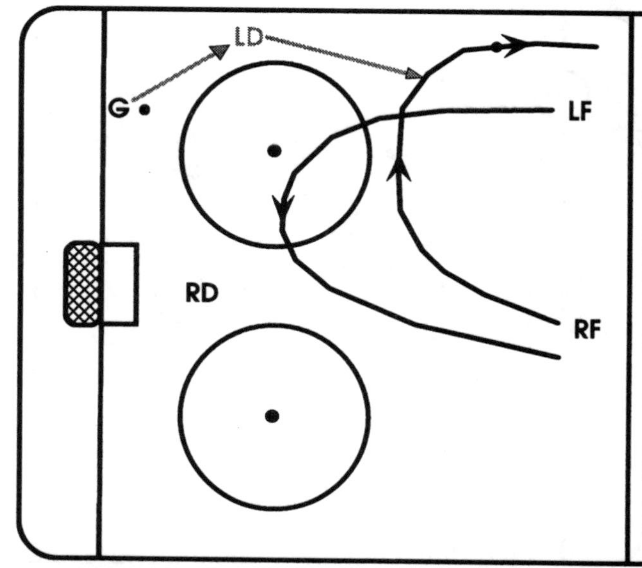

Drill 10-14; Goaltender Breakout

the team has mastered the drill, introduce two defenders (4-on-2) and finally four defenders (4-on-4). As the coach shoots the puck into one of the corners or behind the net, the breakout team skates into the defensive zone and takes the breakout position according to the corresponding diagram. The strongside defenseman retrieves the puck and begins skating with it. Once he moves toward the face-off circle, the weakside defenseman crosses behind the strongside defenseman (reverse) and is available to receive a drop pass if the strongside defenseman gets pressured. As this is occurring, both forwards move toward the center red line to create space and additional passing options for the puck carrier. Practice all options. Execute at half speed initially and move to full speed. Work both sides of the playing surface so that all four players become accustomed to their proper positioning and movement. Monitor and provide feedback to the breakout team on the five breakout criteria described in Drill 10-3.

Drill 10-14; Goaltender Breakout. Line up the breakout team on the center red line. Initiate the drill with no defenders (4-on-0) and then after the team has mastered the drill, introduce two defenders (4-on-2) and finally four defenders (4-on-4). As the coach shoots the puck into one of the corners or behind the net, the breakout team skates into the defensive zone and takes the breakout position according to the corresponding diagram. As the goaltender retrieves the puck, the strongside defenseman positions himself along the boards while the weakside defenseman moves to the slot. The two forwards move in curvilinear patterns, as shown in the corresponding diagram. The goaltender should pass the puck to LD who can quickly pass the puck to either forward. Practice all options. Execute at half speed initially and then move to full speed. Work both sides of the playing surface so that all four players become accustomed to their proper positioning and movement. Monitor and provide feedback to the breakout team on the five breakout criteria described in Drill 10-3.

Recap

After reading and studying the material in this chapter, you should be able to answer the following questions:

1. What is the primary role of a team in the defensive zone?
2. What is the 3PO Principle?
3. Describe the three components that every defensive zone strategy should incorporate. What is roller hockey's tactical triad?
4. Summarize the two fundamental defensive zone coverage techniques. How are they similar? How are they different? What are the roles of the players, including the goaltender, in each technique? Which technique is better to teach beginning roller hockey players?
5. Describe defensive exchanging.
6. Describe three keys to an effective breakout.
7. Describe the five fundamental breakout techniques. When should each be used?
8. What are face-off techniques designed to do?
9. Describe three elements of the defensive zone face-off strategy.
10. What are the two tactical components of the face-off?
11. Describe three face-off alignments. When should each be used? Describe three essential face-off assignments.
12. Describe three ways to win face-offs.
13. What are four points that every center must master to win face-offs?
14. Summarize the overload defense technique in terms of the overload line and defensive overloading.
15. List and describe the four advanced breakout techniques.
16. How will you use the Defensive Zone Team Play Checklist and the drills provided in this chapter to help improve defensive zone team performance and correct existing deficiencies?
17. What eight criteria should the coach use to evaluate all defensive zone coverage drills?
18. What five criteria should the coach use to evaluate all breakout drills?
19. What six criteria should the coach use to evaluate all face-off drills?

JOE'S GARAGE
FULL SERVICE
?
JOE
GAS
JOE'S
7
CAN YOU GET ME IN FOR A TIRE ROTATION AND A FRONT END ALIGNMENT?

11

Offensive Zone Team Play

Highlights

This chapter addresses the role of team play in the offensive zone. Chapter 11 presents the following information:

Discussion

Fundamentals

- *attacking in the offensive zone*
- *triangulation (or the third man in)*
- *2-2 attack*
- *diamond attack*
- *occupied triangle attack*
- *forechecking systems*
- *1-1-2 system*
- *1-2-1 system*
- *0-1-3 system*
- *face-off techniques*
- *3-0-1, 2-1-1 and 2-0-2 alignments*
- *assignments*

Advanced Techniques

- *offensive regrouping*
- *offensive cycling*
- *2-1-1 forechecking system*
- *2-0-2 forechecking system*

Siller Player and Team Evaluation Profile — Offensive Zone Team Play

Drills

Advanced Drills

Recap

The greatest test of courage on earth is to bear defeat without losing heart.
— Robert Green Ingersoll —

Courage is resistance to fear, mastery of fear — not absence of fear.
— Mark Twain —

Discussion

Roller hockey is played from an offensive standpoint; with plenty of shots, rebounds and goals. That's not to say that defense isn't important, but wheeling down the playing surface with lots of room to maneuver, setting up the offensive attack and scoring a goal is how the game is played. All successful roller hockey teams know what it takes to put the puck in the net; and putting the puck in the net is the **primary role of a team in its offensive zone**. That's it, that's all that is required! How a team accomplishes this role is what keeps every coach planning, preparing, designing and revising throughout the season. Scoring goals is accomplished through hard work and discipline by gaining control of the puck, moving it into a high-percentage scoring location, positioning players near the net for a rebound, screen or deflection, and shooting the puck on net. Putting the puck into the opponent's net sometimes comes from luck, but most goals are scored because a team has an effective offensive strategy. **Your offensive zone strategy should incorporate the following six factors**: puck control and movement, positioning of non-puck carrying players with respect to the puck carrier/shooter, defined plays with improvisation, shots on net from a high-percentage scoring location, patience, and reading, reacting and anticipating.

- **Puck control and movement** form the basis of any successful offensive attack. To score goals you must first have control of the puck, and as we know from the *3PO Principle*, puck possession provides opportunities. These opportunities are created by having the puck carrier in motion and constantly looking to pass, shoot or skate on net. The puck carrier should move with the puck to draw the opposition out of position. Forcing the opposition into making bad plays is good offensive roller hockey and is critical in the offensive end. **The success of an offensive attack** is attributed to both the determination and skill of the offensive team as well as taking advantage of mistakes made by the defensive team.
- **Positioning of non-puck carrying players with respect to the puck carrier/shooter** is important because movement by all players creates an attack which is always more difficult for the opposition to cover. Non-puck carriers or supporting players should maneuver themselves into an open position to create options and should base their movement on the puck carrier, the defenders and the open playing surface available. Supporting players should make themselves available to receive a pass, clear an area to allow space for the puck carrier, screen an opponent and offer close support to the puck carrier. To be effective in this support role, a player must anticipate the puck carrier's intentions, read the defensive pressure being applied on the puck carrier and adjust his position in relation to the puck carrier.
- **Defined plays with improvisation** will always create a better organized attack than an ad-lib attack, all things being equal. By working on defined offensive plays, the players develop the confidence and ability to improvise on the defined plays when different situations arise. Though roller hockey is a game in which the players must do a lot of improvising because of ever changing scenarios, they will be able to select the right moves more often if they have learned as many basic offensive plays as possible.
- **Shots on net from a high-percentage scoring location** will improve any team's scoring chances over haphazard shooting. Move the puck from the perimeter scoring areas toward the slot. Once in this area, a direct shot, screen shot or deflection can be executed. After the initial shot, there is always the potential for a second opportunity on the rebound. Remember that each shot is really a potential **one-two punch** — the initial shot and the rebound.
- **Patience** by the offensive team, especially the puck carrier, is required to make effective use of puck control. Since your team has control of the puck, why be quick to get rid of it? If you have the puck in a high-percentage location, shoot. If another player is open in a better scoring location, pass the puck. If neither occurs, be patient and continue to move the puck while your teammates maneuver into better positions. An immediate and direct offensive attack is great, but when nothing is available, use your

head and wheels and be patient while your supporting players set up.

- **Reading, reacting and anticipating** are required during all offensive attacks to best make use of a current situation and to create additional ones. This involves all offensive players knowing the tendencies of their teammates as well as learning the opponent's defensive strategies and incorporating this information into your overall offensive zone strategy. Employing these skills teaches the offensive team to create its own opportunities as well as to take advantage of the opposition's weaknesses by attacking specific positions, areas or players.

Fundamentals

Three fundamental offensive zone team skills covered in this section include attacking in the offensive zone, forechecking systems and face-off techniques.

Attacking in the offensive zone is a team skill that is designed to score goals with the intent of maximizing high-percentage scoring opportunities. Attacking is really a two-stage process; the first stage involves initially moving the puck into the offensive zone. This includes the kind of plays that were described in Chapter 8 in the section on moving the puck into the offensive zone. If the initial attack does not produce a goal or at least a good shot on net, and you still have possession of the puck, set up the second stage of the attack. This second stage consists of maintaining the puck in the offensive zone to initiate a secondary scoring attack. It can also consist of offensive regrouping which will be discussed in the advanced section of this chapter. Maintaining control of the puck in the offensive zone is vital to a team's scoring success.

To be effective at both stages of the attack, use triangulation. **Triangulation** (or the third man in) is the technique of maintaining three offensive players (the puck carrier and two supporting players) in every offensive attack to create the necessary puck movement. The puck carrier moves the puck around in the offensive zone while the two supporting teammates move to create space and options for the puck carrier. One supporting player is a forward and the other supporting player is almost always a defenseman. Utilizing your defensemen in offensive play allows a team to remain on the offensive for a longer period of time because the defensemen provide additional players and locations to maintain puck possession. Employing this triangulation technique increases your presence in the offensive zone and pressures opponents with quick passing, skating and shooting to set up many scoring opportunities. Triangulation places one player (either the puck carrier or a supporting player) in or near the slot to maintain the scoring threat, while the other two players maneuver for an eventual pass, shot, deflection or rebound. This technique guarantees added scoring opportunities and is **the central roller hockey element to maintaining control of the puck and moving it around in the offensive zone**.

Two plays that employ triangulation are shown in the corresponding figures. The first play (Figure 11-1) has the defenseman reading that a scoring opportunity is available and skating in toward the net, receiving a pass from one of the forwards, and putting a shot on net. This play is very effective when the opposition has two or three men deep in the zone, away from the defenseman. That is how I scored a couple of goals in the 1994 NARCh Finals in St. Louis. The second play (Figure 11-2) utilizes both defensemen to create an opening for one defenseman to move into an open area and shoot. This play utilizes the give-and-go technique and is effective when one of the defensemen can get past one of the opponent's forwards. Triangulation allows the defensemen to become part of the offense by putting a shot on net, passing to a player with a better scoring opportunity or moving the puck from a congested area to an uncongested area of the playing surface.

Three strategies used to attack in the offensive zone consist of the 2-2 attack, the diamond attack and the occupied triangle attack. All three of these approaches have advantages and disadvantages and must be evaluated by the coach to determine which strategy will work during any given situation.

- The **2-2 attack**, a basic offensive zone strategy, **is the best strategy to teach beginning roller hockey players** because of its basic design and set of responsibilities. This strategy also allows

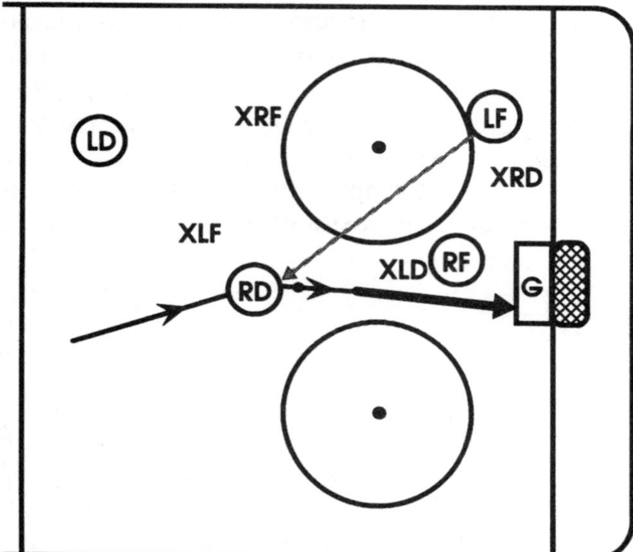

Figure 11-1; Triangulation

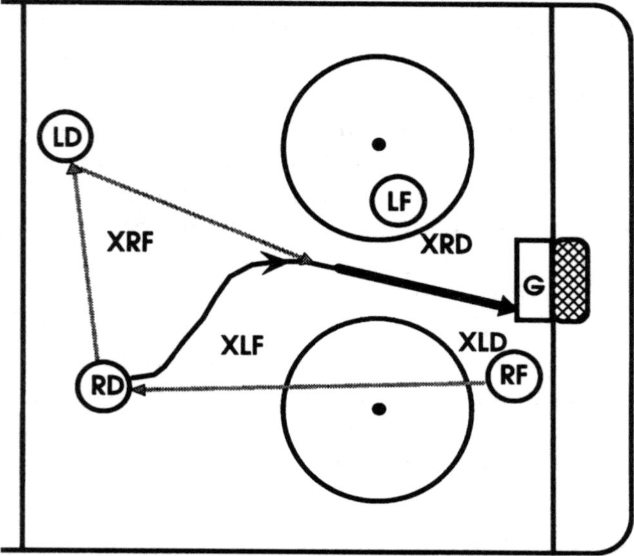

Figure 11-2; Give-and-Go Triangulation

for a more balanced transition to defense when the opposing team gains control of the puck. Figure 11-3 shows quadrants — defined as quadrants one through four — that this attack employs. The 2-2 attack utilizes the offensive players in a boxlike formation (as shown in Figure 11-4), generally with one attacker in each quadrant, to control the puck and move it around the four quadrants with the objective of getting a shot on net from a high-percentage scoring location. When the puck is in quadrant one, the quadrant two player moves near the slot for a scoring opportunity. When the puck is in quadrant two, the quadrant one player moves near the slot for a scoring opportunity. The point men will shift laterally, forward or backward depending on where the puck is, with one of the defensemen being the third man in when the opportunity is available.

When executing the 2-2 attack, the offensive players are not free to skate all over the playing surface with the puck. They should generally remain in their normal quadrant and pass the puck to a player in another quadrant instead of skating all around the playing surface with it.

In Figure 11-4, the offensive team (circled players using the 2-2 attack) positions one forward

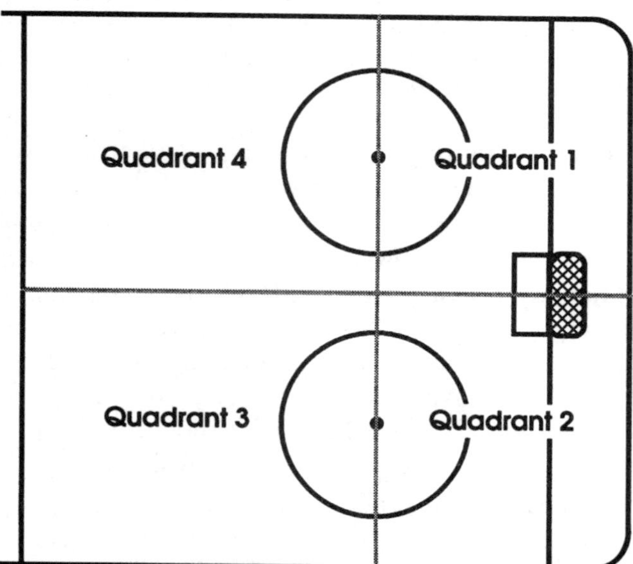

Figure 11-3; Offensive Quadrants

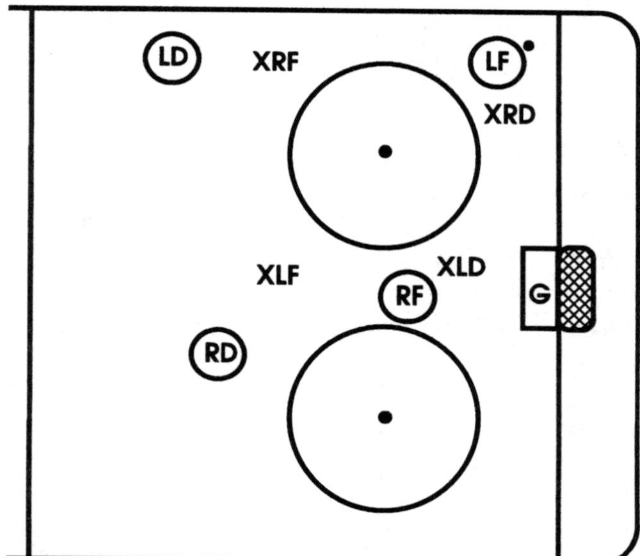

Figure 11-4; 2-2 Attack

(LF) in quadrant one and one defenseman (LD) in quadrant four. The second forward (RF) is placed near the slot in quadrant two, and the second defenseman (RD) is placed in quadrant three. When the puck is deep in the offensive zone, LF can skate with the puck, pass it employing triangulation or shoot. Since LF is in a low-percentage scoring location, the first two options should be chosen. The offensive team should always make use of the space behind the net when setting up a scoring opportunity. Many positional mistakes are made by the defensive team when the puck carrier has possession of the puck behind the net, and those mistakes should always be translated into opportunities by the offensive team.

Offensive players need to be constantly reading and anticipating the play, with the puck carrier moving the puck to set up a high-percentage scoring opportunity, while the supporting players react by positioning themselves appropriately. The puck carrier should always have two supporting players involved in the attack and take advantage of the opportunities created by triangulation. If the puck carrier gets in trouble, either freeze the puck along the boards or dump it in front of the net. By dumping the puck in front of the net, you may get a scoring opportunity; otherwise, the goaltender may freeze the puck and you can start off the next play with a face-off deep in your offensive zone. If the opposing team gains control of the puck, start forechecking and putting pressure on the opponents to regain control of the puck. Above all, be patient and continue to move the puck while your teammates maneuver into better positions.

- The **diamond attack** is an offensive zone strategy that should be used by an experienced roller hockey team. This strategy requires the attackers to be fairly quick and agile and be able to read and anticipate offensive patterns and defensive coverage very well. The diamond attack, as its name implies, utilizes the offensive players in a diamond formation (circled players as shown in Figure 11-5), with one attacker behind the goal line and near the net, one attacker between the left face-off dot and the slot, a third attacker between the right face-off dot and the slot, and the single point man operating above the face-off circles and in the middle of the offensive zone. As the figure shows, triangulation is built into the diamond attack since one of the defensemen is required to play the role of a forward. Although the diamond attack positions players in certain general locations, it is not as rigorous as the 2-2 attack. Players are free to move around the playing surface as long as one player exchanges positions in the location vacated by another player (**offensive exchanging**). **There are two objectives of the diamond attack**; the first is to get the puck to the player near the slot for a scoring opportunity, and second, to move the puck from a position deep in the zone to a position high in the zone, and vice versa, when the player in the slot is not available. Moving the puck in these cycles, when the player near the slot is not open, is an excellent offensive tactic because it keeps the puck moving and does not allow the defensive team time to set up. This may allow the attackers to trap two or even three defenders deep or to one side of the playing surface if the offensive team times its cycles just right. When the puck is deep in the offensive zone, as shown in Figure 11-5, LF can skate with the puck, pass it using triangulation or shoot. Since LF again is in a low-percentage scoring location, the first two options should be chosen.

  Offensive players need to be constantly reading and anticipating the play, with the puck carrier moving the puck to set up a high-percentage scoring opportunity, while the supporting players react by positioning themselves appropriately. The diamond attack should allow two or even all three supporting players to be involved in the attack. Again, if the puck carrier gets in trouble, either freeze the puck along the boards or dump it in front of the net. If the opposing team gains control of the puck, start forechecking and putting pressure on the opponents to regain control of the puck. Be patient and continue to move the puck while your teammates maneuver into better positions.

- The **occupied triangle attack** is another offensive zone strategy that should be used by an experienced roller hockey team. The occupied triangle attack, as its name implies, utilizes three offensive players in a triangular formation (LF, RF and LD as shown in Figure 11-6), with one attacker (RD) occupying the slot. Two offen-

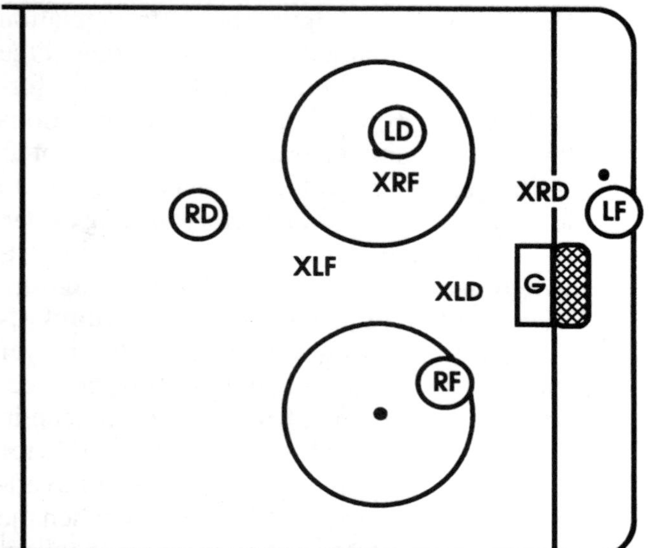

Figure 11-5; Diamond Attack

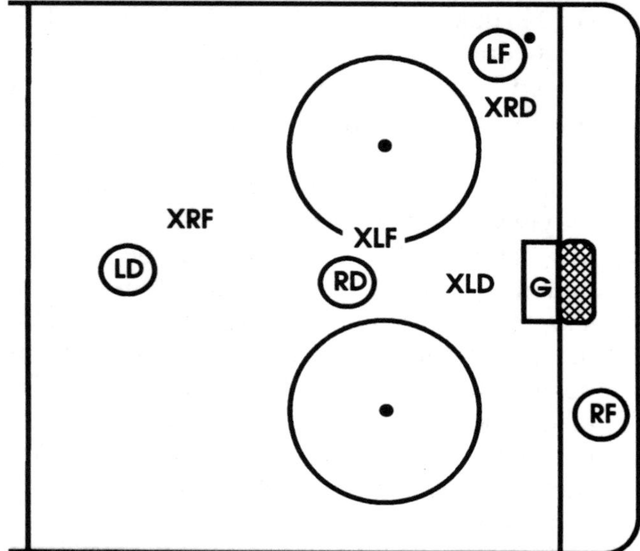

Figure 11-6; Occupied Triangle Attack

sive players maneuver in quadrants one and two, as described in the 2-2 attack, and are the base of the triangle, while the top of the triangle is maintained by a single point man operating above the face-off circles and in the middle of the offensive zone. The attacker occupying the center of the triangle moves around inside the triangle, positioning himself for a scoring opportunity. This offensive attack strategy is similar to the 2-2 attack in that players generally maintain their positions in quadrants one and two and at the point and are not free to move in all areas of the offensive zone. One exception is when the slot man moves away from his position, such as when going after a loose puck. In this case, one of the attackers at the base of the triangle will move to the slot while the original slot man moves to the base of the triangle (offensive exchanging). **The objective of the occupied triangle attack** is to have the players maintaining the triangle move the puck around the perimeter, always reading for the right opportunity to pass the puck to the slot man for that high-percentage shot. When the slot man is continually covered, the point man can execute a shot on net and have the slot man and the two other attackers converge on the net for the one-two punch.

When the puck is deep in the offensive zone, as shown in Figure 11-6, LF can skate with the puck, pass it or shoot. Since LF is in a low-percentage scoring location, the first two options should be chosen. Unless the defending team is executing a man-to-man defense, one of the attackers deep in the offensive zone should be open since one of the defenders will usually be positioned in front of the net. If none of the three teammates is open, LF would skate with the puck until one of his teammates did get open or until he could maneuver into a good scoring position himself. This occupied triangle attack is designed for most of the action down low since most of the attackers are positioned there. The offensive team should always make use of the space behind the net when setting up for a scoring opportunity. Due to the number of players down low, confusion will occur and the potential for mistakes by the defensive team when the puck carrier has possession of the puck behind the net are moderate to high. Those mistakes should always be translated into opportunities by the offensive team.

Offensive players need to be constantly reading and anticipating the play, with the puck carrier moving the puck to set up a high-percentage scoring opportunity, while the supporting players react by positioning themselves appropriately. The occupied triangle attack should allow two or even all three supporting players to be involved in the attack. Again, if the puck carrier gets in trouble, either freeze the puck along the boards or dump it in front of the net. If the opposing team gains control of the puck, start forechecking and

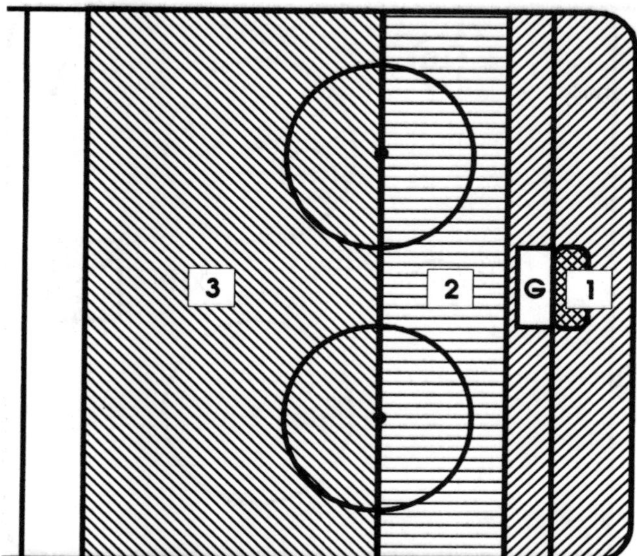

Figure 11-7; Forechecking Zones

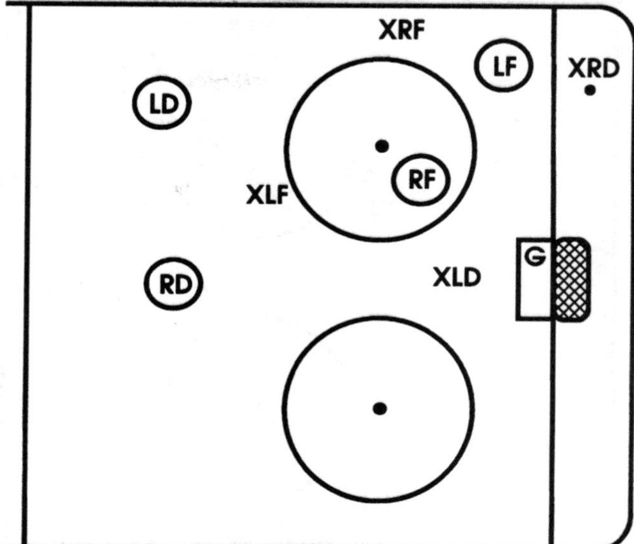

Figure 11-8; 1-1-2 Forechecking System

putting pressure on the opponents to regain control of the puck. Be patient and continue to move the puck while your teammates maneuver into better positions.

Forechecking Systems. As described in Chapter 8, forechecking is a tactic used to gain or regain possession of the puck in the offensive zone and to eventually set up a scoring opportunity. **Three effective roller hockey forechecking systems** presented in this section include the fundamental 1-1-2 and 1-2-1 systems and the conservative 0-1-3 system.

Forechecking systems are described using three numbers (i.e., 1-1-2) corresponding to the three forechecking zones. The numbers represent the number of forecheckers positioned in each zone (see Figure 11-7). For example, the 1-1-2 forechecking system consists of one forechecker (generally a forward) in zone 1, one forechecker (generally the second forward) in zone 2 and the two defensemen in zone 3.

The **1-1-2 forechecking system** is designed to gain or regain control of the puck using fundamental positional play. The objective is to force the opposition to move the puck to locations controlled by the forechecking team. This system attempts to control the strongside boards (the side of the playing surface that the puck is on) and the middle of the playing surface, and negate getting caught too deep in the zone. As shown in Figure 11-8, this system has the strongside forward (LF) forechecking the puck carrier (XRD) in zone 1, trying to force XRD into area 1. For a review of forechecking areas 1, 2 and 3 see Figure 8-13. The zone 2 forward (RF) positions himself inside the face-off circle ready to cover the offensive forward XRF and force him into forechecking area 3 if he gets control of the puck. RF also prevents the opposition from moving up the middle and moves into the slot for a pass if the LF gains control of the puck. The forwards will often have to exchange roles and zones depending on puck and player movement. As the play moves from one side of the playing surface to the other, RF becomes the forechecker in zone 1 and LF assumes a position in zone 2. The strongside zone 3 defenseman (LD) plays about six feet from the boards and can pinch if he is able to gain control of the puck. The weakside (the side of the playing surface that the puck is not on) defenseman, RD, plays at the center of the playing surface guarding against a pass up the middle or around the boards.

Pinching occurs when a defenseman moves in from his point position to pressure a defender with the intent of keeping the puck in the offensive zone. If the defenseman does not beat the opponent to the puck when pinching, the opponents will most likely set up for an odd-man rush (i.e., 2-on-1). Pinching is a calculated risk, but if the odds are in your favor it is an excellent move. Experience and anticipation will help the point men determine when to pinch to keep the puck in the offensive zone and when to retreat.

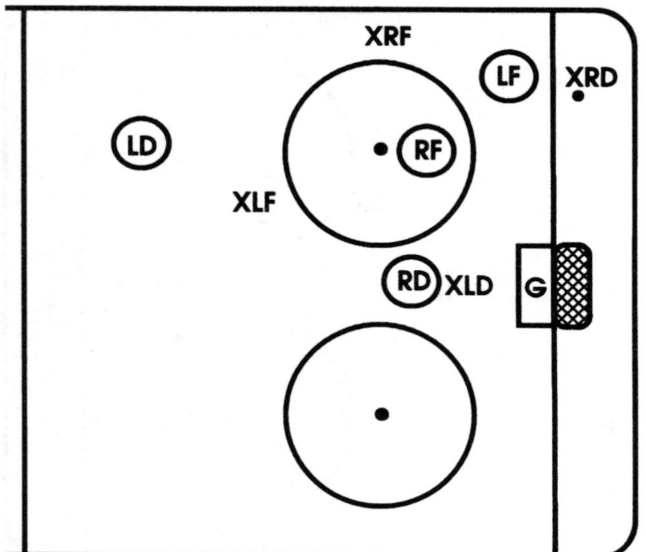

Figure 11-9; 1-2-1 Forechecking System

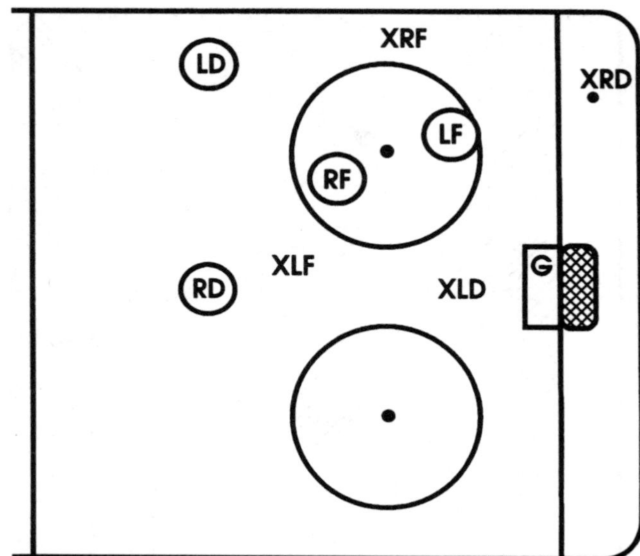

Figure 11-10; 0-1-3 Forechecking System

The **1-2-1 forechecking system** is similar in strategy to the 1-1-2 system, to attempt to gain or regain control of the puck using fundamental positional play. The objective, again, is to force the opposition to move the puck to locations controlled by the forechecking team. The 1-2-1 system has one main difference: it is designed to control the flow of players and the puck in zone 2. Even though there is only one defenseman in zone 3, the two players in zone 2 will become quickly involved in the play if they can cover their opposing players. As shown in Figure 11-9, the 1-2-1 system has the strongside forward (LF) forechecking the puck carrier (XRD) in zone 1. The zone 2 forward (RF) and defenseman (RD) position themselves in the face-off circle and near the high slot, respectively, attempting to force a turnover and move the puck to the slot for a scoring opportunity. As with the 1-1-2 system, the zone 1 and 2 players will often have to exchange roles and zones. All of this transitioning is done quickly, so that a forechecking presence will be maintained no matter what side of the playing surface the puck is on. The zone 3 defenseman (LD) plays on the strong side at a location between the boards and the center of the playing surface. His role is to control the puck if it is passed up the middle or along the strongside boards and pinch only if one of the zone 2 players covers for him.

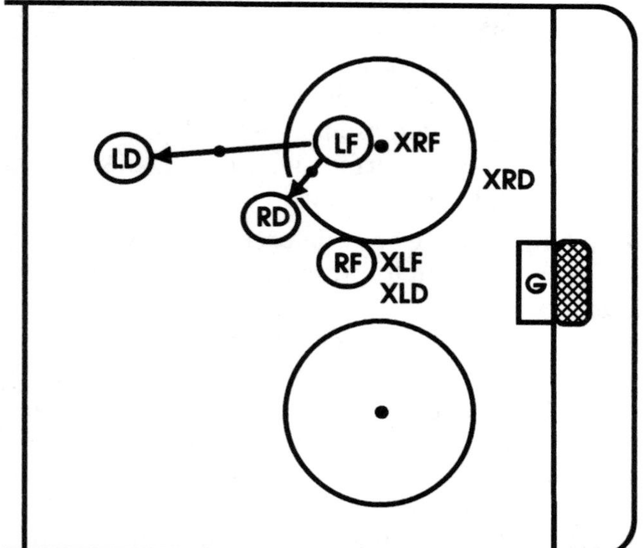

Figure 11-11; Face-off Win

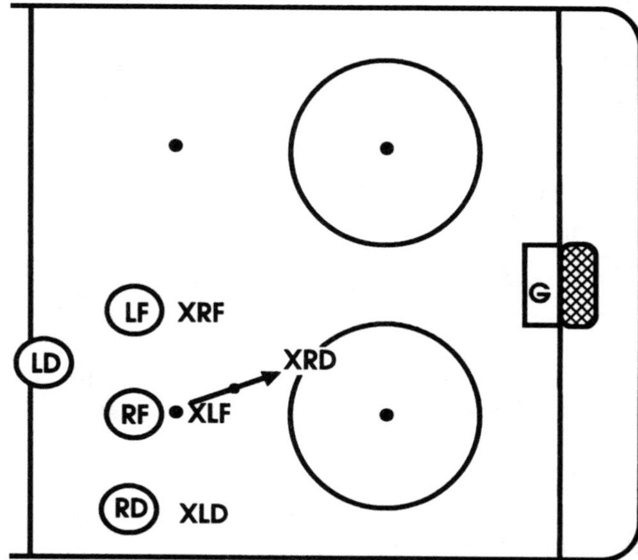

Figure 11-12; Face-off Loss

Face-off Drop

The **0-1-3 forechecking system** uses a conservative approach and can be used when a team is a couple of goals ahead or trying to protect a lead late in a game. The objective of this system is not necessarily to gain or regain control of the puck, but to make sure that zone 3 is protected against any surprise or odd-man attacks. The 0-1-3 system does not utilize any pressure in zone 1 and only utilizes one forechecker in zone 2. As shown in Figure 11-10, the 0-1-3 system employs the strongside forward (LF) in zone 2 to defend against the puck carrier (XRD). His role is to force XRD to pass the puck to one of his teammates (XRF, XLF or XLD), and thereby force a situation in which puck control can be gained. The zone 3 players consist of the two defensemen (LD and RD) and the weakside forward (RF). RF plays near the zone 2 and 3 transition while RD and LD play in the central part of zone 3, with LD playing about 10 feet from the boards. The zone 3 players cover the opposition and attempt to break up any passing plays or, using the various stick checking techniques, attempt to strip the opponents of the puck.

Face-off techniques are used by a team to optimize its chances of gaining control of the puck following a face-off. The ability of a team to consistently gain control of the puck following a face-off, especially in its offensive zone, will allow that team the opportunity to move the puck in for a scoring opportunity (3PO principle) and force the opposing team to immediately go on the defensive. In the **offensive zone, the face-off strategy** should be built around winning the face-off and gaining control of the puck first, initiating an offensive attack second and forechecking the opponents to regain control of the puck third. After understanding these three elements of the strategy, the team should work on the **two tactical components of the face-off — alignments and assignments**.

Alignments are the placement of players by a team to most effectively implement the face-off strategy. Since the strategy is built around winning the face-off and gaining control of the puck first and foremost, player alignments should reflect this. **Three face-off alignments** consist of the 3-0-1, 2-1-1 and 2-0-2 alignments described in Chapter 10. How a team aligns its players in the offensive zone depends upon where the face-off occurs and how the other team's players are aligned. When the face-off is deep in the offensive zone, the players align themselves using either the 3-0-1 or 2-1-1 alignments. Both alignments allow your team to control the puck and set up a scoring opportunity if you win the face-off, and put the most pressure on the opposing team if you lose the face-off. The center (LF as shown in Figure 11-11) positions himself at the face-off dot while the other forward (RF) plays on the edge of the face-off circle closest to the net. One of the defensemen plays just outside of RF if the 3-0-1 alignment is used or between LF and RF and about 10 feet back if the 2-1-1 alignment is used (as shown in Figure 11-11), while the other defenseman positions himself behind the center.

When the face-off is out near the transition zone, the players should align themselves using either the 3-0-1, 2-1-1 or 2-0-2 configurations and should also take into account how the other team lines up for the face-off. Players must be taught to read what the opposition is trying to do with the face-off and then align themselves accordingly. For instance, if the opposing team lines up using a 3-0-1 alignment (as shown in Figure 11-12), your team should read this alignment and also line up using the 3-0-1 alignment. If the opposing team lines up in either a 2-1-1 or 2-0-2 alignment, align your players accordingly. These alignments allow your team to maintain balance during face-offs occurring near the transition zone.

Assignments are each player's responsibilities during and subsequent to each face-off. Assignments must be carried out to perfection for an effective face-off strategy. The center is your quarterback for the face-off, and it is his job to position the players based on what he is planning to do with the puck. On every face-off, each player must have a primary assignment that he will carry out once the puck is dropped. After the puck has been dropped, his assignment may change depending upon whether the draw is won, lost or undetermined (both centers continue to battle for the puck). **Three essential assignments** that each team should understand and employ during and subsequent to every face-off depend upon whether your team wins, loses or neutralizes a face-off.

When the face-off is deep in your offensive zone and your team (circled players as shown in Figure 11-11) wins the face-off, three options are to get the puck back to LD or RD, or have the center move the puck forward himself. During the first two scenarios, LF contains XRF, RF moves to the net for a pass, rebound or deflection, RD contains XLF in the first scenario and shoots the puck in the second. If LD receives the puck, he can shoot, pass or skate in closer to the net. In this situation it is generally best to take the shot unless a teammate is in a better scoring position. When the face-off is near the transition zone and your team wins the face-off, players should move on an offensive attack by either moving toward the net or getting open for a pass. If the puck is at the point, a pass can be executed to an open teammate to initiate the attack.

When the face-off is deep in your offensive zone and your team loses the draw, the intent is to immediately begin forechecking and pressuring the opponents in an attempt to gain control of the puck. All four players position themselves according to the specific forechecking strategy desired. When the face-off is near the transition zone and your team loses the face-off (as shown in Figure 11-12), RF or LF pressures the puck carrier into making a bad play with the intent of gaining possession of the puck.

When the face-off is anywhere in your offensive zone, neither team immediately wins the face-off, and the puck remains in the area of the two centers, your center (LF) contains the opposing center while the second forward (RF) contains XLF and XLD (as shown in the 2-1-1 alignment in Figure 11-13). During this, RD moves in to get the puck back to LD for a shot or another pass. Players should maintain movement during the struggle for puck control. While some players are battling for the puck, the other supporting players maintain movement close to the puck so they can ensure that they are not caught standing still when a play is initiated. If RD gets the puck back to LD (as shown in Figure 11-13), then LD moves to establish the offensive attack, LF moves to an open area on the strong side of the playing surface, RF moves to the net and RD positions himself off to the weak side for a passing option. If both teams are battling for the puck after the face-off and your team does not gain control of the puck, immediately begin forechecking and pressuring the opponents in an attempt to gain control of the puck.

Chapter 10 discusses **several techniques that every center must use to win a face-off.** Each of these methods requires plenty of practice in both drills and scrimmages. Practice specific face-off

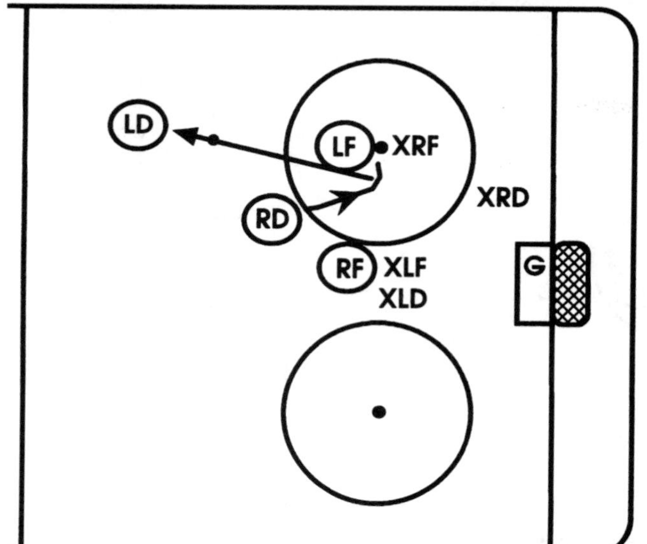

Figure 11-13: Face-off Draw

plays with the left- or right-handed centers. For instance, deep in your offensive zone, it is more effective to have a left-handed center for face-offs in the right offensive zone and a right-handed center for face-offs in the left offensive zone. The reason for this is that in the left offensive zone, a right-handed center will take a backhand draw toward the center of the playing surface (the slot) and the left-handed center (taking a face-off in the right offensive zone) will also take a backhand draw toward the slot.

Advanced Techniques

Three advanced offensive zone team skills covered in this section include offensive regrouping, offensive cycling and forechecking systems.

Offensive regrouping is a technique used to reenter the offensive zone when the offensive team is unable to initially penetrate deep into that zone and is another option to use during the second stage of an offensive attack. Instead of shooting the puck in, and possibly losing possession of the puck, the offensive team keeps possession (3PO Principle) by turning back toward its defensive zone, passing the puck back to one of the point men and regrouping to attack the offensive zone again. The **main purpose of offensive regrouping** is to reorganize the offensive attack for a more effective penetration of the offensive zone. Regrouping can occur anywhere on the playing surface but generally occurs as the puck carrier initially moves into the offensive zone. Although a regrouping play is often started by a simple pass from a forward to a point man, the actions that follow, by both puck carrier and supporting players, determine the effectiveness of this reattack. The flow of the offensive regroup is shown in Figure 11-14.

- Once the puck carrier (RF as shown in Figure 11-14) determines that the initial attack will not be effective, he turns and passes the puck back to one of the defensemen (LD) who, in turn, passes the puck across to his partner (RD). The point men should be positioned so that they are slightly staggered, with one point man deeper than his partner.
- As the puck is passed back to the point men, the forwards move to open playing surface. The forwards should move quickly, in circular and curvilinear crossing patterns, to develop speed and acceleration. The forwards try to challenge and confuse the opposing defensemen using speed and movement and force them to back off, making it easier for the attacking team to successfully penetrate deep into the offensive zone.
- The puck-carrying point man (RD) is now in a position to pass the puck to either forward, to his partner (LD) or skate the puck into the offensive zone. The point men should quickly join the offensive attack to create a numerical advantage. Every second counts during an offensive regroup, and quickness during the transition is imperative for successful execution. Communication, reading, anticipation and quick judgment are key ingredients in producing a successful offensive regroup. Reading the play means not only looking at what the opposition is doing, but also observing the movement of your teammates.

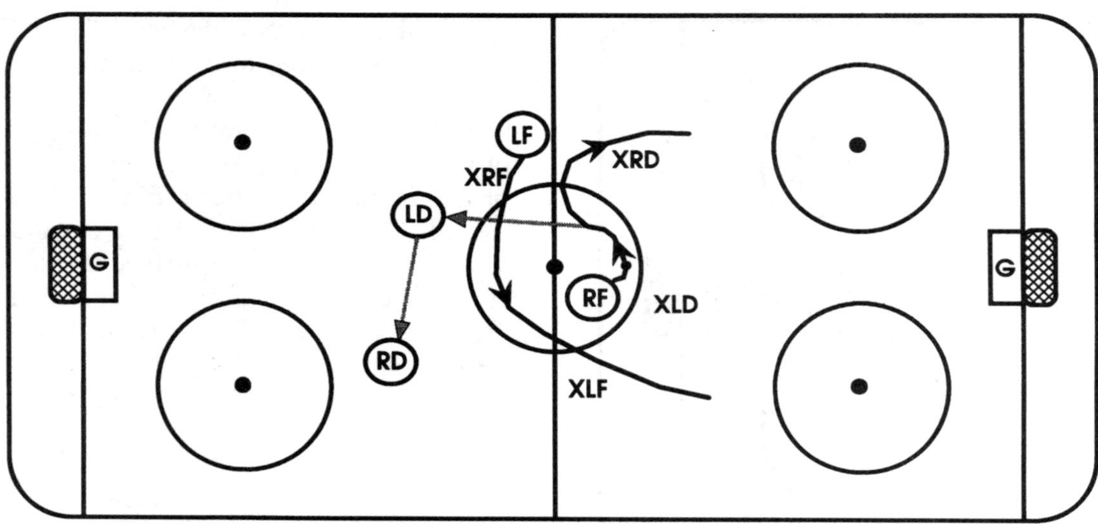

Figure 11-14; Offensive Regrouping

Offensive Cycling is an advanced roller hockey tactic designed to supplement existing tactics and strategies through the use of continuous position exchanging. Position exchanging can occur between two, three or even all four teammates simultaneously. Offensive cycling can be used to complement an offensive attack or be employed in conjunction with a forechecking strategy. **The emphasis of offensive cycling is keeping players in motion**. When used properly, the constant motion of the exchanging players does three things:

1. It creates confusion. Players exchanging positions are confusing the defenders by continually being in motion. Defenders do not have a chance to set up against a single attacker due to constantly changing assignments, and this can result in an attacker becoming uncovered.
2. It creates constant pressure. When using offensive cycling in conjunction with a forechecking strategy, the puck carrier is continually getting bombarded by the cycling defenders. Even if the puck carrier defeats one defender, another is always ready to take the puck away.
3. It buys time. Using this tactic with an offensive attack provides the puck carrier with vacated areas to maneuver in order to maintain puck possession. By creating and using these areas, the offensive team (specifically the puck carrier) buys time until an opportunity develops.

Implementing **two-man offensive cycling** can be done with the 2-2 attack or the 1-1-2 forechecking system described earlier in this chapter. When using the 2-2 attack, if the puck carrier (LF) moves behind the net to the lower portion of Figure 11-15, RF moves to fill LF's vacated area at the top of the figure. LF and RF continue two-man cycling, with the intent of setting up a scoring opportunity and confusing their defenders. While the two forwards are cycling, one of the point men moves toward the slot, ready for a high-percentage shot on net.

Implementing **three-man offensive cycling** can be done with the occupied triangle attack or the 1-2-1 forechecking system described earlier in this chapter. Using the 1-2-1 forechecking system, LF, RF and RD would execute three-man cycling against XRD in the pattern shown in Figure 11-16 to pressure him into making a bad play and to gain control of the puck. This forechecking and cycling combi-

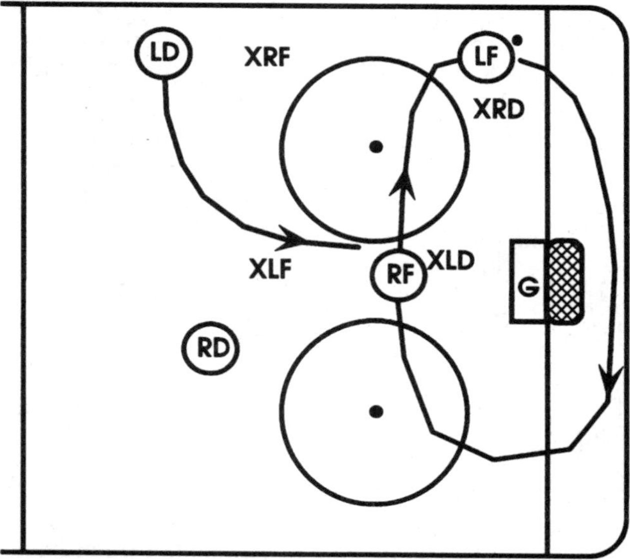

Figure 11-15; Offensive Cycling — 2 Man

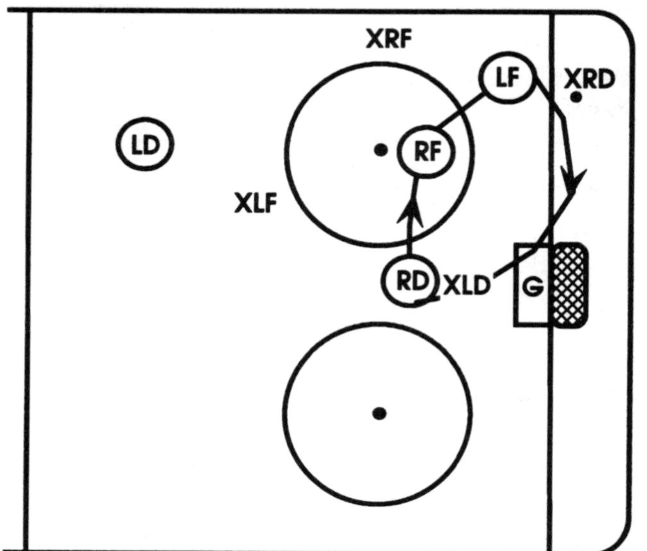

Figure 11-16; Offensive Cycling — 3 Man

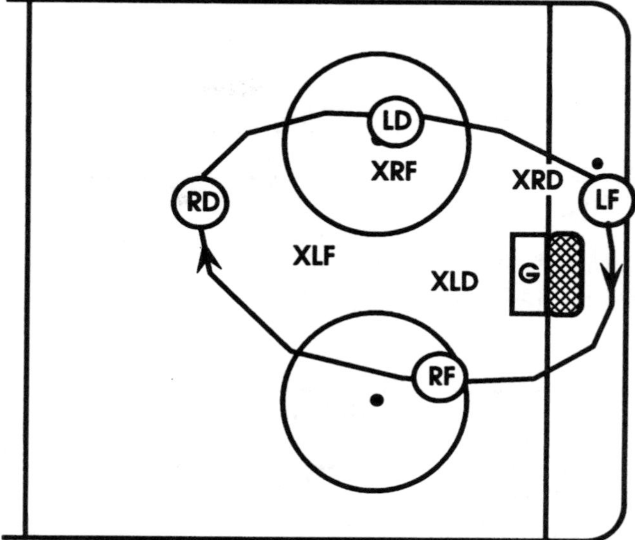

Figure 11-17; Offensive Cycling — 4 Man

nation requires LF, RF and RD to not only focus on XRD, but to read the movement of XRF and XLD as well. During the cycling, LD has the responsibility of covering XLF and becoming a safety valve if XRF gets the puck and begins to move out of the zone.

Implementing **four-man offensive cycling** can be done with the diamond attack described earlier in this chapter. In this approach, LF, RF, RD and LD all become involved in the play. If the puck carrier (LF) begins to move behind the net to the lower portion of Figure 11-17, RF reads the play and moves toward RD. As this occurs, RD and LD move in this clockwise pattern while LF maneuvers for a scoring opportunity. The four-man cycling continues until a scoring opportunity occurs. Offensive cycling is a supplemental tactic. If the basic tactic is not working, supplement it with cycling. Once a scoring opportunity exists, discontinue cycling and take advantage of it.

Advanced forechecking systems presented in this section consist of the 2-1-1 and 2-0-2 systems. The **2-1-1 forechecking system** uses a very aggressive approach and should only be used by a quick, agile and experienced team. This system demands hard work and determination since the players are in constant motion and must move quickly. The objective is to keep constant pressure on the opposition and not allow them to initiate an effective offensive attack. Use this system when the coach instructs the team to do so (such as when the opposing team has an excellent offensive attack) or when a team reads and reacts to specific signals given by the opposition. Some signals are when the defenseman carrying the puck is a poor stick handler or skater, when the opponents appear to be confused about their positioning in their defensive zone or when the forechecking team is quicker than the opposition. The 2-1-1 system is designed to penetrate and pressure the opposition deep in the offensive zone and can create many opportunities to gain or regain control of the puck. A concern of any team executing this system is getting caught with two players deep in the offensive zone if the opposition moves the puck quickly out of its zone. As shown in Figure 11-18, the 2-1-1 system works by sending two forwards (LF and RF) into the strong side of zone 1 in an attempt to dominate the puck carrier (XRD) in that zone; LF controls XLD, while RF gains control of the puck. This forechecking system is similar to the advanced overload defense system described in Chapter 10. The strongside defenseman (LD) moves to zone 2 and positions himself on the strong side between the high slot and the boards. His role is to contain a pass around the boards (to XRF) or through the slot (to XLF). If RF gains control of the puck, LD moves to the slot to create a scoring chance. The zone 3 defenseman (RD) needs to remain in a defensive posture, protecting against a quick transition, and should only move to an offensive posture if he is *very, very* sure that he will not get caught out of position. RD plays in a central location, moving around in zone 3 according to the play.

Siller Player And Team Evaluation Profile©
Offensive Zone Team Play Checklist

Evaluator: Mary | **Date**: 7/10/95 | **Location**: Inline Empire

	Line Number									
Notes: Line 1 - Mark/Paul/Ryan/Birk Line 2 - Will/Matt/Andy/Cliff Line 3 - Josh/Tad/Katy/David	**LINE 1**		**LINE 2**		**LINE 3**					
Fundamental Offensive Zone Team Techniques										
2-2 Attack	8		8		8					
Diamond Attack	7		6		6					
Occupied Triangle Attack	8		8		8					
1-1-2 Forechecking System	8		8		8					
1-2-1 Forechecking System	8		5		5					
0-1-3 Forechecking System	8		8		8					
3-0-1 Face-off Alignment	8		7		7					
2-1-1 Face-off Alignment	8		6		7					
2-0-2 Face-off Alignment	8		7		7					
Advanced Offensive Zone Team Techniques										
Offensive Regrouping	7		5		4					
2-Man Offensive Cycling	6		6		5					
3-Man Offensive Cycling	6		6		5					
4-Man Offensive Cycling	6		6		5					
2-1-1 Forechecking System	7		6		6					
2-0-2 Forechecking System	6		6		5					
TOTAL SCORE	**109**		**98**		**94**					
AVERAGE SCORE	**7.3**		**6.5**		**6.3**					

Comments: Line 1 demonstrated high overall offensive proficiency with a total score of 109 and an average score of 7.3. Lines 2 and 3 demonstrated medium overall proficiency with total scores of 98 and 94, respectively, and average scores of 6.5 and 6.3, respectively. All techniques were performed during this evaluation. The results from Line 1 are very good. They have demonstrated many effective roller hockey skills during this evaluation period. Lines 2 and 3 forwards need to improve on the 1-2-1 forechecking system. Lines 2 and 3 also need additional practice on offensive regrouping. Line 3 needs to work on offensive cycling. Line 3 got caught out of position several times when offensive cycling was combined with an offensive attack and missed several scoring opportunities.

Scale: 0 = Not Performed, 1 - 3 = Low Proficiency, 4 - 6 = Medium Proficiency, 7 - 9 = High Proficiency, 10 = Excellent Proficiency

Table 11-1; Offensive Zone Team Play Checklist

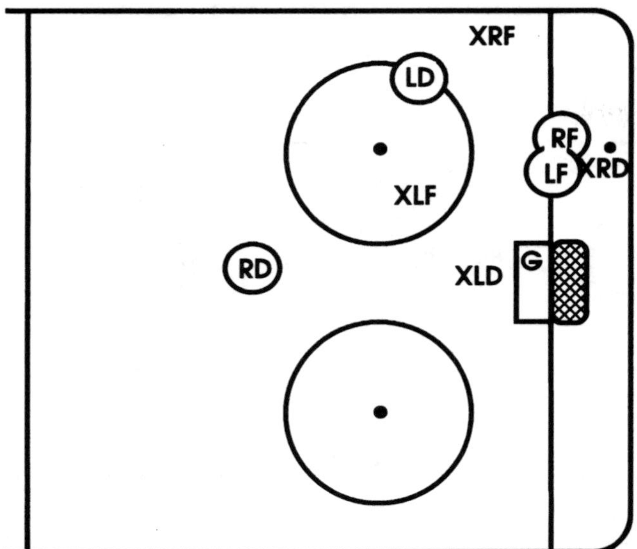

Figure 11-18; 2-1-1 Forechecking System

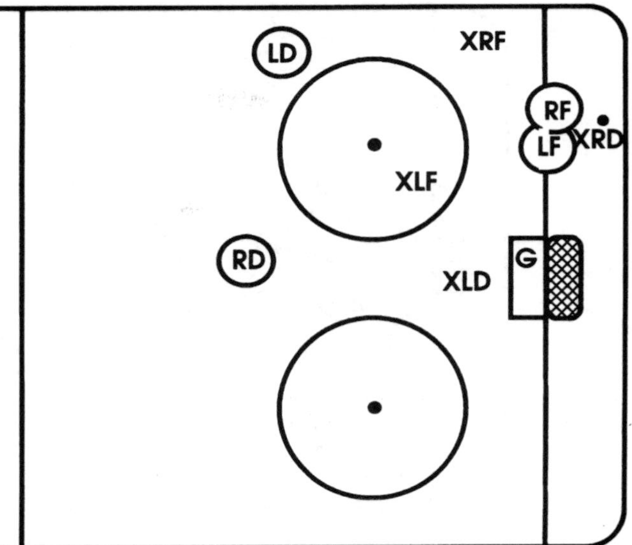

Figure 11-19; 2-0-2 Forechecking System

The **2-0-2 forechecking system** is a less aggressive approach to forechecking than the 2-1-1 system and should also only be used by a quick, agile and experienced team. The 2-0-2 system is also designed to penetrate and pressure the opposition deep in the offensive zone to create many opportunities to gain or regain control of the puck. Since this system keeps both defensemen back in zone 3, the team is less apt to suffer the consequence of getting caught with two players deep in the offensive zone if the opposition moves the puck quickly out of its zone. The 2-0-2 system works by sending two forwards (LF and RF) to the strong side of zone 1 in an attempt to dominate the puck carrier (XRD) in that zone (see Figure 11-19). One forward (LF) controls XLD, while the other forward (RF) gains control of the puck. Since zone 2 is left unprotected, the defensemen will have to read and react to specific situations and determine whether or not to pinch. If control of the puck is gained by the forecheckers, the weakside defenseman (RD) should employ the triangulation technique and move to an offensive role in the high slot (zone 2), while the strongside defenseman (LD) maintains his defensive posture in zone 3. The role of the defensemen in zone 3 is to *read, read, read.*

Drills

Offensive zone team drills should be selected to enable players to adjust to as many offensive zone situations as possible. Offensive zone proficiency comes with knowledge and practice. By learning the material in this chapter, the coach and players will become familiar with the particular skills and strategies required to play the many styles of offense, allowing the individual players and units to become a better overall roller hockey team. As the coach discovers the particular needs of his team, he can select the drills required for team improvement. The coach should employ the Offensive Zone Team Play Checklist to monitor performance and plan improvements for each player and line throughout the season.

Drill 11-1; Third Man In. This drill develops confidence in a defenseman's ability to become part of the offense in the offensive zone and is really two drills in one. This drill requires two coaches to provide feedback to the players, one at each end. If only one coach is available, then the drill could be performed executing one of the plays at a time, or an experienced teammate could provide feedback. Line up the players as shown in the corresponding diagram. The first drill (right side of diagram) has the defenseman (RD) skating in toward the net, receiving a pass from one of the forwards and putting a shot on net. At the whistle, the players should start to maneuver. When the defenseman sees an opening, he moves toward the net, receives the pass

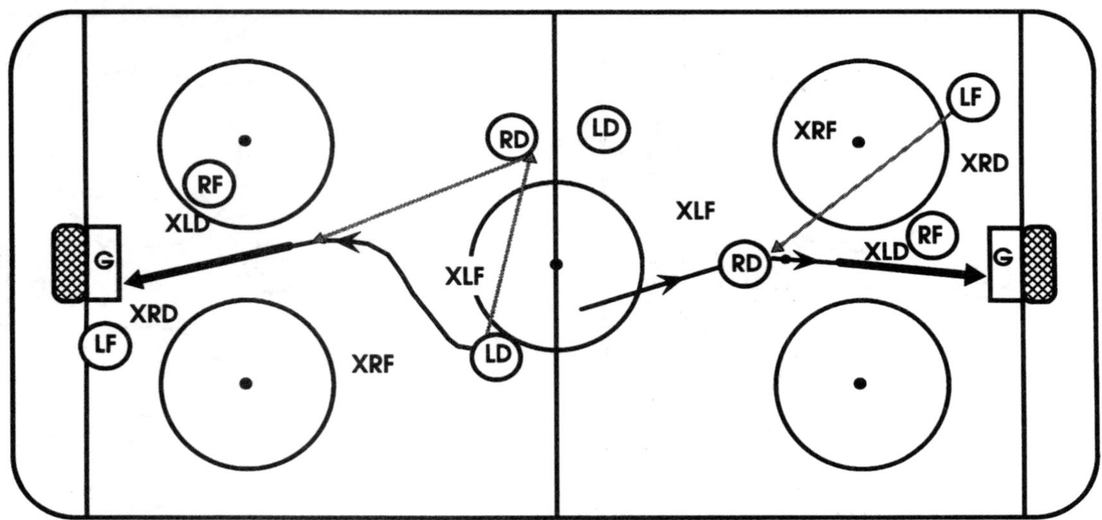

Drill 11-1; Third Man In

and shoots. The second play (left side of diagram) utilizes both defensemen (LD and RD) to create an opening for LD to move into an open area and shoot. At the whistle, the defensemen pass the puck back and forth. Once one of the forwards (XLF) is drawn out of position, the defenseman without the puck moves toward the net, receives a pass from the other defenseman and puts a shot on net.

Drill 11-2; 2-2 Attack. This drill provides practice operating in the offensive zone. Offensive players move in a boxlike formation, generally with one attacker in each quadrant, to control the puck and move it around the four quadrants with the objective of getting a shot on net from a high-percentage scoring location. This drill assumes that the attacking team has already penetrated the offensive zone and is maintaining control of the puck. Position the players as shown in the corresponding diagram. Begin the drill with no defenders (4-on-0). Once the attacking team has mastered the drill with no defenders, introduce two defenders (4-on-2) and then all four defenders (4-on-4). At the whistle, the offensive team begins moving the puck around. Continue the drill for one minute or until the defensive team gains control of the puck. Move the puck to the point men, along the boards, below the goal line, behind the net and to the slot.

The coach should monitor and provide feedback to the offensive team, after the allotted time, on the following **six offensive zone attack criteria:**

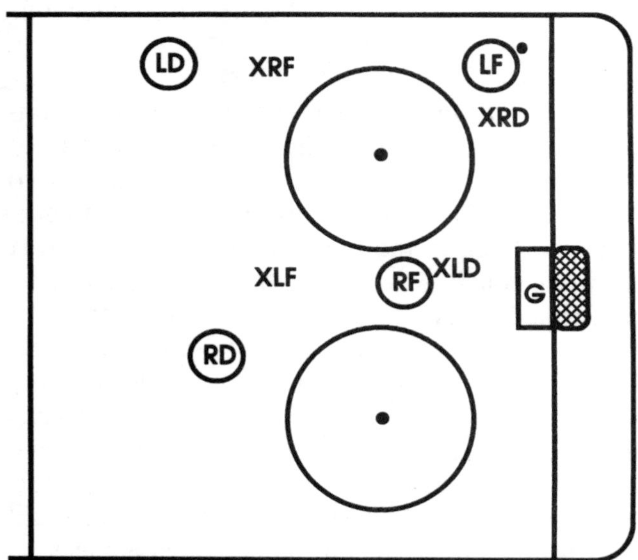

Drill 11-2; 2-2 Attack

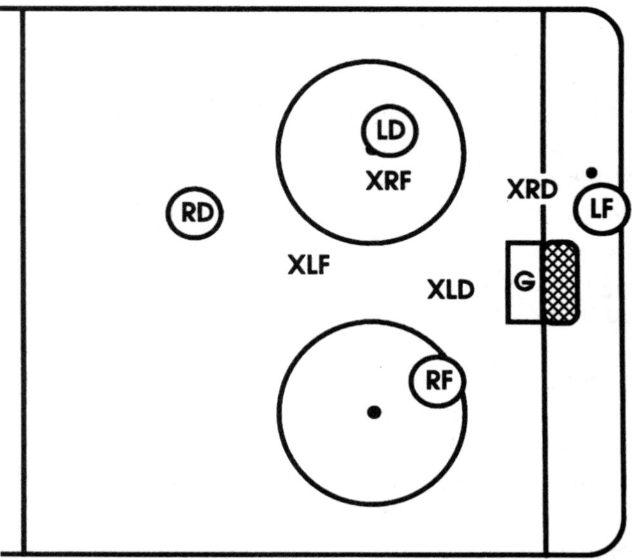

Drill 11-3; Diamond Attack

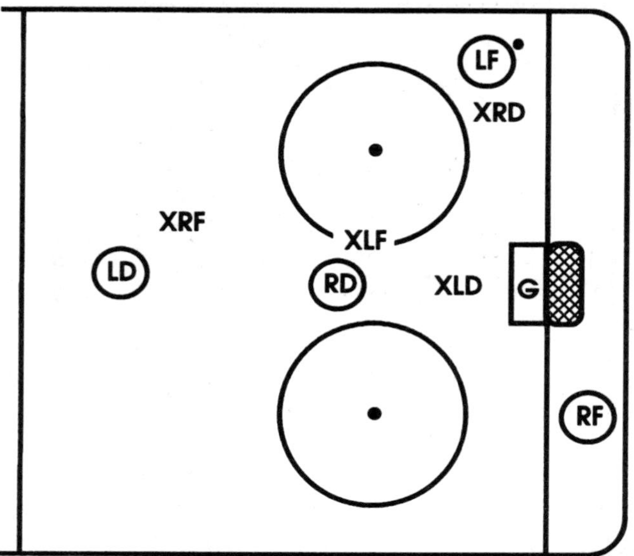

Drill 11-4; Occupied Triangle Attack

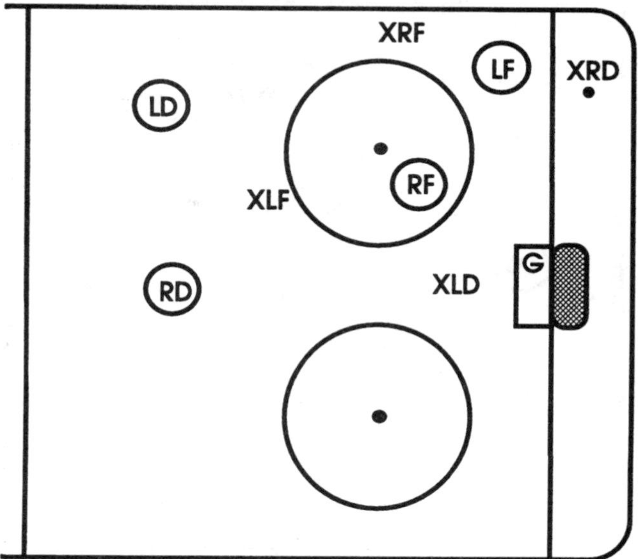

Drill 11-5; Forechecking System

- Puck control and movement
- Positioning of non-puck carrying players with respect to the puck carrier/shooter
- Shots on net from a high-percentage scoring location
- Triangulation
- Patience
- Reading, reacting and anticipating

Drill 11-3; Diamond Attack. Offensive players move around the offensive zone utilizing the diamond formation, with one attacker behind the goal line, two attackers near each deep face-off dot, and the single point man above the face-off circles and in the middle of the offensive zone. The attackers should focus on getting the puck to a player near the slot for a scoring opportunity or cycle it deep and high in the offensive zone if a slot man is not available. This drill assumes that the attacking team has already penetrated the offensive zone and is maintaining control of the puck. Position the players as shown in the corresponding diagram. Begin the drill with no defenders (4-on-0), introduce two defenders (4-on-2) and then all four defenders (4-on-4). At the whistle, the offensive team begins moving the puck around. Continue the drill for one minute or until the defensive team gains control of the puck. Move the puck to the point man, along the boards, below the goal line, behind the net and to the slot. Monitor and provide feedback to the offensive team on the six offensive zone attack criteria listed in Drill 11-2.

Drill 11-4; Occupied Triangle Attack. The players maintaining the triangle move the puck around the perimeter, always reading for the right opportunity to pass the puck to the slot man for that high-percentage shot. The attacker occupying the center of the triangle moves around inside the triangle positioning himself for a scoring opportunity. When the slot man is covered, the point man can execute a shot on net and have the slot man and the two other attackers converge on the net for the one-two punch. This drill assumes that the attacking team has already penetrated the offensive zone and is maintaining control of the puck. Position the players as shown in the corresponding diagram. Begin the drill with no defenders (4-on-0), introduce two defenders (4-on-2) and then all four defenders (4-on-4). At the whistle, the offensive team begins moving the puck around. Continue the drill for one minute or until the defensive team gains control of the puck. Move the puck to the point man, along the boards, below the goal line, behind the net and to the slot. The coach should monitor and provide feedback to the offensive team on the six offensive zone attack criteria listed in Drill 11-2.

Drill 11-5; 1-1-2 Forechecking. Position the players as shown in the corresponding diagram. At the whistle, the offensive team attempts to break out of the zone while the forechecking team attempts to gain control of the puck. The zone 1 (LF) player pressures the puck carrier while the zone 2 player (RF) controls the strongside boards and the middle of the playing surface. The two zone 3 players (LD

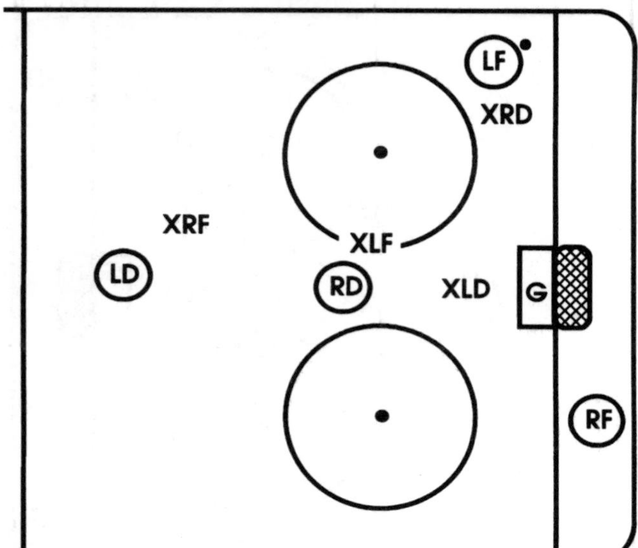

Drill 11-6; 1-2-1 Forechecking System

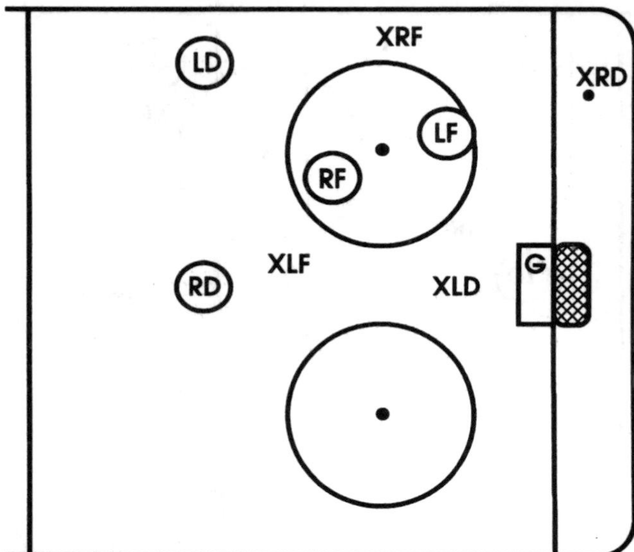

Drill 11-7; 0-1-3 Forechecking

and RD) pinch to keep the puck in, if that opportunity arises. Continue the drill for one minute or until the forechecking team gains control of the puck. Move the puck along the boards, below the goal line, behind the net and up the middle of the playing surface.

Monitor and provide feedback to the forechecking team on the following **six forechecking criteria:**

- Positioning of the forechecking team in the three forechecking zones.
- Quickness in applying pressure to the opponents.
- Ability to force the opposition to locations controlled by the forechecking team.
- Ability of the zone 1 and zone 2 players to exchange roles and zones depending on puck and player movement.
- Zone 3 player pinching.
- The end result.

Drill 11-6; 1-2-1 Forechecking. Position the players as shown in the corresponding diagram. At the whistle, the offensive team attempts to break out of the zone while the forechecking team attempts to gain control of the puck. The zone 1 player (LF) pressures the puck carrier while the two zone 2 players (RF and RD) control the strongside boards and the middle of the playing surface, attempting to force a turnover. The zone 3 player (LD) controls the puck if it is passed up the middle or along the strongside boards and pinches only if one of the zone 2 players covers for him. Continue the drill for one minute or until the forechecking team gains control of the puck. Move the puck along the boards, below the goal line, behind the net and up the middle of the playing surface. Monitor and provide feedback to the forechecking team on the six criteria listed in Drill 11-5.

Drill 11-7; 0-1-3 Forechecking. Position the players as shown in the corresponding diagram. At the whistle, the offensive players attempt to break out of the zone while the forechecking team covers them. The zone 2 player (LF) covers the puck carrier, eventually forcing him to pass the puck to one of his teammates, creating a situation in which puck control can be gained. Zone 3 players (RF, RD and LD) cover the opposition and attempt to break up any passing plays or, using the various stick checking techniques, attempt to strip the opponents of the puck. Continue the drill for one minute or until the forechecking team gains control of the puck. Move the puck along the boards, below the goal line, behind the net and up the middle of the playing surface. Monitor and provide feedback to the forechecking team on the six criteria listed in Drill 11-5.

Drill 11-8; Deep Zone Face-offs. Line up the team in its offensive zone using the 2-1-1 or 3-0-1 face-off alignments at either of the deep face-off circles, as shown in the corresponding diagram. Rotate the defensive team's face-off alignments (using the 3-0-1, 2-1-1 and 2-0-2) so that the attacking team will be comfortable with any opponent alignment. Get both centers in the habit of checking out the opponent's alignment and their own team's align-

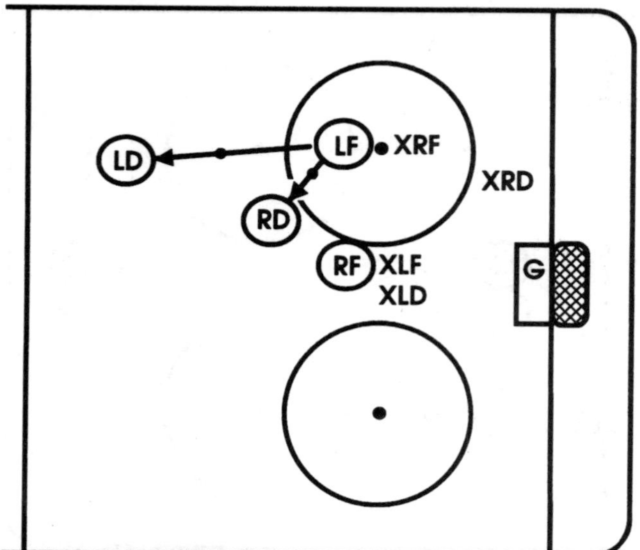

Drill 11-8A; Deep Zone Face-off — Win

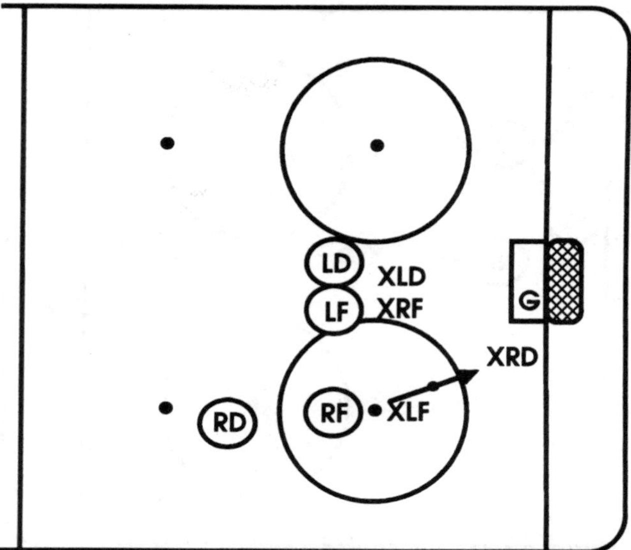

Drill 11-8B; Deep Zone Face-off - Loss

ment before preparing for the face-off. The strategy in the attacking zone should be to win the face-off and gain control of the puck first, initiate an offensive attack second and forecheck the opponents to gain control of the puck third. Instruct both teams on positioning if the face-off is won, lost or drawn. If the offensive team wins the face-off (as shown in Drill 11-8A, 2-1-1 Alignment), it should move to its attack positioning and set up a good scoring opportunity. If it loses the face-off (as shown in Drill 11-8B, 3-0-1 Alignment), it should immediately begin to pressure the opponents using one of the forechecking strategies to gain control of the puck. If neither team clearly wins the face-off, the attacking center should contain his counterpart while the other offensive forward or layer 2 defenseman moves in to get the puck back to the point. Once everyone is ready, the coach should drop the puck. Immediately after the puck is dropped and the outcome of the face-off is known, the coach should stop the play and provide feedback to both teams on the proper positioning of each player. Continue stopping the play immediately after the face-off four more times (for a total of five face-offs). On the sixth face-off, instruct the players that after the puck is dropped, they should continue playing until the whistle is sounded.

The coach should monitor and provide feedback to the offensive team on the following **six face-off criteria**:

- Positioning and movement of all players — creating space.
- Employing a forechecking strategy and pressuring the opponents if the face-off is lost.
- Attacking if the face-off is won.
- Forward or defenseman moving to retrieve the puck if the face-off is neither won or lost.
- Reading, anticipating and reacting.
- Communicating.

Provide feedback to the centers on their quickness, strength, face-off strategy, how they used their stick, skates and body against the opposing center, and how effective both the right- and left-handed centers were in right and left offensive zone face-offs.

Drill 11-9; High Zone Face-offs. Line up the attacking team in its offensive zone, initially using the 2-1-1 face-off alignment as shown in Drill 11-9A. Rotate the defending team's face-off alignments (using the 3-0-1, 2-1-1 and 2-0-2) so that the attacking team will be comfortable with any opponent alignment. Both centers should check out the opponent's alignment and their own team's alignment before preparing for the face-off. Both teams should be instructed on positioning if the face-off is won, lost or drawn. If the attacking team wins the face-off (as shown in Drill 11-9A), it should move on an offensive attack. If it loses the face-off (as shown in Drill 11-9B), it should immediately begin to pressure the opponents using one of the forechecking strategies to gain control of the puck. If neither team clearly wins the face-off, the attacking center should contain his counterpart while the other offensive forward or layer 2 defenseman

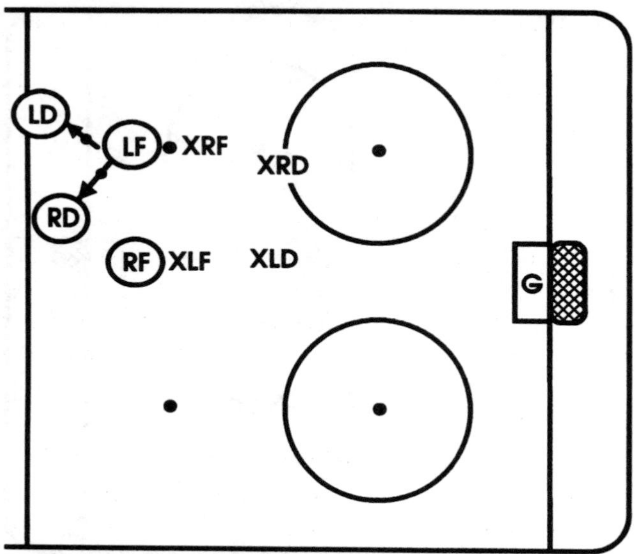

Drill 11-9A; High Zone Face-off — Win

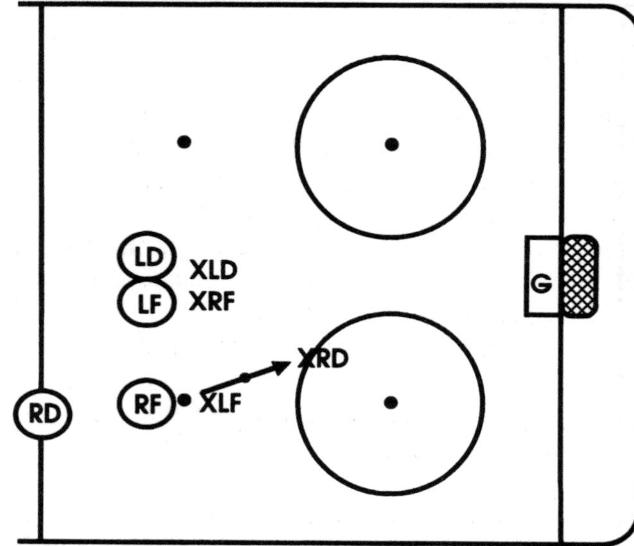

Drill 11-9B; High Zone Face-off — Loss

moves in to get the puck back to the point. Execute the drill like Drill 11-8.

Drill 11-10; Center Face-off Drill. Select groups of three players for this drill. One player acts as the official dropping the puck and the other two players face-off. Have the centers take ten face-offs and then rotate the players in the group so that every player has had two opportunities to play center. Provide feedback to the centers on their quickness, strength, face-off strategy, how they used their stick, skates and body against the opposing center, and how effective both the right and left centers were in right- and left-handed offensive zone face-offs.

Advanced Drills

Drill 11-11; Offensive Regrouping. This drill teaches the offensive team how to reorganize the offensive attack for a more effective penetration of the offensive zone when unable to initially penetrate deep into that zone. Place two pylons along the boards about five feet on the offensive zone side of the center red line. Line up the four attackers in their defensive zone. Begin the drill with no defenders (4-on-0). Once the attacking team has mastered the drill with no defenders, introduce two defenders (4-on-2) and then all four defenders (4-on-4). At the whistle, the attacking team moves the

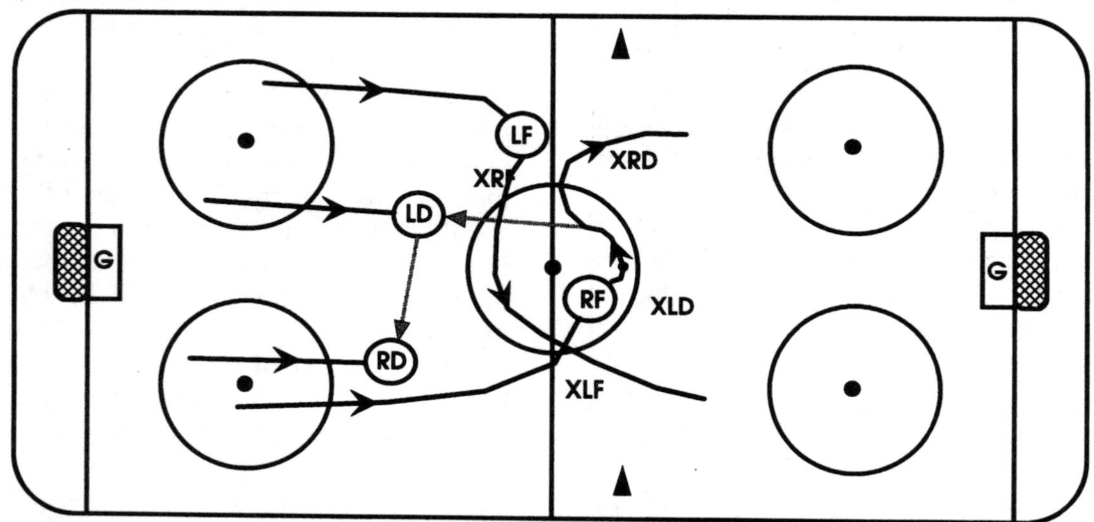

Drill 11-11; Offensive Regrouping

puck toward the offensive zone. Once they reach the pylons, the attackers initiate the regroup. The puck carrier (RF) turns and passes back to one of the defensemen (LD) who passes it to his partner (RD). The forwards turn back toward their defensemen and then turn back up the playing surface, picking up speed. The forwards should be staggered so that they are more difficult to cover and provide added passing options. The new puck carrier can now skate or pass the puck; all options should be practiced. Players continue into the offensive zone until the next whistle.

Drill 11-12; Offensive Cycling. This drill allows the offensive team to supplement existing offensive attacks and forechecking strategies with the use of continuous position exchanging. Employ two-man cycling in conjunction with Drills 11-2 (2-2 Attack) and 11-5 (1-1-2 Forechecking). Employ three-man cycling in conjunction with Drills 11-4 (Occupied Triangle Attack) and 11-6 (1-2-1 Forechecking). Employ four-man cycling in conjunction with Drill 11-3 (Diamond Attack). Begin the drill with no defenders (4-on-0). Once the attacking team has mastered the drill with no defenders, introduce two defenders (4-on-2) and then all four defenders (4-on-4). The coach should ensure that the players' movements are coordinated, the key to offensive cycling.

Drill 11-13; 2-1-1 Forechecking. Position the players as shown in the corresponding diagram. At the whistle, the offensive team attempts to break out of the zone while the forechecking team attempts to gain control of the puck. The two zone 1 players (RF and LF) quickly pressure the puck carrier and attempt to immediately gain control of the puck while the zone 2 player (LD) controls the strongside boards and the high slot. The zone 3 player (RD) controls the puck if it is passed up the middle or along the strongside boards and remains in a defensive posture. Continue the drill for one minute or until the forechecking team gains control of the puck. Move the puck along the boards, below the goal line, behind the net and up the middle of the playing surface. Monitor and provide feedback to the forechecking team on the six criteria listed in Drill 11-5.

Drill 11-14; 2-0-2 Forechecking. Position the players as shown in the corresponding diagram. At the whistle, the offensive team attempts to break out of the zone while the forechecking team attempts to gain control of the puck. The two zone 1 players (RF and LF) quickly pressure the puck carrier and attempt to immediately gain control of the puck. LD and RD read and react to specific situations and determine whether or not to pinch. If control of the puck is gained by the forecheckers, the weakside defenseman should employ the triangulation technique and move to an offensive role in the high slot (zone 2), while the strongside defenseman maintains his defensive posture in zone 3. Continue the drill for one minute or until the forechecking team gains control of the puck. Move the puck along the boards, below the goal line, behind the net and up the middle of the playing surface. Monitor and provide feedback to the forechecking team on the six criteria in Drill 11-5.

Drill 11-13; 2-1-1 Forechecking System

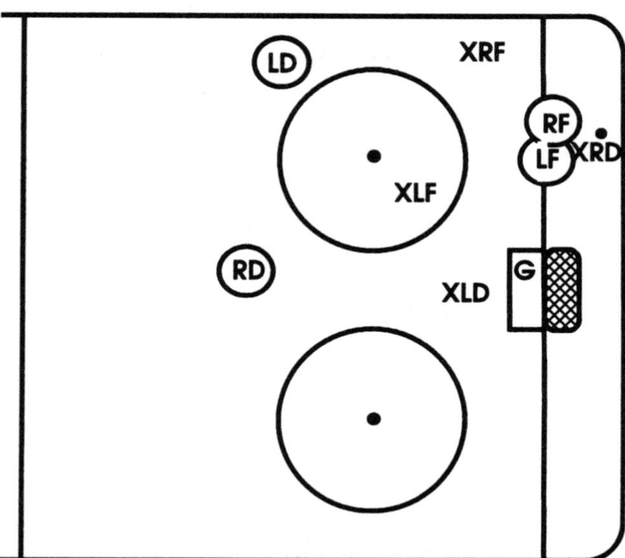

Drill 11-14; 2-0-2 Forechecking System

Recap

After reading and studying the material in this chapter, you should be able to answer the following questions:

1. What is the primary role of a team in its offensive zone?
2. Describe the six factors that every offensive zone strategy should incorporate.
3. The success of any offensive attack is attributed to what three factors? Describe the one-two punch.
4. Describe triangulation. Why is it the central roller hockey element to maintaining control of the puck and moving it around in the offensive zone?
5. Summarize the three fundamental offensive zone attack strategies. How are they similar? How are they different? What are the roles of the players in each? Which technique is better to teach beginning roller hockey players?
6. Summarize the three fundamental forechecking systems. How are they similar? How are they different? What are the roles of the players in each?
7. Describe pinching in an offensive roller hockey context.
8. What are face-off techniques designed to do? Describe three elements of the offensive zone face-off strategy.
9. What are the two tactical components of the face-off?
10. Describe three face-off alignments. When should each be used? Describe three essential face-off assignments.
11. What techniques must every center master to win face-offs?
12. Summarize the offensive regrouping technique. What is its main purpose?
13. Describe offensive cycling. What techniques can offensive cycling supplement?
14. How will you use the Offensive Zone Team Play Checklist and the drills provided in this chapter to help improve offensive team performance and correct existing deficiencies?
15. What six criteria should the coach use to evaluate all offensive attack drills?
16. What six criteria should the coach use to evaluate all forechecking drills?
17. What six criteria should the coach use to evaluate all face-off drills?

12

Getting the Most Out of Your Special Teams

Highlights

This chapter addresses the role that special teams play during the game. Chapter 12 presents the following information:

Discussion

Fundamentals

- *Power play unit*
  - *one-man advantage*
  - *two-man advantage*
  - *face-off strategies and alignments*
- *Penalty killing unit*
  - *one man short*
  - *two men short*
  - *face-off strategies and alignments*
- *Pulling your goaltender*

Siller Player and Team Evaluation Profile — Special Teams Play

Drills

Recap

Believe you are defeated, believe it long enough, and it is likely to become a fact.
— Norman Vincent Peale —

Besides the practical knowledge which defeat offers, there are important personality profits to be taken. Defeat strips away false values and makes you realize what you really want. It stops you from chasing butterflies and puts you to work digging gold.
— William Moulton Marston —

Discussion

Special teams are a subset of a roller hockey team working together to accomplish a specific task. A special team could be established and utilized specifically to win face-offs in the defensive zone, to control the game during the last minute when your team has a lead, or to play against opponents when the two teams are at equal but reduced strength (such as in a 3-on-3 or 2-on-2 scenario). But most special teams focus on situations when they either have a player (or two) advantage or are a player (or two) short.

Use a **power play unit** to take advantage of the team's numerical superiority while the opponent is serving a penalty. The power play consists of the following player scenarios: 4-on-3, 3-on-2 and 4-on-2. The objective of the power play unit is to use your additional player(s) to move the puck into your offensive zone, maintain possession until a scoring opportunity can be set up and score.

Use a **penalty killing unit** to minimize the opponent's numerical superiority and goal-scoring opportunities by using speed, quickness, discipline and strategy. The penalty kill consists of the following player scenarios: 3-on-4, 2-on-3 and 2-on-4. The objective of the penalty killing unit is to force the opponents to the outside of the slot, force them to execute bad passes or poor-percentage shots, eventually gain control of the puck and sometimes even score a goal.

Choosing the right players for your special teams is based on physical and mental factors and the overall special teams strategy. Physical factors include quickness, agility, excellent skating, stickhandling and passing ability, top plus/minus players (refer to your game statistics) and communication. Mental factors include excellent reading, anticipating and reacting ability, determination and desire to either put the puck into a good scoring position or keep it away from one, and knowledge of special teams positioning. The team's strategy should balance specific players with the plays to achieve an optimum approach. Roller hockey special teams should not be made up of forwards, defensemen and goaltenders, but should emphasize a team's strengths through the right mix of skilled players to get the job done. If you have someone with an excellent shot from the point, use screens and create traffic in front of the net so you can take advantage of that shot. Don't be afraid to move players around to take advantage of their specific skills.

Ideally, your power play unit should include a good breakout player, a player with an excellent shot and two players who can screen the goaltender and be ready for a deflection or rebound, as well as stickhandle and pass the puck in and around defenders. All of these players need to be able to work well under pressure. Try to develop two power play units because your first unit is not always going to be ready to go when the opportunity arises. During practice sessions, you may want to mix players from the first and second units together on occasion and note the interplay.

The penalty killing unit should include one of your fastest players who can forecheck and backcheck, and two additional defenders who are quick, can break up a pass and have a strong shot to get the puck out of the defensive zone once they gain control of it. It is also important to have players who are going to react coolly and effectively under pressure. As with the power play, two penalty killing units should be developed so that they can be switched during a penalty.

Fundamentals

The **power play unit** has one objective — to take advantage of a numerical superiority situation by moving the puck and putting it in the net. Performing this objective requires a combination of the individual, positional and team skills described in earlier chapters. The power play unit moves the puck out of its own end (breakout) and into its offensive zone, maintains possession of the puck in the offensive zone, forechecks opponents if they lose possession of the puck, wins face-offs and scores. The power play provides an added opportunity to score because the power play team is playing with one (or even two) more players than the opponent.

There are several keys to an effective power play. After the coach establishes which players to use, he must ensure that the power play unit understands and executes the following **three power play fundamentals**:

- **Player movement and position exchanging.** An effective power play should always be based on plenty of hard work and player movement. Hard work requires quick and agile skaters, with their wheels in constant motion, who can anticipate the flow of play. Player movement should be based on defined plays with improvisation to create passing and scoring opportunities. Movement also creates the potential for disorganizing the opponents through confusion and missed assignments. The power play unit should move players around the perimeter of the penalty killing unit as well as penetrating the perimeter. This will confuse the defenders or force them to move out of position. In some cases, it may cause two defenders to cover one attacker, allowing the remaining attackers to converge on net for a *very* high-percentage scoring opportunity. Position exchanging can be employed using two-man, three-man and four-man cycling described in Chapter 11. Reading, reacting and anticipating skills are essential for an effective power play.
- **Puck control and movement** is essential to an effective power play. By moving the puck around, you force the opponents to move, including the goaltender, creating openings for passes and shots. Position one non-puck carrier close to the puck carrier/shooter to maintain control of the puck. If the puck carrier/shooter gets pressured, at least one teammate is close by to receive a short, low-risk pass or retrieve a loose puck. **The power play is really a series of two-on-ones played by the puck carrier and a support player in an attempt to isolate and defeat a defender** with the objective of making a critical pass or putting a shot on net. Give-and-go and one-time passing plays are very effective on the power play. Passers should use the perimeter of the penalty killing unit to make short, low-risk passes to set up most power plays as most penalty killing units won't pressure passes outside the perimeter.
- **Shots on net.** Some teams pass the puck around and wait for the perfect scoring play. They end up wasting time and getting very few shots on net. Too many passes provide the penalty killers with the opportunity to intercept the puck and shoot it down the playing surface, reducing valuable power play time. Most shots should be taken from high-percentage scoring locations; however, a slap shot from the point with the potential for a rebound, or a one-time shot near the goal post, can be just as effective on the power play. For every two-minute power play, the power play unit should get **at least five good shots** on net. Since a 30 percent power play scoring percentage is considered very good, anything less than five good shots on net will probably not get you a goal. Balancing all-out shooting with patient passing makes each player think about whether a shot at this time has a good chance to score or not. If you have the puck at the point and no teammate is near the net, be patient and either pass the puck or skate with it. This will give your teammates the added time required to increase your scoring chance.

One-man advantage. The three offensive zone attack strategies described in Chapter 11, the 2-2 attack, diamond attack and occupied triangle attack, work very effectively when employed by the power play unit. The coach can modify any or all of these strategies depending upon the players' styles and abilities and the type of penalty killing strategies the opponents use.

- The 2-2 attack is a good power play strategy to use with beginning roller hockey players. The power play unit (circled players) positions players as shown in Figure 12-1. When LF has the puck deep in the offensive zone, triangulation can be used by having RD skate toward the slot for a shot. If the penalty killers collapse their triangle, LF can pass to LD for a shot or give-and-go play. When the puck is at the point (LD), the weakside forward (RF) should move to the slot for a deflection or rebound, while RD and LF maneuver for a pass. The power play unit should also make use of the space behind the net when setting up. If you lose possession of the puck, aggressively forecheck the new puck carrier. Any of the fundamental or advanced forechecking techniques described in Chapter 11 should work.
- The diamond power play attack is used to cycle the puck deep and high in the offensive zone in an attempt to get the puck to a player near the

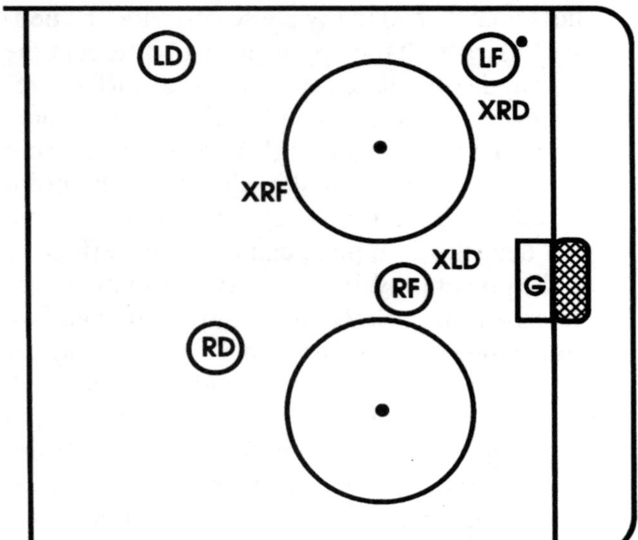

Figure 12-1; 2-2 Power Play Attack

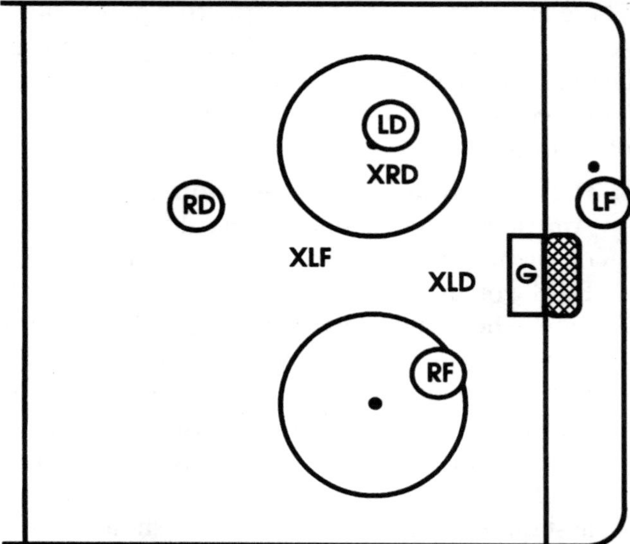

Figure 12-2; Diamond Power Play Attack

slot for a scoring opportunity and to force the defenders to move. The power play unit (circled players) positions players as shown in Figure 12-2. When the puck is deep in the offensive zone, LD and RF move into position for a pass or shot. If they are not available, LF executes a bank pass to RD. LF can also maintain his position behind the net in an attempt to collapse the penalty killing to create traffic around the net. If puck possession is lost, aggressively forecheck the new puck carrier. If RD has the puck, LF should move to the slot for a deflection or rebound, while LD and RF become passing options.

- The occupied triangle power play attack moves the puck around the perimeter, ready for the right opportunity to pass the puck to the slot man for that high-percentage shot. When the slot man is covered, the point man can execute a shot on net and have the slot man and two other attackers converge on the net for the one-two punch. The power play unit (circled players) positions players as shown in Figure 12-3. When the puck is deep in the offensive zone, LD or RF move into position for a pass while RD maneuvers into an open position for a quick shot on net. If LD has the puck, RF should move to an open position for a passing option while LF and RD converge to the slot for a deflection or rebound. If you lose possession of the puck, aggressively forecheck the new puck carrier.

Two-man advantage. When there is a two-man advantage, move the puck into the offensive zone, set up and shoot. A two-man advantage in roller hockey should produce a goal 75 percent of the time; if it doesn't, the coach needs to immediately determine why and make adjustments.

Power play face-off strategies are identical to those described in Chapters 10 and 11 and are summarized at the top of the following page for convenience.

Power play face-off alignments consist of the 3-0-1, 2-1-1 and 2-0-2 alignments, described in chap-

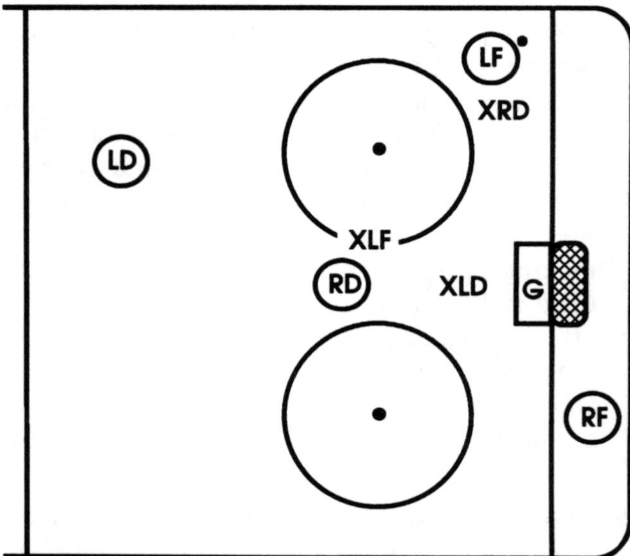

Figure 12-3; Occupied Triangle Power Play Attack

Face-off Priorities	Offensive Zone	Defensive Zone
1	win the face-off and gain control of the puck	win the face-off and gain control of the puck
2	initiate an offensive attack	prevent a scoring opportunity by the opponents
3	forecheck the opponents to regain control of the puck	initiate a breakout play or offensive attack

Table 12-1; Face-off Strategies

Face-off Location	Alignment when 4-on-3 or 4-on-2	Alignment when 3-on-2
Deep Offensive Zone	3-0-1 or 2-1-1	2-1-0 or 2-0-1
Transition Zone	3-0-1, 2-1-1 or 2-0-2	3-0-0, 2-1-0 or 2-0-1
Deep Defensive Zone	3-0-1	3-0-0 or 2-0-1

Table 12-2; Power Play Alignments

ters 10 and 11 in addition to the 3-0-0, 2-1-0 and 2-0-1 depending on how many players are available on the power play and whether your team wins, loses or neutralizes a face-off.

The **penalty killing unit** has one objective — to play the percentages and stop the opposing team from scoring. Performing this objective requires a combination of the individual, positional and team skills described in earlier chapters. The penalty killing unit forechecks the opponents to gain possession of the puck, freezes the puck or moves it out of its own end and into the offensive zone by clearing the puck or skating with it, wins face-offs and occasionally scores. The penalty killing unit must work together very effectively because it is playing with one (or even two) less players than the opponent.

There are several keys to an effective penalty kill. After the coach establishes which players to use, he must ensure that the penalty killing unit understands and executes the following **three penalty killing fundamentals**:

- **Control the area near the slot.** There are at least two ways to do this. The **first** is to physically position a penalty killing player in the slot to control that area. That requires the penalty killing player (generally a defenseman) to stand his ground and prevent any attackers from screening the goaltender, deflecting a puck into the net or receiving a pass or a rebound. Body blocking and stick checking are effective techniques to perform this. Reading, reacting and anticipating skills are essential to effectively kill a penalty.

  The **second** is to position the penalty killing players around the perimeter of the slot and control the slot area using a triangular formation. Quickness and hustle, the desire to gain control of the puck, fast thinking, wheels in motion and the ability to relax under pressure are the penalty killer's greatest assets. The penalty killing team plays a series of two-on-ones between the puck carrier and a support player. This requires the penalty killing team to play the pass, because forcing the attacking team to pass creates an opportunity to intercept, gain control of the puck and shoot it down the playing surface. You can allow the opponents opportunities to pass the puck around the perimeter of the penalty killing triangle while covering passes to the slot, always forcing the play to the outside. Forcing the opposition into making bad plays is good defensive roller hockey and is essential while killing a penalty. Put your stick in passing lanes to spread out power play players. If a pass does get to the slot, one defender should immediately converge on the attacker to block or gain control of the puck and prevent any rebounds. If an attacking player attempts to skate into the slot, angle him toward the boards, execute a stick check or body block, while playing the pass to the most dangerous potential attacker. Learning the opponent's patterns will help the penalty killing team play the percentages by playing strong even with one less player.

- **Coordination with your goaltender.** The goaltender must become involved in each penalty killing situation. Since your team is playing (at least) one player short, involving the goaltender neutralizes some of this. The penalty killing unit and the goaltender must coordinate their efforts to strategically resist offensive attacks. Communication between the penalty killing unit and the goaltender is essential so there is no confusion about loose pucks or possible rebounds. If they play together, with each understanding the other's role, they will have an excellent chance of neutralizing many power plays. The penalty killing unit needs to position itself to give the goaltender a clear and equal chance at stopping shots fired toward him. Once a shot is taken, and there may be plenty of them during a power play, the penalty killing unit should make sure that any rebounds are covered up or can be cleared. If you can gain control of the puck, head for an open area on the playing surface, begin a counterattack, clear the puck out of the defensive zone or have your goaltender freeze it at the side of the net.
- **Work the clock.** When killing a penalty, delay your opponents and run down the clock as often as possible. Delaying your opponents forces them to maneuver for a better scoring opportunity and also reduces the remaining penalty time. When playing a running time game (the clock does not stop until the end of the period or an official requests it to), get as many face-offs as you can. You'll tick off five to 10 seconds for every face-off. When the play is stopped but the clock is ticking, you should also make player changes during your penalty killing effort. Although the referee may object to too many player changes, take advantage of at least one or two per penalty. Every player change reduces the remaining penalty time by at least five seconds.

One man short. The most efficient way to defend against a 3-on-4 penalty killing situation is by using a triangular formation (the circled players shown in Figure 12-4), where two penalty killers play low to cover the deep attackers and one penalty killer plays high in the triangle to cover the opponent's point men. Variations include two- and three-man cycling incorporated into the triangle. Maintain this triangular formation in both the defensive and offensive zones. The penalty killers' role is to force the opponents to pass the puck around the perimeter of the triangle, by controlling the area near the slot. If you can aggressively force the attacking team to pass the puck or shoot it from outside the slot, you have an opportunity to intercept a pass or block the shot and gain control of the puck. If a shot makes it to the net, cover the attackers so that a second shot off of a rebound does not occur. If the goaltender freezes the puck, the remaining penalty killing time is reduced by a few more seconds as both teams ready themselves for a face-off. Give your players plenty of practice in penalty killing situations so that they can experience the best tactics to use. Roller hockey is not a very forgiving sport for penalty killing teams that do not practice.

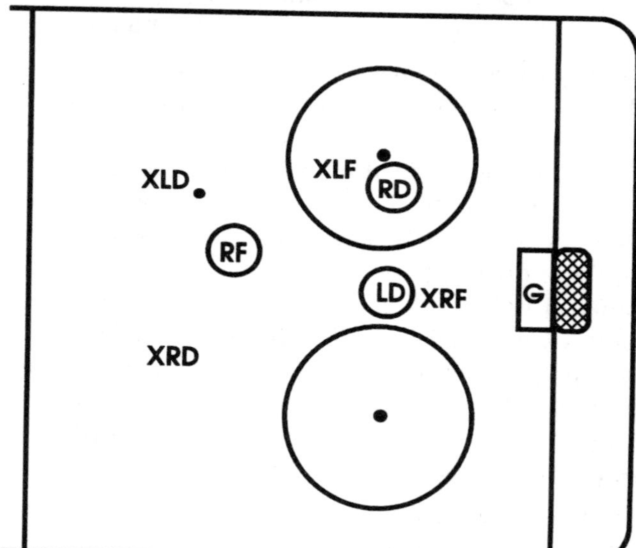

Figure 12-4; Penalty Killing Triangle

When XLD has the puck high in the offensive zone, LD and RD cover the deep attackers while LF plays the pass between XLD and XRD. If XLD attempts to skate into the slot, angle him toward the boards and execute a stick check or body block or employ defensive exchanging, while playing the pass to the most dangerous potential attacker. Put your stick in passing lanes to spread out the power play players. If a pass does get to the XRF, LD should im-

Face-off Location	Alignment when one man short	Alignment when two men short
Deep Offensive Zone	1-1-1 or 2-1-0	1-1-0 or 1-0-1
Transition Zone	2-1-0 or 2-0-1	1-1-0 or 1-0-1
Deep Defensive Zone	3-0-0, 2-1-0 or 2-0-1	2-0-0, 1-1-0 or 1-0-1

Table 12-3; Penalty Killing Alignments

mediately stick check him and gain control of the puck. If the puck carrier is not moving (waiting for something to happen), stand between him and the net moving your stick around in the areas that a potential pass could be made. If the puck is moved behind the net, do not go behind the net because the majority of time you *will* lose that battle! Play the percentages and force the puck carrier behind the net to make the first move. Generally in this situation, while the penalty killing unit is reading the play behind the net, one or even both of the defensemen move in toward the slot for a shot. RF should constantly read the positioning of the attacking point men as well as the puck carrier behind the net. He should move to the slot along with either or both defensemen and communicate with his teammates along the way. If you gain control of the puck freeze it, skate with it or shoot it down the playing surface. Either way, you can knock precious time off the clock. When the puck is in the offensive zone, generally use a conservative forechecking approach such as the 0-1-2 system (similar to the 0-1-3 system described in Chapter 11). However, to keep the opponents from making any assumptions about your forechecking strategy, it is worthwhile to aggressively forecheck your opponents occasionally when you read or anticipate that you can contain that opponent.

Two men short. When you are two men short, your goaltender gets a real workout. During this scenario, players will basically go into a shooting frenzy with shots executed from almost any location. The objective in this situation is to let your goaltender play the shooter while the rest of the team makes sure that passes across the slot and rebounds are covered. Get as many stoppages of play as possible to try and eat away at the clock. If you come away without a goal being scored, you've done a fine job.

Penalty killing face-off strategies are identical to those detailed in Table 12-1. **Face-off alignments** when a team is one or two men short consist of the 3-0-0, 2-1-0, 2-0-1, 1-1-1, 2-0-0, 1-1-0 and 1-0-1 alignments and are presented in Table 12-3. Face-off strategies and alignments are described in more detail in chapters 10 and 11.

Pulling Your Goaltender. Substituting an offensive attacker for your goaltender at the right time can give your team the additional offensive power needed to score a goal and even come from behind to win a game. This move is usually executed during the last minute of the game when your team is down by a goal or two, during the last few seconds of a period when the face-off is deep in your offensive zone, or when you are on a power play. In all three cases, puck movement and control are essential to maintaining your attack, and this task is made easier by adding another player. Although this play may seem risky, there are surprisingly few goals scored against a team that has pulled its goaltender. To be effective, your team should understand and execute both the fundamental and advanced attack, power play, forechecking and face-off strategies. By anticipating plays, maintaining control of the puck and utilizing your extra attacker, this move could be a formula for success.

Drills

Special teams drills should be selected to enable players to adjust to as many situations as possible. Special teams proficiency comes with knowledge and practice. By learning the material in this chapter, the coach and players will become familiar with the particular skills and strategies required to play the many styles of offense and defense, while playing shorthanded or with a numerical advantage, allowing the individual players and units to become a better overall roller hockey team. As the coach dis-

Siller Player And Team Evaluation Profile©
Special Teams Play Checklist

Evaluator: The One **Date**: 7/10/95 **Location**: The Inline Forum

	Line Number											
Notes: PP1 - John/Paul/George/Ringo PP2 - Nick/Jeff/Ron/Dennis PK1 - Jose/Tony/Marty PK2 - Maureen/Todd/Eddy PP - Power Play Line PK - Penalty Killing Line	**PP1**		**PP2**		**PK1**		**PK2**					
Fundamental Special Teams Techniques												
2-2 Power Play												
• player movement/pos. exch.	7		6									
• puck control and movement	7		6									
• shots on net	7		6									
• face-offs	7		6									
Diamond Power Play												
• player movement/pos. exch.	8		7									
• puck control and movement	7		7									
• shots on net	7		7									
• face-offs	8		6									
Occupied Triangle Power Play												
• player movement/pos. exch.	6		6									
• puck control and movement	5		6									
• shots on net	8		6									
• face-offs	7		7									
Penalty Killing Triangle												
• control of area near the slot					6		6					
• coord. with goaltender					5		6					
• work the clock					8		6					
• face-offs					8		6					
Pulling The Goaltender	**0**		**0**		**0**		**0**					
TOTAL SCORE	**84**		**76**		**27**		**24**					
AVERAGE SCORE	**7.0**		**6.3**		**6.8**		**6.0**					

Comments: PP1 demonstrated high overall power play proficiency with a total score of 84 and an average score of 7.0. PP2 demonstrated medium overall power play proficiency with a total score of 76 and an average score of 6.3. Both units need to work on shot accuracy. PK1 and PK2 demonstrated medium overall penalty killing proficiency with total scores of 27 and 24, respectively, and average scores of 6.8 and 6.0, respectively. PK1 is sometimes overly aggressive, and has been beaten because of it. Need to balance patience with the intensity. The Pulling-The-Goaltender technique was not executed.

Scale: 0 = Not Performed, 1 - 3 = Low Proficiency, 4 - 6 = Medium Proficiency, 7 - 9 = High Proficiency, 10 = Excellent Proficiency

Table 12-1; Special Teams Play Checklist

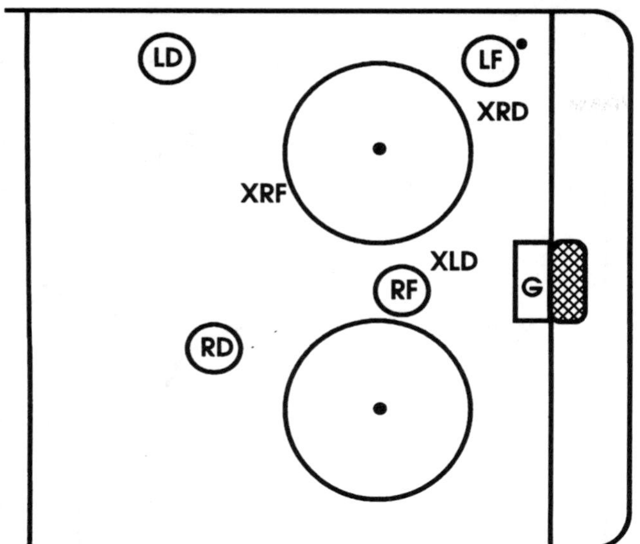

Drill 12-1; 2-2 Power Play Attack

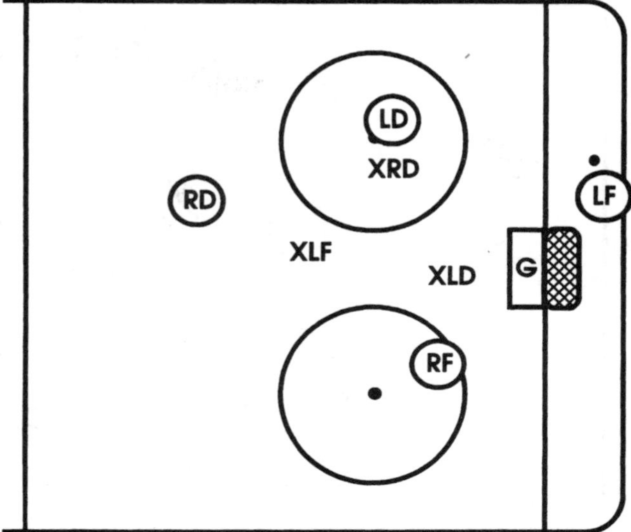

Drill 12-2; Diamond Power Play Attack

covers the particular needs of his team, he can select the drills required for team improvement. The coach should employ the Special Teams Play Checklist to monitor performance and plan improvements for each player and line throughout the season.

Drill 12-1; 2-2 Power Play. This drill assumes that the attacking team has already penetrated the offensive zone and is maintaining control of the puck. However, the attacking team can begin the drill with a breakout play from the defensive zone. Position the players as shown in the corresponding diagram. Begin the drill with two defenders (4-on-2). Once the attacking team has mastered the drill with two defenders, introduce three defenders (4-on-3). At the whistle, the offensive team begins moving the puck around and continues the drill for one minute or until the defensive team gains control of the puck. Work the puck to the point men, along the boards, below the goal line, behind the net and to the slot.

Monitor and provide feedback to the offensive team after the allotted time on the following three power play fundamentals:

- Player movement and position exchanging.
- Puck control and movement.
- Shots on net.

Drill 12-2 Diamond Power Play. The diamond power play attack is used to cycle the puck deep and high in the offensive zone to eventually get the puck to a player near the slot for a scoring opportunity, and to force the defenders to move. This drill can be initiated from either the offensive or defensive zones. The power play unit (circled players) positions players as shown in the corresponding diagram. Begin the drill with two defenders (4-on-2) and gradually introduce three defenders (4-on-3). At the whistle, the offensive team begins moving the puck around and continues the drill for one minute or until the defensive team gains control of the puck. Work the puck to the point men, along the boards, below the goal line, behind the net and to the slot. Monitor and provide feedback to the offensive team, after the allotted time, on the three power play fundamentals listed in Drill 12-1.

Drill 12-3; Occupied Triangle Power Play. The occupied triangle power play attack moves the puck around the perimeter, ready for the right opportunity to pass the puck to the slot man for that high-percentage shot. When the slot man is covered, the point man can execute a shot on net and have the slot man and the two other attackers converge on the net for the one-two punch. The power play unit (circled players) positions players as shown in the corresponding diagram. Begin the drill with two defenders (4-on-2) and gradually introduce three defenders (4-on-3). At the whistle, the offensive team begins moving the puck around and continues the drill for one minute or until the defensive team gains control of the puck. Work the puck to the point men, along the boards, below the goal line, behind the net and to the slot. Monitor and provide feedback to the offensive team, after the allotted time, on the three power play fundamentals listed in Drill 12-1.

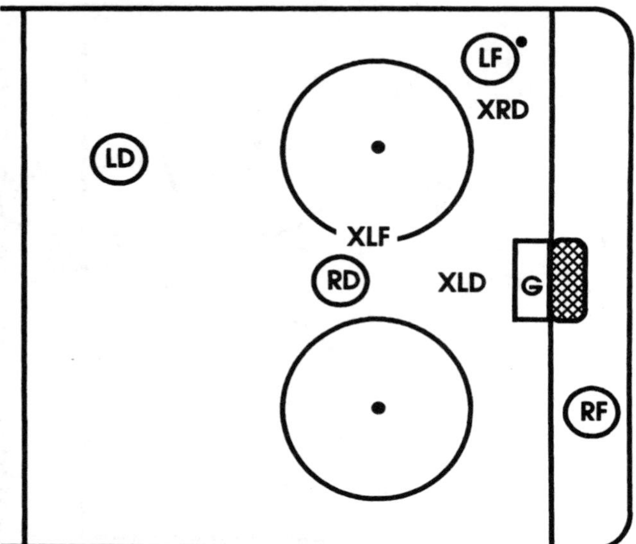

Drill 12-3; Occupied Triangle Power Play Attack

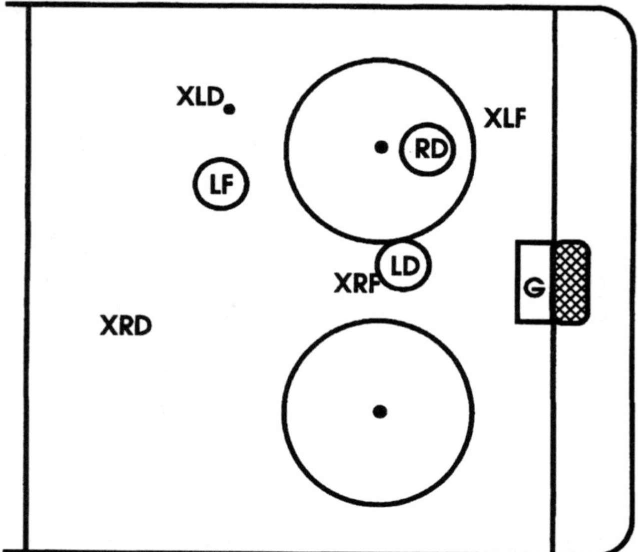

Drill 12-4; Penalty Killing Triangle

Drill 12-4; Penalty Killing Triangle. Use two penalty killers playing low to cover the deep attackers and one penalty killer playing high in the triangle to cover the opponent's point men. The objective is to force the opponents to pass the puck around the perimeter of the triangle (by controlling the area near the slot) or shoot the puck from a low-percentage scoring location. This creates an opportunity to intercept a pass or block the shot and gain control of the puck. The penalty killing unit (circled players) positions players as shown in the corresponding diagram. Begin the drill with three defenders (3-on-4) and eventually introduce two defenders (2-on-4). At the whistle, the offensive team begins moving the puck around and continues the drill for one minute or until the penalty killing unit gains control of the puck. Once it gains control of the puck, the unit should shoot it down the playing surface, skate with it (if there is open playing surface available) or freeze it. Monitor and provide feedback to the penalty killing unit, after the allotted time, on the three penalty killing fundamentals listed below:

- Controlling the area near the slot.
- Using your goaltender.
- Working the clock.

Drill 12-5; Pulling The Goaltender. Rerun Drills 12-1 through 12-3 by pulling the goaltender and adding an extra attacker. Work the drill using 5-on-4 and 5-on-3 scenarios.

Recap

After reading and studying this chapter, you should be able to answer the following questions:

1. Define special teams.
2. What should a power play unit be designed to do?
3. What should a penalty killing unit be designed to do?
4. Describe the factors that each coach should look for when selecting special teams players.
5. Summarize the three power play fundamentals. What are the suggested minimum number of shots on net required for a potent power play?
6. Describe the three power play strategies. What is the objective of each?
7. Summarize the three penalty killing fundamentals.
8. Describe the fundamental penalty killing strategy. How can a coach employ both conservative and aggressive tactics into this strategy?
9. What is the purpose of pulling your goaltender? What are the advantages/disadvantages?
10. How will you use the Special Teams Play Checklist and the drills provided in this chapter to help improve special teams performance and correct existing deficiencies?

Coaches' Toolbox

Highlights

This section contains 13 vital tools for the coach to perform player evaluations and to obtain team and individual statistics, both critical to provide effective feedback and plan improvements for the team as well as individual players.

Team Selection Checklist

Scouting Information Sheet

Siller Game Statistics Worksheet

Skating and Rink Conditioning Checklist

Stickhandling and Puck Control Checklist

Passing and Receiving Checklist

Shooting and Scoring Checklist

Defensive Player Checklist

Offensive Player Checklist

Goaltending Checklist

Defensive Zone Team Play Checklist

Offensive Zone Team Play Checklist

Special Teams Play Checklist

SILLER PLAYER AND TEAM EVALUATION PROFILE©
TEAM SELECTION CHECKLIST

Notes:												
Skating and Rink Conditioning												
Skating--forward/backward												
Stopping												
Turns and crossovers												
Transitioning												
Stickhandling and Puck Control												
Open area												
Around pylons												
Passing and Receiving												
Passing--forehand/backhand												
Give-and-go												
Receiving--forehand/backhand												
Shooting and Scoring												
Wrist shot--forehand/backhand												
Snap shot												
Slap shot												
Rebounds												
Defense												
Stick checking/body blocking												
1-on-1, 2-on-1, 2-on-2												
Rushing												
Third man in												
Forwards												
1-on-1, 2-on-1, 2-on-2												
Moving puck into offensive zone												
Backchecking												
Goaltenders												
Playing the angles												
Glove/blocker/stick/pad saves												
1-on-1, 2-on-1, 2-on-2												
Controlling the puck after a shot												
Team												
Forechecking												
Breakout												
Face-offs												

Scale: 0 = Not Performed, 1-3 = Low Proficiency,
4-6 = Medium Proficiency, 7-9 = High Proficiency, 10 = Excellent Proficiency

SILLER PLAYER AND TEAM EVALUATION PROFILE©
SCOUTING INFORMATION SHEET

Scouted By:_____________ **Team #1:**_______________ **Team #2:**_______________

Date:_________ **Location:**___________________ **Score:**_______________

Team Attribute	Team #1	Team #2
Style at Start of Game		
Face-off Strategies and Effectiveness		
Goaltending Style and Effectiveness		
Defensemen		
Forwards		
Defensive Zone Play - coverage, breakout, backchecking		
Offensive Zone Play - forechecking, offensive defensemen		
Description of Goals		
Power Play Strategies and Effectiveness		
Penalty Killing Strategies and Effectiveness		
Players to Watch		
Team Strengths		
Team Weaknesses		
General Comments		

Siller Game Statistics Worksheet©

_________ **versus** ___________ **Score:** ______ **Location:** _____________ **Date:** ________

Nmbr	**Player Name**	**Shots**	**Goals**	**Assists**	**Points**	**+/- PP PK**	**Face-offs Won/Lost**	**Penalty (mins)**
	TOTALS							

Opponents Stats
Goals Scored
Shots
Penalties

O represents goals, X represents shots

Shooting Percentage:	**Penalty Killing Percentage:**
Save Percentage:	**Power Play Percentage:**
Face-off Win Percentage:	**Shot Distribution:**

Notes:

SILLER PLAYER AND TEAM EVALUATION PROFILE©
SKATING AND RINK CONDITIONING CHECKLIST

Evaluator: **Date:** **Location:**

	Player Name															
Notes:																
Fundamental Skating and Rink Conditioning Techniques																
Forward Skating																
• Front (V) Start																
• Side Start																
• Crossover Start																
• Moving Forward																
• T-Stop																
• Two-Foot Stop																
• Two-Skate Turn																
• Power Turn (Scooting)																
• Crossover																
• Forward-to-Backward Transition																
Backward Skating																
• Figure-Eight Start																
• C-Start																
• Moving Backward																
• Backward Curl Stop																
• Two-Skate Turn																
• Crossover																
• Backward-to-Forward Transition																
Advanced Skating and Rink Conditioning Techniques																
Power Slide (Forward)																
Power Slide (Backward)																
Scissor Jump																
Two-Legged Jump																
TOTAL SCORE																
AVERAGE SCORE																

Comments:

Scale: 0 = Not Performed, 1 - 3 = Low Proficiency, 4 - 6 = Medium Proficiency, 7 - 9 = High Proficiency, 10 = Excellent Proficiency

SILLER PLAYER AND TEAM EVALUATION PROFILE©
STICKHANDLING AND PUCK CONTROL CHECKLIST

Evaluator: **Date:** **Location:**

Notes:____________________

	Player Name															
Fundamental Stickhandling and Puck Control Techniques																
Push																
Side-To-Side																
Diagonal (Left Side)																
Diagonal (Right Side)																
Back-To-Front (Left Side)																
Back-To-Front (Right Side)																
Advanced Stickhandling and Puck Control Techniques																
One-Handed Puck Control																
Puck Control Using The Skates																
• between the skates																
• skate-to-stick																
• stick-to-skate-to-stick																
Incidental Body Contact and Puck Control																
Stickhandling While Skating Backward																
TOTAL SCORE																
AVERAGE SCORE																

Comments:

Scale: 0 = Not Performed, 1 - 3 = Low Proficiency, 4 - 6 = Medium Proficiency, 7 - 9 = High Proficiency, 10 = Excellent Proficiency

SILLER PLAYER AND TEAM EVALUATION PROFILE©
PASSING AND RECEIVING CHECKLIST

Evaluator: **Date:** **Location:**

	Player Name															
Notes:																
Fundamental Passing and Receiving Techniques																
Passing																
• Forehand Sweep																
• Backhand Sweep																
• Snap Pass																
• Flip Pass																
• Around-The-Boards Pass																
• Give-And-Go																
Receiving																
• Forehand																
• Backhand																
• Too Far Ahead																
Advanced Passing and Receiving Techniques																
Passing																
• Bank Pass																
• Open Area Pass																
• Drop Pass																
• Touch Pass																
• Reverse																
• Weave																
• Skate Pass																
Receiving																
• Off The Skates																
• In The Air																
TOTAL SCORE																
AVERAGE SCORE																

Comments:

Scale: 0 = Not Performed, 1 - 3 = Low Proficiency, 4 - 6 = Medium Proficiency, 7 - 9 = High Proficiency, 10 = Excellent Proficiency

SILLER PLAYER AND TEAM EVALUATION PROFILE©
SHOOTING AND SCORING CHECKLIST

Evaluator: **Date:** **Location:**

	Player Name															
Notes:____________________																
Fundamental Shooting and Scoring Techniques																
Wrist Shot - low																
Wrist Shot - high																
Snap Shot - low																
Snap Shot - high																
Flip Shot - high only																
Backhand Wrist Shot - low																
Backhand Wrist Shot - high																
Backhand Flip Shot - high only																
Shooting Power Test - This test lists the distances the __ pound target block has been moved, from __ feet, with a forehand wrist shot, snap shot, and a backhand wrist shot, in inches.																
Advanced Shooting and Scoring Techniques																
Slap Shot - low																
Slap Shot - high																
Rebounds																
Shooting Off The Back Leg																
Deking The Goaltender																
Breakaways																
Screen Shot																
One-Time Shot																
Deflections																
TOTAL SCORE																
AVERAGE SCORE																

Comments:

Scale: 0 = Not Performed, 1 - 3 = Low Proficiency, 4 - 6 = Medium Proficiency, 7 - 9 = High Proficiency, 10 = Excellent Proficiency

SILLER PLAYER EVALUATION PROFILE©
DEFENSIVE PLAYER CHECKLIST

Evaluator: **Date:** **Location:**

	Player Name															
Notes:																
Fundamental Defensive Techniques																
Communicating																
Reading And Reacting																
Poke Check																
Sweep Check																
Diving Sweep/Poke Check																
Stick Lift/Press																
Body Blocking																
Riding A Player Out Of A Play																
Covering In Front Of The Net																
One/Two/Three-On-One																
One/Two/Three-On-Two																
Advanced Defensive Techniques																
Learning Opponents Patterns																
Blocking Shots With Your Body																
Fake Shot																
One-Time Shot																
Rushing																
TOTAL SCORE																
AVERAGE SCORE																

Comments:

Scale: 0 = Not Performed, 1 - 3 = Low Proficiency, 4 - 6 = Medium Proficiency, 7 - 9 = High Proficiency, 10 = Excellent Proficiency

SILLER PLAYER AND TEAM EVALUATION PROFILE©
OFFENSIVE PLAYER CHECKLIST

Evaluator: **Date:** **Location:**

Notes:______________________

	Player Name															
Fundamental Offensive Techniques																
Communicating																
Reading and Reacting																
Fake Pass																
Against the Boards																
Flip Out																
Forehand and Backhand Shifts																
Backhand-To-Forehand Shift																
Forehand-To-Backhand Shift																
Slip Through																
Slip Across																
Change of Pace																
The Weave																
Shoulder Turn/Drop																
Flip Through																
Body Blocking																
One/Two/Three-On-One																
One/Two/Three-On-Two																
Forechecking																
Backchecking																
Advanced Offensive Techniques																
Learning Opponents Patterns																
Rebounds																
Screen Shot																
Deflections																
One-time Shot																
Fake Shot																
Spin-O-Rama																
TOTAL SCORE																
AVERAGE SCORE																

Comments:

Scale: 0 = Not Performed, 1 - 3 = Low Proficiency, 4 - 6 = Medium Proficiency, 7 - 9 = High Proficiency, 10 = Excellent Proficiency

SILLER PLAYER AND TEAM EVALUATION PROFILE©
GOALTENDING CHECKLIST

Evaluator: **Date:** **Location:**

	Player Name															
Notes: ________________																
Fundamental Goaltending Techniques																
Stance																
• maintain proper balance																
• cover maximum area of net																
• move efficiently																
Knowing Where You Are In Net																
Crease Movement																
• forward and backward																
• left and right																
• down and up																
Playing The Angles																
Glove Saves																
Blocker Saves																
Pad Saves																
Skate Saves																
Upper Body Saves																
Stick Saves																
Plays From Behind The Net																
Controlling The Puck After A Shot																
Handling An Offensive Attack																
Advanced Goaltending Techniques																
Learning Opponents Patterns																
Handling The Puck																
Stopping The Puck Behind The Net																
Active Deflections																
Stick Checking																
TOTAL SCORE																
AVERAGE SCORE																

Comments:

Scale: 0 = Not Performed, 1 - 3 = Low Proficiency, 4 - 6 = Medium Proficiency, 7 - 9 = High Proficiency, 10 = Excellent Proficiency

SILLER PLAYER AND TEAM EVALUATION PROFILE©
DEFENSIVE ZONE TEAM PLAY CHECKLIST

Evaluator: **Date:** **Location:**

	Line Number											
Notes: ______												
Fundamental Defensive Zone Team Techniques												
Zone Defense												
Man-to-Man Defense												
Strong Side Breakout												
Weak Side Breakout												
Defenseman Skating Breakout												
Around-the-Boards Breakout												
Fast Breakout												
3-0-1 Face-off Alignment												
2-1-1 Face-off Alignment												
2-0-2 Face-off Alignment												
Advanced Defensive Zone Team Techniques												
Overload Defense												
Defense-to-Defense Breakout												
Behind-the-Net Breakout												
Defense Reverse Breakout												
Goaltender Breakout												
TOTAL SCORE												
AVERAGE SCORE												

Comments: ______

Scale: 0 = Not Performed, 1 - 3 = Low Proficiency, 4 - 6 = Medium Proficiency, 7 - 9 = High Proficiency, 10 = Excellent Proficiency

SILLER PLAYER AND TEAM EVALUATION PROFILE©
OFFENSIVE ZONE TEAM PLAY CHECKLIST

Evaluator: **Date:** **Location:**

	Line Number											
Notes:___________________												
Fundamental Offensive Zone Team Techniques												
2-2 Attack												
Diamond Attack												
Occupied Triangle Attack												
1-1-2 Forechecking System												
1-2-1 Forechecking System												
0-1-3 Forechecking System												
3-0-1 Face-off Alignment												
2-1-1 Face-off Alignment												
2-0-2 Face-off Alignment												
Advanced Offensive Zone Team Techniques												
Offensive Regrouping												
2-Man Offensive Cycling												
3-Man Offensive Cycling												
4-Man Offensive Cycling												
2-1-1 Forechecking System												
2-0-2 Forechecking System												
TOTAL SCORE												
AVERAGE SCORE												

Comments: ____

Scale: 0 = Not Performed, 1 - 3 = Low Proficiency, 4 - 6 = Medium Proficiency, 7 - 9 = High Proficiency, 10 = Excellent Proficiency

SILLER PLAYER AND TEAM EVALUATION PROFILE© **SPECIAL TEAMS PLAY CHECKLIST**												
Evaluator: **Date:** **Location:**												
	Line Number											
Notes: ______________________												
Fundamental Special Teams Techniques												
2-2 Power Play												
• player movement/pos. exch.												
• puck control and movement												
• shots on net												
• face-offs												
Diamond Power Play												
• player movement/pos. exch.												
• puck control and movement												
• shots on net												
• face-offs												
Occupied Triangle Power Play												
• player movement/pos. exch.												
• puck control and movement												
• shots on net												
• face-offs												
Penalty Killing Triangle												
• control of area near the slot												
• coord. with goaltender												
• work the clock												
• face-offs												
Pulling The Goaltender												
TOTAL SCORE												
AVERAGE SCORE												
Comments: ______________________												
Scale: 0 = Not Performed, 1 - 3 = Low Proficiency, 4 - 6 = Medium Proficiency, 7 - 9 = High Proficiency, 10 = Excellent Proficiency												

Glossary

AAPMD Level — individual player's ability, age, physical and mental development level.

Aerial Angle — created by drawing a line from the crossbar to the puck. By drawing these lines, angles are created (with respect to the net) which are used by the goaltender to guide his body and glove/blocker to the most effective placement. Angles are classified into three general categories: slight, moderate and extreme.

Alignments — placement of players to most effectively implement the face-off strategy.

Anticipation — combination of skill, intellect, judgment, intuition and experience; it is the one element that sets upper echelon roller hockey players apart from average roller hockey players. Anticipation is the ability to read a play, predict a teammate's or opponent's probable course of action and execute the best option available.

Assignments — each player's responsibilities during and subsequent to each face-off.

Backchecking — skating back toward your defensive zone to cover an opposing player.

Blade — portion of the stick that comes in contact with the puck.

Body Deception — body movements a player, puck carrier or non-puck carrier makes to deceive a defender.

Breakout Techniques — used by a team to move the puck out of its defensive zone on an offensive attack.

Center — player taking the face-off.

Changing On The Fly — changing a line during active play as opposed to during a stoppage of play.

Defensive Exchanging — transfer or exchange of coverage in the defensive zone from one defender to another.

Defensive Overloading — tactic of employing two defenders to pressure any puck carrier when the puck is deep in the defensive zone.

Defensive Team — team trying to gain control of the puck.

Defensive Zone — side of the playing surface occupied by your team's goaltender.

Deking — skill used to defeat an opponent during a one-on-one confrontation using exaggerated and camouflaged player and puck movement.

Diameter — height (in millimeters) of a roller hockey wheel.

Durometer — hardness of a roller hockey wheel.

Face-off Strategy (Defensive Zone) — winning the face-off and gaining control of the puck first, preventing a scoring opportunity by the opponents second and initiating a breakout play or offensive attack third.

Face-off Strategy (Offensive Zone) — winning the face-off and gaining control of the puck first, initiating an offensive attack second and forechecking the opponents to regain control of the puck third.

Five-Hole — shooting space between the goaltender's legs.

Forechecking — tactic used to gain or regain possession of the puck in the offensive zone.

Front Door/Back Door — front door refers to the area between the shooter and the goaltender and back door refers to the area between the goaltender and the net.

Goaltender's Alley — area formed by drawing lines from each goal post to the puck.

Heel — bottom portion of the stick blade closest to the player.

Individual Skills — fundamental abilities required to play roller hockey. Consists of skating and rink conditioning, stickhandling and puck control, passing and receiving and shooting and scoring.

Integrated Individual and Positional Skills — applying individual skills to the forward, defense or goaltender positions.

Interval Between Skating and Resting — a ratio (such as 1:4) of the amount of active time a drill is performed to the amount of resting time required following a drill.

Keeping a Book — maintaining mental notes on favorite moves and plays of the opposing players, various line combinations and goaltending styles.

Level — the most efficient placement of the goaltender's eyes to focus on the puck.

Lie of a Stick — angle between the shaft of the stick and the playing surface.

Man-to-Man Defense — defensive strategy normally used when the defending team has an equivalent number of players or a numerical advantage in the defensive zone where each defensive player is responsible for covering one opponent and staying with him as long as the opposing team has control of the puck.

Offensive Cycling — continuous position exchanging between two, three or even all four teammates simultaneously.

Offensive Exchanging — transfer or exchange of positioning in the offensive zone from one attacker to another.

Offensive Regrouping — technique used to reenter the offensive zone when the offensive team is unable to initially penetrate deep into that zone.

Offensive Team — team with the puck.

Offensive Zone — side of the playing surface occupied by the opposing team's goaltender.

One-two Punch — executing an initial shot followed by a rebound shot.

Overload Line — imaginary line drawn in a team's defensive zone between the boards and the deep face-off dots.

Penalty Killing Unit — used to play the percentages and minimize the opponent's numerical superiority and goal-scoring opportunities by using speed, quickness, discipline and strategy.

Pinching — a defenseman moving in from his point position to pressure a defender with the intent of keeping the puck in the offensive zone.

Player's Space — area surrounding your body with the horizontal component equal to the distance of your outstretched arms, generally two feet to the front, back and sides of your body.

Playing the Man — requires a defender to focus on the movement of the attacker (specifically his chest).

Playing the Pass — requires a defender to maintain a position between two attackers with the intent of breaking up a pass, while covering the player with the best scoring opportunity.

Playing the Puck — requires a defender to focus on the movement of the puck.

Point Man — defenseman in the offensive zone.

Power Play Unit — used to take advantage of the team's numerical superiority while the opponent is serving a penalty by moving the puck and putting it in the net.

Puck Control — maintaining possession of the puck against one or more opponents. Can be performed either individually or as a team.

Puck Fake — technique used to deceive a defender and to create offensive opportunities from anywhere on the playing surface.

3PO Principle (Puck Possession Provides Opportunities) — With possession of the puck, you can transition from defense to offense and create potential scoring opportunities as well as control the overall flow of the game.

Puck Protection — process in which the puck carrier keeps his body between the defender and the puck to maintain control of the puck.

Pulling Your Goaltender — substituting an offensive attacker for your goaltender to give your team additional offensive power.

Reading and Reacting — ability of the individual or positional unit to perceive the play (of both teammates and opponents) around them and to respond appropriately.

Running Time — the clock is started and continues until the period ends.

Rush — a player carrying the puck up the playing surface on an offensive attack.

Sanctioning — performed by organizations recognized to do so. In the United States, major sanctioning organizations and their phone numbers (at this printing) are listed in Chapter 1. These organizations help get a league started, provide insurance coverage and keep you informed of events in the world of roller hockey.

Scramble — period of transition where each team is trying to gain control of the puck.

Scrimmage — controlled intrateam game designed to execute various team skills in a gamelike manner at a pace consistent with the competition.

Selling — ability of a player to make a puck fake or body deception move believable to a defender.

Shaft — portion of the stick that the player holds onto.

Slot — area bounded by the crease and a portion of each face-off circle.

Soft Hands — ability to control and manipulate the puck quickly, accurately and consistently by feel.

Special Teams — subset of a roller hockey team working together to accomplish a specific task.

Stickhandling — process of moving the puck with the eventual goal of setting up a scoring opportunity.

Stop Time — the clock is stopped at each stoppage of play and started again at the drop of the puck.

Stride-then-glide Technique — method used to continue skating.

Strong Side — side of the playing surface that the puck is on.

Strongside Defenseman — defenseman who is on the side of the playing surface that the puck is on.

Surface Angle — created by drawing a line from the center of the goal line to the puck.

Tactical Triad — reading, reacting and anticipating.

Team Skills — consolidation of integrated individual and positional skills used by all players on a team with the objective of winning the game.

Telegraph — give away the intention to pass or shoot.

Telescoping — technique used by a goaltender when trying to find that point where his body most effectively blocks the shooter's open net area.

Third Man In — third player, usually a defenseman, moving up into the offensive attack.

Toe — end of the stick blade farthest from the player.

Trailing Support — teammates who are skating back toward your defensive zone while covering or attempting to cover an offensive player. Opponents who are entering the offensive zone behind the initial play to provide secondary attacking support.

Transition Zone — area approximately 20 feet on either side of the center red line where team play is considered neither offensive nor defensive.

Triangulation — technique of maintaining three offensive players in every offensive attack to create the necessary puck movement.

Weak Side — side of the playing surface that the puck is not on.

Weakside Defenseman — defenseman who is on the opposite side of the playing surface that the puck is on.

Zone Defense — a basic defensive strategy which utilizes the defensive players in a boxlike formation to cover opponents in the left, central and right defensive zones with the objective of gaining control of the puck or at least neutralizing the opponent's attack.

Reference Material

The following is a list of the published or released resources used to support the development of this book.

Books

- Chambers, Dave. *Complete Hockey Instruction: Skills and Strategies for Coaches and Players*. Toronto: Key Porter Books, 1989.
- Chartraw, Rick. *Strong Side Hockey*. 1993.
- Kirkham, Roger. *Pearls of Wisdom for the job and for life*. Salt Lake City: Crystal Publishing, Inc., 1994.
- National In-line Hockey Association. *NIHA Official Rulebook*. Executive Printing Services, Inc., 1994.
- Orlick, Terry. *In Pursuit of Excellence: How to Win in Sport and Life Through Mental Training*. 2nd Edition. Champaign: Leisure Press, 1990.
- Percival, Lloyd. *The Hockey Handbook*. Toronto: McClelland & Stewart Inc., 1992.
- Perron, Jean and Chouinard, Normand. *Shooting to Win: A Coach's Guide to Playing Better Offensive Hockey*. Toronto: McGraw-Hill Ryerson, 1991.
- Roller Hockey International. *1994 Official Rules Book*.
- Smith, Michael A. *A Hockey Coaching Manual*. 1985.
- Smith, Michael A. *Hockey Drill Book*. West Tisbury, MA: Codner Books, 1983.
- Walford, Gerald A. and Walford, Gerald E. *Youth Hockey for Parents and Players*. Indianapolis, IN: Masters Press, 1994.
- Young, Ian and Gudgeon, Chris. *Behind the Mask: The Ian Young Goaltending Method, Book One*. Vancouver: Polestar Press Ltd., 1993.
- Young, Ian and Gudgeon, Chris. *Beyond the Mask: The Ian Young Goaltending Method, Book Two*. Vancouver: Polestar Press Ltd.
- Zulewski, Richard. *The Parent's Guide to Coaching Hockey*. Cincinnati, OH: Betterway Books, 1993.

Instructional Videos

- In-Line Hockey Partners. (1994). *Winning In-Line Hockey* [30-minute videotape]. Featuring instruction by Herb Brooks and Mike Butters.
- Neilson, Roger. (1986). *Hockey with Roger Neilson* [60-minute videotape]. NHL Pros in action. Distributed by Atlantis Direct Marketing Inc., Toronto.

Magazines and Periodicals

- *Hockey Player*, various articles and authors, 1994-1995.
- *Inline Hockey News*, Volume 1, Issue 1, April/May 1995 and Volume 1, Issue 2, June/July 1995. General information.
- *NIHA hockeytalk*, Volume 2, Issue 2 July 1995.
- *Roller Hockey*, various articles and authors, 1994-1995.